NOUS·SOMMES·PRETS

SIMON FRASER UNIVERSITY
W.A.C. BENNETT LIBRARY

Britain, Germany and the Cold War

This book examines British policy towards the German Question and détente during a crucial period in Cold War history, and draws on unpublished British and American archives. British policy strove for both good relations with West Germany and détente with the Soviet Union. West Germany's hard line towards the Soviet bloc and the issue of German unification was a permanent source of East–West tension during this period. This policy was initially endorsed by the United States, and these factors cast British policy onto the horns of a dilemma. On the one hand, the quest for détente required recognition of the status quo in Central and Eastern Europe; on the other, close relations with West Germany required at least minimal support for the revisionist aims of Bonn's *Ostpolitik* ('Eastern policy'). It was not until the United States revised its approach towards the German Question that this stumbling block to détente was removed. But it took some time for British policy-makers to accept the reduced role that Britain could play on the international stage.

This well-researched book seeks to further our understanding of British policy on détente (and East–West relations) and on the adjustment to the loss of 'great power' status, thereby offering a considered appreciation of British foreign policy in the Cold War.

R. Gerald Hughes obtained his PhD from the Department of International Politics at the University of Wales Aberystwyth where he is now a lecturer. He is the co-editor of *Intelligence, Crises and Security* (forthcoming, Routledge, 2007) and *Exploring Intelligence Archives* (forthcoming, Routledge, 2007).

Cold War history series
Series Editors: Odd Arne Westad and Michael Cox
ISSN: 1471-3829

In the new history of the Cold War that has been forming since 1989, many of the established truths about the international conflict that shaped the latter half of the twentieth century have come up for revision. The present series is an attempt to make available interpretations and materials that will help further the development of this new history, and it will concentrate in particular on publishing expositions of key historical issues and critical surveys of newly available sources.

Britain, Germany and the Cold War

The search for a European Détente
1949–1967

R. Gerald Hughes

LONDON AND NEW YORK

First published 2007
by Routledge
2 Park Square, Milton Park, Abingdon, Oxon OX14 4RN

Simultaneously published in the USA and Canada
by Routledge
270 Madison Ave, New York, NY 10016

Routledge is an imprint of the Taylor & Francis Group, an informa business

© 2007 R. Gerald Hughes

Typeset in Baskerville by Wearset Ltd, Boldon, Tyne and Wear
Printed and bound in Great Britain by TJI Digital, Padstow, Cornwall

British Library Cataloguing in Publication Data
A catalogue record for this book is available from the British Library

Library of Congress Cataloging in Publication Data
A catalog record for this book has been requested

ISBN 10: 0-415-41207-2 (hbk)
ISBN 10: 0-203-08908-1 (ebk)

ISBN 13: 978-0-415-41207-0 (hbk)
ISBN 13: 978-0-203-08908-8 (ebk)

Poor old H.M.G. Whether it's Germany, or Europe, or Africa, or Cyprus, we are always trying to conciliate both antagonists, and getting nothing but suspicion and abuse from both sides.

Harold Macmillan, diary entry for 25 November 1959

We were dissatisfied with the broad and beautiful Reich of 1914 and got the frontiers of 1937. We disliked the frontiers of 1937 and got the frontiers of 1945. What frontiers shall we get next time?

Golo Mann, 'Mit den Polen Frieden Machen', *Stern*, 12 July 1964

Contents

Illustrations

Acknowledgements

In writing this book I have incurred many debts, and I should like to acknowledge them here. In the full knowledge that I will have forgotten some of these debts, this is more a reflection of my failing memory than any lack of gratitude on my part. I should like to thank the Department of International Politics at the University of Wales for awarding me a studentship to study for the PhD that formed the basis for a large part of this book. I should like to pay tribute to Len Scott, whose patience and understanding I have benefited from for over a decade now. Thanks to Peter Jackson for his long-standing friendship, enthusiasm and prudent advice. I should like to thank Klaus Larres, who spent a considerable amount of effort in examining my PhD thesis. Thanks also to Gottfried Niedhart for his helpful comments. I should also like to thank a number of other friends and colleagues who live and work in Aberystwyth. These include: Martin Alexander, Michael Foley, Ian Clark, Björn Weiler, Martyn Powell, Robert Harrison, Karen Stöber, Andrew Priest, Roger Price, Jeff Davies, Siân Nicholas, Paul O'Leary, Will Bain, Patrick Finney and Graeme Davies. My special thanks go to my good friends and colleagues Jim Vaughan and Peter Lambert for their support. I should like to thank the staff of the Department of International Politics, past and present (including dear Ardwyna), who have been so supportive of myself over the years. I would like to express my grateful thanks to the libraries and archives that I visited in the course of the research for this book, and in particular the staff of the Public Record Office, Kew (now a part of the National Archives), who were unfailingly helpful in the many months I spent there. Archival visits are expensive, and I gratefully acknowledge the hospitality of Michael, Pauline, Michael Jnr, Brigid, Freddie, Judy and Gerry-Anne in Boston; Mark and Helen in Oxford; Laura and Jamie in Manchester; and Whitelegg and Grant in North London. Special thanks to my brother, David, for his willingness to put up with my frequent extended stays at his place in London. I also wish to thank many of the people I have known over the years in Aberystwyth: Treacle, Synge, Llewis, Twiney, Wurz, Wolf, Melzer, Flares, Steve Mahoney, Guy Evans, Susie Carruthers, Adie Roderick, George Welton, Matt Dafforne and Greg Moore. Thanks to

Roland Vogt for his help and loans of material over the last couple of years. My thanks for many years of special friendship to all the good folk I met at Stirling University (and Kudu *et al.* in Dundee) between 1986 and 1990 – especially Mark Enright, Maxi, Lindy, Claypole and Babar. I have never forgotten, either, the encouragement in all matters pertaining to education that dear Philip gave to me all those years ago. Thanks to Edward Ingram and the *International History Review* for allowing me to reproduce portions of the article 'Unfinished Business from Potsdam: Britain, West Germany, and the Oder–Neisse line, 1945–1962', and similar to *Diplomacy and Statecraft* for the reproduction of portions of ' "Possession is nine tenths of the law": Britain and the boundaries of Eastern Europe since 1945'. Thanks to the Image Library of the National Archives for permission to reproduce the map contained in this volume (and to Hugh Alexander for his expertise). My thanks to Wearset Publishing Services and to Georgina Boyle for her patience and professionalism. I wish to express my thanks to the readers who took time to read the manuscript of this book, and to the series editors, Odd-Arne Westad and Michael Cox, for their exertions. My warm wishes go out to my godchildren, Anna and Cameron, for being such a source of joy to me whenever we meet. My thanks to Bangor City FC and all at Farrar Road for keeping the Spirit of '62 alive. My love to my grandmother, Muriel: I still treasure her gift of a book on twentieth-century leaders (*Portraits of Power*) given to me when I was ten. Very special thanks to Rachel Juliet for her love and encouragement over the last few years. My most intense feelings of gratitude are extended to my family: Ma, Arnie, Rachel, Owen and David. Their support has never wavered, and it is to them that this book is dedicated.

Glossary and abbreviations

Abstammung Blood principle of German citizenship.

Adenauersche Konzeption Adenauer's conception. Term used to denote Adenauer's policies.

Aktion Oder–Neiße (AKON) Extremist expellee group formed in the FRG in 1962.

Alleinvertretungsrecht Right of sole representation. Claim by the Federal Republic to be the only government representing Germans.

Auswärtiges Amt (AA) West German Foreign Office (created 1955).

BAOR British Army of the Rhine.

BHE Block der Heimatvertriebenen und Entrechteten – the political party of the expellees in the FRG.

Bund der Vertreiben The League of the Expellees – the umbrella organisation for the German expellees.

Bundestag West German parliament.

Bundeswehr West German armed forces.

CDU *Christlich Demokratische Union Deutschlands.*

Co-existence Concept for mutual bloc toleration.

CSU *Christlich-Soziale Union.*

Détente Agreement for peaceful resolution of differences. Usually applied specifically to the late 1960s/1970s.

Deutschlandplan Plan drafted by the SPD (q.v.) for moving towards reunification in 1959.

Deutschlandpolitik Germany policy. Policies of Bonn relating to all Germany and/or its reunification.

Die zone The zone. West German term for the GDR.

Disengagement Concept of neutral/demilitarised belts in Europe.

Drang nach Osten Drive to the East. Centuries-old, semi-mythical German expansion eastwards with a somewhat missionary zeal.

Dreikaiserbund The understanding between Germany, Austria–Hungary and Russia after 1873.

ECSC European Coal and Steel Community.

EDC European Defence Community.

Eden Plan 1954 proposals to reunify Germany and the basis of subsequent Western negotiating position.

EEC European Economic Community.

FDP *Freie Demokratische Partei.*

Gaitskell Plan Disengagement (q.v.) plan of Hugh Gaitskell.

Grundgesetz (West) German Basic Law of 1949.

Hallstein Doctrine Named for the State Secretary in the *Auswärtiges Amt* (q.v.), Walter Hallstein. West German pledge to sever relations with any state that maintains relations with the GDR, enunciated in 1955.

Hauptverwaltung Auflärung (HVA) Main Intelligence Directorate. Foreign Intelligence Service of the GDR.

Heimatrecht Right of domicile (see *Recht auf Heimat* q.v.).

Kleine schritte Little steps. Tentative modification of *Ostpolitik* under Dr Gerhard Schröder (FRG Foreign Minister 1961–6).

Lebensform Political life.

MdB *Mitglied des Deutschen Bundestages* (member of the West German parliament).

Munich Agreement Agreement of 30 September 1938 between Britain, France, Germany and Italy whereby the Sudetenland area of Czechoslovakia was transferred to the *Reich.*

Oder–Neiße line Rivers that acted as the (provisional) boundary between Soviet zone of occupation (later the GDR) and Poland. Agreed at Potsdam in 1945.

Odra–Nysa line Polish version of above.

Odsun 'Transfer' (Czech), sometimes translated as expulsion. Term for the removal of the Sudeten Germans from Czechoslovakia after the Second World War.

Offset costs Financial compensation paid by the FRG to Britain (and the US) for the expense incurred in the stationing of troops in West Germany as part of the NATO commitment.

Ostabteilung Eastern Office of the *Auswärtiges Amt* (q.v.).

Ostausschuss der deutschen Wirtschaft Eastern Committee of German Industry.

Osteuropapolitik East Europe policy. West German policy to Communist states of Eastern Europe (excluding the USSR but including Yugoslavia).

Ostforschung East research. Defined by Bonn as research into the lands to the east. Defined by the Poles as 'the scientific elaboration of political ideas of revisionism'.

Osthandel Trade with the East.

Ostkunde East (European) studies.

Ostpolitik East policy.

Pankow Suburb of East Berlin where the GDR Government was based. Euphemism for the GDR.

Politik der Bewegung Policy of Movement. Flexible eastern policy adopted by Dr Gerhard Schröder.

Politik der Stärke Policy of Strength. Intransigent policy towards the Communist bloc adopted by Konrad Adenauer (Chancellor 1949–63). Sometimes characterised by the slogan 'No Concessions'.

Rapacki Plan Disengagement (q.v.) scheme initially proposed by Adam Rapacki, Polish Foreign Minister, in 1957.

Rapallo factor Fear that Germany might turn to the Soviet Union (Russia) rather than the West for an alliance. So-named for the German–Soviet Rapallo Treaty of 1922.

Recht auf Heimat Right to the Homeland. West German concept asserting the rights of those expelled after 1945 to return to their place of origin.

Sackgasse Dead-end. Term given to the impasse in West German foreign/eastern policy by 1966.

Schaukelpolitik Pendulum politics or politics of swing. Traditional oscillation of German policy between East and West (i.e. neither **Ostpolitik** nor **Westpolitik**).

Sicherheit Security.

Sowietpolitik Soviet policy. Policy of West Germany towards the USSR.

SPD *Sozialdemokratische Partei Deutschlands.*

Sudetendeutsche Ethnic Germans from the Sudetenland in Czechoslovakia.

Torschlusspanik Shut-gate panic. Term used in reference to the exodus from the GDR in the last few months before the Berlin Wall's construction in 1961.

Volksdeutsche Ethnic Germans living outside of Germany.

Wandel durch Annäherung Change through rapprochement. Term coined by the SPD foreign policy specialist Egon Bahr in June 1963.

Westpolitik West policy.

Wirtschaftswunder The economic miracle in West Germany after 1949. Often identified with the economist and CDU (q.v.) politician, Dr Ludwig Erhard.

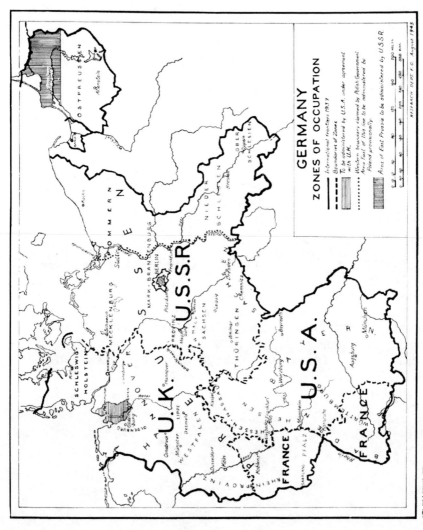

Map of the division of Germany as agreed at Potsdam, August 1945 (Research Department of the Foreign Office). Reproduced with the kind permission of the National Archives in Kew (file reference: MPI 1/694).

Introduction

Britain, Germany and Europe in the Cold War

There can be no revival of Europe, without the active and loyal aid of all the German tribes ...

Winston S. Churchill, 28 October 1948

This is a study of ambiguity in British policy during the Cold War. From the early 1950s, Britain's policy in Europe was caught between a need to support its ally West Germany on the one hand, and a desire to achieve détente with the USSR on the other. West Germany's rejection of the post-war settlement in Eastern Europe after 1949 created a dilemma for British policy-makers. Détente required a broad acceptance of this settlement. West Germany's hard-line Eastern policy thus posed a challenge to British policy-making elites seeking both the continued strength of the Western Alliance and a durable understanding with the Soviet Union that might bolster European security.

In the immediate aftermath of the Second World War, perceptions of aggressive Soviet intentions led Britain and the United States to engineer the creation of a (West) German state, politically and militarily aligned with the West.[1] At that time a consensus within the policy establishment believed that dealing with the USSR on terms acceptable to Britain was impossible.[2] This provided West Germany, under Konrad Adenauer, with the opportunity to construct a hard-line Eastern policy (*Ostpolitik*) that was endorsed by its allies.[3]

Recent scholarship has suggested that the Soviet Union was genuine in its desire for a rapprochement, while the West was uninterested.[4] However, Soviet terms for any such détente were unacceptable as they were designed to undermine West Germany. Thus, opposition to Soviet attempts at détente characterised the policies of the USA and the Federal Republic of Germany (FRG) after 1949. This was not the case with Britain, and serious efforts at détente began in earnest after Stalin's death in 1953. Indeed, the British were accused by Bonn, Washington and Paris as bring still enamoured of 'appeasement', and the term 'English disease' was employed to describe London's desire for an East–West accommodation.[5] While the secondary literature on British détente policy is extensive,[6] little attention has been paid to the effect of Germany's Eastern policy upon London's goals.[7] The historiography of Anglo-German relations has certainly presented the question of Germany's Eastern policies as an irritant,[8] but while British policy towards the *Ostpolitik* of Willy Brandt in the 1970s has attracted some attention,[9] the period after 1949 is only sporadically addressed.

The Potsdam Conference of July and August 1945 was supposed to herald a peace treaty to solve the German Question.[10] In 1919, the Versailles Peace Settlement had at least tried, albeit unsatisfactorily, to address the root causes of the problems within the European system. Even this was lacking after 1945, and as East–West consensus evaporated the Potsdam Agreement remained 'provisional'. This lack of a final peace treaty became something of a destabilising force as Cold War politicking replaced wartime hopes for an enduring international system.[11] As Marc Trachtenberg observes, 'victory did not mean peace'.[12] By 1949, Europe had divided into two armed camps. Germany was at the heart of the conflict, and would remain the biggest obstacle to improving East–West relations in the global Cold War.[13] As Carolyn Eisenberg notes, 'divided Germany was not simply a symbol but a stimulus to East–West confrontation'.[14]

From the British perspective, all of this was compounded by the fact that Germany occupies a unique place in the national psyche. In 1961, the US ambassador in London concluded that if the division of Germany were to be made permanent, this would be overwhelmingly popular in a country where the word 'Hun' was still in common usage.[15] Relations between the FRG and Britain are traditionally characterised as alternating periods of hostility and harmony.[16] This is reflected in the literature on Anglo-German relations during the Cold War.[17] This ambiguity is a product of the process whereby Britain and Germany evolved from deadly enemies to alliance partners. The weight of history casts a long shadow over Anglo-German relations, and Christopher Coker has observed that 'Whenever the British discuss Germany's role they tend to do so in terms of [Britain's] past, in terms of German hegemony ... of old policies that still seem threatening forty-five years on.'[18]

In the ultimate place, West Germany was able to create a hard-line policy on the German question by virtue of the indulgence of the United States.[19] This was acceptable to Britain while the West German state was being consolidated. Once this had been achieved, Britain desired an arrangement with the Soviet bloc that implied the 'closing' of the German question. The West German state insisted that the German question was open. Roger Morgan frames it thus: '"If you Germans want to go on with this exciting rhetoric about the openness of the German question, then please tell us what you intend to do about it."'[20] The West German position was based upon a rigid legalism which insisted that all questions were provisional pending 'a peace treaty which can rightfully be concluded only by an all-German Government, democratically elected by the entire German people.'[21] This was anathema to a traditional British diplomatic strategy aimed at reaching accommodation by mutual compromise. This belief in 'pragmatism' regarding the conduct of diplomacy pervaded official British attitudes and perceptions. In the quest for a European détente, West German adherence to a self-serving legalism thus came to be regarded as an obstacle. As former West German President Richard von Weizsäker later termed it: 'British pragmatism came face to face with German principle.'[22]

History and geography dictate that Eastern Europe has always been more important to Germany than it is to Britain. Traditional differences in priorities, combined with the specific political results of the Second World War, and the subsequent development of the Cold War, explain the divergent positions adopted towards the Soviet bloc by Britain and West Germany. First, West Germany, unlike Britain, was a power limited in scope to the continent. Second, West Germany shared borders with the potential aggressors of the Communist bloc. Third, given its position on frontiers and related questions, West Germany was widely perceived as a revisionist power. Fourth, Germany's nominal capital, Berlin, was deep within the Soviet bloc. Fifth, Germany had a long history of economic and commercial links with the East. Finally, West German sovereignty was constrained by its status as a defeated nation.[23] These factors limited the scope for manoeuvre in Bonn's foreign policy.[24] Most significantly of all, the issue of national division placed unique constraints on both domestic and external policy in West Germany that had no parallel in the rest of Europe.[25] British policy towards Germany was primarily shaped by three factors: Britain's special relationship with the United States;[26] its possession of nuclear weapons after 1952; and, finally, Britain's role as one of the four powers with special responsibility for Germany and Berlin.[27]

In assessing British policy on Germany we might view matters through the perspective of what Arnold Wolfers termed 'possession' and 'milieu' goals. Possession goals are direct and concrete; milieu goals are indirect and more abstract. Wolfers identifies the nature of possessive goals as meaning that they are praised by some for being in the national interest, and condemned by others as 'indicating a reprehensible spirit of national selfishness or acquisitiveness'. Milieu goals, by contrast, are characterised by nations seeking not to defend or increase possessions they hold to the exclusion of others, but instead to 'shape conditions beyond their national boundaries'.[28] In Wolfers' model, Soviet hegemony in Eastern Europe did not represent a mortal threat to British interests. For West Germany, conversely, Soviet domination of Eastern Europe posed both a mortal security threat and perpetuated German division. For the FRG, the ending of German disunity was a 'possession goal'. For the British, it was a 'milieu goal' at best.

From a British perspective, encounters with the German Democratic Republic (GDR) and Eastern Europe were strictly a matter for consideration as part-and-parcel of foreign policy. For the Federal Republic, by contrast, there was a strong domestic imperative in the formulation of its policy towards the East. Consequently, West German *Aussenpolitik* (foreign policy) after 1949 was often virtually indistinguishable from its *Deutschland-politik*.[29] Furthermore, the post-1945 situation meant that there was an intrinsic link between domestic and foreign policy in Germany, and the casting of the international system.[30] In this respect there were historical precedents. The Treaty of Westphalia of 1648 and the Congress of Vienna of 1815 shaped both German domestic and German constitutional arrangements, as well as international society. Such examples are unique in European history.[31] It was the relationship between the breakdown of relations between the Potsdam signatories and the division of Germany that caused domestic considerations to become paramount in West German Eastern policy.[32] Policy-makers in London all too often forgot the domestic immediacy of the German question for Bonn. Viewed from London the nature of the settlement to be reached over Germany after the Second World War was but one factor in a number of competing interests for a global power like Britain.[33]

Britain played a significant role in achieving West German membership of NATO by 1955. However, Britain failed to anticipate two developments: first, the will and capacity of Bonn to create a hard-line Eastern policy, and second, the totality of the Franco-German rapprochement that would provide the impetus for West European integration. London consequently found itself at odds with West German Eastern policy and outside of the attendant process of European integration. The subsequent British pursuit of détente with Moscow only heightened existing German suspicions by means of efforts to manipulate European integration[34] and Harold Macmillan's much-criticised diplomatic efforts during the Second Berlin Crisis of 1958–62.[35] By the time the Paris Summit collapsed in May 1960, Britain found itself at odds with the Eisenhower administration over East–West relations and frozen out of Western Europe by the Adenauer–de Gaulle axis. The idea that détente could bolster British power was fallacious. Likewise, much of Macmillan's policy towards Germany was ill advised and self-defeating. However, Britain emerged from this period with a clearer idea of the direction of national priorities than for some time past. Britain was now committed to seeking membership of the European Economic Community (EEC). The United States, in the guise of the Kennedy administration, was now more receptive to the idea of a détente with Moscow. In pursuit of such an arrangement it was clear that Washington would find a far more willing partner in London than in either Paris or Bonn. Once US indulgence of the West German hard-line waned then so did the ability of Bonn to defy the realities of the international situation. The recognition of these 'realities' was something that British policy-makers had long since insisted was essential before any lessening in East–West tension could be achieved. By contrast, the construction of the Berlin Wall in August 1961 left West German policy in some disarray. Although the intimacy of Bonn and Paris contributed to de

Gaulle's '*Non!*' to British EEC membership in January 1963, Adenauer's successors refused to embrace de Gaulle's anti-American vision of a 'Europe from the Atlantic to the Urals'. This augured well for Anglo-German relations.

From the early 1960s, the British government realised its limitations. This came after a period in which Britain's position in the world, and therefore its interests, were far from clear. With regard to policy on détente, this had concrete results. In 1962, the British government made a secret assurance to Poland regarding the inviolable nature of its western frontier – the Oder–Neiße line. This frontier, established at Potsdam, had severed a quarter of Germany's territory from the Reich, and its recognition was opposed across the political spectrum in the FRG. Its 'provisional' status had been regarded by London as a source of instability ever since the late 1940s.[36] Despite this, Britain had endorsed its German ally's position that the frontier should remain 'provisional', 'pending a peace treaty'. London now accepted that only Bonn could recognise the line. Moreover, this recognition, while inevitable, would be all the more valuable for its having not been imposed on the Federal Republic. The secret assurance to Poland was a revolutionary development in British policy. It 'squared the circle' between British disenchantment with Bonn's Eastern policy and the desire to achieve a détente in Europe. Britain's secret guarantee was designed to calm Polish fears and instil a greater measure of stability in Europe, and, in terms of this study, the secret guarantee of 1962 is the axis about which British policy revolves.

After 1964, the new Labour government of Harold Wilson pursued a cautious but supportive policy towards Bonn in its modification of its Eastern policies. London now sought to provide reassurance by means of its remaining influence in Eastern Europe and via its links with Washington. In turn, the Wilson government sought Bonn's support for a second application to join the EEC. The collapse of the Erhard government in late 1966 signalled the end of the transition of Bonn's Eastern policy from Adenauer's 'Policy of Strength' to the genesis of Brandt's *neue Ostpolitik*. The year 1967 saw three signal events in the final demise of Britain as a World Power and its acceptance of European Power status. The first was the devaluation of Sterling, the second was the decision to withdraw from 'East of Suez', and the third was the second application for British membership of the EEC. By this time, British policy choices increasingly reflected an acceptance of a role as a medium-sized European power. This study sheds new light on the evolution of Britain from a state that had 'lost an empire' to one that had found a 'role'. Falling between the 1930s era of Appeasement and that of Détente in the 1970s, British policy on Germany in the Cold War often steered a path that invited comparisons with both of these terms. This journey was an essential part of the making of modern Europe and a European Britain.

1 *Stunde null* to *Deutschlandvertrag*

It looks as though Dr Goebbels' disciples may still be able to say 'I told you so'.

John Colville, diary entry for 7 March 1945

Tsar Alexander got to Paris!

Stalin at Potsdam, 1945

Now please do not commit suicide. You would cause me no end of trouble. You're seventy years old and your life is over anyway.

Prison warden to Konrad Adenauer, autumn 1944

Wartime diplomacy

There were two central consequences of the fact that the wartime 'Grand Alliance' was forged by the actions, and the continued existence, of National Socialist Germany. The first was that the Allies would never end the war until Nazism had been completely destroyed. The second was that the Allies, united in their determination to destroy Germany, would find themselves at loggerheads after the war given their radically different political viewpoints and strategic ends. After all, as recently as 1938–9 the British had baulked at the idea of deterring Nazi adventurism by virtue of a military arrangement with Moscow – for fear that the Soviets might use it as an opportunity to expand into Eastern Europe. When Josef Goebbels foresaw the limited shelf life of the Soviet alliance with the West he was quite right.[1] But, for the *Reichsminister*, this fact was of limited utility given that his regime's continued existence provided sufficient common ground to ensure that the 'Grand Alliance' would persist until after the extinction of the 'Thousand Year Reich'.

Whilst the war continued, the West could, on occasion, match the East in its desire for the absolute destruction of the German nation; US Secretary of the Treasury, Henry Morgenthau, proposed a plan that would have effectively ended the life of Germany as a modern, industrialised nation.[2] For his part, President Roosevelt believed that the every German would have to recognise their guilt as their whole nation had 'been engaged in a lawless conspiracy against the decencies of modern civilization'.[3] Churchill similarly stated that 'Retribution for [German] crimes must henceforth take its place among the major purposes of war'.[4] In the spirit of co-operation engendered by the struggle against Hitlerism, the wartime alliance dictated that foundations of a post-war settlement must be laid. Thus, the UK, USSR and US agreed to establish a European Advisory Commission (EAC) in October 1943.[5] The EAC duly began work in London in January of 1944, and agreed that Germany should be dealt with on the basis of its borders of 1 January 1938 (i.e. without the Sudetenland and Memel).[6] On 12 September 1944 an agreement on zones of occupation and the division of Berlin was drafted for post-war Germany (this was revised in July 1945 to include a French zone).[7] Despite this acquiescence regarding Soviet dominance in Eastern Europe, the British were alarmed at what they saw as the US willingness to grant every Soviet demand at the wartime conferences of the 'Big Three'. Jock Colville, Churchill's Private Secretary, noted that Churchill and Foreign Secretary Anthony Eden feared that their willingness to trust the Russians had been 'in vain' and, furthermore,

> It looks as though Dr Goebbels' disciples may still be able to say 'I told you so'; but God knows, we have tried hard to march in step towards the broad and sunlit uplands. If a cloud obscures the sun when we reach them, the responsibility is with Moscow and the bitter, though for the Germans empty, triumph is with Berlin.[8]

Fear and hostility to the USSR had, of course, been the norm in British policy since 1917: the years 1941–45 were the exception.[9] Even before the war had ended, the British feared the 'naïve' Roosevelt was neglecting British advice and blithely allowing the USSR to move towards continental hegemony under the pretence of preventing any resurrection of German militarism.[10] Eden resolved not to 'allow [the Americans] to dictate our foreign policy and if they were wrong we would have to show independence'.[11] Colville noted with trepidation early in 1945:

> The Americans have become very unpopular in England; the Russians are losing their glamour and a few publicised examples of their incorrigibly bad manners and brutal methods of getting their own way will awaken that dread of their future intentions which twenty-five years of Red Bogy [*sic*] propaganda (preceded by a century of the eastern Question) has left close to the surface in most Englishmen's minds.[12]

The British feared the creation of a post-war situation where the Soviet Union replaced Germany as the primary threat to British interests. Thus, German recovery had a security dimension in British minds as well as an

economic one: the increasing menace of the Soviet Union.[13] When
Hitler's Germany had been in the ascendant, Britain had fully co-operated
with Moscow so as to defeat Nazism. Traditional British policy, though,
meant that the advance of the Soviet armies into the heart of Europe was
creating hostages to Europe's future. In March 1944, the historian E.H.
Carr wrote that there could be no viable security system in Europe without
accepting that the Soviet Union was to be allowed to have considerable
influence in Eastern Europe.[14] That same month, Eden confessed to a
'growing apprehension that Russia has vast aims, and that these may
include the domination of Eastern Europe and even the Mediterranean
and the "communizing" of much that remains'.[15] But, in the short term,
Britain had little option but to accept this, and the interdepartmental
Post-Hostilities Planning Sub-committee recommended in May 1944 that
the British government should not 'oppose any reasonable demands of
the USSR where they do not conflict with our vital strategic interests'.[16]
Indeed, Churchill had originally divided the states of Eastern Europe with
Stalin by using percentages.[17] Thus, the original aim of British policy-
makers for the post-war world was a 'concert system' along the lines of that
operated with Metternich and Bismarck.[18] As late as July 1945 the British
embassy in Moscow could report on the growth of Soviet power with a
somewhat detached equanimity.[19]

Realising the implication of US connivance at Soviet aims, however inad-
vertent, Churchill wrote that 'There are a lot of ... terms implying the
German ruin and indefinite prevention of their rising again as an armed
power'.[20] Soviet policy persuaded the British government that Moscow
sought to dominate Central and Western, as well as Eastern, Europe. As
with Hitler, initial acquiescence to Soviet domination of Eastern Europe
gave way to a realisation that such power could lead to Soviet domination
over the entire continent. Antagonistic Soviet policy over the nature of
regimes in Eastern Europe and post-war European frontiers was at the very
heart of the decline and collapse of British–Soviet relations between 1944
and 1947. Indeed, Prime Ministers from Clement Attlee to Harold Wilson
considered the fate of East European boundaries to be an important facet
of British policy.[21] Logically enough, as British policy on frontiers had been
initially used to appease Stalin as an ally, it came, in time, to be used as a
weapon to resist Soviet expansionism.

The 'provisional' arrangements for the territorial re-ordering of
Europe were rooted in the Second World War.[22] The onset of the Cold
War, and the absence of any final peace treaty, meant that these arrangements became part of the problem rather than part of the solution. And
British policy-makers were far from blameless. In the light of the subsequent policy claims under consideration here, it is worth examining
their role in this wartime diplomacy. At the Tehran Conference in 1943,
Churchill had agreed to Stalin's demand for the adoption of the Curzon
line as the Soviet–Polish frontier. Britain duly put pressure on the Polish

government-in-exile to accept the Curzon line,[23] planning, with its Allies, to compensate Poland for the lands lost to the Soviet Union in 1939 with German territories in the west. Following his return from Tehran, Churchill conferred with the Polish Prime Minister in-exile, Stanisław Mikołajczyk – and his Foreign Minister Tadueuz Romer – urging upon them the notion of moving their state westwards at the expense of Germany.[24] In the Commons in December 1944, Churchill stated: 'The Poles are free, so far as the Russians and Great Britain are concerned, to extend their territory at the expense of Germany, to the West ... they gain in the West and North [German] territories more highly developed than they lose in the East.'[25] *The Times* noted that this seemed a 'satisfactory and lasting solution' to the problem of Germany and its eastern neighbours.[26] The Yalta Agreement of 11 February 1945 stated that the USA, the USSR and Britain 'recognized that Poland must receive substantial accessions of territory in the north and west ... [and] will hereafter determine the status of Germany or of any area at present being part of German territory'.[27] No geographical areas were actually identified at Yalta, but the specification and transfer of what became known as the Oder–Neiße territories was enunciated in Article IX (b) of the Potsdam Agreement of 2 August 1945. This 'provisionally' awarded the lands to the east of the Oder–Neiße line to Poland and the USSR:

> [P]ending the final determination of Poland's western frontier, the former German territories east of a line running from the Baltic Sea immediately west of Swinemunde, and thence along the Oder River to the confluence of the western Neisse River and along the western Neisse to the Czechoslovak frontier [excluding that area of East Prussia placed under Soviet control] ... shall be under the administration of the Polish state and for such purposes shall not be considered as part of the Soviet zone of occupation in Germany.[28]

Article XIII of the Potsdam Declaration provided for what was termed the 'orderly and humane' transfer of the German population from the Oder–Neiße territories, as well as from Czechoslovakia, Hungary and Poland proper.[29] Such drastic measures seemed close to effectively finalising the post-war territorial arrangement. Those Germans expelled from the Oder–Neiße territories were replaced with ethnic Poles, and also with Ukrainians, Belorussians and Lithuanians, displaced by the Soviet annexation of formerly Polish lands. Poland also expelled ethnic Germans from Poland proper and the Polish Corridor. The wholesale deportation of Germans (including those in the area between the western and eastern Neiße), from lands under 'temporary' Polish administration, elicited British concern that while '[t]hese transfers of the German population have already been accepted in principle ... but they must be affected in an orderly fashion'.[30]

Eden warned the Poles that, in 1920, 'they made a mistake . . . on going too far East . . . this time, I fear, they are making a mistake in . . . going too far West'.[31] Harold Macmillan recalled that Churchill wanted the eastern Neiße not least to avoid the expulsion of three million more Germans westwards, creating further burdens in the British zone of occupation.[32] Churchill, having declared in the Commons that the decision at Potsdam was 'not a good augury for the future map of Europe', later wrote that 'One day the Germans would want their territories back and the Poles would not be able to stop them', and he would never have agreed to extend Poland to the western Neiße.[33] In fact, Foreign Secretary Ernest Bevin had strongly argued the case for the eastern Neiße[34] but, having lost power in the July 1945 election, Churchill had the luxury of now being able to declare his lack of responsibility for the Potsdam declaration.[35] This was all rather disingenuous given Britain's having previously repeatedly agreed to Poland's 'moving west' – regardless of any distinction between the eastern and western Neiße. Churchill advised Sir Alexander Cadogan[36] in April 1944 that '[we] have promised the Poles that they shall have compensation both in East Prussia in and, if they like, up to the line of the Oder'.[37] In November 1944, Cadogan, in turn, assured Polish Foreign Minister Romer that, even if the US government failed to agree the changes to Poland's western frontier, Britain would advocate them at a peace conference.[38]

But just as in 1944 it was politic to agree to 'moving' Poland westwards, so ten years later it was equally politic to say that the boundaries of Germany could only be settled by a final peace treaty. In 1954, by contrast, the Soviet Union was seen as irreconcilable, and Polish feelings were of little or no consequence in comparison to those of the new West German ally. Therefore, Britain resolved that the West must not allow the Soviets to manipulate the Oder–Neiße line in order to detach the FRG from the Western Alliance.[39] Bonn saw that Western fears of the Soviet threat could be exploited, and Herr Lukaschek, the Minister for Refugees, stated that Bonn would 'never recognise the Oder–Neisse line' and those who advocated doing so in France and Britain would simply create another Versailles.[40] The prospect of a German state detached from the West, and inclined to *revanchiste* tendencies, was the last thing that London wanted to see.

In 1944–5 Germany unambiguously remained the defeated enemy, and there was extensive debate within British circles regarding the practicalities of splitting up the Reich by encouraging 'separatist' movements.[41] However, the consensus, as articulated by Frank Roberts, the British Minister in Moscow, was that German partition would be unsuccessful. The Minister held that any fragmentation could only be temporary, as the splitting up of such a nation 'which is racially, economically, geographically and within certain limits historically a unit, is a step which goes fully contrary to the development of history'.[42] Thus, while Germany must be prevented from waging another war of aggression, it also had to be given a stake in the future of Europe. Oliver Harvey, Eden's Principal Private Secretary, asserted that 'It is utopian to think of a West Germany which is not in the long term united again with East Germany'.[43]

In March 1946, Bevin summarised British aims in Germany to the Cabinet. There were five main points: first, security from a revival of German aggression; second, reasonable economic well-being in Germany and Europe; third, a reduction of the British costs of occupation of Germany; fourth, the creation of a democratic and Western-minded Germany; and fifth, the restriction of Soviet influence as far to the east as possible.[44] The Soviet threat meant that Bevin was aiming for a non-aggressive, democratic, prosperous Germany that would prevent any further westward expansion. This was given greater urgency by British economic and political requirements. The British government had poured £80 million into its occupation zone in 1945–6, and bread rationing was introduced into Britain so as to divert wheat to Germany.[45] Bevin simply declared that 'The Germans must work and produce like everyone else'.[46] While the Labour MP Manny Shinwell regretted that the non-implementation of Potsdam meant that Britain was being forced into expensive, unilateral policy in its zone in Germany,[47] the government did not draw the same conclusion. Crucially, though, Bevin himself conceded that the Western presence in Berlin would be 'fatal to any plans which [the USSR] may have for the political assimilation of the eastern Zone'.[48] Consequently, in spite of rhetoric affirming a commitment to German unity, the British were a driving force in the creation of the Bonn republic. This was in spite of initial American indifference and French hostility to such a move. British policy was derived of a pragmatism borne of a set of three central factors: first, the parlous state of the British economy; second, British commitments worldwide which threatened to stretch resources to breaking point; and, third, the need to reconstruct Western Europe against the USSR.

The most obvious manifestation of the end of the fragile East–West consensus was the dispute over the future frontiers of eastern Germany. Amid growing fears of Soviet intentions, the British protested their alarm at the brutality of the expulsion of the Germans.[49] Policy-makers in London now saw a torrent of criticism – both in public and private – of the continuation of the population transfers and their rationale in the first place.[50] President Truman, less than one year after Potsdam, now referred to the manner in which the Poles had occupied the Oder–Neiße territories of Germany as a 'high handed outrage'.[51] This was accompanied by sharp criticism of Soviet behaviour in their zone of occupation. Allen Dulles, future chief of the CIA, serving in Germany in 1945, told the Council on Foreign Relations that 'An *iron curtain* has descended over the fate of these people and very likely conditions are truly terrible. The promises at Yalta to the contrary, probably 8 to 10 million people are being enslaved'.[52] As the Soviets resisted attempts to modify what they believed they had been granted at the wartime conferences,[53] the West increasingly saw itself, in turn, as free to interpret the wartime agreements in whatever manner it saw fit. This began to question the very essence of previously agreed positions. The mutual and escalating hostility of the early post-war period was reflected in increasingly divergent attitudes towards the Potsdam Agreement, on either side of the Iron Curtain. At the epicentre of the problem lay the matter of German reunification and the status of the Oder–Neiße line. In 1946, Bevin had informed the Cabinet that

> [I]t has been generally assumed that no change in the Potsdam line will be made in Germany's favour. But the Potsdam decision places Russia in a very strong position. The Poles will never be able to dispense with Russian protection in order to hold their newly acquired lands. At the same time the Soviet Government will always have a means of enticing the Germans into their camp by offering to return some of the lost territory.[54]

In order to forestall such a possibility, Secretary of State James F. Byrnes called into question the validity of the Oder–Neiße line as it stood. While the US would

> support revision [of Germany's eastern] frontiers in Poland's favor ... the [exact] extent of the area to be ceded to Poland must be determined [only] when the final settlement is agreed upon ... [but] the United States will not support any encroachment on territory which is indisputably German or any division of Germany which is not genuinely desired by the people concerned.[55]

Byrnes did not say that Potsdam was going to be revised; indeed, he was merely stressed that 'the extent of the area to be ceded to Poland must be determined [only] when the final settlement is agreed upon'.[56]

Byrnes' neat dovetailing of 'self-determination' rhetoric with Cold War politics, whilst mirroring West German tactics after 1949, was part of a wider American strategy. This strategy, as outlined by Eisenberg, deliberately sought to resurrect the German economy as the engine-room of post-war European capitalism. The United States would on no account settle for a neutral Germany, and aimed instead to ensure that the Ruhr and the greater part of Germany entered the Western sphere.[57] Ahonen notes that 'the advocacy of revising the Oder–Neisse line would allow the western Allies to pose as resolute champions of German reunification, even as their real priorities increasingly centred on the establishment of a separate West German state'.[58] Thus, the Americans, like the British, sought to distance itself from the expulsion of Germans from the 'eastern territories':

The fact that the United States signed the Potsdam Agreement does not mean we bear co-responsibility for the wholesale expulsion of Germans from Eastern Europe ... [as] a very large proportion of the Germans had already been expelled ... when the Potsdam Agreement was signed. [Further], the United States ... [only] supported ... German [expulsions] because ... we wanted to make more orderly and humane the inevitable expulsion of those Germans who still remained in Eastern Europe.[59]

Such self-serving logic had an eye on encouraging the German people into a position of permanent antagonism towards the USSR by means of a heavily slanted presentation of decisions reached at the wartime conferences. Thus, reservations about the Oder–Neiße line evolved into the position whereby the United States was actually proposing rectifications by the time of the Foreign Ministers' Conference in Moscow in 1947.[60] Signally, the US delegation, led by the new Secretary of State, George C. Marshall, went to Moscow 'unwilling to compromise'.[61] Anglo-Saxon thinking converged on such matters at the London Conference in December 1947. Britain strongly backed Marshall in his demands for a reassessment of Germany's frontier with Poland.[62] Bevin warned Soviet Foreign Minister Molotov that deadlock on the German Question meant deadlock in East–West relations at the Moscow Conference in 1947,[63] but, as Eisenberg notes, the British and Americans were determined to break with the Soviets by this stage.[64] Stalemate absolutely suited British strategic goals, particularly the wooing of the emerging western Germany. Frank Pakenham, the Minister for Aviation, advised Bevin,

Today, Soviet Russia threatens us just as certainly as the Nazis did before the war. Today, Germany is led by democratic, civilised men, proved anti-Nazis and socialists or Christians, or both. Let history never say that with the lessons of the immediate past in front of us, we solemnly and methodically replied to the Communist aggressor by further weakening the best ally we were likely to find on the Continent.[65]

In this atmosphere, grievances which would have previously been the preserve of the most anti-Soviet elements in the West now became part of the armoury of British diplomacy. British diplomats bluntly informed the Soviets that their occupation of part of East Prussia (endorsed at Potsdam) was evidence of the USSR being 'an expanding imperialist power'.[66] The Carthaginian Peace hinted at at Potsdam, and feared across the political spectrum in the Federal Republic, never arrived. Instead, East and West cultivated their own German client.[67] As Roger Morgan has noted, from the late 1940s 'Britain's Deutschlandpolitik concentrated on consolidating the links for the Federal Republic with the West'.[68] While the resurrection of any German state would be viewed with alarm in Moscow, the British government felt impelled to ignore Moscow's sensibilities. Bevin commented in January 1948 that 'We cannot accept the Russian view that Germany should be kept strictly in hand under an over-centralised government, nor can we let continued poverty and discord cause havoc in Germany and weaken all of Europe'.[69]

Establishing West German legitimacy

The need to strengthen West Germany caused the Western allies to deny the legitimacy of the East German regime following its establishment in October 1949. Secretary of State Dean Acheson declared that, 'the so-called German Democratic Republic is without any legal validity of foundation in the popular will . . . As long as an autocratic Communist regime remains fastened upon the people of eastern Germany . . . it would be meaningless to speak of a peace treaty.'[70] The British were in absolute agreement on this point, and endorsed an official strategy of non-recognition of the GDR on 15 December 1949.[71] The Western purpose in this strategy was two-fold. First, it recognised West German sensibilities by removing any perceived rival as legitimate successor state to the German *Reich*. Second, it would guard against Germany reuniting in a neutral guise and thereby denying the West of the resources of the three Western zones of occupation. As Chester Wilmot pointed out in 1953, a divided Germany offered Britain far more security than a neutral, reunified one.[72] Paradoxically, cementing these two strands together was an undertaking to support Bonn's efforts at reunification. On 18 September 1950, the Foreign Ministers of France, the UK and the USA declared in New York that they considered 'the Government of the Federal Republic as the only German Government free and legitimately constituted and therefore entitled to speak for Germany as the Re-presentative (*sic*) of the German people in international affairs'.[73]

This was to accept the West German claim of *Alleinvertretungsrecht* (right of sole representation) as laid out in the *Grundgesetz* (Basic Law) of the Federal Republic. The Western acceptance of the principle of 'sole representation' was to become a key pillar of the West German foreign policy. The lengths to which Bonn went in the name of 'sole recognition' were considerable, and included a refusal to pay compensation to Nazi victims in countries (such as Poland) that maintained relations with the GDR. While, in strictly formulaic legal terms, this was defensible, it posed obvious problems for British policy-makers in terms of the moral gap in left in propaganda defences against enemies of the West German state.[74] Furthermore, for the Soviet Union, Potsdam remained a blueprint for a treaty with Germany. Thus, Moscow's 'Peace Note' of 10 March 1952 stated that '[t]he territory of Germany is fixed by the borders which were specified by the resolutions of the Great powers at the Potsdam conference'.[75] The 'Peace Note' of March 1952 has long been the subject of dispute as to Stalin's motives; most historians believe that Stalin's offer of a free, neutralised, reunited Germany was a largely tactical device designed (as Adenauer suspected) to prevent the integration of the FRG into the West.[76] Regardless, Moscow was determined that the territorial status quo would prevail in Europe, and, on 9 April 1952, it reiterated its position, reminding the West of its role in bringing about this state of affairs.[77] In rebutting Soviet demands, Adenauer specifically insisted that the 'lost territories' remained part of Germany.[78] This, he knew, would be unacceptable to the USSR whilst, at the same time, popular in the Federal Republic. By such strategies, Adenauer sought to ensure that there was nothing in the Soviet stance that could be seized upon for the negotiation of a peace treaty, whose permanent provisions could only be worse than the 'limbo' legal status that existed in 1952. While British High Commissioner Sir Ivone Kirkpatrick believed that Adenauer had developed a 'Versailles complex',[79] it was undeniable that the Chancellor had managed to wedge his republic between the Potsdam signatories.

Paradoxically, while the Cold War caused the division of Germany it also saved Germany from the punitive peace, a 'Super Versailles', which the Potsdam Agreement of 1945 had seemed to portend. Of course, such a peace settlement was dependent upon on a continued consensus on Germany between the Western Allies and the USSR. Adenauer was unambiguous with regard to the danger of this.

> Every Soviet reference to this agreement constitutes [an] invitation to the West to conclude such a bargain on our backs . . . Bismarck spoke about his nightmare of coalitions against Germany. I have my own nightmare: Its name is Potsdam. The danger of a collusive great power policy at Germany's expense has existed since 1945, and it has continued to exist even since the Federal Republic was founded. The foreign policy of the Federal Republic has always been geared to an escape from this danger zone. For Germany must not be lost between the millstones. If it does it will be lost.[80]

Adenauer had solid backing for his anti-Potsdam stance. The three main parties in the FRG (the CDU/CSU, FDP and SPD) were all, in one historian's words, 'engaged in an ongoing tussle over the mantle of the truest and earliest champion of the Oder–Neisse cause'.[81] In July 1953, the Chancellor told the *Bundestag* that 'I am very happy about the unanimity among the parties in the Bundestag that the content of the Potsdam agreement must be sharply rejected'.[82] In that same year, a typical FDP document demanded that any future policy 'must never lead to a German recognition of the Oder–Neisse line'. Similarly, the SPD's first post-war leader, Kurt Schumacher, himself from West Prussia, declared that his party would 'fight with all peaceful means . . . over every square kilometre east of the Oder–Neisse'.[83]

That Soviet strategy was aimed at splitting the West was readily apparent to London.[84] Eden, restored as Foreign Secretary when Churchill returned to power in 1951, was careful to assure Adenauer that such attempts would not succeed.[85] Given this, Eden was thus uninterested when Moscow proposed the reimposition of four-power occupation whilst an all-German government was formed.[86] Despite commitments to reunification from all sides, Selwyn Lloyd, Minister of State for Foreign Affairs, now advised Churchill that

> Dr Adenauer, the Russians, the Americans, the French and ourselves – feel in our hearts that a divided Germany is safer for the time being. But none of us dare say so openly because of the effect upon German public opinion. Therefore we all support a united Germany, each on his own terms.[87]

When in Berlin in January and February 1954, Eden proposed a plan for the reunification of Germany with free elections for an all-German government. He was surely aware that this would be unacceptable to the USSR.[88] This position was to remain the Western negotiating position for some years to come; this was never going to be accepted by Moscow, especially as the West was now proposing to re-arm the Federal Republic.

Rearming Germany

There is evidence that Stalin had feared the West might use German troops against the USSR during the Second World War.[89] Certainly, in May 1945 Churchill had ordered contingency planning for the use of German troops in the event of a Soviet sweep across Northern Europe.[90] Publicly, the idea of a German military contribution to Western defence was first given respectability in Britain when Montgomery raised it in 1948.[91] Bevin was more cautious over any re-militarization of Germany.[92] At this time, Britain was still officially opposed to German rearmament.[93] The United States had hitherto only mooted such ideas on a hypothetical level, and the French were still resolutely opposed.[94] As late as 28 March 1950, Bevin informed the Commons that 'I have sometimes been urged to win Germany for the West. This raises the question of arming Germany. All of us are against it . . . Talk in any form of arming the Germans is going to set the clock back for a considerable time.'[95] However, as a number of prominent Labour MPs termed it in 1954, 'The real clue to the western attitude on German rearmament is to be found in the fact that the struggle against Germany has become part of the western strategy in the Cold War'.[96]

Adenauer[97] and Sir Ivone Kirkpatrick later identified the Korean War as being of major assistance in the argument for (West) German rearmament.[98] This may have been true for the US policy, but the British position was more ambiguous. A new state that could facilitate West European security via economic means was one thing; a rearmed sovereign state with some measure of policy autonomy was quite another. In the period between May 1950 and September 1951 the Attlee government, after some initial enthusiasm, stressed its continuing fear of offending Moscow.[99] A group of ministers, led by Attlee, even advocated using German rearmament as a bargaining chip in negotiations with the USSR. This proposal foundered on opposition from Washington.[100] The resolve of the Truman administration on German rearmament caused Attlee to see its implementation as being inevitable. Therefore, the Prime Minister resolved it best that Britain involve itself in the process so as to ensure safeguards against any possible resurgence of German militarism.[101] Having decided upon this course, the British government aimed to integrate West Germany into the Western camp in order to nullify the historic military and strategic danger posed by Germany.[102] A balance between a rearmed (West) Germany and the sensibilities of its Western neighbours was essential if the NATO alliance was to present a credible barrier to Soviet expansionism.[103]

Additionally, West German rearmament was seen in London as providing an essential economic role. Paying for the defence of a prostrate Germany was one thing; allowing this to continue after Germany was a sovereign state was quite another. The economic strains of paying for the defence of vital British interests was quite bad enough without having to incur additional, unnecessary expense which would place further strain on the Treasury. Indeed, the years when West Germany had incurred no defence costs were later identified as having 'given the German economy a relative advantage over that of the UK particularly in the export field'.[104]

Adenauer sought to make the FRG the linchpin of the Western Alliance, arguing that 'Germany will be a useful partner to the limit of the strength and resources; she will be a reliable partner to the limit of her strength and resources'.[105] British initiatives on German rearmament were often accepted by the FRG for different reasons than those intended. The consensus on action therefore often masked different motives. In later years, these motives would cause severe policy differences between London and Bonn. From Bonn's perspective, as well as enhancing security the possession of an army would significantly advance its desire to attain the trappings of a 'normal' state. In the FRG's campaign to enhance its status within the West, Adenauer was an undoubted asset. In the eyes of British officialdom, Adenauer personified the new democratic, Western republic, while avoiding the neutralist and pacifist tendencies inherent in the SPD. The SPD, less inclined towards the West and adopting a more 'national' stance than Adenauer's CDU, was regarded with suspicion in London for the manner in which it seemed to entertain Soviet overtures such as the 'Peace Note' of March 1952.[106] Many in Britain feared the 'old' Germany was simply awaiting the demise of the democratic experiment of Adenauer to return to centre stage.[107] Eden noted that 'The Germans are always awkward allies and are likely to be more so after Dr Adenauer has left the scene'.[108] A delegation from the Conservative Party concluded that the CDU lacked cohesion, as did the population of West Germany, and noted that reunification was the one issue that drew a broad consensus in the Federal Republic.[109] The two forces for stability in the 'fragile' democracy of West Germany were, therefore, the person of Adenauer, and the aspiration to reunification.

Adenauer and the West: tied to a new *Drang nach Osten?*

Chancellor Adenauer was under severe domestic pressure to ensure that West German adherence to the Western camp did not necessitate the abandonment of territories outside the boundaries of the Federal Republic. Adenauer carefully wove together the German contribution for the defence of Western Europe with the refusal to recognise the Oder–Neiße line as permanent. The West German refusal to accept the post-war territorial status quo was to become one of the defining characteristics of Bonn's foreign policy. The German case on the Oder–Neiße line rested on two fundamentals rooted in strict legalism. First, Potsdam held that only a 'final peace settlement' with an *all-German* government could adjudicate as to the final status of the permanent boundaries of Germany. Advocates of the German case continued to stress the continued relevance of Potsdam and, hence, the continued existence of the Oder–Neiße question as an unresolved international legal issue. Even following the Eastern treaties of Willy Brandt, signed between 1970 and 1973, the German scholar Claus Arndt wrote that treaties entered into by the *West* German government were very limited in their application to the *whole* of Germany as 'a final settlement for Central Europe' remained the long-term goal.[110] Second, the Basic Law identified the FRG as the sole successor to the German *Reich* and the representative of the entire German nation until that nation was reunited in its entirety. In actual fact, West German constitutional arrangements after 1949 had the effect of obstructing any progress towards finalising German borders in advance of reunification. Article 23 of the Basic Law identified Germany as existing – in strictly legal terms – within the boundaries of the Reich of December 1937 (the FRG described itself as 'identical with the German Reich within the frontiers of December 31, 1937').[111] In order to ensure that this would be difficult to circumvent, Article 146 stated that the *Grundgesetz* would only become ineffective the day that a new constitution was adopted having been freely enacted by the German people. In sum, since Potsdam had specified that the boundaries of Germany could only be fixed by a treaty with an all-German government, West Germany could not recognise the Oder–Neiße line even if it wished to do so. This, of course, was used to reinforce the unwillingness of Bonn to recognise the line in traditional terms of national interest. Federal Foreign Minister Heinrich von Brentano asserted in 1956:

[T]here is no German Federal Government, either today or tomorrow, which can recognise the Oder–Neisse Line as frontier. Firstly, it will not do so because it is not entitled to do so ... Secondly, it will not do so because it is not entitled to do so towards the people, the German people, who have lived there for centuries.[112]

From its inception, the GDR took immediate advantage of the opportunity to demonstrate that it was, unlike the FRG, keen to recognise the Oder–Neiße line in order to try and facilitate German–Polish relations. Thus, the GDR recognised the boundary as permanent in the Treaty of Görlitz (Zgorzelec) on 6 July 1950. The treaty declared the Oder–Neiße boundary as 'inviolable',[113] and charged the British and the Americans with failing to do likewise so as 'to drive Germany, the trouble spot of Europe, to war against Poland and the Soviet Union'.[114] The GDR claimed that it, unlike its Western neighbour, was keen eradicate the 'tragic experiences of the Hitler-system era'.[115] Unmoved by such emotive language, the West German *Bundestag* formally denounced the GDR–Polish statement of 6 June 1950: '[the] Bundestag knows that in rejecting this action it is also speaking in the name of the Germans in the Soviet zone of occupation'.[116] Those in sympathy with the Polish case were moved to suggest that this constituted the 'peace settlement' now held in abeyance by the Cold War.[117] In reality, however, this was wishful thinking, as the status of the territories had not in fact yet received the final approval by means of a peace settlement.[118] The West German case rested upon the premise that the Oder–Neiße line was not a bilateral German–Polish dispute but rather a decision in the gift of the Four Powers, and it was the failure to negotiate a peace treaty that meant that the line remained 'provisional'. Adenauer had ensured that the West, and especially the United States, would have nothing to do with the Treaty of Görlitz. Thus prompted, the West denounced Görlitz as a violation of the Potsdam Declaration of 2 August 1945, which saw German boundaries as provisional 'pending a final peace treaty'.[119]

In January 1951 the British Control Commission for Germany expressed alarm when it saw, in a statement that Adenauer intended to deliver at a press conference, a passage stating that 'A genuine all-German solution can ... only be achieved if it applies to all those areas which belonged to Germany on 31st December 1937'. The British advised that it would be wise to inform Adenauer that such statements were imprudent because 'The Chancellor thus spurns German unity on the basis of the four existing zones even as an interim measure; and in doing so lays down a new condition for all-German elections'.[120] The Federal government suspected, however, that to accept the idea of reunification as being the unification of the four occupation zones, even as an 'interim measure', would mean the effective loss of the Oder–Neiße territories. West German political rhetoric showed that this was simply unacceptable. In August 1951 the

Minister for All-German Affairs, Jakob Kaiser, demanded the return of the eastern territories, stating 'We must once more have a German Breslau, a German Marienburg, a German Stettin'.[121] Soon afterwards, Adenauer told a refugee meeting in Hannover: 'Be convinced of this, that in the negotiations which I have to conduct the recovery of your homelands, which is of such importance to you, will never be left out of account.'[122]

In November 1951, the three Western Allies' representatives met Adenauer at Wahnerheide and, on an American-inspired initiative, informed the Chancellor that when they referred to a reunified Germany they were referring to the reunification of the Federal Republic, the Soviet Zone and Berlin. The Western Allies 'were not referring in any way to the territories east of the Oder–Neisse line'. Adenauer reacted very sharply towards this and said that he had assumed the Western Allies backed the 1937 boundaries, highlighting the impossibility of passing anything in the *Bundestag* without this proviso. The British High Commissioner, Kirkpatrick, recounted that he insisted that the new element in the situation was 'not our refusal to admit that a unified Germany must include these territories but the Chancellor's insistence that that we should agree to include them'.[123]

Adenauer retorted that he took the protest at the Treaty of Görlitz as a sign that the Western powers endorsed the West German position. Bonn's nascent foreign policy was effectively challenging British policy for the first time. Kirkpatrick complained that Adenauer refused to be 'pinned down' over a future German eastern frontier, and would only try and secure Western backing for the recovery of the Oder–Neiße territories at the peace treaty. Refusing to be 'pinned down' in advance of a peace treaty was, however, precisely Adenauer's policy. The Treaty of Görlitz was dismissed in an official Federal statement noting that the 'so-called' GDR had no right to speak for the German people. Instead, 'In future peace negotiations the Federal Government will seek a just solution of this question between a really democratic Poland and a democratic, united Germany'.[124]

The failure of the Western Allies to stand behind this, Adenauer lamented, would mean an adherence to Potsdam in a manner that would 'lose' the West the peace treaty. Adenauer then outlined a black scenario with remorseless logic. The failure of negotiations would mean the end of European integration; there would be no Schuman or Pleven Plan; no more European movement in Germany; subsequently, the Federal Republic would be easy prey for neo-Nazis and socialists, and Germany would fall victim to the Soviets through neutralism. Furthermore, the fact that the allies were asking Germany for 400,000 troops would be rendered redundant as 'Germany would not be ready to supply them if they were told that the Allies retained complete freedom of action for the future in respect of the territories beyond the Oder–Neisse line'. The French High Commissioner, François-Poncet, observed sharply that Adenauer was being asked to help defend Western Europe, and not prepare for the eastern expansion of Germany.[125]

Willy Brandt records that Adenauer stated in conversation in Hamburg that the twelve divisions would be useful behind him when he was talking to the West. His interlocutor stated that surely he meant the USSR. Adenauer replied 'No, Herr Ollenhauer, the West. That's where the pressure comes from. The other lot are much more realistic; they have enough on their own plates.'[126] Nevertheless, even in West Germany's relatively prostrate position in the early 1950s, Adenauer managed to lever the Western Allies, including Britain, into association with his stance on the Oder–Neiße line.[127] While Britain did not actively desire that Germany renounce the eastern territories, the status of the Oder–Neiße line was a sensitive issue for London. Eden stated in 1951 that if Adenauer asked him about the eastern territories he would simply be evasive and make some platitude about awaiting the final peace treaty.[128]

In response to Eden, Churchill simply noted that the West Germans should be aware that the British had desired the Oder–Neiße line to run along the eastern rather than the western Neiße.[129] This was an ominous portent for the future: in 1953 a West German official confided that while there was the possibility of a compromise with Poland and Czechoslovakia over Germany's eastern boundaries, rearmament would instinctively harden Bonn's attitude towards these questions.[130] The British ambassador in Paris, Gladwyn Jebb, concurred: 'an armed Germany will speak a very different language. If ... the Germans should then use their twelve divisions in an effort to come to terms with the Soviet Union we should not, I suppose, be able to say that we were not warned.'[131]

The waning fortunes of the refugee parties in the FRG were seen by London not as a decline of sentiment on the eastern territories question, but rather as a reflection of the mainstream parties' adoption of a position favoured by the refugees. Furthermore, public feeling over the eastern territories was unlikely to decline in the foreseeable future.[132] The West German state was assimilating the refugees but, at the same time, assimilating their policies too. This was especially the case in the Konrad Adenauer's CDU/CSU, which held power in the Federal Republic (as dominant partners in a coalition) in no small part due to its stance on the 'eastern territories'.[133]

The British desire to keep the door open on détente

In 1945, the differences between Britain and the USSR seemed by no means certain to lead to open hostility. Yet, as Clark and Wheeler have argued, 'concern about the Soviet Union had already become fabric of [British] post-war security', and the alliance inherited from the war was 'not strong enough to bear the burden of post-war settlement but not sufficiently adversarial to be abandoned altogether'.[134] Although the Attlee government had supported the creation of a West German state, this was accompanied by fears of a Soviet reaction that might lead to war. After all, West Germany was supposed to increase security, not to act as a catalyst for war with the Soviet Union. British frustration with Stalin and Molotov culminated in the Moscow Conference in December 1947, and negotiation was subordinated to the creation of a Federal Republic. Prior to this, Alan Bullock points out, a deal with the Soviet Union would have suited Bevin, the Labour Party, the British economy and the Americans – who were not yet committed to an anti-Soviet crusade.[135]

Even staunch anti-Communist Bevin was concerned with keeping the door to the East open as well as ensuring the United States stayed in Europe. In consequence, one must see the alliance as providing a foundation for negotiation with the East rather than ensuring success in the military sphere.[136] Thus Bevin resisted pressure from the Foreign Office and the military to turn to the expedient of anti-Communist rhetoric. In November 1947, he stressed that the British had been 'scrupulously careful not to encourage subversive movements in Eastern Europe or anti-Russianism, or to lead the anti-communists to hope for support that we cannot give'.[137] Three years later, Bevin cautioned that German rearmament 'might provoke just that action which it is our aim to prevent'.[138] Such attitudes were often at variance with the hardening stance of the United States, and the US ambassador to Moscow warned that to think in terms of appeasing the USSR over Berlin ignored previous experience of dealing with Moscow since Potsdam.[139] In the wake of the 'Peace Note' of March 1952, the Soviets again put pressure on access routes to Berlin in order to try and pressurise the West. When the three Western Allies (represented by French Foreign Minister Robert Schuman, Acheson and Eden) discussed their possible response at meetings in Paris on 26 and 28 May, it was Eden who was the most pessimistic about the prospects of resisting Soviet pressure.[140] Britain continued to exercise caution, and in the autumn of 1953 the Eisenhower administration terminated its major propaganda effort in East Germany in the face of British (and French) protests against 'unnecessary' provocation of the Soviet Union.[141]

Anglo-German differences

Even before Konrad Adenauer became the first Chancellor of West Germany, he publicly declared of the Oder–Neiße line: 'This frontier we will never recognise!'[142] He reiterated this in his first speech in office. The Adenauer government's refusal to recognise the Oder–Neiße line was a central facet of its hard-line *Politik der Stärke* – 'Policy of Strength' – although the Chancellor himself dismissed the term as a cliché.[143] The Federal Republic had little to gain by negotiation which, if successful, would most likely lead to the general recognition of the Oder–Neiße line and the setting aside of the question of German reunification in the interests of better relations between East and West. It was easy for the British to see the 'tidying up' of the Oder–Neiße question as a price worth paying for a general settlement. This was not, of course, the way things would look in Bonn. Alliance did not create a symmetry of interest between Bonn and London as *The Times* cautioned in welcoming German friendship, 'it does not follow that Europe accepts and supports all-Germany's claims for frontier revision'.[144] Or, as Adenauer stated in 1963, 'Britain did not have the same perception of threat as continental Europeans. This was certainly the best explanation for the British attitude in all questions which interested us.'[145]

Despite such obvious policy differences, there was little real doubt amongst British policy-makers as to the peaceful intentions of the Adenauer government. On 20 October 1953, the Chancellor told the *Bundestag* that 'The problem of the Oder–Neisse line is not to be solved by force but by peaceful means only'.[146] However, as an important corollary of this, the FRG emphasised that all it would guarantee was that Bonn would not rectify the Oder–Neiße line by force. Thus, the refusal to recognise the Oder–Neiße line meant that Soviet bloc charges of West German intransigence and revisionism were extremely hard to refute on a straightforward level. The West German government, however, had its reasons. For one thing, Adenauer was severely limited in his room for manoeuvre in policy by virtue of the presence of large numbers of expellees (from the Oder–Neiße territories and elsewhere) in the FRG. By 1950, there were at least eight million expellees in the Federal Republic (as well as some four million in the GDR).[147] Yet any indulgence of expellee demands by the Federal government was an open goal for Communist propaganda. This drove British diplomats to distraction, as these groups, and their patrons in West German politics, were seen to exert a wholly unhelpful influence on the search for meaningful East–West dialogue. Internationally, Adenauer had little option but to renounce force on the issue of the Oder–Neiße line, but at the same time, domestically, he simply could not recognise – or even negotiate over – the loss of the 'eastern territories'. Numbering approximately one-fifth of the population, the expellees had an entire ministry of the Federal government (*Bundesministerium für Vertriebene, Flüchtlinge und Kriegsgeschädigte*) to look after their interests, and the strong overlap between this ministry and the expellee organisations meant that the latter's charter was an official publication.[148] It is against such realities that Sabine Lee has noted that, for Adenauer, there was a great deal of difference between an *Ostpolitik* designed and controlled by him and any détente arranged for him by the United States and Britain to which he was expected simply to subscribe.[149]

Nevertheless, the rights and wrongs of history were not for those seeking to make broad sweeps to effect great change. For the British, the issue of *rapprochement* between Bonn and the East had long been seen as fundamental to the issue of progress in East–West relations. Clement Attlee articulated the fears of many when he stated in the Commons:

> There is ... a great danger in [the Germans] looking backwards ... I think that there are dangerous irredentist forces in Germany. Any number of re-allocations of territory can be made ... [as noted in the] five points of the Bundestag with regard to territorial settlements but for 700 years the Slav and the Teuton have quarrelled about the division of those areas. I should have thought it was about time that they ... tried to settle down to make the best of what they have got.[150]

The period after Stalin's death in March 1953 saw intensified pursuit of a summit breakthrough.[151] Churchill stated in the Commons 'that a conference on the highest level should take place between the leading powers without delay'.[152] Amongst the issues requiring resolution was the 'provisional' nature of German eastern frontiers. Churchill invoked the 1925 Treaty of Locarno, which had guaranteed the frontiers of the Weimar Republic and its western neighbours:

> the master thought that animated Locarno might well play its part between Germany and Russia ... Russia has a right to feel assured that ... the terrible events of the Hitler invasion will never be repeated, and that Poland will remain a friendly power and a buffer, though not, I trust, a puppet State.[153]

This was precisely what Adenauer feared, and he stated at press conference in London that this concept was unsuitable for Eastern Europe and the idea of the West German state attacking the Soviet bloc was absurd. While he did like the notion of a 'Locarno spirit', he saw the question of Germany's eastern frontier as being the business of a future all-German government and a 'free' Poland.[154] To the Chancellor's relief, Eisenhower rejected Churchill's proposal as being 'untimely'.[155] In reality, the US attitude was derived of hard-line 'roll-back' policy rhetoric (which Adenauer well understood and played up to). To this end, the President had already drafted a resolution 'reject[ing] any interpretations or applications of any international agreements or understandings, made during the course of World War II, which have been perverted to bring about the subjugation of free peoples'.[156] Such rhetoric, linking the promotion of post-war anti-Communism with a rejection of wartime diplomacy, encouraged the West German government to seek specific US backing for its hard line on the eastern territories. Realising this, Adenauer sent a memorandum to the US President on 29 May 1953 requesting that the West refuse to recognise the Oder–Neiße line in any East–West deal.[157] The memorandum insisted that any peace treaty accord 'the right of all people to their homeland', while stressing that 'No German government will ever be able to recognize the Oder–Neisse Line. [Although] Germany will … endeavour to settle the territorial questions bound up therewith in a new spirit of peaceful international co-operation.'[158] While the ability to obstruct Churchill confirmed Adenauer as one of the most influential foreign figures in Washington,[159] Eden concluded bitterly: 'It must be a long time in history since any one speech did so much damage to its own side.'[160]

Although Churchill lamented the loss of the opportunity afforded by the demise of Stalin,[161] suspicion of him in Moscow was widespread due to his anti-Communist past.[162] Thus, there was little chance of the Prime Minister prevailing in the face of such widespread opposition.[163] Indeed, many members of Churchill's own Foreign Office actually shared Adenauer's fears regarding the dangers of dabbling in horse-trading over Germany (as did Foreign Secretary Eden).[164] A Foreign Office memorandum pointed out that the neutralisation of Germany would ruin NATO defensive strategy, based as it was on the Elbe. It would also upset the FRG and its Chancellor, provide an opening for the USSR, and maybe even encourage the USA to disengage from Europe.[165] The speech on 11 May 1953, and British behaviour at the Berlin Conference of Ministers of Foreign Affairs of the four powers in January and February of 1954, were two major causes of Adenauer's belief that the British would sacrifice major German national interests in order to achieve a settlement with Moscow.[166] This eventuality was one Adenauer was determined to frustrate, as he, and Germans from across the political spectrum, feared precisely what the British seemed increasingly keen to arrange: a Four-Power agreement on Germany.[167] In June 1953, the *Manchester Guardian* reported that 'Dr Adenauer's suspicion that Four-Power talks might be exploited as a tactical weapon of delay by the Russians is unfortunately based on much long and frustrating experience.'[168]

Diplomacy impelled Adenauer to sound as reasonable as possible publicly. In July 1953 the Chancellor called for East–West negotiations, correctly anticipating, with American collusion, that the USSR would rebuff his proposals.[169] Adenauer saw the Soviet threat as wedding Russian nationalism with an inherently hostile ideology: Communism. The Chancellor despaired of his Western Allies' inability to see the malignant intent in Soviet policy on occasion. The death of Stalin was an early example of the different readings of Moscow applied by London and Bonn. This event had prompted Churchill to make his 'eastern Locarno' speech. The feeling that the death of Stalin was a major opportunity was genuinely felt in Britain. Sir William Hayter, the then ambassador to Moscow, recalled that in 1954 Malenkov was a man, despite his toughness, with whom 'business could be done'.[170] Politicians such as Aneurin Bevan made 'much headway' with the idea that Premier Georgy Malenkov would happily negotiate the withdrawal of Soviet troops from Germany.[171] Conversely, Adenauer was in the USA making speeches expressing scepticism about any real change in Soviet policies.[172] For Adenauer, 'the Soviet Union aimed at a period of détente in order to solve the problems the Soviet leadership found itself confronted with. Yet, there was no indication the USSR had changed its inner goal . . . to conquer the world through communism.'[173]

For Adenauer, Soviet Communism was an irreconcilable enemy, and he made little secret of this: 'The conditioning factor of our policy and the root of historical developments of the past several years has been the aggressive expansionist policy of Soviet Russia.'[174] He believed that 'The danger of atheist materialism in Europe, threatening the whole Christian world, is great because of the political power behind it'.[175] Adenauer remained unyielding, advising Kennedy in 1961:

> The Soviet Union will in essence remain what it is, even if a certain degree of understanding is now reached. In the centuries of Czars, at least since Peter the Great, Russia was already aggressive and intent upon constantly increasing its territory, especially towards the West. . . . Communism has not weakened Russian nationalism; on the contrary, it has strengthened it. Mr Khrushchev, too, in my opinion is primarily a Russian nationalist and only secondarily a Communist.[176]

With American backing, it was Adenauer who prevailed in his vision of non-negotiation with the Soviet bloc. Not for the last time, British advocacy of détente won few converts. However, if there was to be no 'negotiation', then Britain hoped that there would at least be 'strength' via a European Defence Community (EDC).

Britain and Europe

In the EDC, London had seen a workable mechanism for resurrecting the military potential of (West) Germany in a controlled fashion (in the same manner as the European Steel and Coal Community (ECSC) was doing with industry). In May 1952, the Western Allies and Bonn signed a convention confirming the integration of the Federal Republic with the West.[177] This 'Bonn War Treaty' was violently attacked by the USSR and the GDR,[178] as was the treaty on the EDC signed one day later in Paris. When Eden was asked in the Commons how he could support EDC membership for the 'same people we fought twice', he replied

> 'What is the alternative? It is to see Germany a vacuum, in the centre of Europe with a national army, and perhaps giving herself away to the highest bidder. . . . If Germany is to be neutral and disarmed, who will keep her disarmed? If Germany is to be neutral and armed, who will keep her neutral?'[179]

Adenauer was in absolute agreement: 'A neutral country is one which has the power . . . of defending its country against all-comers. A country that survives only by the tolerance of others is not neutral.'[180]

When the French Assembly set aside the EDC in 1954 Churchill informed Eisenhower that it must be the Anglo-Saxons' number one priority to see that the EDC gain acceptance.[181] It was Eden's sophistry that rescued the situation by proposing to extend the 1948 Brussels Pact, which now became the Western European Union, to include West Germany. Furthermore, Adenauer expressed to Eden in September 1954 the absolute necessity of British participation in any military arrangement involving West Germany, so as not to be left alone with France.[182] In order to calm continental fears, Eden announced on 30 September 1954 that the UK would maintain four divisions in Europe in perpetuity to 'prevent a war and not win a war', as Eden put it at the Conservative Party Conference on 6 October 1954.[183] Symbolically, West Germany was proposed for membership of NATO by the French Prime Minister Pierre Mendes-France, and on 23 October 1954 the Paris Treaties – the *Deutschlandvertag*, as Adenauer insisted they be termed – were signed.[184] On 15 January 1955, in an attempt to prevent the ratification of the Paris Agreements, Moscow offered to establish normal relations with Bonn.[185] The rebuttal of this Soviet offer led to the formation of the Warsaw Pact. However, even in resolving to form the Communist alliance the USSR had been deliberately vague about the terms of the pact, in the continued hope of delaying or preventing the implementation of the Paris Agreements.[186] On 5 May 1955, the Federal Republic attained full sovereignty (albeit with residual allied rights).[187] Adenauer assessed the implications of the *Deutschland-vertag* in a memorandum:

> The German Treaty prevents an agreement between the western Allies with the Soviet Union at ... the Federal Republic's expense. ... This foreign policy line is, even though the circumstances are very different, the same as that followed by Bismarck, who considered his success after [1871] in preventing the creation of a coalition against Germany.[188]

An enraged Molotov declared: 'The German militarists and revenge-seekers ... will yet, when the time comes, remind the French, British and American Ministers of [their folly].'[189] But the West was not listening. The Paris Agreements ended the Allied occupation regime, made West Germany a full member of NATO and created the Western European Union (WEU). Article seven of the agreements also specified that a 'significant goal' of Western policy remained 'a settlement for the whole of Germany freely entered into by Germany and its former opponents ... and a final determination of Germany's borders must be postponed until such a settlement is achieved'.[190] On 11 May 1955, Adenauer declared: 'We are now part of the strongest alliance in history. It will bring us unification.'[191] The British had given encouragement to such thinking, and Churchill informed Adenauer that 'We shall not betray you. If the West is strong enough, the Soviet Union may possibly yield and agree to a reunification of Germany.'[192] As a sop to those who feared Soviet ire over the resurrection of German military power, Adenauer declared that 'We must prove to the Soviet Union again and again that our loyalty to the Western alliance ... does not pose a threat to the Russian people, but will make a real contribution to the relaxation of tension'.[193] What the Paris Agreements had done, however, was to deepen the division of Europe, as the Soviet Union responded with the formation of the Warsaw Pact. Foreign Secretary Sir Anthony Eden told a Commonwealth Prime Ministers' meeting that he did not believe that the Paris Agreements would achieve the ultimate German aim of reunification. However, in a curious mirror-imaging of Adenauer's 'magnet theory', Eden suggested that if the Western European Union became a reality then eastern Germany might be increasingly drawn to the West, and the USSR might thus be impelled to negotiate.[194] Eden was certainly correct in assessing that there would be no German reunification in the foreseeable future, and the Minister of Defence, Selwyn Lloyd, conceded as much in the Commons.[195]

In place of a united Germany, Adenauer was going to concentrate on integration with the West. Only by reassuring its neighbours in such a fashion could Germany, Adenauer believed, move towards unity, and thus he could assert 'I am the only German Chancellor in history who has preferred the unity of Europe to the unity of the Reich.'[196] But Adenauer's integrationist *Westpolitik* was intimately linked with an intransigent *Ostpolitik*:

> Only when the West was strong enough might there be a genuine point of departure for peace negotiations to free not only the Soviet zone but all of enslaved Europe east of the Iron Curtain, and free it peacefully. To take the road that led to the European Community appeared to me the best service we could render to the Germans in the Soviet zone.[197]

Bevin stated in the Commons in 1948 that 'We should do all we can ... to foster both the spirit and the machinery of co-operation ... Britain cannot stand outside Europe and regard her problems as quite separate from those of her European neighbours.'[198] But Britain saw its role as a catalyst of, rather than a participant in, European integration.[199] Adenauer stated in 1949 that 'I would be glad if the British Government and people would accept the facts that England (*sic*) is a European Power, and that her history is bound up with that of Western Europe, and that she is in duty bound to play her part in European development'.[200] In May 1951, Adenauer complained to Foreign Secretary Herbert Morrison that without British participation in the ECSC and the EDC, Western Europe 'had not enough strength firmly to resist communist pressure from the East in the long run'.[201] Although Churchill had called for a 'United States of Europe' in 1946,[202] once in government after 1951 he demonstrated that, while supporting West European integration, any previous calls for British participation were essentially rhetorical and had been deployed for political advantage.[203] Eden declared in January 1952 that Britain's real interests lay outside Europe, and joining a European federation was 'something which we know, in our bones, we cannot do.'[204]

Adenauer pleaded for British participation in Europe in order to assuage French fears of Germany; the German people would be psychologically devastated if the European project that they had placed so much faith in were to fail. Eden was unmoved, citing domestic pressure to concentrate on traditional overseas ties rather than continental Europe.[205] Adenauer saw the detrimental effects of such British policies – namely the prospect of the *Westpolitik* failing – as allowing the USSR to impose 'neutralism' on the Federal Republic.[206] This was Adenauer's worst fear, for, having rejected Soviet domination, 'The Federal Republic cannot exist without the support of other states ... in the case of a neutralization depending solely upon international agreement there is no assurance that the march of events might not trample ruthlessly over it'.[207]

The manner in which the Americans and the British pushed through West German rearmament and membership of NATO in 1954–5 meant that France and West Germany would be forced together in a West European framework. This was to cause problems later when de Gaulle built upon these foundations to work against the Anglo-Saxons.[208] Adenauer believed that reconciliation with France was essential because 'Without a Franco-German understanding we shall not attain the unification of Europe, and without the unification of Europe there will be no unification of Germany'.[209] Against this, Eden's willingness to commit Britain to the continent militarily seemed to signal the ascendancy of Britain and the demise of French attempts permanently to enfeeble Germany. This link between security and economic strategies, inherent in the *Adenauersche Konzeption*, was lost on the British and, as a result, after 1958 de Gaulle was able to harness West Germany to his vision of Europe.

Conclusion

Potsdam was originally intended to foreshadow a peace treaty in Europe. That this was not the case was due to the manner in which the common ground between the former wartime allies rapidly disappeared. Any peace treaty was dependent upon continued Four-Power co-operation in Germany and, although each Power had supreme authority in its own occupation zone, joint authority was stipulated for Germany as a whole.[210] For the British this became untenable after the USSR displaced Germany as the major threat to British security. This rapid switch in threat perception was well rooted in British thinking historically. Duff Cooper, the British ambassador in Paris after 1945, reflected that 'So far as the continent was concerned British policy had always been, and must in my submission remain, to prevent its domination by any one too powerful nation'.[211] British policy therefore concerned itself with the resurrection of a German state to balance against the USSR. West Germany was accepted as the sole legitimate representative of the German people, while the GDR was a 'non-state'. Adenauer exploited this endorsement of West German policy in order to strengthen the position of the Federal Republic and ensure that Potsdam would not be implemented. While London concerned itself with the construction of a viable Western security system, West German policy seemed not unduly at odds with British policy. Echoing American 'roll-back' rhetoric, Adenauer declared that Western strength might cause 'a complete reorientation of large segments of the peoples of eastern Germany, Czechoslovakia, Hungary, and other Russian satellites'.[212] In the face of Soviet power, such rhetoric was far more seductive to US policy-makers than were British pleadings for détente. The idea, as articulated by 'Cold Warriors' like Adenauer, that there could be no accommodation with Moscow because the latter represented an implacable ideological opponent was not one that British policy-makers would find easy to accept.

The underlying thrust of British Soviet policy after 1945 was the dual approach of 'armed vigilance' allied to 'a search for détente ... when opportunities presented themselves'.[213] Sir Duncan Wilson, former British ambassador to Moscow, believed that '[with regard to] intergovernmental relations, we cannot confine ourselves to dealing with states whose general policies we approve'.[214] Lord Strang referred to such attitudes as being born of a 'conciliatory quality'; a policy characterised by Strang as one seeking 'compromise' rather than 'victory', settlement by mutual compromise.[215] In short, as Harold Nicolson argued, Britain had a 'civilian' as opposed to a 'warrior' method of conducting diplomacy.[216]

British policy-makers were disposed to think of the Cold War in a less doctrinaire fashion than their American and West German counterparts. In 1950, Churchill spoke out in Edinburgh on the need for high-level talks in order that East and West might co-exist.[217] The driving consistency in Churchill's thinking was a policy of negotiation from strength.[218] This was also the supposed guiding principle in Adenauer's thinking. The crucial difference was that any successful negotiations would inevitably be at the expense of Germany – otherwise they could never be acceptable to Moscow. British policy-makers constantly asked the same questions of themselves. Would the reunification of Germany as a neutral state be a safe option? Was German reunification a necessary prerequisite to European stability? And if Germany continued to assert that its eastern frontier lay to the east of the Oder–Neiße line, was Polish–German reconciliation possible? Finally, if the military strength of the Federal Republic were increased, would this inevitably heighten the tension between East and West?[219]

George F. Kennan's original conception of 'containment' had not been wholly pessimistic. Kennan had not advocated cutting off diplomatic links and any prospects of negotiation, but rather counselled pressure to 'modify' Soviet behaviour by what Kennan referred to as 'positive' and 'negative' reinforcement.[220] Yet the manner in which the Federal Republic refused to accept the status quo was a direct challenge to Soviet plans to consolidate their hold on Eastern Europe and the GDR. The logic of the West's endorsement of Adenauer's 'no concessions' would be the infinite perpetuation of a state of mutual hostility with the Soviet Union. As early as the late 1940s, the British had fretted that Western policy on Germany was making war more likely by causing alarm in Moscow.[221] Adenauer had brilliantly exploited the Cold War by constantly advancing worst-case thinking to present the Soviet danger as posing an immediate threat to the security of West Germany and, hence, of the Free World.[222] As the Soviet ambassador to East Germany was later to note, 'The cold war planners in Bonn ... had always vigorously opposed any negotiations between the western Powers and the Soviet Union on a German peace settlement.'[223] To Britain, continued indulgence of Bonn's position could outweigh the potential deterrent value of a West German contribution to the Western Alliance. The Western endorsement of West German Eastern policy was intended to bolster Adenauer's claim to legitimacy domestically and avoid a nationalist or neutralist alternative in the Federal Republic. It was not intended as the foundation of a revisionist position with designs on Eastern Europe. Such a position could only create alarm across the Elbe, perpetuate the division of Europe and increase the likelihood of war.

2 Détente or *Politik der Stärke?*

I believe that God has given the German people a specific function: to be the defenders of the west against the powerful influences that affect us from the east.

Konrad Adenauer

We arm to parley.

Winston Spencer Churchill

Accepting revisionism?

The Final Act of the London Conference of 3 October 1954, signed by Britain, France and seven other NATO powers, endorsed the frontiers of Germany as provisional pending a comprehensive peace settlement with a future all-German government.[1] This effectively accepted the West German government's refusal to recognise the status quo. Little wonder that the creation of a strong German state, aligned with the West, had been something Moscow had determined to prevent.[2] The West's position flew in face of the fact that much of the post-war status quo had been agreed during the wartime conferences. The Soviets[3] (and Poles, Czechs and others for that matter) certainly believed in the permanence of the post-war arrangements – and the British well knew this.[4] Moscow determined at every turn to highlight its belief that it was the British (and the Americans) who were reneging on agreements given that 'the Soviet Government hold as adequate and final the decisions ... of the Potsdam Conference'.[5] But, as Joseph Joffe later noted, this meant that

> [While] the grand settlement of 1954 precluded an autonomous German *Ostpolitik*, it also denied the West a free hand in Eastern Europe and Moscow. By underwriting Bonn's maximal objectives, the West had minimized its freedom of manoeuvre in the East ... the German Problem was now the decisive barrier in the overall East–West relationship, and the Federal Republic was the guardian at the gate.[6]

This was reinforced by the fact that Britain and the USA had come to regard the loss of power by Adenauer as being, in Churchill's words, a 'big disaster'. US Secretary of State John Foster Dulles even sought to intervene on the Chancellor's behalf in the 1953 *Bundestag* elections, while President.[7] Eisenhower believed that the West's entire European policy was predicated on 'Adenauer's continuance in power'.[8] The path taken by British policy reflected these concerns, and London's policy-makers were intimately involved with the process whereby support for the policies of Adenauer was proffered so as to secure German adherence to the Western Alliance preventing West Germany from concluding an agreement with the Soviet Union.[9] Adenauer's visit to Moscow in 1955 raised the spectre of the Treaty of Rapallo with the Soviet Union in 1922 in the minds of British officials.[10] Bonn's alliance partners began to fear that West Germany, having re-established its sovereignty, might use its considerable weight to play off East against West in a nuclear age *Schaukelpolitik*.[11] Eden's diplomacy sought both to avoid such an eventuality by Bonn's integration with the West and, at the same time, ensuring that the British role in that process bought London permanent influence in the new Germany.[12] Adenauer certainly believed that 'by its entry to the WEU in the year 1954, Great Britain showed its substantial commitment to, as well as community of interest with, the countries of Europe'.[13]

For Moscow, the Western endorsement of Bonn's position implied that German reunification could only take place after the demise of Communism in the Eastern bloc. In the early 1950s this seemed a distant prospect, even with the American enunciation of the doctrine of 'roll-back'.[14] War to regain the eastern territories was not an option. The NATO alliance, at least in terms of possible territorial aggrandisement, was a defensive alliance, as confirmed in 1954: 'As the initiation of a war by NATO would be contrary to the fundamental principles of the Alliance, it has been ruled out as a possibility. War, therefore, can only come about as a result of Communist aggression.'[15] In line with this, Adenauer declared on 5 October 1954 that the FRG 'undertakes, in particular, not to induce ... reunification ... [or] a change in the present frontiers ... by means of force, and to solve by peaceful means all ... disputes ... between the [FRG] and other states'.[16]

In principle, the West German position was a model of democratic correctness, fully in accordance with international law. The Federal government identified the restoration of sovereignty, economic reconstruction, political stability, Western integration and peaceful reunification as its priorities.[17] These were all laudable goals in the eyes of Bonn's alliance partners (so long as they remained fairly unlikely to be achieved). What Adenauer had done was to erect an uncompromising *Ostpolitik* that was both the cement of, and the result of, a liberal integrationist *Westpolitik*. But, as Lawrence L. Whetten later wrote, 'Adenauer [had] adopted an even harder, more hostile policy towards the [East European] countries than Stresemann ... The cumulative impact of [West German] claims was that the Federal Republic had far larger grievances against the East Europeans than did Stesemann' in the inter-war period.[18] Furthermore, Bonn's allies were intimately associated with this policy. Thus,

> The formal extension of the [NATO] alliance to its natural defensive perimeter occurred simultaneously with the formal assumption of a pledge to extend western political influence beyond that perimeter. The completion of an alliance championed from its inception as defensive involved the reassertion of revisionist political goals.[19]

The British were under no illusions about this; a Foreign Office Research Department paper in 1953 made the point that the term 'reunification', for the West German government, was more than the idea of the fusion of the FRG with the Soviet zone. The Foreign Office was acutely aware of domestic pressure on the West German government, where 'opinion is strongly united in calling for its return as an inalienable German right'. Therefore, 'no plan for German re-unification would be considered final which neglected this issue [and, furthermore,] radical protagonists of this cause, led by certain groups of refugees themselves, are less cautious in their approach, and [their] territorial ambitions . . . show no signs of diminishing with time'.[20]

This West German commitment to reunification was inextricably bound up with its adherence to the Western Alliance. Conversely, the GDR was intimately linked with the Soviet desire to prevent Germany reunifying within the Western bloc. The FRG was therefore both a product and a proponent of a 'Policy of Strength' against the USSR.[21] Bonn explicitly declared itself dependent upon its Western allies to achieve security and reunification, which meant that it could be vulnerable to those allies' pursuit of their own goals. West German policy would therefore have to strive to keep reunification synonymous with the goals of the NATO alliance.[22] The intransigent policies of Adenauer, the three Western Allies' acceptance of the principle of *Alleinvertretungsrecht* and the 1955 Cabinet decision not to make any concessions to Moscow without the consent of Bonn,[23] meant that Britain's dealings with the USSR were now subject, in effect, to a West German veto. This was reinforced in Cabinet in succeeding years, and, in 1957, it was agreed that the British government 'should not propose a Conference with the Soviet Union . . . unless [Adenauer] wished one to be held'.[24] The key to Adenauer's leverage lay in the attitude of Washington, and he, accordingly, shamelessly courted the United States:

> A free Germany is an absolute necessity for the integration of a free Europe. A free Europe is absolutely essential for the free United States. Our fate, the fate of the Federal Republic of Germany, is inseparably linked up with the fate of Europe. The fate of Europe is inseparably linked up with the fate of the United States of America.[25]

The identification of West German policy with American interest was Adenauer's strongest card. How long this state of affairs could be sustained was, however, outside the Federal Republic's control.

Keeping the flame of détente alive

Whilst endorsing Bonn's position, the British government was ready to contemplate concessions to the Soviet Union so as to achieve an agreement over the question of Germany. Whether the British were in a real position to achieve anything of substance is a moot point.[26] Be that as it may, the British certainly believed in their own continued relevance at this juncture. In March 1955, Cabinet discussion of possible concessions ranged from the dropping of the demand for a realistic prospect of success before addressing the German problem on an official level, to the participation of the GDR and its leader Walter Ulbricht in reunification discussions.[27]

The USSR was resolutely opposed to Adenauer's position that Germany be reunified on Western terms. Further, Bonn's demand for the return of German lands lost after the Second World War was, when combined with West German economic growth and rearmament, viewed as a threat to Soviet security and its control of Eastern Europe.'[28] In December 1955 Khrushchev stated in Rangoon that now the West had drawn the Federal Republic into NATO, and was rearming it rapidly, 'Many leading figures in the western countries do not even consider it necessary to conceal the fact that they are preparing a West German army against the Soviet Union.'[29]

The Soviet Union realised that many in the West were uncomfortable with this resurrection of German power, while periodic British overtures suggested their dislike of the intransigent position of Adenauer. The Soviet invitation for Adenauer to visit the USSR in 1955 was designed, at least in part, to expose the fact that the Federal Republic was the least enthusiastic proponent of détente in the West.[30] Despite objections from Heinrich von Brentano and the State Secretary at the *Auswärtiges Amt* (*AA*), Walter Hallstein, that there should be no diplomatic relations without concessions on reunification, Adenauer visited Moscow in September 1955 and agreed to diplomatic relations with the USSR. This meant that Bonn had, in effect, allowed the status of the GDR to rise internationally, although, in typically rigid legalistic fashion, Adenauer stressed that 'There is no genuine security in Europe without the re-establishment of German unity'.[31] This was reiterated in a letter to Premier Nikolai Bulganin asserting that diplomatic relations did not mean the recognition of the present frontiers or abandoning the claim to speak for all of Germany.[32] Adenauer's goals in making the trip remained rather obtuse, and the US State Department noted the disappointment of the German people over the lack of any progress on reunification.[33] Herbert Blankenhorn, Adenauer's diplomatic adviser, wrote in his diary that 'In our principle objective, the reunification of our country, we made no progress. There was no talk of free elections. We had the impression that the Soviet point of view has significantly hardened, and that the Russians will not – certainly for a long time – let the East zone out of their sphere of influence.'[34] The domestic opposition to Adenauer saw their suspicions regarding the benefits of NATO membership as being vindicated as Adenauer's claim 'that the inclusion of the Federal Republic in NATO, the unity and power of the West, would force the Soviet Union to renounce the zone of Germany which it occupies, has thus collapsed.'[35]

This was fundamentally to misunderstand what Adenauer was seeking by means of his Moscow diplomacy (admittedly, like all politicians, he had made grandiose claims about the potential of his policies). British Foreign Secretary Harold Macmillan stated in Cabinet that Adenauer's Moscow visit represented a major triumph for Soviet diplomacy.[36] Now that Adenauer had seen the Soviets in negotiations at first-hand, he might appreciate how difficult they could be. This, Macmillan concluded, would 'At least ... will stop the Germans rebuking us (as they are apt to do) for our weakness towards the Russians.'[37]

Fears of a new Rapallo

What Macmillan failed to grasp was that the Moscow trip convinced Adenauer that there was little point in substantive negotiations, as the Soviets sought only to undermine the FRG by exacting concessions by offering a distant prospect of reunification at some future date. On the contrary, Adenauer recognised that he had indefinitely deferred Potsdam by exploiting the Western desire to guard against a new *Schaukelpolitik*: 'Now it is essential – and this is the next task of German foreign policy – to induce the fourth of the powers, the Soviet Union, to make the necessary concessions. Not by war; no one has any such idea, and I least of all.'[38]

Macmillan feared that the USSR might be tempted to try to detach West Germany from the Western Alliance by offering up the GDR. If this was insufficient then Moscow would offer the Oder–Neiße territories, and if this was still inadequate, then 'another part of Germany'.[39] The Cabinet feared that the 'strong desire of the German people to move towards the reunification of Germany' might cause the Germans to rethink the *Westpolitik* if the Soviets offered something more than the Western Allies could.[40] The Labour MP Denis Healey summed up the British dilemma: 'A major objective of western policy is to ensure that a resurgent Germany does not produce a third world war either by fighting Russia or by allying itself with Russia.'[41] Eden warned that 'Unless we make a serious effort to reunify Germany, which the Germans will regard as serious, they will be restive, and cannot be relied on to resist Russian blandishments. So long as Germany is divided, the attachment of West Germany to the western Group will be precarious.'[42]

Eden's successor as Prime Minister, Harold Macmillan, advised his Foreign Secretary Selwyn Lloyd that he saw 'obvious and immediate' dangers if West Germany felt any such pledge lacked real commitment – especially in the event of a rising in the GDR or elsewhere in Eastern Europe.[43] This even led him to speculate on the possibility of a new Ribbentrop–Molotov Pact![44] Fear as to what the Federal Republic would be prepared to do in order to attain unity caused Britain to believe that it was vital 'to hold West German opinion firmly attached to the West'. In 1955, Eden informed the Cabinet that

> On the main issue of the relationship between European Security and German unity, it would be right that the offer of a Security Pact should contain guarantees for the Russians; but any concessions we offered should only be made in return for, and at the same time as progress was made towards, German reunification.[45]

British policy-makers believed that this was necessary to bind the Federal Republic to the West in order to prevent a return to the era of Rapallo: that is, to establish and utilise a diplomatic link with the Soviet Union in order to lever concessions from the West as had been done in the 1920s. Of this era, Stephanie Salzman notes that, 'Rapallo has always been a byword for Russo-German secret and potentially dangerous collabora- tion'.[46] The British Cabinet of the 1950s concurred with this view: '[t]he conclusion to be drawn from the Geneva Conference ... is that we are faced with a protracted period of "competitive co-existence" during which the Russians will seek to undermine the strength and unity of the West and lure the Germans into the eastern orbit.'[47] Consequently, a Cabinet memorandum of 1956 held that 'The Germans cannot be bound to the West by institutional links alone. The solidity and permanence of Germany's connection with the West will depend on a sense of community and common interest.'[48]

It was felt necessary to observe West German sensibilities in order to avoid the overriding British fear – German neutralism. A neutral Germany would 'be [at best] an element of doubt and instability in the middle of Europe playing off one side against the other'.[49] A Germany cast loose from the Western Alliance would not only increase the Soviet danger; it might also become a potential menace in itself. Thus, despite British urgings to negotiate, the 'Rapallo factor' continued to loom large. When Adenauer put a proposal for direct Soviet-German talks before the NATO Council, Macmillan asked Lloyd for an immediate study into the attitude of the Federal Republic of Germany towards neutrality.[50] In response, the Foreign Office continued to display an essentially monolithic opposition to German neutrality, viewing Adenauer as being the best guarantee against this eventuality.[51] The problem of how to introduce any movement into East–West relations constantly seemed to founder on the danger of undermining West Germany's links with the West.

'We belong to the West': Adenauer and the *Westbindung*

Adenauer's policy of integration with the West provided his government with a rock-solid platform both at home and abroad. It was the cornerstone of his policy, and of his popularity at home. In an election broadcast of 1956, Adenauer proclaimed 'The admission of the Federal Republic into the federation of the free peoples of the West protects our liberty against any aggression ... Only the security of this position makes possible a future ... initiative to achieve reunification.'[52]

In reality, the Federal Republic had little option but to choose the Western camp, given the fact that isolationism and communisation were both very unpopular in the FRG.[53] Adenauer knew this, but he determined to maximise the uncertainties of his allies. (Even as wily an observer as Bevin had feared that the USSR might make a more attractive proposition than the West – unless the West took steps to ensure the loyalty of the Federal Republic.)[54] Kirkpatrick, Permanent Under-Secretary at the Foreign Office, was thus reassured by the West German ambassador that Adenauer was bent on a *Westpolitik*. Furthermore, Adenauer, having little faith in the German people, wished to ensure that any future German government could not embark on a war-like course or rapprochement with the Soviet Union.[55] The Chancellor wrote that 'I believe I can confidently state that for us attachment to the East is out of the question ... we Germans belong to the West.'[56] Heinrich von Brentano told the *Bundestag* in 1957 that moves towards an Eastern accommodation would 'cost us the confidence and friendship of the free world and gain for us the contempt of those who threaten us'.[57] Consequently, as Northedge and Wells have suggested, 'In reality it should not have been the NATO alliance which was courting the Germans in 1955, but the other way round.'[58] Further, as Henry Kissinger later reflected, West German security and prospects for a successful Eastern policy rested upon the support of the Western Alliance, and 'Failing this the Federal Republic would be unable to motivate the Soviet Union to compromise'.[59]

This was not lost on the British. As early as 1953, a Foreign Office research paper had concluded that the charge that Western integration was obstructing reunification was making little headway in 'informed circles' as the Soviets were seen as bearing the responsibility for the perpetuation of division. Furthermore, reunification was 'not [seen as being] more likely to be overcome by a policy of isolation than by a policy of solidarity with the West'.[60] Regardless of the fact that West Germany had little option but to join the Western bloc, the West Germans received the backing of the *Ostpolitik* as part of the dowry for their marriage to NATO.

Thus the West ensured the loyalty of Bonn by its commitments on the *Ost-* and *Deutschlandpolitik*. As Alec Douglas-Home later commented,

> That [West] Germany should have confidence in NATO was essential from many points of view, not least because, if Germany felt that the NATO alliance could not guarantee her security, a school of thought would be sure to develop which would look for insurance with the East.[61]

By rubber-stamping Bonn's policy, the Western Allies ensured a period of sustained Soviet–German hostility. By Potsdam's deferral, the West had ensured there would be no second Rapallo. In order to avoid another Rapallo, the West also managed to deepen the East–West divide by adhering to the *Politik der Stärke*.

Obstacles to détente

Once the Western defence system was consolidated, pressure for negotiation became irresistible. Eden had laid down a three-stage path to détente in March 1955: first, the establishment of an East–West equilibrium; second, a period of co-existence; and, finally, a stable situation bringing a genuine settlement.[62] Thus, only five days after West Germany acceded to NATO, the three Western Allies (in consultation with West Germany) issued an invitation to the Soviet Union to a summit conference. Adenauer asserted that membership of NATO did not mean that Bonn was abandoning reunification; rather it was a prerequisite for it. Furthermore, Adenauer won Western support for the view that German reunification by free elections and disarmament had to be negotiated together, and that further European security arrangements could only be negotiated after Germany had been reunified.

The Soviet Union knew that its trump card in negotiations on Germany was the prospect of reunification. Its tactical deployment was designed to prevent the integration of a remilitarised Germany into the Western bloc. To this end, Soviet Premier Bulganin had proposed a European security pact at the July 1955 Geneva Summit to encompass a reunified Germany resulting from bilateral negotiations.[63] However, the question of Germany proved again to be insurmountable – and so it would be while the Cold War continued. After the failure of Geneva, Foreign Secretary Macmillan could assuage the fears of the British public ('There ain't gonna be no war')[64] but he could not disguise the very real blow British policy had suffered, as British hopes for success had been high and extremely obvious.[65]

Adenauer adopted an essentially defensive position of refusing to accept the legitimacy of the GDR or to recognise the borders of Germany (i.e. FRG and GDR) as they stood in 1955. Geneva in 1955 heralded what the future course was to be. Adenauer's achievement was to make reunification the centrepiece of Western diplomacy at what was supposed be an exercise in détente.[66] Eisenhower effectively conceded this point in the language of his initial speech at Geneva on 18 July 1955: 'The division [of Germany] does a grievous wrong to a people which is entitled ... to pursue together a common destiny ... That is why we insist a united Germany is entitled at its choice, to exercise its inherent right of collective self-defense.'[67] Eisenhower later recalled that Soviet talk of a neutral and disarmed Germany could only be a prelude to Communist domination of Germany and that, in any case, the West had certain obligations to Adenauer and the Federal Republic.[68] As part of this obligation, the Western Allies were committed to regarding the GDR as a non-state and refusing to accept the 1945 boundaries of Germany as final. These positions were to prove a fundamental obstacle to détente, as 'On these two vital issues, the three western Powers had predetermined their positions before meeting their Russian partner at Geneva [in 1955], and, of course, without consulting them.'[69] Gladwyn Jebb, the then British ambassador in Paris, was much opposed to the Western backing for reunification in such strong terms, implying as it did that the failure to reunify Germany would lead to increased 'tension' and the danger of war. For,

> [I]n practice reunification could only come about either by the liberalization of the DDR or by the Sovietization of the Federal Republic. I was certain that the first, given the reaction of the Russians to anything of the kind, was impossible; it was equally clear that the second was undesirable ... 'reunification' seemed to me to be highly dangerous as a slogan, and to describe it as 'the cardinal aim of our foreign policy' nothing less than folly.

Jebb thus advocated that if an intransigent policy was going to be operated, then negotiations were not only futile, they were actually detrimental:

> [A] good many people ... even in the Federal Republic, thought that the present frontiers had come to stay and I should not at all be surprised if these included Chancellor Adenauer. Whatever we might say for propaganda purposes, surely the real justification for the rearmament of western Germany was to defend the existing *status quo* and ... to ... graft western Germany onto the body politic of the Atlantic Community.[70]

Despite official support for German reunification and Bonn's *Ost-* and *Deutschlandpolitik*, the British privately debated the possibility of circumventing the policy straitjacket imposed by Bonn.[71] Occasionally, this question reared its head in the public domain. *The Economist* criticised the adherence to the 'pedantic insistence on a particular set of priorities', asking 'Must peace wait German reunion?'[72] The Cabinet recognised that many of the British public would have supported the perpetuation of the

division of Germany.[73] This was, of course, at variance with the stated official British position of endorsing the reunification of Germany. While
reunification was the national aim of the Federal Republic, for the
Western Allies, including Britain, it was at best a peripheral matter in
terms of the national interest.[74] By 1957, the British belief that the West
should not allow the issue of German reunification to take priority had
hardened into a determination that it could not be allowed to take priority. In December 1957, Macmillan advised his Foreign Secretary, Selwyn
Lloyd, that 'Of course we have always said that our aim is a reunified
Germany, with free elections.... What is the real view? Do we want a
united Germany on any terms that we are likely to get in the next decade
or so?'[75]

Adenauer viewed the East–West situation in very different terms from
British policy-makers. In 1959, Adenauer asserted to Macmillan that what
the British failed to comprehend was that the settlement of the German
Question (on whatever terms) would not remove the underlying cause of
tension: namely, Soviet expansionism. Therefore, for Adenauer, the only
way in which to reduce the tension between the Superpowers was to achieve
the build-up of nuclear weapons.[76] There was therefore little to be achieved
by talks with the USSR. Adenauer's demand for a firm line with the USSR
seemed, to the British, to be closing the door on détente unnecessarily.

Economic pressures for détente in British policy

Not only was Adenauer's policy seen as perpetuating the state of tension;
it was, from a British perspective, expensive. In any analysis of post-war
British policy, it must be remembered that economics dominated
decision-making by virtue of almost perpetual economic decline. The
Treasury constantly sought to reduce expenditure, and one Treasury official stated in 1951 that Chancellors of the Exchequer had 'no business to
be in favour of *any* expenditure programme'.[77] Following the integration
of the FRG into the Western Alliance, a pre-Geneva Treasury memo
hinted that, in future, British policy-makers would be less inclined to fail
to reach agreement with the Soviets simply to further any (remote)
chance of German reunification: 'Geneva will be of peripheral interest to
HM Treasury, apart from the consideration that a satisfactory détente
leading to a general scaling down of armaments offers the best prospect of
relief for the heavy burden of defence expenditures.'[78]

In any case, while the West Germans saw the defence of their territory
via conventional means as being of paramount importance, this was not
the way it appeared to many British policy-makers. Macmillan had written
to R.A. Butler in August 1955 arguing that nuclear rockets had rendered
most conventional defence spending as being pointless, whilst he
informed Eden in 1956 that 'We ... know that we get no defence from ...
defence expenditure.'[79] Economics was less a factor in West German

policy, while its defence spending was entirely for the defence of the homeland. Unlike Britain, Bonn did not have to wrangle over strategic priorities 'East of Suez' when allotting funds for armaments.[80] Thus, when the British demanded German financial remuneration for their troops in West Germany, the Federal Finance Minister, Fritz Schäffer, argued that Allied troops were in Germany to defend all free peoples, not just those who were citizens of the Federal Republic.[81] British demands for money were often mistaken for a lack of commitment in Bonn, but at this time, Britain was stretched across the globe. As Chancellor of the Exchequer, Macmillan had argued that a reduction in British contribution to the NATO infrastructure was imperative because 'If we do all this, we may escape our greatest danger – which is not war but financial collapse'.[82] In 1962, Macmillan advised Kennedy that

> [G]iven our wide-spread commitments and deployment, we believe that for us regular forces are the most suitable instruments of policy in a long period of tension like the struggle in which we are now engaged with the Communist countries.... But in present circum-stances a premature calling up of reserves means keeping a lot of men doing nothing in particular in Germany. This injures our economy and in my view does not effectively add to the deterrent. Indeed, if we were to yield to these successive pressures the Communists could do us grievous injury all over the world without ever firing a shot. This is very likely one of their objectives.[83]

NATO was maintained at a high opportunity cost and participation pre-vented Britain from diverting resources elsewhere – unfortunate, given both Britain's worldwide commitments and its limited economic base.[84] Britain had supported the resurrection of (West) Germany to share the burdens of Western defence and not, as it transpired, to commit the Western Alliance to a number of (West) German goals that ensured the maintenance of a state of (expensive) tension with the Soviet Union. However, having created a West German state to contribute to the defence of the Free World, one could hardly entirely direct the aspirations of that state in a non-democratic manner.

The creation of an independent *Ostpolitik*

The tone for the *Ostpolitik* of the newly sovereign Adenauer government was set not by the Moscow trip of September 1955, but rather by the intro-duction of the so-called 'Hallstein Doctrine' in December of that year.[85] The doctrine was the cornerstone of the emerging *Ostpolitik*, which was characterised by intransigence. The doctrine, named after the State Secretary in the *AA*, as announced on 9 December 1955, enunciated that Bonn would sever relations with any country that recognised the GDR, and would not establish relations with any Communist state other than the Soviet Union.[86] In June 1956, this was clarified:

> The recognition of the German Democratic Republic would mean international recognition of the partition of Germany into two states ... [Bonn] will feel compelled in future to regard the establishing of diplomatic relations with the so-called German Democratic Republic by third States with which the Federal Republic maintains diplomatic relations, as an unfriendly act calculated to intensify and aggravate the partition of Germany.[87]

This doctrine evidenced that Adenauer meant to rely on strength, rather than negotiation, to achieve his goals. As Sir Christopher Steel, the British ambassador in Bonn from 1957 to 1963, stated: 'Although Dr Adenauer has often bowed to the desirability of negotiation, he has never had much faith in it.'[88] Adenauer made no secret of this: 'the Soviet Union will be interested in a German settlement only when the Soviet Union believes that it is in her own best interests to have such a settlement. That would be if the integration of Western Europe had so developed that the Soviet Union was forced to abandon all hope of ever dominating Europe.'

If the USSR got financial aid to develop her resources and did not fear attack, Adenauer asserted, the West would achieve a settlement.[89] In practice, this meant that West German policy would adopt an intransigent face. The initiation of such a period of sterile hostility coincided with Harold Macmillan's assertion of his international credentials in the field of détente. From a British perspective, West German policy was simply too inflexible to act as a starting point for improving relations.[90] British policy towards the Communist bloc was designed to bridge gaps in a pragmatic fashion. West German *Ostpolitik* was a fortress of principle, an end in itself.

If one accepts the logic of the argument that Germany remained at the epicentre of the East–West dispute, one must accept that a deal with the Soviet Union was virtually impossible without the acceptance of the status quo in Europe. In other words, the Federal Republic must pay the price for securing peace by accepting the GDR and the loss of its eastern territories. This would mean the acceptance of the de facto boundaries of Potsdam without any quid pro quo, and in advance of a peace settlement and a reunited Germany. Timothy Garton Ash has identified at least some of the reasons why Bonn would not do this. First, the recognition of the Oder–Neiße line was still a diplomatic card for Germany to play, and one not to be sacrificed for nothing. Second, the legal status of Germany as a single state was at least maintained as long as Potsdam was in suspension. Any tinkering with this could simply entrench division by removing the legal basis for unity whilst failing to bring reunification.[91]

Sir Christopher Steel saw the logic in the West German position. Steel asserted that if, as had been pointed out, the Poles were unlikely to be reconciled to Bonn, why should the FRG give up something that could help in the negotiation of a final settlement?[92] The West German stance caused the historian Elizabeth Wiskemann to write in 1956 that 'it is difficult for Germany's neighbours not to smile sourly over this post-1945 legalism'.[93] The Bonn government endorsed the idea of German expellees returning to their former homes east of the Oder–Neiße line. Additionally, Bonn advocated that ethnic Germans (*Volksdeutsche*) expelled from their homes in areas *outside* of the 1937 *Reich* should also be allowed to return if so desired.[94] This concept was known as the *Recht auf Heimat* ('Right to the Homeland'), and supposedly articulated the denial of forcible expulsion as recently enacted, in theory at least, in the Dayton accords of 1995 with regard to Bosnia. While a laudable principle, in practice this was bound to be strongly opposed by the East Europeans as, while not being land transfer deals, this would cause fundamental and ominous shifts in East European demography; in essence, a *Drang nach Osten* by stealth. The British High Commission in Germany identified the manner in which the FRG was essentially espousing revisionism but conspiring to 'wrap this up in verbiage about international co-operation and the rights of the individual as applied to minorities'.[95] The Germans expellees even cited the Atlantic Charter of 1941 in support of their case, specifically highlighting the Anglo-American pledge

> to see no territorial changes that do not accord with the freely expressed wishes of the people concerned ... [and] the right of all peoples to choose the form of government under which they live and wish to see sovereign rights and self-determination restored to those who have been forcibly deprived of them.[96]

Thus, a statement originally designed to demonstrate solidarity with the Czechs, Poles and other victims of German aggression was, within a few years, utilised by German 'victims' of Czech, Polish, Yugoslav and Soviet retribution. Such was the turn-around in events engendered by the defeat of Nazi Germany and the onset of the Cold War. The issue of the Czech Sudetenland region was a particularly difficult one for British policymakers. British Prime Minister Neville Chamberlain had, after all, been the architect of the transfer of the Sudetenland to Germany in 1938 at Munich. The British had unilaterally abrogated the Munich Agreement following the punitive measures adopted by the Nazis in Bohemia-Moravia in response to the assassination of *SS-Obergruppenführer* Reinhard Heydrich in 1942.[97] Moreover, the Czech expulsion of the ethnic Germans from the Sudetenland after 1945 (the *Odsun*)[98] had received the sanction of the Allies at Potsdam.[99] The Adenauer government, however, refused formally to repudiate the Munich Agreement. Britain thus found itself allied with a state that seemed to question a status quo that British policy had done much to create and that, at least in theory, was committed to uphold.

By the second half of the 1950s, Adenauer's policy towards the East was characterised by four central tenets. First, Adenauer's personal outlook was virtually indistinguishable from that of the Federal Republic. While the AA might envisage any number of scenarios with regard to Eastern policy, Adenauer's opinion was what counted in the foreign policy sphere. Second, the AA was often bypassed by Adenauer and his circle of close confidants. Third, the *Politik der Stärke*, although in principle allied to flexibility, was in practice rigid in the extreme. Finally, Moscow was regarded (especially by Adenauer) as the only place in which meaningful progress could be made with regard to dealing with the Eastern bloc. Adenauer discounted the alienation of the satellites as being of any real relevance, claiming their best hope lay with the West: 'If we fail ... we will offer no prospects for the liberty and the fate of the satellite states'.[100] Such reasoning removed any incentive for coming to an accommodation with the East Europeans directly. Pressure for the pursuit of measures to alleviate tension from within the Western bloc were, however, more difficult for the FRG to ignore.

'Disengagement'

The popularity of 'disengagement' schemes[101] in Britain with politicians across the spectrum alarmed the Federal Republic. While the strongest proponents of these schemes were in the Labour Party, Eden and Macmillan also showed interest in the concept. In July 1955, Eden proposed a zone of 'equalized armaments' in Europe. This raised Bonn's suspicion that Britain was willing to recognise the GDR de facto, as any 'disengagement' scheme would use the inner German border as a demarcation line.[102]

The British did, however, recognise the inherent dangers in any such plans. The prospect of German neutralism would mean the loss of any meaningful strategic position on the Central Front, and the withdrawal of the forces of the United States from Europe.[103] Because of this, the Conservative government was noticeably more cautious than the Labour Party on this issue. Selwyn Lloyd warned in Cabinet that, while desiring disarmament, the UK must be aware of

> [the] attempt [by the USSR] to interweave into the disarmament discussions something which will lead to the neutralisation of the whole of Germany ... a vigorous Germany with seventy-five million inhabitants even if possessing only conventional armaments, would, if reunited outside the western alliance, be a menace to peace and stability in Europe.

Thus,

> We would have to convince the Germans that any scheme of disen-
> gagement which we favoured would improve rather than hinder the
> prospects of eventual reunification.[104]

However, Bonn was unlikely to be in favour of such schemes, as West
Germany was adamant that any defence against a Soviet attack should be
conducted as forward as possible.[105] In the German experience, any land
occupied by the Communists was likely to remain occupied and, as the
British deputy commandant in Berlin from 1958 to 1961 later recalled,
disengagement was a 'red rag to the German bull'.[106] The opposition to
'disengagement' in Bonn remained absolute. Having worked for Western
acquiescence in the goal of German reunification, Adenauer was not
about to embrace any mechanism that de-coupled the FRG from the West.

'Prisoners of Adenauer': British obligation to West Germany

To the British, the intransigent stance of Bonn appeared more a
stonewalling exercise rather than a viable diplomatic stance. If Bonn was
to reject schemes like 'disengagement' out of hand, then what did it
propose? Bilateral talks with the USSR? To the British this seemed unrealistic in the extreme – especially after the visit of Adenauer to Moscow –
and Eden believed that 'They [the West Germans] ... think themselves
able to outsmart the Russians. Although, of course, they had no real
power to play at hands.'[107] From the British perspective, Germany
remained a divided country that was still awaiting a peace treaty as a
defeated nation.[108] This was added to the fact that the British over-
estimated their ability to negotiate with the USSR, especially where
Germany was concerned. The reality was that Western agreements with
the Federal Republic had greatly limited room for manoeuvre. In January
1958, D.A. Logan, Assistant Private Secretary to Lloyd, lamented that

> Personally I do not see why our insistence on the non-recognition of
> the East German régime need necessarily be sacrosanct. I would not
> be unwilling to see the two Germanys meeting together, provided that
> we could be reasonably satisfied as to the eventual outcome. But in
> this matter we are for the time being largely the prisoners of Dr Ade-
> nauer's policy.[109]

The NATO alliance, by its stress on German reunification in negotiation,
provided the foundation of the *Ostpolitik*. Thus, Adenauer could express
the alliance in somewhat more positive terms than Logan:

> The Federal Government has ... continually directed its policy against
> the threat from the East ... to secure freedom for the millions of

people in the free part of Germany, and to win back freedom for the millions who since 1945 have had to live under the foreign rule of Soviet Russia ... Today free Germany is bound in an alliance with three of her opponents in the last war – an alliance in which today and in the future these opponents of yesterday have the obligation to defend with us the freedom of Europe.[110]

The British, and Macmillan in particular, were well aware of Adenauer's dominant role in the conduct of West German foreign policy. Unfortunately, this was accompanied by a belief that Adenauer was isolated in his thinking, and that led the British to under-estimate the underlying strength of feeling within the Federal Republic. Macmillan recorded in his diary that his 'plain speaking' on Adenauer's intransigent attitude to the USSR had pleased the Chancellor's entourage,[111] but feared they would 'relapse into ... suspicions and fears. The trouble is that they [von Brentano, Erhard, the AA etc.] are all afraid of him.'[112] Wishful thinking amongst the British held that the German diplomats and the AA were as one in desiring a more flexible policy. The Foreign Office Western Department's Clive Rose (previously of the High Commission in Germany) wrote early in 1958 that 'The German press and public are quick to welcome any signs of flexibility in official German thinking – of which the rigidity has been so marked during recent years'.[113]

Ernst Lemmer, Minister for All-German Affairs, visited London in February 1958, and stated that Adenauer was being too stiff and inflexible in his view of the Soviet bloc. While being somewhat sceptical of Lemmer's influence, the British, at least, drew some comfort from the statement.[114] The belief that the Chancellor and his immediate entourage were the obstacles to a more flexible *Ostpolitik* ignored a number of factors. First, there existed a large expellee lobby in West Germany that was well organised, rich and influential in West German political life. Second, the first two years of a 'sovereign' *Ostpolitik* (1955–7) had ended with the CDU/CSU achieving an absolute majority in the *Bundestag*. Third, Adenauer was immensely popular. Fourth, what possible benefits would accrue for the Federal Republic if it modified its *Ostpolitik*? In June 1957, the West German Foreign Minister publicly called for Germany's 1937 borders to be still legitimate in law, the principle of *Recht auf Heimat* for Sudeten Germans, and negotiations on the Oder–Neiße line with a 'free' Poland. Sir Christopher Steel concluded that, 'As ever with this question, Government statements like Brentano's fall between two stools and seem bound to annoy both the refugee extremists by their moderation, and Poland and Czechoslovakia by their irredentist character'.[115]

In essence, Steel was identifying an inner contradiction in West German policy: the attempt to pursue 'revanchist' goals by democratic means. In any case, the fact that such goals alienated the satellites was not seen as so important in Bonn. Adenauer saw the satellites as being nothing other than Soviet stooges of Moscow and, consequently, only dialogue with Moscow could have any meaning. London believed that this was to ignore significant movements within the bloc states themselves. The British therefore despaired when Franz Blücher, West German Vice-Chancellor, offered a pledge on non-aggression to the UN, while rejecting Czech suggestions of establishing diplomatic relations. The British embassy in Bonn noted that 'The Vice-Chancellor's somewhat naïve comment & proposal do less than credit to Czech intuitions, which were directed to the growing body of opinion in Germany which does not distinguish between Moscow and the other satellite capitals'.[116] In fact, West German policy simply hardened Eastern bloc attitudes. In September 1957 Polish Premier Władysław Gomułka made a speech in Warsaw, stating that

> Adenauer realises only too well that no Pole will ever negotiate with anyone on a change of Poland's western frontiers ... So, if Adenauer puts forward the question of the revision of our western borders and at the same time says he has no intention of revising the frontier by force, we may ask him what other means he would use. For Adenauer knows only too well that to realise the demands of the German militarists no other means but force exist.[117]

The Poles also expressed disquiet over the fact that Selwyn Lloyd declared the question of Germany's eastern frontiers to be open pending a final peace treaty. British–Polish relations would not progress unless Britain was itself to recognise the Oder–Neiße frontier. Furthermore, the Polish government was of the opinion that West German persistence in refusing to accept the western frontier of Poland was only sustained by the manner in which its allies indulged Bonn. While the British ambassador in Warsaw appreciated the importance of the West German state as an ally, he saw little practical purpose in supporting West German policies that contemplated the revision of the de facto borders of 1945.[118] In the wider sphere, it was judged better to tolerate Polish disquiet rather than to risk a disenchanted West Germany turning its back on the *Westpolitik* because of a Western reluctance to support its vital interests. The British ambassador in Bonn advised that 'Since we can no longer physically control Germany, the best hope of dealing with this latent risk remains in my opinion to assimilate the Federal Republic as closely as possible to Western Europe and to have it as an ally on our side'.[119]

The uncompromising attitude of Bonn was an open goal for Eastern bloc propaganda, and this in turn elicited press criticism in a Britain. When, in 1957, Tito and Gomułka issued a joint statement noting that 'a Polish frontier on the Oder–Neisse line is the only solution possible',[120] *The Economist* ventured that a Western guarantee of the 'Oder–Neiße frontier, would remove one important obstacle on the Polish road to a limited independence from Moscow'. Furthermore, it was pointed out that if the East Europeans did manage to establish a greater degree of freedom from Moscow, 'The problem may become acute when a German government becomes seriously interested in Germany's relations with Eastern Europe'.[121] Despite reports that the Polish and West German governments could reach agreement by agreeing to differ over the Oder–Neiße line, the positions of Bonn and the East Europeans were, in fact, becoming increasingly polarised.[122] Hugh Sykes, an experienced *Ostpolitik* 'watcher', believed that changes in West German Eastern policy were only likely to develop slowly, although

> I know that some members of the *Ostabteilung* [eastern Office of the *AA*] and many politicians on the Left Wing of the C.D.U. and in the S.P.D. would like to see a change and resent the inhibitions of the Federal Government and especially of the more legalistic members of the Foreign Ministry. The *Ostabteilung* were in my day always rather keener on the development of relations with Poland than their masters. Dr von Brentano himself would probably like to see a gradual thaw in relations with the Satellites.[123]

From London's perspective, Bonn's *Ostpolitik* remained 'wholly negative' and the influence Britain could wield in this direction was limited.[124] To Britain, West German intransigence meant that the West was passing up an opportunity to exploit potential schisms in the Communist bloc. The satellite states of Eastern Europe were seen as the 'Achilles heel' of Moscow, and Britain believed the West should encourage them in every way in their aspirations for greater freedom from Moscow. Selwyn Lloyd advised the Cabinet that he saw the refusal to negotiate with the East as being of no value to anyone save those interested in the perpetuation of Soviet rule in Eastern Europe. Lloyd believed that

> If we appear to lose heart in our dealings with the Russians or to lose interest in negotiating with them, the satellite populations may begin to lose hope . . . History shows that ideas of independence continue to survive in Eastern Europe generation after generation in the most discouraging conditions. The rebellion of the Hungarians proved that their spirit had not been damaged by twelve years of Communist occupation. Nevertheless there is a limit to what these peoples can be expected to accomplish in the way of actual resistance if they are deprived of any gleam of hope that their condition may one day be changed. One of the demands which the Russians are now putting forward most insistently that we recognise the *status quo*. We should never do this.[125]

Thus, British policy-makers advocated that the Federal Republic recognise certain aspects of the status quo (the Oder–Neiße line, for instance). In doing so the Federal Republic would undermine wider, more negative aspects of the status quo, such as the Soviet domination of Eastern Europe. Certainly, there was a lot of attention paid to statements by various bloc leaders that seemed to assert a loosening of Soviet control over Eastern Europe in the post-Stalinist era.[126] For the British, the West Germans, wrapped in their hard-line positions, failed to see the distinct advantages for the West to be accrued by an improvement of relations with the satellites. In any such improvement the Federal Republic had by far the most important role to play, as it was the fear of Germany that caused the satellites, and Poland and Czechoslovakia in particular, to align with the USSR.[127] Federal Foreign Minister Heinrich von Brentano recognised this fact in a speech in 1956:

> [T]he expulsion of millions of people and the annexation of territory historically belonging to another country cannot be the basis for a permanent settlement since they violate all the tenets of natural, human and divine law. However, a just solution . . . can be agreed only between free peoples. Today the Polish people are not free. A totalitarian Government, illegitimate at home and dependent abroad . . . will never be in a position even to strive for a just solution. One of the main planks in Stalin's foreign policy was to chain Poland to Russia by offering her a quarter of Germany's territory.[128]

While West German policy asserted that the expulsions were a wrong that had to be addressed, from a British perspective the expulsions were an unfortunate but irreversible fact of history.[129] Bonn was possessed of a domestic constituency of millions of expellee voters that could effectively block modifications in the *Ostpolitik.*[130] British policy-makers saw von Brentano's assertion that Bonn could deal with a 'free' Poland as nonsense. No Polish government would accept the loss of its new 'western territories'. Further, the Poles (like the Czechs) were only too aware of the problems that their German minority had caused them between 1919 and 1939 – especially when the *Reich* claimed to speak for them.[131] Faced with such intractable positions, the British took comfort in the fact that the German case could only diminish over time, as the German population in the 'eastern territories' was reducing incrementally. This was to ignore some basic facts about the West German position at this time. The preamble to the basic law of 1949 not only committed the 'whole' German people to work for unity – it also claimed to speak for 'those Germans who were prevented from participating in this process'.[132] As a corollary of this, all ethnic Germans, wherever they were domiciled, were entitled to West German citizenship as *Volksdeutsche* (ethnic Germans). An extremely complex historical and legal pattern had gone into the formulation of this stance. Essentially, it was based on two principles; those of *Alleinvertretungsrecht* and *Abstammung* (the right of anyone of German blood to citizenship). *Abstammung* was derived from the 1913 *Reich* Citizenship Act that held that nationality was determined by 'blood' ancestry, rather than by place of birth or residency. Such complex legalistic formulae often simply invited misunderstanding.[133] Nevertheless, in March 1957, the British embassy in Bonn reported that the upsurge in German emigration from Poland had caused speculation that Warsaw intended to clear Poland entirely of Germans. This was alarming for the refugee groups and nationalist elements in the Federal Republic, as it further strengthened the hand of the Poles in any future negotiations while making the German claims to *Recht auf Heimat* even less realisable.[134] Such demographic reality served only to further reinforce the hostility to West Germany within sections of British society.

Such hostility was reinforced by the suspicion that the West Germans themselves knew that these policies were unrealistic. It was generally recognised in Britain that, even in the event of German reunification, the Oder–Neiße territories were unlikely in the extreme to return to Germany. Privately Adenauer admitted this, as, for instance, when he snapped to Erich Ollenhauer, the SPD leader, in 1955: '[The] Oder–Neisse, eastern provinces – they're gone! They don't exist anymore!'[135] Willy Brandt, Mayor of West Berlin, certainly suspected that Adenauer had little faith (or interest) in German reunification or in the eastern territories. Brandt suspected that disinterest in things Prussian was at least partially responsible for Adenauer's policies. In January 1958, when calling specifically for the development of a positive *Ostpolitik*, Brandt noted that its need was more pressing in Berlin that it was from Adenauer's vantage point 'on the left bank of the Rhine'.[136] The 'eastern territories' were certainly regarded by many West German policy-makers as forever lost, and, privately, many were willing to concede this point. A West German embassy official in London stated in December 1956 that Bonn was considering a compromise with Poland over the Oder–Neiße territories (although the British representative concluded that Bonn had written off East Prussia).[137] The British embassy in Prague reported in 1957 that the French ambassador had recently had talks with von Brentano in which the latter hinted at eventual diplomatic relations with Poland. Although the FRG could not publicly accept the frontier, von Brentano accepted that Poland had moved west. Therefore, in any settlement Bonn would content itself with the smallest of border adjustments. With regard to Czechoslovakia, the Sudetenland, asserted von Brentano, was nowhere near as much of an obstacle to eventual diplomatic relations as were the Oder–Neiße territories.[138] Gladwyn Jebb, having spoken to his Polish counterpart in Paris, concluded:

> Generally speaking, the Poles were torn in two. A neutral Germany . . . might at least have the result of getting Russian troops out of Poland. On the other hand any reunification of Germany would no doubt

raise the crucial issue of the Oder–Neisse line ... His conclusion seemed to be that for the time being the *status quo* would be more or less endurable.[139]

If the Federal Republic could come to an arrangement with Poland, Czechoslovakia and its other eastern neighbours, the dependence of those states upon Moscow would be completely undermined. Historically, these countries feared Russia at least as much as Germany. The British therefore viewed the establishment of diplomatic relations between the FRG and the East Europeans as an essential first step.[140] Macmillan told Dulles in 1959 that if the West could secure the liberation of Poland, Czechoslovakia and perhaps even Hungary by some concessions to the Soviet point of view on Germany, then it would be a price worth paying.[141] Until such time that there was a West German acceptance of the de facto borders in Europe, the satellites would always prefer the existence of a GDR that recognised the status quo to any future united Germany that did not. The East Germans recognised that this was their strongest means of preventing West German gold from ever separating them from their East European allies. In 1957 the East German Premier, Grotewohl, asserted that 'In the interests of peace and of friendly relations with the Polish people we continue ... to stand by the inviolability of the Oder–Neisse frontier as the peace treaty between Germany and Poland'.[142]

The recognition of the Oder–Neiße line by Bonn would make the FRG a much more attractive partner to the Poles by virtue of West German economic power if nothing else. Furthermore, if Bonn sought reunification by consent, the British believed that some move towards recognition of the Oder–Neiße line by the FRG would serve as a basis for future discussion of the eastern boundary of a reunified Germany.[143] Against this, Bonn asserted that the Oder–Neiße line would be settled at some future date by an all-German government with a 'free' Poland. However, this was absolutely at variance with official British opinion on the matter: 'In the foreseeable future no Polish Government, Communist or free, could accept any cession of territory except just conceivably the smallest of frontier rectifications.'[144] The logic behind this seemed lost on many in the British political scene. West Germany could not continue to ignore the Oder–Neiße line and the GDR forever. The East European satellites naturally sought to exploit British feelings on this matter for their own ends. In Poland, Vice-Chairman Jan Izydorczyk declared that if the United Kingdom and the United States would clarify their attitude towards the frontier, 'this would unquestionably exert a serious and positive influence on the future stabilisation of international relations'.[145] Communist propaganda targeted the rich vein of anti-German feeling in British society, in the Beaverbrook press and elsewhere, in areas where West German society was most vulnerable to attack (such as the prominence of ex-Nazis, the obstruction of détente, revanchism and militarism).

Britain, the Hallstein Doctrine and '*die Zone*'

While the British government remained faithful to the West German demand that there be no official contact with the GDR, certain individuals and groups wilfully ignored this.[146] At the centre of the West German campaign against the GDR was the Hallstein Doctrine, which, in British eyes, had little legal basis. Bonn managed to use the lever of economic aid when persuading non-aligned countries not to have full diplomatic relations with the GDR. The GDR was thus limited to only twelve embassies (all in Communist countries), while being restricted to Consulates-General in countries such as Burma, Indonesia, Iran, Cambodia and the UAR.[147]

The Foreign Office, whilst conceding the success of the doctrine in isolating East Germany in diplomatic and trading terms, saw all too clearly that the drawbacks were significant.[148] In fact, as William Glenn Gray has recently argued, the doctrine achieved a high degree of success in limiting the number of countries recognised by the GDR.[149] What the British disliked was the manner in which its rigidity affected them. Such a dogmatic stance, not unnaturally, imposed severe restrictions upon the West's capacity for having any contact with the GDR. Further, it meant that relations with third countries maintaining links with the GDR were placed in jeopardy. When Yugoslavia established relations with the GDR in 1957, the Federal Republic broke off relations – and the East Germans had a significant political victory in as much as they had managed to get a third party to ignore Bonn's dictates.[150] London found it hard to see what exactly this had achieved, and the episode was seen as more harmful to Bonn than to Belgrade, given that 'if obliged to choose between Polish and German friendship Tito would decide for the Poles'.[151] British officialdom simply concluded that, due to the Hallstein Doctrine's rigidity, West Germany had contrived to alienate Yugoslavia and destroy any nascent relationship with Warsaw.[152]

The doctrine was a propaganda gift to the GDR and an easy target for 'blackmail' by non-aligned states, especially in the Third World. When, for instance, the Federal Republic began flexing muscles against the UAR in 1960 by threatening funding for a dam, London saw the root of Bonn's dilemma. 'If [the West Germans] recall July 1956, they will know that Cairo retaliated on the withdrawal by western countries and the World Bank to finance the [Aswan] High Dam.'[153] To the British, the West German obsession with the German Question was blinding them to the wider consequences of their *Deutschlandpolitik*. Macmillan especially sought to win over the non-aligned states in order that the West might reap the economic and political benefits on offer.[154] In the propaganda war amongst the non-aligned, the Hallstein Doctrine served little purpose other than in allowing the GDR to portray its western neighbour as a bully. Furthermore, the West German policy was fundamentally handicapped by the diplomatic doublethink that required third parties to deny that the GDR existed when confronted with contrary physical evidence. The head of the West German National Olympic Committee gloomily acknowledged this in a letter to the Minister of the Interior in Bonn, noting that the 'yardstick of sporting practice' internationally 'unfortunately already regard[s] the GDR as a sovereign state' as much as a 'satellite state of Russia'.[155] Such attitudes on the part of third parties were derived of three main factors: first, hostility to the West German state; second, incomprehension of Bonn's position; and third, national goals at variance with that of Bonn. Pankow[156] was, of course, aware of these considerations and the part they could play in East German policy – in everything from Olympic representation to academic conferences. A British Information Research Department paper noted that Klaus Baltruschat, of the GDR's State Secretariat for Higher Education, had publicly written that the aim was to use attendance by GDR nationals at international conferences so as to 'ensure that ... DDR delegation[s]' are 'recognised as legitimate *independent representation of our state.*' Signally, an official in London noted that, in the long-term, 'I think the W[est] Germans will just have to lump this'.[157]

The East Germans had always been alert to the latent hostility (and incredulity) towards the Federal Republic's *Ost-* and *Deutschlandpolitik* in Britain such as that engendered by the Hallstein Doctrine. In March 1960, the SED's official newspaper reported that British Labour Party politicians at the annual Königswinter Conference had demanded the recognition of the DDR and of the Oder–Neiße line.[158] Whilst over-stated, these reports were not fiction. Sir William Hayter reported the dispute over the necessity of making a declaration on the Oder–Neiße line as '[s]ome of the British thought that there would be an advantage in doing that in order ... to clear the decks for an advance on German reunification'. Hayter accepted that, even if such a statement were to be made, there would be no prospect of an immediate return of the eastern territories to Germany, and recognition by *any* Western government, including that of West Germany, would not result in reunification.[159]

Conclusion

In the dynamic of Anglo-German relations, the perception of the best course of action with regard to the German Question highlighted the most serious differences. Hans von Herwarth (Federal ambassador to London, 1955–61) identified the 'no-win' situation West Germany found itself in:

> Public opinion in Britain understands and accepts the Germans' desire to be reunited with their brothers on the Iron Curtain. At the same time their demand for reunification is often regarded as the main obstacle in the way of an East–West *détente* and is consequently resented. Strict adherence to the so-called Hallstein doctrine has sometimes earned us the reproach from the British public that of all

the countries in Europe Germany alone insists on maintaining the cold war indefinitely. If, however, German diplomacy puts out cautious feelers in Eastern Europe ... the spectre of Rapallo is immediately seen in Britain.[160]

After 1955, West German foreign policy was based on a formula that derived its legitimacy from a strict legalism underpinned by Western power as the basis of a 'Policy of Strength'. The Western endorsement of West German policy represented a sort of de facto peace treaty that, in excluding the Soviet Union, implied that Potsdam seemed no more acceptable to the German people than Versailles had been. Thus, paradoxically, Potsdam, by its non-implementation, became a source of strength for West German policy. In the process of integrating West Germany into the Western bloc, the distinction between West German and Western interests had become blurred – often to the point of being indistinguishable. Adenauer ensured that this overlapping, blurring process advanced as far as possible.

The fear of a new Rapallo, or of a neutral Germany, leading to uncertainty in British security planning in Europe caused Britain to accede to German national aspirations. Progress on disarmament and co-operation was made conditional on progress on the question of German reunification. Although the USSR was unsuccessful in its attempts to split the Western Allies from Bonn, Soviet suspicion that Britain was uncomfortable with its association with West German intransigence was not at all wide of the mark. Britain saw a 'Policy of Strength' as a starting point in policy: a basis for negotiation. By allowing the Communists to raise the possibility of a new revanchist 'German' war, Bonn provided the Soviet bloc with virtually unlimited propaganda material. Despite this, the British Cabinet had accepted that negotiations on Germany should be subject to Bonn's assent. Such inflexibility was anathema to the British tradition of seeking pragmatic compromise. This was reinforced as the British suspected that they were in a better position than the West Germans to negotiate with the Soviet Union.

Adenauer realised that the adherence of the Western Alliance to his stance placed him in a formidable position, letting him sit tight and allow his 'magnet theory' to work towards his (long-term) goal of reunification. Adenauer viewed the Soviet Union in far more rigid ideological terms than did the British. These views formed the basis of West German policy, and dictated that an arrangement with the Communist bloc was virtually impossible. For Britain, not only was détente required to avoid war but it was also increasingly a pressing economic imperative. It was ironic that the same economic weakness that had driven Britain to support the creation of the West German state now drove the imperative for détente as that state now provided a significant factor in perpetuating East–West tension.

Britain subscribed to the concept of reunification in the realisation that

West German opinion would not settle for anything less. However, the uncomfortable prospect of German reunification could safely be assumed to be out of the question by virtue of Soviet intransigence. The suspicion was that the West Germans knew this too. The unfortunate consequence was that Bonn, therefore, had even less incentive to negotiate with the Soviet Union. The fact that the NATO alliance had made negotiations with the East dependent upon progress on reunification meant that Adenauer could dictate the line of the Western Alliance. Since any deal with Moscow would inevitably involve some concessions on Germany, the Federal Republic had, in effect, more interest in the (provisional) status quo, awaiting reunification at some more propitious date in the future. In consequence, if the prospect of reunification was so slight, the Chancellor reasoned, the abandonment of central policy goals would serve no purpose other than the alienation of the significant refugee lobby in the FRG. Many British policy-makers recognised the dichotomy between the recognition of the unlikely actuality of reunification and the *Politik der Stärke*. At Geneva in 1959, Selwyn Lloyd stated the long-held British official line on Germany: 'Under international law the international entity known as Germany remains in existence. This is not affected by what has happened since 1945 as an incident of Four-Power occupation.'[161] In private, two days later, Selwyn Lloyd adopted a somewhat different tone:

> Some of the Germans are genuinely frightened of a détente between East and West. They want a divided Germany but dare not say so ... If the *status quo* is to persist it is reasonable to give more recognition to East Germany. If they give recognition to East Germany it will start the rot in West Germany. Standing pat is easier than thinking out the future.[162]

Adherence to a hard-line policy was increasingly reinforced by West German augmentations to its economic and military strength. Furthermore, the strength of the refugee lobby and its adherents within the Federal Republic seemed to ensure that this obstruction was anything but temporary. For Britain, intransigent West German polices only entrenched Soviet domination of Eastern Europe and was therefore counter-productive. Thus, Macmillan could muse on the possible benefits to be accrued with Eastern Europe in return for concessions on Germany.[163] While von Brentano agreed with Bevin that Potsdam had placed Germany and Poland at loggerheads, the German did not follow the logic of the British case. Bonn believed that there had been a number of wrongs committed to which it could not reconcile itself. By contrast, Britain, whilst conceding certain wrongs, could only assert that it was now time to make the best of a bad job and deal with the de facto situation.

3 Macmillan and the search for détente

We must all drop the habit of making allowances for the Germans. It isn't fair to ourselves.

Lord Vansittart

It is very dangerous to underestimate German shortsightedness.

Henry Kissinger

I don't know why you use a fancy French word like détente when there's a good English phrase for it – Cold War.

Golda Meir

Détente versus *Sicherheit*

From 1958, the Macmillan government pursued a more self-assured policy in Europe. Its chief aim was to achieve a durable arrangement with the Eastern bloc that would bolster Britain's international position but also ease the financial strains that came with a large armed presence in Europe. Such an arrangement would have to address the German Question and would require the support and co-operation of the United States. British policy-makers over-estimated their own influence in Europe and under-estimated American opposition to concessions to the Soviets. Implicit in Macmillan's strategy was the belief that, in order to achieve an understanding, West German goals with regard to reunification, frontiers and the GDR would have to be considerably modified. In part consequence of this, the FRG moved closer to de Gaulle's France, and Britain became increasingly isolated on the European continent. The Berlin Crisis from 1958 encouraged this trend, and Macmillan's attempt to use the Crisis to further his aims was to prove deleterious in the extreme to relations with the FRG.

The antagonisms in Anglo-German relations were personified by the relationship between Macmillan and Adenauer. Macmillan had little time for the complex West German legal formula with regard to the Oder–Neiße line, and saw its continued 'provisional' basis as an unnecessary obstacle to progress: '[At Potsdam the] Russians, by way of compromise, proposed that a final adjudication [of the status of the Oder–Neiße line] should be left for the peace conference; but this was an illusory concession, since by the time any conference might meet, possession would have become nine tenths of the law.'[1] Macmillan believed this of all the gains made by the USSR since 1940, telling the exiled Estonian Prime Minister in 1951, 'I find it difficult to imagine conditions in which Russia will evacuate these territories'.[2] Thus the animosity that arose between Adenauer and Macmillan mirrored, and built on, the clash of 'pragmatic' and 'principle' demonstrated in the attitudes of Bonn and London. In short, national policy was shaped in a significant manner by the search for détente by Britain and for security (*Sicherheit*) in West Germany.

In the story of British decline since 1945 the myth of Britain's ability to broker a détente is a rather sorry saga, and misperceptions about Bonn, Moscow and Washington played a central role in this. Following the failure of the Geneva Conference in 1955, Eden stated that the Soviets 'were looking ahead, and saw in ten or twenty years a very strong China to the east ... and perhaps a strong Germany to the West, and were looking for someone to hold their hands a little. They could not expect anything from the USA, and they saw that the French were no use, *so they were looking to us.*'[3]

While Macmillan differed in many ways from Eden, he shared similar delusions regarding the role détente could play in propping up British power.

'Blessed are the Peacemakers': Macmillan and détente

Selwyn Lloyd once remarked that 'Summiting is an occupational weakness of any incumbent of No. 10 ... Since the war Winston was the principle advocate. Eden disapproved when Foreign Secretary, but not when P.M.'[4] In this assessment, Lloyd had no better example than Harold Macmillan. For Macmillan, the role of peacemaker was the best way for Britain to stay in the front rank of the global powers whilst simultaneously assuring his own role in history, and the Geneva summit of 1955 was, 'never far from his thoughts'.[5] Since the central problem in Europe was Berlin and Germany, it was thus logical that Macmillan should pursue these issues with the utmost vigour. In 1946, Macmillan predicted that the importance of Germany to the international system would remain undiminished:

> Unless an accommodation can be found, and a formula established between the eastern and western hemispheres, you can have no sound policy regarding Germany ... she will once more become a menace to peace ... Germany ... will once more be courted by each of the two groups, and from a starving outcast she will become the pampered courtesan of Europe, selling her favours to the highest bidder.[6]

For Macmillan, time was of the essence, and he wondered in 1963, 'Will the Germans be democratic for long? Will ... the Generals return?'[7] Macmillan confided to Kennedy his view of the enduring mutual enmity felt by Moscow and Bonn:

> The Russians both hate and fear the Germans. They hate them, inspired by cruel memories which we have decided to blot out: they fear them as an efficient hard-working, brave and determined people. Nor can they fail to be conscious of the pressure which they put continually upon German patience by the obstinacy with which they enforce the division of Germany.[8]

Such opinions were not confined to Macmillan. Anatoly Dobrynin, Soviet ambassador to the United States, 1962–86, later recalled: 'Germany was ... the historic balance at the centre of Europe, as well as our historic enemy, the cause of two world wars, and now the main battleground of the cold war, with Berlin ... as the front line.'[9] In 1966, the head of the British Chancery in Bonn concluded that 'Soviet fear of the Germans is associated with a great, perhaps possibly undue, respect for German ability and strength ... the Germans have somewhat the same attitude towards the Russians'.[10] The widespread belief that there was a psychological barrier between the Germans and the Soviets, impervious to bilateral diplomacy, led Macmillan to conclude that *he* would have to broker a détente. In February 1958, Macmillan told the Commons that he believed that the dangers of Soviet Communism might be 'blurred, blunted and perhaps softened'.[11] However, prior to any grand initiative, Macmillan recognised that he must first consolidate Britain's position.

Following the Suez debacle in 1956, Britain, drawing the opposite conclusion from France, rapidly drew back into the American orbit.[12] The restoration of the 'Special Relationship' meant that Britain's position improved dramatically during 1957. Macmillan, like Churchill, half-American by birth and at ease with Americans, paid a visit to Washington in October 1957 which confirmed in him the ability of Britain to play an active East–West role via the 'Special Relationship' and the British possession of nuclear weapons.[13] This British determination to pursue détente was heralded by the NATO meeting of December 1957.[14] But Macmillan over-estimated British power, and saw the US as being in far greater need of London's good offices than it actually was. In essence, Macmillan demonstrated a paternalism towards the United States that, on the personal level, manifested itself with President Kennedy in the 1960s. Not uniquely, Macmillan sought to explain Britain's much-reduced power in terms of highfalutin historical analogy: the Americans being militarily powerful Romans, the British the politically astute Greeks.[15] Unfortunately, the USA did not see it that way, and Macmillan's metaphor only reinforced British delusions of grandeur.

In 1954–5, the diplomacy of Eden facilitated West German member-ship of NATO and won the gratitude of Bonn.[16] This period of cordial Anglo-German relations was to persist until 1957–8, and Macmillan described the relationship as 'very friendly ... sometimes gay'.[17] Macmil-lan had concluded after his first meeting with Adenauer in 1954 that the only way to achieve results with regard to German foreign policy was to have Adenauer on side,[18] and when meeting the Chancellor in New York in 1955 he had found the his ideas on the future of Europe 'sensible enough'.[19] Subsequently, Macmillan over-estimated his influence in Bonn, believing, incorrectly, that Adenauer would back British plans on Euro-pean integration.[20] This was reinforced by reports Macmillan received from British officials in Germany (the Chancellor having supposedly returned from London in 1958 'encouraged' by British attitudes to détente and 'disengagement').[21]

Yet by the late 1950s, the incentives for avoiding offence to the Ade-nauer government were much reduced. First, the FRG had clearly moved towards de Gaulle's France. Second, the British were recovering their self-confidence after the nadir of Suez.[22] And finally, Adenauer's domestic popularity was waning after having achieved an absolute majority in the 1957 elections,[23] whilst Macmillan won a resounding election victory in 1959. This encouraged the pursuit of an East–West arrangement, as the British public continued to share his belief that 'Summitry' would yield the hitherto elusive breakthrough.[24] This put the Prime Minister on a col-lision course with the many in the West German elite. *Bundespräsident* Theodor Heuss publicly warned against the flashy conferences that turned diplomacy into propaganda.[25] Federal Defence Minister Franz Josef Strauß poured scorn on the 'conferences and super conferences' with the Soviet Union since 1945, none of which had fundamentally altered Soviet attitudes, and which were just 'Hocus Pocus'.[26] Such sentiments were perhaps under-standable, as the legal intricacies of West German positions on frontiers and the GDR were unlikely to withstand the popular scrutiny that would be engendered by 'populist' diplomacy. Thus, from London's perspective, con-ciliatory proposals from Adenauer were usually tactical, designed for public consumption and to prevent exclusion by the Four Powers.[27]

The commitment of troops to West Germany was an important part of the leverage wielded by Britain over the Federal Republic. Unfortunately, as with so many decisions in post-war British policy, economic constraints were to have unfortunate consequences when the 1957 Defence White Paper (the 'Sandys Paper') reduced the size of the BAOR.[28] Adenauer believed the Sandys Paper presaged a British withdrawal from the conti-nent and, pleaded with Macmillan in May 1957 not to cut the British defence commitment to the continent.[29] Macmillan dismissed such fears as a failure to understand the strategic and economic logic of nuclear deterrence. Whilst claiming to understand Bonn's fears, Macmillan 'frank[ly]' told Adenauer that the fault lay with Bonn and its insufficiently rapid re-armament'.[30] Such sharp exchanges were only too representative of the relationship between Macmillan and Adenauer.

Der Alte and Supermac: the personal as political

Personal relationships are often overlooked in discussions of international affairs,[31] but the animus between Adenauer and Macmillan merits special consideration. The deterioration in relations was particularly detrimental to Anglo-German relations, given the 'presidential' mode of personal diplomacy that both men operated by virtue of their character and strong political base. Adenauer especially dominated foreign policy, often with minimal reference to the rest of his party, public opinion and the *Bundestag*.[32] As Willy Brandt later recalled, Adenauer governed 'like a nineteenth-century patriarch'.[33]

Alastair Horne, Macmillan's official biographer, is unambiguous regarding Harold Macmillan's attitude to the Germans: 'Like so many of his generation, he could never quite overcome his distrust and dislike of the Germans or of anyone who supported them.'[34] As his limousine swung past a guard of honour at Adenauer's funeral in 1967 Macmillan commented to Harold Wilson's Private Secretary, Michael Palliser, 'Marvellous aren't they! They scare me stiff!'[35] Like many of his opinions, Macmillan's dislike of Germany was derived from the trauma of the Great War, in which he had been wounded and lost many friends.[36] This was accompanied by a strong dislike of contemporaries who had not fought in the Great War and, typically, Adenauer was contemptuously referred to as the 'arch-civilian'.[37] Macmillan constantly invoked the First World War as a reference point in much of his thinking, littering his diplomatic rhetoric with allusions to it. Early August was always marked in Macmillan's diaries by sad reflections, both on his fallen comrades and on the state the world had fallen into since 1914. In 1961, he wrote that

> Yesterday ... was the anniversary of the 1st war ... from which fatal date spring all our troubles – the beginning of the end of Empire's supremacy; the predominance of the White man in the world. From this date began the end of the British Empire & the capture of the greatest Euro/Asian country – Russia – by the strange doctrines of a German Jew Intellectual – Karl Marx. Happily we did not realise all this when we were young.[38]

Macmillan therefore conceptualised Franco-German relations in terms of Verdun rather than the Treaty of Rome. This was a serious miscalculation. As Lord Home's Private Secretary later phrased it, 'Adenauer had a very close relationship with General de Gaulle. On the contrary he had no sort of relationship at all with Harold Macmillan – and that was cordially reciprocated.'[39] For his part, Adenauer is on record as having listed as his chief dislikes, in no particular order, as being 'Russians, Prussians and the British'.[40] The latter were therefore unfortunate in their news press as Adenauer had an endemic suspicion of the media generally, referring to them as 'perverse and destructive'.[41] It was small wonder that he regarded Fleet Street, with its populist anti-German bent, as 'hostile, vindictive and outdated'.[42] The Chancellor saw no place for the media in policy formulation,[43] and was driven to complain to Macmillan about the British press on more than one occasion.[44] Sir Frank Roberts later recalled that some British correspondents were under instructions to write bad things about Anglo-German relations if at all possible.[45] Small wonder that the *Daily Telegraph* conceded in 1959: 'When ... [the West Germans] ... hear ... news reports ... about them in Christian, democratic, capitalist Britain, they often find no difference from what is being said about them by the atheist, Communist collectivist regime in eastern Germany.'[46]

The Foreign Office was only too aware of the damaging effects of popular British anti-German sentiment.[47] The popular view that West Germany was thoroughly infiltrated by ex-Nazis,[48] press abuse (from the right) and rhetorical outbursts (from left-wing MPs)[49] was compounded by what the Foreign Office saw as the activities of 'professional anti-Germans, [such as] A.J.P. Taylor'.[50] Adenauer, however, was certainly no innocent, and Anglophobia was a feature of his daily rhetoric: 'If the English worked six days a week, they would be a lot better off. But they finish work Friday lunchtime and don't start again until Monday morning. They should not complain when they do not succeed.'[51]

Adenauer was often careless in his language regarding the British,[52] and Noel Annan, who served in the British zone of occupation after the war and had personal dealings with Adenauer, recalled that the Chancellor seldom failed to make a barbed remark concerning the Attlee government's partisan attitude with regard to the SPD in the British zone.[53] (Adenauer had something in this. The cause of 'International socialism' meant that the Labour Party (which was in power) forged close links with the SPD after 1945, offering advice and material assistance.[54]) Annan further stated that 'Since 1918 [Adenauer's] life had been devoted to coming to an understanding with the French, and he regarded Protestant England (*sic*) with the same scepticism as did de Gaulle'.[55] Hans von Herwarth recalled that 'The British mentality was less familiar to him than the French. In my opinion, he was irritated by the inherent self-confidence of the English political class. Such likes and dislikes certainly influence politics.'[56]

This is a somewhat fatalistic point of view. Annan knew Adenauer at a time when clashes with an occupying power were perhaps inevitable. Sir Ivone Kirkpatrick did not concur with the traditional view that Adenauer bore a grudge against the British over his sacking as Mayor of Cologne in 1946. Further, '[h]e does not allow any feeling of resentment to sway his conduct of affairs. He has every reason to feel resentment against the ... British Military Government ... But whilst he is a dour and relentless adversary, he keeps a cool head and the achievement of his aim takes precedence over self-indulgence in resentment.'[57]

Sabine Lee concludes that the traditional picture of Adenauer as the Catholic, anti-British Rhinelander has been much overstated. Certainly Adenauer seems to have had a rather neutral attitude to Britain, at least in the early 1950s.[58] Personal chemistry apart, that Adenauer 'chose' de Gaulle over Macmillan was the result of the perceived national self-interest.[59] It is perhaps unfair to reproach Macmillan too harshly for his failure to appreciate just how close the relationship between Adenauer and de Gaulle would become (especially as the Chancellor told Macmillan in March 1958 that he was apprehensive about de Gaulle's high-handedness and his tendency to view himself as an 'absolute monarch').[60] A Foreign Office Research Department paper concluded in 1953 that 'French fears of growing German strength ... are expressed in an almost equal dislike of the idea of possible West German hegemony in Western Europe'. These anxieties were only exacerbated by German claims to its eastern territories. The return of these territories, and the subsequent augmentation of German power, might even prompt France to side with Poland and the Soviet Union.[61] The apparent depth of Franco-German antagonism reinforced Macmillan's existing preconceptions: 'The French are frightened of the Germans; the Germans are frightened of themselves.'[62] By discounting a Franco-German rapprochement the British believed, wrongly, that Adenauer would side with London over issues such as the Free Trade Area.[63] This was a fundamental miscalculation.

Khrushchev turns the screw in Berlin

Following Suez, Gladwyn Jebb later recalled that 'it must now be obvious that the French would turn more and more to the West Germans ... the [days of an] *Entente* based on British leadership were over'.[64] The behaviour of Macmillan over Berlin from 1958 was to accelerate this process considerably, and John Gearson, Sabine Lee and Victor Mauer (especially) all highlight the Prime Minister's visit to Moscow in February 1959 as representing a major setback for Anglo-German relations.[65] Macmillan failed to understand that Khrushchev's machinations over Berlin and related questions represented no real opportunity for his diplomacy at all. Khrushchev believed in the inherently strong position of the USSR, and planned to exploit weakness and division in the Western camp by means of his bullish diplomacy in the 1950s and 1960s.[66] Thus, Khrushchev's diplomatic initiatives were aimed at weakening the linchpin of the western alliance – the Federal Republic – and not at lowering tension.

Renewed crisis over Berlin was sparked by a Khrushchev speech at the Polish embassy on 10 November 1958 (leading to a diplomatic note of 27 November demanding the de-militarization of West Berlin in six months or all Soviet powers would be handed over to the GDR).[67] This implied recognition of the GDR and called into question the right of access of the three Western powers.[68] This alarmed the West Germans on two points. First, they feared a weakening of their links with the West by an East–West deal. Second, any deal would enhance the status of East Germany and make reunification much more difficult to achieve. Khrushchev linked the drive to strengthen the GDR with wider grievances, reasoning that successful attacks on Bonn could only strengthen Pankow. One of the General Secretary's constant themes was the equation of a rejection of the status quo with the desire for *revanche*:

> If you ask Mr Adenauer whether he believes that a part of German territory, lost as a result of war unleashed by the Hitlerites, can be recovered by means of a policy of cold war, then in public he would certainly believe it, but at home that he did not ... At the present moment the situation is such that both sides are sufficiently reasonable not to go so far as military action for the sake of a frontier change. One must therefore recognise those frontiers which exist at the present moment.[69]

Khrushchev understood as well as anybody the fact that West German legitimacy had always been derived in no small part from the weak position of the GDR, a position that Bonn had done all it could to institutionalise and perpetuate.[70] Adenauer believed, accurately as it turned out, that reunification would only be achieved by the collapse of the GDR and not by any 'growing together' of the two Germanies,[71] and he demanded that the GDR be left isolated. The Federal Republic would remain as a rump state of German self-determination until '*die Zone*' came on board. Thus, British 'flexibility' on the question of the GDR, reflected Bonn's fears of the willingness of London to 'appease' the Soviet Union.[72] Adenauer's long game with regard to the GDR was anathema to the British, who were more concerned with the 'here and now': the non-recognition issue was an irritating obsession.[73] British acquiescence on the question of the GDR was conditional, and the prospect of war over Berlin caused a re-think: 'It is not that we want to recognise the DDR in the least ... But ... faced with a choice between recognising and fighting we would certainly not have the support of public opinion here or in other western countries for fighting.'[74] Selwyn Lloyd was unambiguous as to the implications of this: 'Dealing on a de facto basis with the East Germans is a reasonable course and I would not much mind if it ended up with the recognition of the DDR Government.'[75]

Given that the State Department resolved to make no concessions over Berlin under duress,[76] Eisenhower was startled to learn that Lloyd had told the US ambassador, Whitney, that there was no reason why dealing with the GDR – in order to avoid war – should lead to Western expulsion from Berlin.[77] Lloyd claimed that French Foreign Minister, Couve de Murville, shared this view, and Jebb concurred, reporting that Couve had told him that Berlin was not worth a war and that it had been a mistake not to recognise the GDR 'ages ago'.[78] Legal experts at the FO agreed: 'There is no fundamental legal reason why we could not recognise the DDR authorities as a *de facto* Government ... and yet maintain quite consistently that the status of Berlin and our right to remain there as Occupying Power have not been thereby affected.'[79]

Thus, rather than the contemporary West German charge that the British desired to abandon the Western position in Berlin, it would be fairer to say that the British were unwilling to indulge the West Germans in their absolutist line on Berlin. The British saw their rights in Berlin assured by their status as victors in the Second World War, not as guarantors of the integrity of the legal status of Germany. This was somewhat at variance with the West German assumption that West Berlin was the capital (*Hauptstadt*) of a German state within the boundaries of 1937. In fact, Article 23 of the Federal Constitution had stated that Greater Berlin was the Twelfth Land of the FRG. However, the Western Commandants had abrogated this in 1950. Undaunted, the West Germans continued to hold annual *Bundestag* meetings in Berlin so as to reaffirm their commitment to Berlin as *Hauptstadt*. In 1960 Selwyn Lloyd was forced to assure the Commons that, whatever West German assertions, Berlin was not a part of the FRG.[80] *The Times* opined that 'To hold the Bundestag meetings in Berlin ... is unnecessary and provocative. It is no concern of the western Powers to jeopardize themselves or others in its furtherance.'[81] The insistence of holding such meetings in Berlin was seen as one of the emptier of the gesture politics so beloved of West German policy.[82] Sooner or later, the British felt, Bonn's posturing would be exposed as just that, and to hold meetings of the West German parliament in Berlin served only to provoke the Soviets.[83]

Adenauer's policy represented the worst of all possible worlds for Macmillan. It precluded détente and risked nuclear war without enhancing the prospects of reuniting Germany. Furthermore, the Chancellor's public stance was seen as being at variance with a fatalistic private view that viewed war as almost inevitable, whilst 'Adenauer is in a bad way and ageing (*sic*) rapidly. The rest of them (Brentano etc.) are unable or unwilling to think out anything new in these circumstances.'[84] Consequently, Macmillan believed that '[the West must] decide whether we (including Adenauer) *really* want a Unified Germany or not, recognising that it hardly seems possible to get any unified Germany except as neutral or neutralised'.[85] This was absolutely unacceptable to the Americans, and Eisenhower warned such a prospect meant that 'we might have to put even more US forces in that country'.[86] Macmillan's diaries reveal that he was not averse to floating ideas involving the thinning out of forces 'without national discrimination. We might even prepare something more ambitious – Russian troops to leave Poland, Hungary and Czechoslovakia – at a price. This price might even be the neutrality of Germany.'[87] When such possibilities loomed large, pressure within the Western Alliance for Bonn to modify its intransigent position was intense. If Adenauer wanted allied backing, he had to demonstrate flexibility. Adenauer therefore let it be known if an otherwise satisfactory arrangement could be concluded, Bonn might perhaps make concessions such as the recognition of the Oder–Neiße line and on diplomatic relations with Poland and Czechoslovakia.[88]

Macmillan was determined that war would not result from technical arguments about who 'stamped passes'.[89] De Gaulle concurred, stating there could be no war for German reunification, but angered Macmillan by refusal to make this public in order that he might continue 'to impress Chancellor Adenauer, and keep his support in their protectionist attitude towards European economic problems'.[90] It would be left to the Anglo-Saxons to make the Germans face facts,[91] but Macmillan, to his fury, was now being compared with Chamberlain at Munich in 1938: 'We want a negotiated settlement because we do *not* believe that the allies will face war over . . . Berlin. However, we must not get into the position we got into at Munich (1938). I will be no Mr Chamberlain . . . What would be the worst thing for the West would be a humiliating climb-down *after* talking big.'[92]

Nevertheless, Macmillan's attempt to use Berlin as a lever to extract concessions elsewhere from the West Germans looked like an attempt to take advantage of an ally's distress for personal gain. The Prime Minister therefore sought to push the 'Six' into the acceptance of a 'Free Trade area'. In attempting this, Macmillan saw an intimate, and exploitable, link between his economic aspirations and the security fears of the West Europeans. In June 1958, Macmillan wrote:

> We should not allow ourselves to be destroyed little by little. We would fight back with every weapon in our armoury. We would take our troops out of Europe. We would withdraw from NATO . . . [We] would say to the Germans, the French and all the rest of them; 'Look after yourselves with your own forces. Look after yourselves when the Russians overrun your countries.'[93]

De Gaulle recalled in his memoirs that Macmillan had told him on 29 June 1958 that 'The Common Market is the Continental System all over again. Britain cannot accept it.'[94] Macmillan expressed his annoyance to Adenauer about French policy and the demise of the Free Trade area, stating his astonishment at the 'British public's' forbearance of being knocked about by 'the Six'. Furthermore, while de Gaulle had withdrawn the French fleet from NATO and France had no troops in Germany, the UK had four divisions in Germany at the cost of £30 million a year. In these circumstances, people in Britain were inclined to feel that a war over Berlin was not worth the cost.[95] Macmillan bluntly declared: 'the French are fundamentally in a very strong position politically, I believe that we shall not succeed in bullying them into accepting us as a partner in Europe ... The Germans, however, are not in a strong political position, and I would have thought there was some chance of bullying them.'[96] But such threats were largely bluff, and they did little to advance Macmillan's cause.

Macmillan's trip to Moscow and its aftermath

Contemporary West German opinion would have been even more alarmed had the West Germans known the nature of the concessions contemplated by the British. Prior to his 1959 visit to Moscow, Macmillan asked Jebb to examine fundamental questions such as whether the NATO alliance could survive without Germany. While Jebb was very much against the neutralisation of Germany, he stated that Britain should be willing to consider the evacuation of West Berlin. Furthermore, German reunification was 'something we should do our best to avoid'.[97]

Forearmed with such advice, Macmillan's Moscow trip was the ultimate expression of the divergence of his agenda from that of Bonn. Although Andrei Gromyko (Soviet Foreign Minister 1957–85) recalled that 'the British position as presented by Macmillan excluded the least possibility of any understanding or the slightest movement',[98] Macmillan had in fact been willing to listen to proposals involving the GDR, the Oder–Neiße line and Berlin that would have, in effect, destroyed Adenauer's foreign policy. As it was, Macmillan did not reveal, even to Cabinet, the price the Soviets had exacted for a foreign ministers' conference – a British willingness to recognise the GDR. Macmillan justified this by the assertion that the Berlin Crisis was 'likely to compel the West to give increasing de facto recognition of the DDR'.[99] The Prime Minister returned to an ecstatic welcome from press, politicians and public alike, declaring in the Commons that 'our purpose [in Moscow] was not to negotiate. It was to try and seek a better understanding of our respective views ... The main point is that ... we reached agreement that the great issues which separate East and West must be settled by negotiation'.[100] Macmillan then announced he was to visit de Gaulle, Adenauer and Eisenhower consecutively.

In Bonn, Adenauer lectured Macmillan that what the USSR desired – the status quo plus concessions – was no basis for negotiation. Macmillan retorted that Khrushchev would win the propaganda war if the West refused to negotiate. The Anglo-Soviet communiqué following the Moscow trip had made reference to a 'Possible Zone of Limitation of Armaments', prompting von Brentano to state that this was tantamount to 'disengagement'. The Chancellor added that nuclear weapons were required to offset Soviet conventional superiority, and inspections limited only to Europe would not be in the West's interest. Macmillan retorted that Adenauer exaggerated the extent of what had passed between the

British and the Soviets. The fact was that the public liked the idea of disengagement, and therefore Macmillan had little option but to bow before popular pressure to discuss such topics. Indeed, the government might fall from power over such an issue, and the disengagement propaganda had to be dealt with by means such as the communiqué. Macmillan believed that disengagement was an idea to be discussed, but the real question was whether or not 'We were going to war about Berlin and, if so, how should we prepare for it?'[101]

While the British saw the threat of war as being sufficient incentive to talk (the substance of such talks was seen as of secondary importance), Bonn saw Khrushchev's threats of war as attempts to exact concessions under duress and, in line with this, von Brentano told Lloyd that Bonn had abandoned plans for a declaration on the Oder–Neiße.[102] In West German eyes, and Adenauer's especially, Macmillan had opted for dialogue with the Soviets rather than solidarity with Bonn.[103] As Adenauer later made clear, the suspicion that Macmillan was more concerned with increasing his parliamentary majority than with Bonn's sensibilities was a strong one.[104] Little wonder that the Foreign Office was to conclude that Adenauer believed that Macmillan's trip had been arranged secretly, and was 'perhaps the single most important contribution to German distrust'.[105]

Arranging a détente: then what?

Eisenhower was increasingly irritated with Macmillan's obsession with summitry, and his upbeat descriptions of his visits to Paris and Berlin (which contrasted with the reports he received from de Gaulle and Adenauer).[106] Macmillan himself noted that British policy now stood in stark contrast with Eisenhower's stated belief in the absolute necessity and obligation of the West to defend Berlin.[107] Dulles had told the British in no uncertain terms that the Western position in Berlin was 'legally and morally impeccable',[108] and he reiterated this to Macmillan and Lloyd (in the presence of Eisenhower) from his hospital bed in March 1959. Further, the Secretary of State sought to disabuse the Prime Minister of any notions that he may have had regarding the possibility of negotiating away Western interests:

> I said [to Macmillan and Lloyd] that I thought the free world allies should not give the people of the world the impression that that we are frightened of the Soviets or that the Soviets are in the driver's seat. In some parts of the world, notably in Asia, Africa and parts of Latin America, people are watching closely to see whether they think the Soviet Union or the western Allies are the more powerful. We cannot, of course, prevent Khrushchev from strutting across the stage and making his grandiloquent speeches. But we can avoid the impression

that whenever he sounds conciliatory we rejoice and whenever he sounds threatening we are fearful as though he were the Lord of Creation.[109]

A frustrated Macmillan retorted that the First World War had resulted from the refusal of the leaders of 1914 to meet 'at the summit'.[110] Eisenhower was unmoved and, echoing Dulles, attacked the British for their lack of resolution. Macmillan could only console himself with the knowledge that a note to the Kremlin proposing a meeting of foreign ministers' for May was agreed upon.[111] Macmillan's suggestions to Eisenhower only increased Adenauer's ire, and Steel warned that the 'Chancellor's suspicions of us are not only alive but more rampant than they have ever been'.[112] Unhelpfully, Macmillan judged Adenauer to have 'gone a bit potty',[113] comforting himself with delusion that the *Austwärtiges Amt* was 'rather ashamed' of Adenauer's increasingly Anglophobic stance.[114] Macmillan believed that, although isolated, he had Western public opinion on his side in seeking détente,[115] and if the West refused to negotiate then Khrushchev had 'every moral justification for immediately making his peace treaty with the eastern Germans and handing over all Russian obligations'.[116] This was to accept at face value Khrushchev's assertion that he only wanted a peace treaty, and if the West had a problem recognising the GDR then the West should have allowed the USSR to sign a treaty solely with the GDR.[117] If Eisenhower now seemed to accept the logic of negotiation, Macmillan noted that 'This is good. For the Germans and the French can accept as "prudent" from Washington suggestions which would be "defeatist" if made from London.'[118] Macmillan's desire for détente had, in addition to saving the world from war, the objective of restoring British influence internationally to a commensurate height. Thus, Macmillan was greatly distressed when Eisenhower unilaterally extended an invitation for Khrushchev to visit the United States in September 1959:

> People will ask 'Why should [the] U.K. try to stay in the big game? Why should she be a nuclear power? You told us that this would give you power and authority in the world. But you have been made fools of ... [The] U.K. had better give up the struggle and accept, as gracefully as possible, the position of a second-rate power.' All this trouble stems from one act of well-meant but incredibly naive diplomacy.[119]

Macmillan could not have it both ways; if Eisenhower accepted his view, then why would he take a 'back seat'? The President himself wanted a place in history before his term of office ended and, if there was to be a détente, he wanted the credit.[120] As Dulles stated: 'Ours is the 'king-pin' of power; therefore our views are in the last analysis compelling on the UK and our other allies.'[121] However, while the Western powers had accepted his calls for a summit, the relationship between Bonn and London seemed to verge on open hostility.[122] By late 1959, Adenauer believed Macmillan 'had absolutely no notion what a dangerous situation [West Germany was] in'.[123] A meeting of Eisenhower, Macmillan, de Gaulle and Adenauer in Paris in December hardly aided the situation. This was partly because tripartite meetings (adopted as a sop to de Gaulle) were included in the schedule, to the frustration of Adenauer. At least a date for the Paris Summit was fixed, even if what was to be discussed (and on what terms) was not.[124] Macmillan's hopes were high, but Adenauer remained as hostile to the whole idea as ever.

The Paris Summit and the collapse of Macmillan's policy

Adenauer now sought to counter Macmillan's 'summitry' by visiting Berlin in the 'Prussia' for which he had such dislike between 11 and 13 of January 1960.[125] Adenauer repeatedly stated that since the USSR had rejected the Western formula proposed at Geneva on 28 July 1959, the status quo was the optimum position until reunification.[126] The British were alarmed that, yet again, Adenauer was trying to put a straitjacket on policy by demonstrating his solidarity with West Berlin, and the Chancellor even concurred with Brandt's demand for a new agreement on Berlin (upholding the Western presence in the city and the right of West Berlin to choose its own economic and political system).[127] Adenauer was effectively treating Berlin in accordance with the abortive Article 23 (that is, as part of the Federal Republic and the future capital of Germany). British consternation was raised when the *Bundestag* introduced a bill to establish a Federal radio authority with headquarters in Berlin without consulting the Western allies as President Lübke followed Adenauer in visiting Berlin.[128] Macmillan recognised the increasing intransigence of the West Germans,[129] but this seemed much diminished in importance when Eisenhower told Macmillan that a deal in Berlin could be achieved by the recognition of the Oder–Neiße line and other frontiers in Europe.[130] This sort of quid pro quo was exactly what Macmillan had wanted – the moderation of the Bonn's positions in exchange for stabilisation of the Western presence in Berlin. Macmillan now speculated that things had progressed to the stage whereby one big push would attain a comprehensive agreement.[131]

The Prime Minister believed that all parties now seemed set for real negotiation, and he 'entertain[ed] high hopes'. But '[b]efore the third week of May had reached its close the grand edifice which I had worked so long and so painfully to build seemed totally and finally destroyed'[132] by the shooting down of an American U-2 spy plane over the USSR. This was rightly seen as a total disaster for Macmillan.[133] Philip de Zuleta recalled Macmillan's complete depression at the realisation that the United Kingdom lacked the status to significantly affect events.[134] Macmillan confessed to his diary: 'The *Summit* – on which I had set such high hopes and for which I worked for over 2 years

– has blown up, like a volcano! It is ignominious; it is tragic.'[135] The demise of the Paris Summit set the seal on British isolation.

Macmillan was now very bitter: 'Dr Adenauer has deceived me before, over the [Free Trade area] ... under French pressure, he went back on his promises. Having a guilty conscience, he then accused me of defeatism vis-à-vis Soviet Russia'.[136] Yet Macmillan, against his better judgement, was persuaded to accept an invitation to visit the Federal Republic.[137] Macmillan believed that Adenauer's 'friendly welcome' was the result of 'his delight at the failure of all my attempts at "détente" with the Soviets. It is rather a bitter pill.'[138] The Chancellor lectured Macmillan on the perils of World Communism, and warned of the danger of his losing the 1961 election to the SPD. Macmillan replied that if this were so, then why had the French and the Germans left the lion's share of the defence of the Free World to the Anglo-Saxons?[139] The Prime Minister was depressed, as 'Adenauer had not understood the economic dangers and only thought of the political gains of the Franco-German friendship'.[140] However, Adenauer's victory was hardly complete. Adenauer may have fended off Macmillan's attempts to make concessions on Germany, but Eastern Europe remained as antipathetic as ever to the Federal Republic. Just because Macmillan could not harness an agreement to bolster British standing did not mean that Bonn could obstruct movement indefinitely.

The 'Brown Past' of the Federal Republic

Throughout the Berlin Crisis, the Soviet bloc was unbounded in its denunciations of West Germany. The issue of Berlin, however, was a complex one to the uninitiated, and the Communists were aware that threats to West Berlin could make them look like aggressive bullies. The Nazi past (and the 'revanchist' present) of the Federal Republic, by contrast, offered a rich target for propaganda. Khrushchev informed Eisenhower that:

> Chancellor Adenauer is your ally and, as the saying goes, noblesse oblige ... [West Germany shows] an unwillingness to conclude a peace treaty; a definite refusal to recognise the state boundaries in Europe which resulted from the defeat of Hitlerite Germany; a refusal to establish diplomatic relations with several European states, including those which, in the last war, were subjected to attack by Hitler's Germany and whose territory at present is the object of Bonn's claims; [this was allied to] the appointment of former active champions of Hitler's policy, including war criminals, to leading positions in the government and ... a poorly concealed desire to gain possession of nuclear weapons.[141]

To some extent, the FRG was responsible for giving such charges substance. Heinrich von Brentano told Soviet ambassador Smirnov, 'If

England and other powers have nuclear weapons, why should the FRG not have them?'[142] Furthermore, a large number of high-ranking individuals found that a 'Brown Past' (i.e. intimate involvement with the Nazi regime) was no obstacle to advancement in Adenauer's Germany.[143] Adenauer's closest confidant, State Secretary Hans Globke, had written one of the official commentaries on the racial Nuremburg Laws in 1935, and in April 1951 introduced constitutional articles 131 and 132 allowing for the return of those civil servants who had been expressly removed by the Allies as Nazis.[144] Adenauer publicly supported Globke and his ex-Nazis when it was obvious to many in his own party that their 'Brown Past' demanded their removal.[145]

In 1958, an SPD international newspaper listed a large number of Nazis in receipt of West German state pensions.[146] However shocking this might have appeared, the fact of the matter was that, as 'successor state' to the *Reich*, Bonn was simply discharging its obligations to former servants of the German state.[147] The obsessive focus on the principle of *Alleinvertretungsanspruch*, of the need to deny East German legitimacy, meant that domestic political decisions in the FRG often appeared at odds with the image the Bonn Republic sought to portray internationally. Indeed a recent author has noted that Bonn's decision to embrace the *Deutschlandlied* (and hence inherit the mantle of the 'national' German state), as the national anthem was indicative of 'the West German government's willingness to compromise with the Nazi past'.[148]

Given all this, it is unsurprising that the KGB and the East German secret service, the HVA, viewed the discrediting of eminent West Germans as ex-Nazis as a top priority.[149] One of the chief denouncers was a British defector, John Peet, recruited by the NKVD as an agent in the 1930s, and editor of the *Democratic German Report* from 1952 to 1975.[150] This paper, often acting on information supplied by HVA chief Markus Wolf, was constantly denouncing West German politicians, diplomats, industrialists, lawyers, generals and police chiefs as ex-Nazis. Peet himself regarded Globke as his 'prize exhibit'.[151] The prominence of former Nazis in the Federal Republic, particularly in the judiciary, led an SPD newsletter to conclude, in 1960, that 'today we find a high percentage of people in the very positions they had held during the Third Reich. This unhealthy state of affairs has produced an atmosphere conducive not only to forgetting the past but even to condoning it.'[152]

While the SPD actively pressed the issue of former Nazis, the CDU seemed content to let matters lie. Daniel E. Rogers argues that Adenauer simply recognised that the continued 'persecution' of German nationals for their actions during the Nazi era 'had become as wildly unpopular as the Treaty of Versailles had been a generation earlier'.[153] There were certainly serious shortcomings in the West German approach to these matters. Prominent examples included judicial appointments (Arthur Lewis MP referred to 596 current jurists who had also served in 'Hitler's

Special Courts' in a Parliamentary Question of 17 February 1959); the 'soft' treatment of war criminals; and Bonn's failure to compensate all of the victims of Nazism.[154] In the Commons in February 1960, the Labour MP, Barbara Castle, charged that the 'allies are in fact conniving with the West German government' in its reluctance to pursue Nazi war criminals. Lloyd retorted that Castle was talking 'nonsense', and refused to be drawn any further on the matter.[155] The Conservative government rather wished the issue would go away, and Lloyd, according to a Labour Party report, 'completely evaded the issue' so as to avoid embarrassment to either London or Bonn.[156] Certainly, an FO brief warned Macmillan:

> There is a tendency, as press articles often illustrate, for people in the U.K. to believe that the Federal Republic is too soft towards the more extreme type of ex-Nazi. This is a matter which is important for Anglo-German relations. It would be disastrous if the impression, which the East Germans are trying to create, that elements of the Federal Government were seriously infiltrated by ex-Nazis, should gain ground.

Understandably, Pankow's propaganda equated Bonn's refusal to recognise the post-1945 frontiers and expulsions with the prominence of ex-Nazis in the FRG.[157] A particularly favoured target were the expellee organisations and their patrons in the *Bundestag*. British officialdom was certainly aware of the strength of the expellee influence over West German policy,[158] and in 1950 the British Control Commission for Germany noted that:

> As a body, the refuges naturally feel the lack of social equality, a sense of being uprooted, and nostalgia for their home lands – hence a certain tendency to accept opportunistic compromises and to fly to extremes, especially to that of conservative nationalism. Besides the possibility that this party may increase its representation, the fact also has to be borne in mind that, given a fairly equal distribution of power, it might come to tip the scales between the SPD and [the CDU].[159]

The expellees initially had their own political party, the *Bund der Heimatvertriebenen und Entrechteten* (BHE), which, having won twenty-seven seats in the 1953 Federal elections, actually joined Adenauer's ruling coalition. That the BHE failed to secure representation in the 1957 *Bundestag* (by failing to get over 5 per cent of the overall vote) was not necessarily indicative of the dissipation of expellee sentiment with regard to the Oder–Neiße territories. Rather, the 1957 result reflected the degree to which the expellees saw the major political parties as representative of their interests.[160] Unsurprisingly, the real power base of the expellees in the Federal Republic was increasingly on the Right. Subsequent to 1957, if the CDU/CSU (and, to a lesser extent, the FDP and the SPD) assimilated the refugee vote it was because of that constituency's satisfaction with the foreign policies of the major parties in the FRG.[161]

The Federal government provided enormous financial backing for expellee organisations whilst publishing a constant stream of books, pamphlets and magazines – at the Federal and Land level – explaining the West German case. These works usually contained a detailed history of the Oder–Neiße line, and always referred to the territories to the east of that line as being *unter polnischer Verwaltung* and, for the northern section of the former East Prussia, *unter sowjetischer Verwaltung.*[162] Prominent politicians often wrote the forewords to such works (usually stating the importance of understanding the 'East'). In March 1964, for instance, Albert Höft, Land minister for expellees in Lower Saxony, recommended a volume as a 'valuable source' for the problem of those living in 'central Germany [the GDR]' and 'under foreign administration' east of the Oder–Neiße.[163] Academic institutes provided scholarly weight to the West German denial of the international legality of the permanent loss of the Oder–Neiße territories. To this end, research bodies specialising in the study of the 'German east' (or *Ostforschung* – 'East research' – and *Ostkunde* – 'East (European) studies') proliferated in West Germany throughout the 1950s. These included the *Osteuropakunde* (established in Stuttgart in 1948), the *Osteuropa-Institut* (established in Munich in 1952) and the *Ostkolleg der Bundeszentrale für Heimatdienst* (established in Cologne in 1957).[164] Such bodies saw their mission as the proclamation of the historical German role in the East, and were often staffed by persons who had an unsavoury past in *Ostforschung* during the Third Reich. Not unnaturally, they were often closely associated with the BHE, whose first leader, Waldemar Kraft, had been a member of the SS,[165] and the refugee umbrella organisation, the *Bund der Vertriebenen* (BdV).[166]

As a definitive work on the saga of the expulsions, the Federal Ministry for Expellees, Refugees and War Victims published a comprehensive five-volume collection of documents on the expulsion of the Germans from eastern and central Europe in the early 1960s.[167] The editor of this collection, the historian Theodor Schieder, a former academic practitioner of *Ostforschung* in the Third Reich, had been closely associated with Nazi settlement policy in the occupied east. From 1953 onwards, Schieder worked on the series under the direction of the BHE leader and *Bundesvertriebenenminister* Theodor Oberländer (with whom he was on '*Du*' terms), having been colleagues in Nazi *Ostforschung* before 1945.[168] Schieder employed former colleagues from Königsberg (such as Hans Rothfels and Werner Conze) on the collection, all of whom were, in the words of one recent historian, 'consciously committed to ... propagandistic activity in their government's service.'[169]

Political conservatives and expellee leaders in West Germany utilised anti-Communism to claim the impossibility of any détente with the East, in order to keep the status of the 'eastern territories' open. Jakob Kaiser, the expellee leader and first Minister for All-German Affairs, articulated this publicly in November 1950 when he declared 'The Potsdam solution is not a German, not a Polish, not even a Russian solution; it is a Bolshevik solution. What we need is a European solution.'[170] Ruling out the possibility of any meaningful dialogue with the Communist bloc therefore conveniently precluded any agreement on the final status of the Oder–Neiße line. It was armed with such evidence that the Soviet bloc would denounce West Germany, in one Polish phrase, as 'a renaissance of Hitlerite ideas in all their murderous splendour'.[171] It was less that the British believed in the reality of the threat of West German 'revanchism', but rather that they saw the manner in which the Communists could make such political capital out of a key Cold War ally.

'East Prussia will be restored to you': Britain and the expellees

As if the presence of individuals of highly dubious pasts (and questionable presents) was not bad enough, the rhetoric of some of the leaders of the Federal Republic drove their allies to distraction. From the perspective of the allies, since Bonn had been given so much freedom as to the timing and nature of any future agreement on the Oder–Neiße line, it could at least avoid making inflammatory statements. For Bonn, if the German question was to remain 'open' then it had to be at the forefront of international affairs. Whilst rejecting the status quo, West Germans sought refuge in democratic phrases, using the rhetoric of the 'victim'. Worse, Bonn appeared to be legitimising 'revisionism' (by the 'back door' at least). Foreign Minister Heinrich von Brentano told an expellee meeting in 1956 that:

> You have shared this fate [of expulsion] … with millions of other people all over the world. The problem … has now become one which is of interest to the whole world and calls out for a permanent ethical, ethnographical and political solution. The basis of any just solution must be the right of the individual to self-determination in his own homeland, and the firm intention to make this a permanent part of international law for the future.[172]

The electoral calculations underpinning much of Adenauer's rhetoric barely seemed to diminish over the first decade of the Federal Republic's life. In a speech entitled '*Recht auf die Heimat*', Adenauer told a rally of Silesians in June 1959 that 'Homeland, peace, liberty, justice … should be … our passwords for the work of the coming years'.[173] In September of that same year, Adenauer pointed out his appreciation of the fact that 'the

questions of Poland, Oder–Neisse, and so on [remained] of great importance to the expellee circles' in the Federal Republic'.[174] Politicians could ill-
afford to upset such groups, and they railed against the wrongs visited upon
millions of expelled Germans, causing consternation in Eastern Europe.[175]
Vice-Chancellor Ludwig Erhard told a rally in 1960 that 'No words can
undo the crimes which have been committed against the Polish people in
the name of the German people. We deplore with deepest regret all the
happenings of this dark period of German history. At the same time we
cannot overlook the wrongs inflicted on the Germans after 1945.'[176]

As the 1961 election loomed, it was noted that the Adenauer government was stepping up its wooing of the refugee vote. The rhetoric of the
politicians to these groups was deliberately vague.[177] Nevertheless, such
rhetoric made for shocking headlines, such as 'Bismarckian frontiers seen
as Bonn's aim – Professor Erhard's advice to the Poles'.[178] Some of the
rhetoric by other MdBs was even less restrained. At an expellee meeting in
August 1960, the CDU MdB Hermann Ehren, vice-chairman of the Upper
Silesian *Landsmannschaft*, denounced Ulbricht as a traitor for handing
over Upper Silesia, adding that whilst they did not want war 'they would
fight for freedom' as they had at Annaberg! The British embassy in Bonn
noted wearily that 'Herr Ehren's remarks will of course provide yet more
ammunition for Soviet bloc attacks on German revanchism, and one
S.P.D. paper has already criticised him on this score'. The British especially saw such statements as grist to the mill of the Communists when they
were made, or endorsed, by the Chancellor himself.[179] In a particularly
notorious case, Adenauer himself told a gathering of East Prussian
expellees that 'We can hope that if we firmly and truly adhere to those
principles, to peace and freedom and firmly and truly stand at the side of
our allies as they do at ours, then peace and freedom will ultimately be
restored to the world and thereby your beautiful Motherland East Prussia
will be restored to you'.[180] The head of the Northern Department saw this
as virtually 'open incitement'.[181] Sensing the discomfort over such rhetoric
in the West, the Polish government communicated an *aide-mémoire* asserting that the alliance seemed to support the 'restoration' of the 'eastern
territories' to Germany.[182] This was not lost on the British, but, as Sir
Christopher Steel pointed out, in electoral terms no West German party
could afford to ignore the refugees, and it was the domestic imperatives
that gave rise to the adverse foreign policy implications.[183]

But Adenauer's domestic constituency could be conveniently neglected
in London. Adenauer's CDU had managed to construct a solid conservative base by assimilating the national elements that had so conspicuously
deserted the mainstream right in the Weimar Republic.[184] After achieving
sovereignty in May 1955, the Adenauer government found that its 'opportunistic' indulgence of expellee demands 'imposed strict limits on their
freedom of movement in Ostpolitik'.[185] By 1960, the expellee umbrella
organisation, the *Bund der Vertriebenen*, had over 2,000,000 members and

was headed by the CDU MdB and member of *Bundestag* Commission on Foreign Affairs, Hans Krüger.[186] The expellee organisations were the most outspoken mass movement in Western Europe, and significant elements within the *BdV* were unhappy even with the claim that Germany still existed in its ('limited') 1937 borders. Associated groups like *Aktion Oder–Neiße* (AKON), which was founded in 1962, issued violent anti-Polish propaganda, with maps depicting the 1914 boundaries of the German *Reich.* On occasion, the flights of fancy of the refugee organisations seemed incredible. In April 1960, Wenzel Jaksch[187] regretted the 'restricting' nature of the official West German claim to the 1937 borders, proposing a 'Benelux' solution to the Sudeten German 'problem' given that 'No Sudeten German would go back to his homeland if he felt that he would have to belong to a minority … namely the union (Anschluss) of the German-speaking territories with Germany would seem to [Jaksch] to be the most sensible solution'.[188]

The danger of such schemes came not in the remote chance of their implementation, but rather in the distorting influence they could have on West German foreign policy. Additionally, West German semi-official endorsement of the expellee groups was damaging to the reputation of the Federal Republic in Britain.[189] The question of the Oder–Neiße territories seemed to permeate every facet of West German life. Towns in the Federal Republic had 'patronage' of towns in the Oder–Neiße territories, and there were 350 settlers' dailies and periodicals, with a circulation of approximately two million. There were even fifteen 'refugee' periodicals produced outside of the Federal Republic. The expellee organisations had a high degree of political influence, and in December 1956, for instance, a Conference of *Land* Ministers' of Culture decided to introduce the study of *Ostkunde* in West German schools.[190] The status accorded the expellees and their demands moved the Labour MP Frank Allaun to ask of the British government their opinion on expellee leader Herr Seebohm's (CDU deputy and Minister of Transport) recent inflammatory statements on the Sudetenland. What were the implications of this, given that Seebohm was also a minister in the Adenauer government? John Profumo, Minister of State for Foreign Affairs, replied that the German had acted in such a role as a 'private citizen'.[191] This was a tenuous defence (to say the least), and the activities of men like Seebohm only allowed the Soviets to make capital out of the genuine fear of Germany in the Eastern bloc.[192]

Krüger, the *BdV* leader, spoke out repeatedly of continuing Soviet pressure for the recognition of the status quo, and the increasing tendency in the West to show 'weaknesses' with regard to the Oder–Neiße territories. At least, Krüger noted with satisfaction, the political parties in West Germany 'were united in acknowledging the legal standpoint in this question'.[193] The presence of such influential and intransigent lobbyists was anathema for British foreign policy professionals. They asked how a proper discussion of the Oder–Neiße line could be conducted with such people at Adenauer's and the *Auswärtiges Amt's* backs? This was reinforced by a belief that the problems in German foreign policy were partly structural, as 'The Government in Bonn simply does not function in the way that H.M.G. does – there is no question of close collaboration between other ministries and the Foreign Ministry nor is there anything like "speaking notes for Ministers" '.[194] That is to say, it was suggested that the formulation of West German foreign policy was far more prone to the shifts of public opinion. In Britain, at least, Foreign Office professionals could apply objective experience to guide ministers, without the intrusion of such distorting factors. Not only was West German foreign policy far from this shallow; the domestic climate in which it operated was also fundamentally different from that in which the British Foreign Office operated. Within the Federal Republic, for instance, the Ministries for All-German Affairs and the Ministry for Refugees[195] would often hold diametrically opposed opinions to those of the *AA*. British policy-makers constantly bemoaned the fact that the *AA* was not given a greater voice in policy-making. However, for Bonn any *Ostpolitik* was a domestic as well as a foreign policy issue, and the *AA* had to contend with the negative connotations of any such policy, just as the British Foreign Office did. For many in the *AA*, Steel was therefore preaching to the converted when he pointed out the harm done to West Germany internationally by 'pandering' to the refugee organisations.[196]

Defending the kettle against the pot: Macmillan at the UN

In September 1960 Macmillan made a spirited defence of the Federal Republic at the United Nations, appearing as Bonn's 'Champion' at the UN (of which neither Germany was a member). One can only conclude that this was part of a deliberate strategy (Lord Home's maiden speech as Foreign Secretary in November also made several favourable references to German foreign policy)[197] designed to rebuild relations with Bonn.

After hearing that Khrushchev was to lead the Soviet (and satellite) delegations in person, Macmillan had resolved to go the United Nations (in his words) 'if only to rally the West'.[198] The Soviet bloc did not disappoint. At the UN on 4 September, Polish Premier Gomułka charged that Bonn 'was reaching out his revisionist paw for Silesia ... The facts indicate more and more significantly that the West German Government has raised the revanchist policy to the ranks of official state policy.'[199] Macmillan obviously hoped to impress Bonn when he, in Gromyko's words, 'started using particularly strong language against the Soviet Union and her friends'.[200] Macmillan told the UN assembly that

> There has been a great deal of communist denunciation ... against the Government and the people of the Federal Republic of Germany ... I am amazed at how reactionary and backward-looking much of

the communist argument is. Both the Polish and the Czech representative talks of revanche which they alleged was reviving in West Germany. I am bound to say that their own speeches were not flowing over with the spirit of reconciliation.[201]

In his memoirs, Macmillan stated that attacks on NATO as the 'instrument of West German militarism' were 'completely unjustified. [And] I thought it right to defend Dr Adenauer's Germany.' Macmillan did not pull his punches:

> I represent a country that has no particular reason to regard German militarism with any special favour. Twice in my lifetime the British people have suffered most grievously both in blood and treasure as the result of German militarism. But we must look forward and not backward. Nor can you ... 'draw up an indictment against a whole people'. Germany is divided ... and so the German people in spite of their great population and importance cannot be represented in this assembly today. Eastern Germany is armed. Great Soviet forces are stationed there. That is part of the unhappy state of the world today. Yet at the same time western Germany is condemned for rearming. We have an old proverb in our country about the pot calling the kettle black.[202]

While Macmillan was satisfied that his speech 'went well',[203] Sir Evelyn Shuckburgh in Moscow noted that he was the only Western leader to speak up for the FRG, earning Adenauer's gratitude. It also meant that the British felt the wrath of the East Europeans, in particular of the Czechs and the Poles.[204] This was inevitable for, as the British ambassador Sir George Clutton opined from Warsaw, 'The flood of anti-German propaganda continues ... This ... seems to have developed a momentum all of is own. The West Germans have not recently done or said anything which could be seized on.' Despite this 'the Poles seem to have begun to create opportunities for beating the anti-German drum to coincide with the meeting of the United Nations General Assembly.'[205]

The Poles delivered a second *aide-mémoire* to the British, and Dr Rodzinski, the Polish ambassador, informed Ted Heath, the Lord Privy Seal, that the official backing these revisionist groups had in the Federal Republic disturbed Poland. Furthermore, the Polish government believed that NATO backed these German policies, endangering peace. Rodzinski said that he saw echoes of Munich in the present policy of the British government, and wondered how this squared with the British desire for détente? Ted Heath replied that West Germany was a free country and could formulate its own policy on the Oder–Neiße line, had renounced force and, while not a member of the UN, subscribed to its Charter. The Pole countered that it seemed that the FRG was increasingly seen to be 'running

NATO', and if senior figures like Adenauer, Erhard and Lübke could speak at 'revanchist' meetings they could only do so with NATO backing. Heath concluded a stormy exchange by stating that if anyone was 'running NATO' it certainly was not Bonn – whose internal political situation bore no resemblance to the 1930s.[206] For the British, the Polish charges at least had the plus of 'provid[ing] a fair opportunity for us to prod the Germans, confidentially & in a NATO forum, to think about the difficulties which their present eastern policy (or perhaps rather, their means of expressing it) causes us & their other Allies'.[207]

The head of the Northern Department deplored Rodzinski's charges (especially the references to Munich), noting the attack on the West Germans was part of the general Communist offensive, 'against the solidarity of the NATO alliance ... [and] the Poles will continue their barrage against alleged revisionist territories, whether they are worried by them or not'.[208] Nonetheless, there was real disquiet over West German policy in Britain. The Conservative MP Gilbert Longden questioned the wisdom of issuing an official West German publication (*The German View*)[209] in Britain, given that, amongst other things, its cover portrayed Germany as existing within its 1937 borders. 'In view of the latent anti-German feeling in this country, it seems to me rather tactless to put this out.' The official reply tells us much about the quandary the British government found itself in:

> The problem of the eastern territories is a very troublesome one for us, and one which will probably become more so as the campaign for next year's German elections get underway. That is inevitable, considering that there are several million voters from the eastern territories in the Federal Republic. Our own position ... is that the final delimitation of Germany's eastern frontier can only be formalised in a peace treaty; meanwhile they are under Polish administration. In fact we accept (tacitly) that there would be virtually no possibility of the territories being returned to Germany, even if we could get as far as a peace treaty. The Federal Government probably accepts this too, in its heart of hearts, but could not possibly say so for the reason given above. But it has renounced the use of force in its efforts to regain the territories, and recent official statements on the subject, unlike those of the various expellee organisations, have been quite moderate.[210]

Clutton stated that the Polish *aide mémoire* was part of Gomułka's election campaign to rally Polish people behind him. This was the classic method of seizing the nationalist 'high-ground' employed by East European Communists (i.e. playing the 'German card').[211] In the meantime, the East Europeans determined to maximise pressure on the British by co-ordinating their attacks. Rudolf Barák, the Czechoslovak Deputy Premier, railed against Macmillan for having 'played a lamentable role in the

General Assembly, having 'whitewashed the West German militarists'. Barák posed three questions for Macmillan to ponder. First, was the Munich Agreement still valid? Adenauer, Barák believed, implied that it was. Second, did Britain recognise the frontiers of Czechoslovakia? Adenauer did not. Finally, what was Britain's view of the Oder–Neiße frontiers? Adenauer did not recognise the de facto frontiers in Europe.[212]

These claims were only partially accurate. First, Adenauer's government did not regard the Munich Pact as being valid, but rather refused to concede that it was invalid *ab initio*. Second, and following on from the previous point, Adenauer did not claim the Sudetenland should 'return' to Germany (indeed it had only been part of modern Germany between 1938 and 1945), but rather only viewed the boundaries of Germany as being 'provisional' prior to any final peace settlement. In strictly legal terms, Bonn claimed the legitimate boundaries as being those of 31 December 1937. Bonn did, however, reject the legitimacy of the Beneš Decrees[213] that led to the expulsion of over 3,000,000 Sudeten Germans following the Second World War. On the final point, however, it was true that Adenauer's government did not recognise the *de facto* frontiers of Europe. Given this, all the British delegation in Prague could do was discreetly inform the Czechs that Britain was none too keen on West Germany's '*Recht auf Heimat*' rhetoric either.[214] Cecil Parrott, British ambassador in Prague, believed that

> [W]hatever we may say about our position regarding the Munich agreement, the present Czechoslovak frontiers and the Oder–Neisse line, there is no question so long as Dr Adenauer continues to associate himself with the expellee demands and we not disassociate ourselves from these views our position will continue to be regarded with suspicion … But if some kind of action … could be taken it might help stem the tide of anti-British feeling which is showing signs of rising here and which will gain a wide measure of support if we can be misrepresented as favouring the German case.[215]

Parrott candidly informed Labour MP James Callaghan that the main motive behind the angry Czech response was Macmillan's failure to condemn the revisionist groups in the FRG. Indeed, Parrott believed that it would have been more helpful had Macmillan done so, instead of going 'out of his way to praise Dr Adenauer's administration'.[216] This was to ignore the manner in which the Cold War had long since dictated British policy towards the Federal Republic and its disputes with eastern neighbours. For while the British government had denounced the Munich Agreement in 1942, by 1948 it was refusing to make a statement declaring the inviolable nature of Czech frontier as Prague slipped into the Soviet bloc. Pierson Dixon, ambassador in Prague, advised the Foreign Office in brutally frank terms:

It is usually considered to be one of the principles of British foreign policy that we do not make any statement about what we should do in a hypothetical situation unless it is absolutely obvious in advance where our interest would lie if such a situation arose. A situation which called in question the future of the Sudetenland is a hypothetical one in which the proper course of action for us to take would depend very much on the circumstances which gave rise to the situation. If it came about as the result of war with Russia ... it might be necessary for us in self defence to pay a price for the support of Germany, and it might in such a case not suit us at all to have been committed to the present frontier between Germany and Czechoslovakia: and, *a fortiori*, it is impossible to foretell where our interests might lie as regards frontiers generally in the event of our winning a war against Russia.[217]

Thus, despite a private acceptance of the rectitude of Prague's position,[218] subsequent Czech requests to declare the Munich Pact null and void *ab initio* foundered upon British deference to its (increasingly important) West German ally and its sensibilities. Indeed, the question of British attitudes to the Munich Agreement was to become entirely dependent upon West German moves towards its own repudiation of that pact.[219] Association with intransigent West German positions was far from a new problem for the British, but there seemed little prospect of lessening the tension between the Soviet bloc and the Federal Republic, as 'The chief political and psychological factor in keeping alive the expellees' claims to their homeland is, I think, the continuous opposition and tension between the Federal Republic and the ... Soviet bloc'.[220]

Signs of American disenchantment with the *Politik der Stärke*

Following his plea at the UN, Gomułka complained to the new US Secretary of State, Christian Herter that West German 'revisionist tendencies' were increasing due to the rising strength of the *Bundeswehr*. This was particularly dangerous, Gomułka asserted, as the restraints upon West Germany were loosened by French involvement in Algeria and British military commitments elsewhere. Herter reassured Gomułka that 'the Potsdam Agreement gave the Polish Government complete administrative authority east of the Oder–Neisse line and what they did was no concern of the United States Government'.[221] The Western Department of the FO advised that:

We are not in fact much inclined to suggest that you should have discretion to speak similarly. Neither we nor the Americans are in any position to object to such Polish measures; the Poles are fully aware of this, and to go out of the way to justify ourselves would merely encourage them to think that we are being flustered by their anti-German propaganda campaign.[222]

Clutton reported that his US counterpart, Jacob D. Beam, asserted that the Americans had only made oblique references to the 'eastern territories' with the Poles in the 'the wider context of the whole problem of the Polish western frontier'.[223] The Northern Department pointed out that Herter's remarks had in fact gone further than anything the British had done. It was therefore advocated that Clutton should make similar assurances to the Poles in order to achieve three goals. First, it would stop the Poles playing off Britain against the USA.[224] Second, it would lessen the affront to the Poles caused by Macmillan's UN speech (without the need for retraction). Third, it would improve Britain's position with Poland in the event of a Berlin crisis. Furthermore, such an undertaking, '[given that] there would be little chance of its becoming public, would not damage our present good standing in West Germany'.[225] It was agreed that Ted Heath should therefore tell Rodzsinki, at the next opportunity, that the British government was of a similar mind to the US government.[226]

The Head of the Northern Department, Heath Mason, wondered just why the Poles were unhappy with the formal government line on the Oder–Neiße line (i.e. that the line was provisional pending a final peace settlement). Furthermore, given that Herter had spoken to Gomułka in such terms in New York, there was a danger that the Poles would think that the US has moved in its direction: 'They might regard these statements as evidence of the success of their propaganda campaign against the Federal Republic.' Mason feared the 'Danger of being out of line with [the] US [and] Fr[ance] on this (e.g. Nixon in Buffalo)', advising that 'we perhaps need a policy review'.[227]

Consequently, although the demise of the Paris Summit had seemingly signalled the triumph of Adenauer's *Politik der Stärke*, the victory had been a Pyrrhic one as it became increasingly obvious that West German intransigence represented an insuperable obstacle to détente. The chief inhibition in Macmillan's attempt to disregard the straitjacket imposed by West German policy had been the need to maintain allied solidarity. The shift in US perceptions was to prove instrumental in undermining the Western acquiescence to the Adenauer government's goals.

The British increasingly resolved that the intransigent West German stance on the Oder–Neiße line should be addressed in order to achieve a number of objectives. First, it would remove a major pretext for anti-Western Communist propaganda. Second, it would elicit reconciliation between Germany and the East Europeans. Third, it would allow the East Europeans to move away from Moscow as fear of Germany was diminished, and the Soviet role as defender of the Slavs would be exposed as a sham. Yet, any British departure from Bonn's policy on this issue risked a serious rupture in the Western Alliance:

> The Federal Republic is vastly more important to us as a N.A.T.O. ally and an important element in the solution of the Six/Seven problem

than Poland so long as she remains firmly within the Soviet bloc ... It is true that our present position gains us nothing on the positive side from the Germans. They take it for granted. But if on the other hand we were to change our position significantly before the Germans have come, of their own volition, publicly to accept the inevitability of the existing Oder–Neisse line, we should lose a great deal *vis-à-vis* the Germans.[228]

Shuckburgh concurred with this, adding that the Oder–Neiße line was a 'moderate-sized card which we should not play yet'; better that West German policy develop in the direction of better relations with Poland to the point of a 'final acceptance of the present frontiers'. In any case, the chances of any meaningful reciprocity from Warsaw were judged as being minimal. De Gaulle may have aimed at the improvement of Franco-Polish relations by his statement on the Oder–Neiße line on 25 March 1959, but there was little evidence of this having been the case. Furthermore, Adenauer would not have demonstrated the restraint he showed with de Gaulle if the British had followed the French leader in breaking ranks over the Oder–Neiße line.[229] As it was, Adenauer's gratitude for French backing in Berlin caused the Chancellor to avert his gaze somewhat and accept de Gaulle's personal assurances that, despite his having seemingly having endorsed the status quo to the Poles, he favoured a peace conference to adjudicate on the final decision with regard to the line.[230]

Britain and the economics of East–West relations

Harold Macmillan saw economics as a valuable Western weapon in the Cold War, believing that 'Work and production were the best defences against Communist subversion'.[231] Macmillan thus impressed upon Adenauer the belief that the USSR was increasingly diverting its resources against the West into economic and propaganda struggle, and therefore there was a need for greater Western vitality to counter these measures.[232] However, the problem with using economics as a political weapon is that occasionally the needs of the latter are defied by the dictates of the former. Britain itself tried to establish a trade relationship with Eastern Europe, even at the height of the Cold War, reflected in the five-year trade agreement concluded with the USSR in May 1959 and renewed throughout the 1960s.[233] Britain, however, had a far less thorough political agenda than did West German *Osthandel* (trade with the East).

In the static political climate of the second half of the 1950s, Adenauer's *Ostpolitik* fell back on West Germany's strongest card – its economy. But West Germany signally failed to make progress on reunification by exploiting the Soviet desire for trade following the establishment of diplomatic relations in September 1955.[234] Although trade with Moscow grew appreciably after 1955, von Brentano cautioned the *Ostausschuss der deutschen Wirtschaft*[235] that 'economic considerations [must] be subordinated to political principle' in all Communist bloc trade.[236] While it was true that Moscow would welcome Bonn's economic assistance, the price of Soviet security was the neutralisation of West Germany and not 'x' million Marks. According to the *AA* German–Soviet relations' specialist, Boris Meissner, there were two main tendencies discernible in West German policy prior to 1961: first, a desire to develop relations with Eastern Europe (especially Poland); and second, the belief of the necessity of a 'Moscow First' when dealing with the Soviet bloc.[237] Khrushchev later claimed that Adenauer had offered DM500 million as reparations in 'exchange' for the GDR. As this would mean a unified German within the Western bloc this was rejected,[238] and in June 1956 Khrushchev told French Premier Guy Mollet that he preferred to have eighteen million Germans as allies rather than seventy million against or, at best, neutral.[239]

The USSR was similarly uninterested when, in 1958, Adenauer offered to recognise Soviet gains in Eastern Europe in return for 'Austrian' status for the GDR.[240] With uncharacteristic flexibility, Adenauer concluded a trade agreement with the USSR in 1958 – which *TASS* hailed as a milestone in détente between states of different systems.[241] This, as Robert Spaulding has noted, highlighted a subtle shift in West German policy from revisionism to seeking an improvement of relations with Moscow.[242] However, trade was limited in the political gains it could yield without fundamental changes in Bonn's position. Demonstrating this, Khrushchev wrote to Adenauer, differentiating between political conciliation and economic co-operation: 'Even with its allies, the Federal Republic would not be able to equal our strength and power ... [But economically we] are not competitors. On the contrary, the economies of our two countries complement each other ... cooperation would be advantageous to both countries.'[243]

In order to maintain the Hallstein Doctrine whilst maximising its own influence, West Germany tried to develop non-political economic links with the Eastern bloc states. The Polish and Hungarian insurrections of 1956 sharpened the *Osthandel* debate within the Federal Republic. The SPD decried Adenauer's idea of the Soviet bloc as monolithic, asserting that trade could accentuate the differences between Moscow and the satellites. As Hélène Seppain has written, 'the *Bundestag* debate [of December 1956] highlighted the ambivalence in the Federal Government position on trade with the Soviet bloc. It condoned economic contacts, whilst simultaneously denying official government support to these contacts.'[244] But since trade with Poland, for instance, was a very small proportion of West German trade, it was perhaps inevitable that political considerations outweighed economic ones.[245]

In 1958, the Foreign Office saw the prospect of a West German trade mission in Warsaw as 'a stepping stone to the establishment of full diplomatic relations'.[246] But London concluded that the West Germans were 'deluding themselves', as 'Poland, if not the other satellites, has good and genuine political reason for requiring that the Germans pay a suitable political price (recognition of the Oder–Neisse line & full diplomatic relations) for improving trade'.[247] Although the Adenauer government was not particularly keen to trade with the GDR (so as not to strengthen it), it certainly did not want other Western states doing so and lessening Pankow's dependency on the FRG.[248] But British economic difficulties meant that no market could be overlooked – including the GDR, regardless of Bonn's feelings.[249] The policy of non-recognition of the GDR, at even de facto level, was increasingly solely in deference to West German wishes. This deference was increasingly questioned because, despite all of Bonn's high-sounding declarations on the illegitimacy of the Ulbricht regime, there were many links between the FRG and the GDR. The East German *Reichsbahn*, for example, ran the rail network of West Berlin, and annual Inter-zonal trade negotiations were hardly 'low-level'. Nevertheless, Bonn resolutely upheld the myth of non-contact so as to avoid any hint of recognition of the GDR, and Adenauer was adamant that his allies abide by this.[250] This irritated the allies, as it meant that their officials were forbidden the kind of contacts the West Germans themselves maintained with the GDR.[251] (The lengths that the Western powers had to go to in order to avoid acknowledging the existence of the GDR led to some cynicism. The French ambassador in Bonn explained that he was late for a meeting in Berlin because, whilst travelling through the 'so-called GDR', his car had hit a 'so-called tree').[252] In April 1958, Macmillan wrote that Britain was losing out on significant opportunities for trade with the GDR and that, in deference to West German wishes, the British government was unable to officially involve itself with matters relating to the GDR: 'I think this question of trade with eastern Germany ought to be looked at.'[253]

The Trade Fair in Leipzig provided an annual headache for Bonn as, despite official British policy, a profusion of MPs, industrialists and journalists accepted East German invitations to the fair.[254] In March 1961, Lord Boothby, the Conservative peer, led a weighty delegation to Leipzig and, with his penchant for publicity, began attracting headlines in the British press like 'Britain losing East German Orders'.[255] The Labour MP Arthur Lewis stated that 'It's about time Britain realised East Germany exists. Why shouldn't the Board of Trade come to some arrangement to help British manufacturers sell more?' Lord Boothby declared that 'I do not see why we should be dictated to by Dr Adenauer. The West Germans are doing 50 times more trade with the East than we are.' For many in Britain, West German policy was being designed to maintain an unfair advantage in its 'intra-German' trade. *The Times* declared that, 'rightly or wrongly, the west [*sic*] German iron and steel industry regards itself as the natural and traditional supplier of the east German market, and it resents the massive intrusion of an outsider like Britain'.[256] The West Germans countered that trade between the FRG and the GDR was classed as inner-German trade and governed by the occupational laws laid down after the

Second World War. West Germany made the continued acceptance of this conditional in its signing of international agreements. In 1957, for instance, a protocol of the Treaty of Rome exempted trade between the Federal Republic and 'German' areas outside of Bonn's jurisdiction (i.e. the GDR) from the regulations of the Treaty.[257] Early in 1961, the GDR launched a campaign to reduce its dependence upon West German raw materials in favour of indigenous and bloc supplies; despite its failure the campaign signalled the desire of East Germany to break away from economic subservience to Bonn. As Ulbricht termed it in May 1962: 'The essential pre-condition for new successes ... was the strengthening of the economy of the D.D.R.'[258] In the pursuit of this goal, British economic necessity was an ally of the East German state.

Nevertheless, under West German pressure the Foreign Office urged the Federation of British Industries (FBI) to desist in their attendance at the Leipzig Trade Fair. The Board of Trade was also urged to withdraw its subsidy from the event, as 'the political disadvantages of F.B.I. participation in the Fair do indeed outweigh the commercial advantages'. The President of the Board of Trade, however, resisted Foreign Office pressure.[259] This was only to be expected: the Board of Trade's *raison d'être* was the maximisation of British exports, and not the maintenance of the 'fiction' of Germany as a unified state. Withdrawal from the Leipzig Fair was all well and good in terms of maintaining alliance solidarity, but, for British industry, West German motives were perceived as practices in unfair trade. In Bonn's eyes, the British were stooges in Pankow's attempts to break its dependence upon West German trade. Von Herwarth lamented that any West German activity, however trifling, on the other side of the Iron Curtain meant that 'German commerce and industry are accused of wanting to ensure the lion's share of lucrative East–West trade'.[260] A Board of Trade memo to the Cabinet concluded in 1962: 'The *bloc* offers possibilities of a sizeable increase in our exports, say from the present 3 per cent to about 5 per cent. It is not the answer to our export problem, but it is a valuable and growing market.'[261] But the Foreign Office made clear that British trade with the Eastern bloc was insignificant (and incidental to a largely emotive argument) whilst clearly identifying the GDR's crude attempt to use the issue of trade to raise its political status. In any case, the prospects for British trade with the FRG would always be more lucrative than with the Eastern bloc, given the extreme limitation of hard currency in the latter.[262]

General economic opportunities in Eastern Europe did contribute to some diminution in West German trade with the GDR, despite the fact that tariffs were unfavourable for East German trade with other West European countries. This was as a result of the fact that France and Britain sought openly to promote their business contacts with the GDR. In this, the East Germans in every way possible encouraged them. By 1965 the dependence of the GDR on the FRG had been much reduced by the increased availability of 'necessary' goods elsewhere in the West.[263] However, Britain did not get the kind of benefits touted by Boothby *et al.*

Conclusion

Harold Macmillan once described the life of a Foreign Secretary as being 'Forever poised between a cliché and an indiscretion'.[264] In his attempts to initiate a détente, Macmillan neglected to recall that clichés in diplomacy are a necessary device in order to avoid giving offence to ones' allies. The Prime Minister's private and public stance on much that could be regarded by Bonn as being in its 'vital interests', on the other hand, fell under the heading of 'indiscretions'. The key to diplomacy, as with poker, is being able to bluff when your opponent is unsure as to the strength of your hand. Macmillan acted as if he were the equal of the superpowers; Adenauer knew well the limits of his position and recognised British folly.[265] The one factor that Konrad Adenauer had always appreciated was that it was the superpowers alone who had the power to determine whether or not détente was achieved. Consequently, of all the major players, it was Macmillan that suffered most when the Paris Summit collapsed in 1960. This seemed to leave Britain isolated and without a clear direction in its foreign policy. Macmillan's subsequent defence of the Adenauer government at the UN was an attempt to build bridges with the Germans. It also had the unfortunate consequence of stirring the Eastern Europeans to fury. The cause of German reconciliation with Eastern Europe seemed to be advancing not at all. Meanwhile, Britain faced a Franco-German axis in Europe and a US administration that was unwilling to pressurise the West German state to modify its Eastern policy.

That Adenauer and Macmillan disliked each other and each other's countries is undoubted. However, both had subordinated their personal prejudices when *Realpolitik* dictated. Personal animosities only came to the fore when policy imperatives led. For this reason, perhaps, personal feelings have been the subject of much comment since. Adenauer's good personal relations with John Foster Dulles and de Gaulle should not mask the fact that their interests coincided on vital issues. One might observe that Macmillan's *Deutschlandpolitik* was based on the idea that Germany had its place in the community of Nations, but at the same time it must *know* its place in that community. On the policy level, whatever Macmillan's selfdelusion, Adenauer had only flirted with British proposals for a Free Trade Area prior to the initiation of his intimate collaboration with de Gaulle. As it was, the Free Trade Area was correctly identified by Adenauer as a naked attempt to steer European integration in a direction deemed beneficial to British interests.[266]

The trip to Moscow in 1959 demonstrated the inability of the British to circumnavigate West German policy objections unilaterally. In reality, the best way of pressurising Bonn in this direction was through Washington, not Moscow. Unfortunately, when the Americans were willing to talk it was to be on their terms and not on those set by Macmillan. When referring to the British as being 'Greeks' to the American 'Romans',[267] Macmillan should have recalled the minimal influence of the former on the conduct of policy in the Roman Empire. While Macmillan and British officialdom were almost certainly correct in their belief that France agreed with their stance on the German question, the French, at least, served their own interests by their staunch backing of Adenauer. As Jebb later concluded '[French policy] in the light of hindsight ... was probably, as it turned out, the best policy in the circumstances'.[268]

Selwyn Lloyd reflected a widely held opinion in London when stating privately that if the Second Berlin Crisis resulted in the de facto recognition of the GDR he would not regret it. The diplomatic 'non-status' of the GDR was, in the opinion of the British, a rather cumbersome impediment in negotiations with Moscow. Yet the West Germans seemed to have no other alternatives to legalistic obstructionism. The Adenauer government thus tried to pursue an economic strategy in Eastern Europe so as to avoid unpalatable political choices. However, since the GDR itself was unwilling to become an economic dependent of the FRG, the ability of West Germany to affect a 'hostile take-over' was increasingly limited. Furthermore, while the Foreign Office may have recognised the logic in Bonn's position, to British industry and the general public it seemed as if the West Germans were simply seeking to monopolise East German trade for themselves. It was also clear that Poland required more than West German economic philanthropy to ensure its security. As the British ambassador in Warsaw noted, Bonn would have to make a choice between continued intransigence and conciliation, as the current Eastern policy was actually deepening rather than alleviating German division.[269]

The end of Macmillan's 'Summitry' at Paris in 1960 foreshadowed the demise of Adenauer's policy by just over a year. The Berlin Wall's construction in August 1961 confirmed that the new Kennedy administration was unwilling to allow Bonn to dictate alliance policy on the German Question any longer. Adenauer's success in entrenching the stalemate in Europe so effectively now alienated a United States' administration that was turning its attention elsewhere in the global Cold War. As the 1960s opened, the key to the future of the unresolved German Question, and its place in the Cold War, lay in Washington.

4 The fall of the *Politik der Stärke* and rise of the Anglo-Saxon consensus

A great furore about a speech by Dean Acheson, wh[ich] seems to indicate that Britain's role is played out. Of course, Dean Acheson was always a conceited ass.

Harold Macmillan diary entry, 7 December 1962

Every human benefit, every virtue and every prudent act, is founded on compromise.

Edmund Burke

Rescued from isolation: Macmillan, Kennedy and the Germans

The early 1960s witnessed a sea change in the relationship between West German policy and the wider goals of NATO. The key to this change lay in Washington. During the final years of the Eisenhower administration there were increasing signs of weariness regarding the underwriting of Adenauer's policy at the expense of any possible arrangement with the Soviet Union. Privately, Dulles sympathised with Soviet fear of Germany, believing the latter should be prevented from doing 'a third time what they had done in 1914 and 1939'.[1] Publicly, Dulles even stated that free elections were not necessarily a prerequisite for German reunification.[2] But the shift in US policy was far from clear in early 1961. Macmillan lamented privately that while all his economic and détente schemes had failed, Bonn had none of his problems,[3] being, as it was, 'rich and selfish – and German'.[4] Yet the development of US policy, especially over Berlin, is fundamental to understanding how the British were rescued from their isolation after the collapse of the Paris Summit.[5] Anticipating a flashpoint crisis like Berlin, Eisenhower had written in 1956 that 'peacemakers are blessed ... [and] the most effective peacemaker is one who prevents a quarrel from developing, rather than one who has to pick up the pieces remaining after an unfortunate fight'.[6] The President informed Adenauer in 1959 that 'We do not want to perpetuate the present situation in Berlin and keep our Occupation troops there forever. We hope to find a way out with honor.'[7] The Kennedy administration would be even less willing to indulge Bonn.[8] Unfortunately for Macmillan, the emerging Anglo-Saxon consensus on the German Question (in which the British were very much the junior partner)[9] pushed Adenauer further into the arms of de Gaulle, helping to ensure the exclusion of Britain from the EEC in 1963.[10]

Following the Paris Summit, the British desire to arrange a general détente was replaced by a series of more limited initiatives towards the Eastern bloc. In line with this, Britain gave Poland a secret undertaking in 1962 with regard to the Oder–Neiße line. This undertaking represented an effective abrogation of British assurances to West Germany since 1949. This limited initiative on outstanding issues affecting Germany was dictated by three factors: first, by a belief that West Germany would accept such an eventuality in any case; second, by the desire that when a reconciliation was realised between the Germans and the East Europeans, the British would not be placed at a disadvantage compared to, say, France; and, third, after January 1961, by virtue of the fact that the new Kennedy administration recognised that to support Adenauer's absolutist position meant an unacceptable deferment of détente.

Macmillan made two predictions in his diary late in 1960, both of which turned out to be fairly accurate. First, he wrote 'I do not feel that Kennedy will be bad for us. He will perhaps have ideas and be attracted by ideas.'[11] (The US ambassador in London later described the intimacy of the Macmillan–Kennedy relationship as having 'few parallels in modern [diplomacy]').[12] Second, he predicted that '1961 will be a pretty tricky year, for it is quite clear that Mr Kruschev (*sic*) means to press the German question.'[13] Macmillan was right on both counts. The construction of the Berlin Wall in August 1961 exposed the frailties inherent in the *Politik der Stärke* by pushing the West into a de facto acceptance of the status quo in Germany based on the minimalist position of a Western presence in, and access to, West Berlin. In short, whatever the West German position, NATO was for the defence of *West* Berlin and *West* Germany. It was not a vehicle for endorsing the German claim to the unity of the German nation within (as yet) undefined boundaries.

Initially, the British saw the Wall as an opportunity to move towards a *modus vivendi* between East and West, but the subsequent need for support over the EEC meant that criticism of Bonn's policies became more muted. Furthermore, from 1961 onwards, the modified Eastern policy of the new foreign minister, Gerhard Schröder, ameliorated the negative effects of West German policy somewhat. The British effectively took a back seat over the conduct of East–West diplomacy as the Kennedy administration embraced détente. The United States could, and should, now prevail upon Bonn to make unpleasant choices. As Macmillan made clear to Foreign Secretary Lord Home in March 1962: 'The Americans must get accustomed to being unpopular. We got accustomed to it when we were strong.'[14]

Kennedy and Eastern Europe

In order to understand the importance of the US government's role in the evolution of West German policy on Eastern Europe, some discussion of Kennedy's thinking is necessary. Many hailed John F. Kennedy's inauguration in January 1961 as a new dawn for American diplomacy, where détente would play a more prominent role. The fact that, as a senator, Kennedy had taken such an active interest in Eastern Europe led Bonn to fear him as being pro-Polish and anti-German.[15] The West German ambassador in Washington at the time, Wilhelm Grewe, later testified that Bonn feared, correctly, that a Kennedy administration would be more détente-oriented.[16] This, according to the British ambassador in Washington, David Ormsby Gore, was wedded to a more 'British' attitude to defence spending.[17] In a speech at the Annual Awards of the Overseas Press Club on 6 May 1957, Kennedy referred to Eastern Europe as the 'Achilles heel of the Soviet Empire'. Kennedy's new administration aimed to avoid the military risks of Eisenhower's (largely rhetorical) liberation diplomacy. Trade, aid and cultural initiatives (such as the radio station 'Voice of America') were to be utilised in order to undermine Soviet influence in the Eastern Europe so as to work for what Kennedy described as 'the liberation of captive peoples'.[18] Eisenhower's policy towards Eastern Europe, which had been somewhat dormant since 'roll-back' had been quietly moved down the agenda, was to be replaced by something altogether more positive.[19]

In 1957, Kennedy wrote in *Foreign Affairs* that Eisenhower and Dulles had bound the West far too closely with the person of Adenauer and his intransigent *Ostpolitik*. Kennedy even declared that 'the age of Adenauer is over'.[20] Once he became President, Kennedy told Theodore Sorenson, one of his closest advisers, that while personal relations with Adenauer were cordial, talking to the Chancellor was like talking to someone from 'another world, another era'. This was, Sorenson noted, in marked contrast to the warmth of the relationship between Kennedy and Macmillan.[21]

West German fears of US attitudes

It was, however, not only the Democrats that the West Germans had to fear in the changing American attitudes. Kennedy's opponent in the 1960 presidential election, Richard Nixon, told a Polish-American audience that 'all Poles in Poland as well as abroad are united in their determination to defend the new western frontier'.[22] While this was dismissed in the Foreign Office as 'pure electioneering',[23] it did signal that Adenauer's veto on Western policy was weakening. For the Foreign Office this was logical, for 'The Poles have a cast iron claim to the territory beyond the Oder Neisse. Their claim is based on historical, legal, moral and practical grounds. The practical claim is that the territories whatever they were before the war have been effectively Polonised (*sic*) and are now an integral and essential part of Poland.'[24] The United States did not, however, pursue the matter, and, to British chagrin, put no pressure on the West Germans on the issue of the Oder–Neiße line.[25] Nevertheless, in the period between Kennedy's election and his inauguration, West German ambassador Grewe heard persistent rumours that a possible 'Berlin border deal' was being mooted in the United States. This would require the definite recognition by Bonn of the Oder–Neiße line, in exchange for a Berlin settlement.[26] In the United States, academics such as Zbigniew Brzezinski saw opportunities for rapprochement with the Eastern bloc, which they urged upon the new Kennedy administration.[27] Given the Kennedy administration's penchant for employing academics at the highest levels, this was something that made Bonn very nervous.

Bonn determined to influence Western thinking by proclaiming the success of the alliance strategy hitherto. In *Foreign Affairs*, von Brentano argued for the continuation of the tough line the West had adopted against the Soviet threat since 1949 in the current situation in Berlin.[28] However, as Trachtenberg notes, while the security system may have been successful thus far, continued adherence to Bonn's line threatened to increase tension to new heights.[29] In any case, the FRG now had two good reasons for to modify its diplomacy. First, initiatives had to be forthcoming to demonstrate the 'flexibility' of Bonn to international opinion; second, it was necessary to ensure that the German Question was not left off the agenda in East–West negotiations.

In June 1961, an all-party *Bundestag* resolution – the Jaksch Resolution – called for the opening up of trade and other links in Eastern bloc countries.[30] The resolution was passed unanimously, which said something about its non-committal nature, and called for the Federal government to 'seize every available opportunity ... to achieve a normalisation of relations between the Federal Republic and the East European states'. To the British embassy in Bonn, this was yet another example of employing modest language to mask essentially inflexible aims. It was concluded that initiatives such as the Jaksch Resolution amounted to little more than exercises in public relations.[31]

The Anglo-American search for a solution in Berlin

While, in 1959, Kennedy identified the Berlin Crisis as a test of Western 'nerve and will',[32] the sacred cows of Adenuaer's foreign policy were no longer inviolable.[33] In February 1961, Kennedy approved a planning paper that called for 'alternative approaches' to Germany – including a possible linkage of access to Berlin and the Oder–Neiße line.[34] Kennedy turned to Dean Acheson, Secretary of State during the Berlin Airlift, who proposed that the President adopt a tough line as there was no 'solution that would not weaken the western position ... Berlin is of the greatest importance. This is why the Soviets press the issue. If the West funks then Germany will become unhooked from the Alliance.'[35] Acheson finally identified three objectives that, if violated by the USSR or the GDR, might require the United States to escalate the situation. These were: first, the freedom of West Berlin to choose its own political and social system; second, the presence of Western troops as long as required and desired by the West Berliners; and third, the guarantee of unimpeded access to Berlin from the west. [36] Despite the tacit acceptance of much of the British position, doubts persisted about their resolution, and national security advisor McGeorge Bundy observed that 'It is agreed that the Acheson memorandum is a sound guide here, although if you let any Englishman (*sic*) see it, he will probably faint.'[37]

The objectives outlined by Acheson were certainly short of what the West Germans would have liked, and Frank Mayer judges that 'Kennedy was ... in search of a response that could avoid both humiliation and a nuclear holocaust'.[38] For the time being this meant steering a path between the British and the German positions, although Kennedy was still too close to the Adenauer line for Macmillan's liking. At an Anglo-American meeting in Washington in April 1961, Lord Home warned that the West had to speak to the Soviet Union on substantive issues – otherwise Khrushchev would sign a peace treaty with the GDR. Acheson concurred, warning against undermining the 'German spirit' by talking about a peace treaty. When Home wondered whether Khrushchev really wanted to pass control to the GDR, Secretary of State Dean Rusk stated that the West was not in Berlin by the grace of Khrushchev and, furthermore, any transfer of rights to the East Germans would only be the first step towards a 'slippery slope' in the recognition of the GDR. For his part, Home said he did not like going into a conference knowing he had nothing to offer.[39] This the British deemed essential, as a growing sense of Soviet intransigence led Macmillan to conclude that there was a real prospect of general war over Berlin.[40]

David Ormsby Gore (British ambassador to Washington, 1961–5) recalled that the lack of progress between Khrushchev and Kennedy at Vienna in June 1961 meant that the impasse would continue, as the West Germans and the French talked 'tough' but essentially relied upon the Anglo-Saxons in the last resort'[41] – although Couve de Murville later testified that while de Gaulle wished to stand firm, Kennedy and Macmillan doubted the ability of democracies to explain intransigence to the electorate.[42] To Macmillan, no solution to Berlin seemed attainable, because 'if anyone tries to talk sense, he is at once called a coward and a traitor',[43] and he was determined that the United States would at least join the British in exposing the false bravado of Paris and Bonn. As Ormsby Gore recalled, 'We all had any amount of evidence that the Germans didn't care so much about West Berlin, that they thought the whole of Germany ought to be destroyed in order to defend it, which is what ... it required.'[44]

Yet throughout all of this British policy had to be seen to strike a balance, and Lord Home, like Macmillan, was anxious to avoid the charge of 'appeaser'.[45] The Foreign Secretary thus advocated 'quiet diplomacy' over Berlin in a Cabinet memorandum of July 1961. In reality, this approach aimed at keeping the West German government from raising difficult questions. Since Home believed that this mode of diplomacy was also favoured by Dean Rusk, he advocated that bilateral discussions with the United States be undertaken. This would ensure that the West Germans and the French would understand that their policy of 'talking simply of standing firm' while 'making no effective contribution' was unacceptable. Home had some sympathy for the Soviets, as

> one can see their fear of an increasingly powerful ... West Germany, clearly devoted to ... reunification ... [maybe] too powerful a magnet for all Germans [and undermining the GDR, unless the latter can be stabilised]. If this is so, Mr Khrushchev's immediate objectives will be closely related to the strengthening of the D.D.R.

In order to achieve a solution over Berlin, Home was willing to discuss subjects that West German sensibilities had hitherto decreed taboo:

> We could ... accept the ... Oder–Neisse line. Nor, in fact, do we really want German reunification, at least for the time being, though we cannot abandon the principle of self-determination for the Germans. The same is ... true of the rest of [NATO], including the Germans. German reunification now would upset what has been achieved in Western European integration since the war.[46]

Furthermore, Home had no desire to see the collapse of the GDR through the emigration of its most valuable citizens. The strengthening of the Ulbricht regime would not be detrimental to 'freedom' in Germany, 'For the East Germans ... will not reach the end of its troubles merely by acquiring a degree of international recognition'. By taking this line Home was in effect denying the most fundamental constitutional West German position – its legitimacy as the sole government representing the German people. Home saw West German policy as an obstacle to agreement with the USSR and, to this end, castigated Bonn for its lack of imagination:

> It is at least arguable that the influence of 47 million West Germans could be brought to bear more effectively on the 17 million East Germans if the Federal Government would pursue a different policy and be prepared to enter into closer relationships with the East German régime. They have hitherto shown [a] remarkable lack of courage in this respect.[47]

Home proposed de facto recognition of the GDR, fully accepting that this would raise the diplomatic status of the GDR worldwide, and urged that the FRG move towards a confederal arrangement with the GDR[48] and recognise the Oder–Neiße line. In return for all this, a Soviet guarantee of the Western presence in Berlin with full access rights could be obtained without having to abandon 'any really crucial position'. For Bonn, the shelving of reunification, the abandonment of the Hallstein Doctrine and the recognition of the Oder–Neiße line would mean the end of the 'Policy of Strength'. In practical terms, Home was reverting to treating the Federal Republic more as a defeated state than as an alliance partner, and their acquiescence would ensure that the three Western allies' rights as victors in the Second World War were secured. Recognising this, Home suggested that 'it might well be easier to persuade the West German Government to accept a compromise German settlement if this originated in the United Nations and was acquiesced in, rather than promoted by, the western Powers'.[49]

West German suspicions of equivocation in Western policy were reinforced when the US Senate Majority Leader, William Fulbright, remarked in a television interview on 30 July: 'I don't understand why the East Germans don't close their border because I think they have a right to close it.'[50] The emphasis on the West's rights in *West* Berlin meant that Kennedy was later accused of having given tacit approval for the construction of the Wall. Certainly, there was no mention of free movement in the city of Berlin at the meeting of the Western powers in Paris in August of 1961.[51] Following this, Macmillan noted in his diary, as he had not been privy to internal deliberations in Washington, that the Americans had done 'a complete volte face on the issue of Berlin'. The previous American hard line, personified by Acheson, had been abandoned in favour of immediate negotiation with Moscow. The negotiations were proposed for October 1961, that is, 'after the German election, [and] *before JFK's* Party Conference'. Macmillan reflected that he had advocated negotiations prior to the conclusion of any Soviet treaty with the GDR but 'if necessary, at a later stage if any pressure is in fact put on access to Berlin'. Macmillan was thus pleased to note that 'The French and the Germans are shocked by the new American policy'.[52]

What Macmillan saw as a 'volte face' in US policy was, in reality, the culmination of a longer process. In February 1961, the US ambassador in Bonn advised Rusk that the Soviets saw an intimate link between Berlin and the whole German Question. Since there was no chance of reunification, the administration should concentrate on achieving a 'modus vivendi' with the Soviets whilst ensuring the maintenance of the allied presence in West Berlin.[53] Although von Brentano had assured the President on 17 February 1961 that there was no question of Bonn recognising the Oder–Neiße line or the GDR,[54] George C. McGhee, ambassador in Bonn from 1963, prepared a paper that advocated recognition of the line.

Criticising the existing ' "Maginot line complex" ', McGhee advocated the recognition of Germany's present frontiers and de facto, even de jure, recognition of the GDR in order to enhance the 'possibility of a future settlement'.[55]

An 'Outline on Germany and Berlin' was drafted for the National Security Council meeting of 19 July 1961 by Rusk, his assistant, Foy D. Kohler, and the Office of the German Affairs Director, Martin Hillenbrand. The paper stated the administration's aims to be the maintenance of West Berlin and the Federal Republic, and, signally, noted the elements of the German problem not of vital interest to the United States. The continued non-recognition of the Oder–Neiße line was not perceived by US policy-makers to be in the general interest. Frank Mayer argues that the outline's objectives 'were nothing short of a total rejection of a crucial part of Konrad Adenauer's foreign policy' and 'developments in German–American relations ... to August 1961 attest to the [Kennedy administration's] attempt to reduce what was perceived as the unwanted Adenauer "veto" over U.S. foreign policy.'[56] In this, the United States was moving towards the position on the German Question long-advocated by Macmillan. By this time, however, Macmillan had other factors to consider in the formulation of policy.

On 9 August 1961, Macmillan drafted a letter to Erhard formally applying for British membership to the EEC (the latter of which was 'a historic affair!').[57] Economic difficulties would therefore be addressed by an application for entry into the EEC, rather than by achieving détente.[58] Better still, Britain could benefit from any American-initiated détente whilst avoiding West German ire for being the harbinger of a deferral of German reunification. The about-turn in American thinking meant that Macmillan was well disposed to Home's proposal that, '[Britain] show some solidarity with the French & Germans ... quite safe now that the US wants to negotiate and ... secondly, [it would] prevent the US press accusing us of 'defeatism' for wanting negotiations instead of being "tough".' [59] Macmillan might well have better exploited this opportunity had not the gulf between the Anglo-Saxons and Adenauer been brought to a head by the Berlin Wall's construction on 13 August 1961.

The Wall

After 1957, Adenauer constantly expressed anxiety that *Sputnik* would undermine the US commitment to the Federal Republic.[60] This was reinforced by an increasing sense of frustration over both the Eisenhower and Kennedy administrations with regard to the question of Berlin.[61] The aftermath of the construction of the Berlin Wall confirmed Adenauer's fears.[62] The Wall became, in Jain's phrase, 'a living testimony to the failure of Adenauer's *Ostpolitik*'.[63] Andrei Gromyko later judged that Adenauer probably did not abandon the idea of a united Germany until the night of

13 August 1961.[64] In the *Bundestag*, Adenauer was reduced to asserting that the West was united behind the demand for German self-determination.[65] Heinrich Krone, one of Adenauer's closest advisers, later referred to this as the 'hour of disillusionment', lamenting that '[t]he German people expected more than just a protest note from the West'.[66] Martin Hillenbrand, US Minister in Bonn, recalled that the *Torschlusspanik*[67] that seized the GDR in the early summer of 1961 meant that the GDR 'had to do something'. Indeed, if the GDR was to remain a viable entity it had little option but to take measures to staunch the flow of refugees to the West.[68] But the cessation of the free movement of citizens from the GDR was not a matter of vital interest to Washington, and Dean Rusk recalled that 'We quickly decided that the wall was not an issue of war and peace between East and West; there was no way we would destroy the human race over it'.[69]

Kennedy himself remarked of the Wall that, 'It's not a very nice solution, but a wall is a hell of a lot better than a war'.[70] This opinion was shared by the British and an official in the British Military Government from 1963 believed that '. . . E[ast] Germany would have collapsed if the Wall had not been built . . . The continuing loss of qualified people was just too great . . . the Wall . . . stabilised the situation'.[71] On 14 August, Sir Christopher Steel informed London that 'I personally have always wondered that the East Germans have taken so long to seal this boundary'. Furthermore, Britain's vital interests were not at stake, and any action risked an 'increase [in] tension or to stimulate an uprising in East Germany'.[72] While West German policy sought to cast *all* Berlin as being of vital interest, the Wall Crisis exposed this as a sham. Kennedy confessed to his adviser Walt Rostow in early August 1961 that 'I can get the alliance to move if he [Khrushchev] tries to do anything about West Berlin but not if he just does something about East Berlin'.[73] In such a fashion the United States demonstrated that Berlin was not to be treated as the capital (*Hauptstadt*) of a future reunified Germany as Adenauer wished. Rather, Berlin's status was to remain that of an occupied city, as agreed at Potsdam. The Wall was thus viewed by the British embassy in Bonn as essential shock treatment: 'The Germans are at long last waking up to realities . . . ask[ing] themselves "has Adenauer's policy on the German question been so clever after all?" '[74]

Official US surveys noted that more than 70 per cent of the British population rejected war over Berlin, while 'public opinion in Western Europe has all but written off the lands behind the Iron Curtain'.[75] The Oder–Neiße territories and the cause of the eastern refugees elicited little sympathy outside of Germany. When full-page adverts appeared in West European newspapers highlighting the millions expelled from the eastern territories at the end of the Second World War, the FO dryly noted that this 'Crude stuff . . . gives the Poles free ammunition: they will themselves fire it off at us before long. The reference to 7 million expellees only serves as a reminder that an equal number of bodies were left behind at Auschwitz and elsewhere in Poland.'[76] In similar vein, Pandit Nehru, Prime Minister of India and a leading light in the Non-aligned Movement, encouraged Macmillan in his belief that the Oder–Neiße line was an obstacle that he should seek to remove. Nehru stressed the intransigence of the Soviet position, and asked whether the West was really serious about German unity. Adenauer's hard-line policies were particularly singled out for criticism, and West German statements about the Oder–Neiße meant that:

> All this becomes a symbol of Germany seeking revenge and recovering the losses she suffered in the last war. It is the reminder of expansionist aims of German Governments in the past ... Khrushchev ... [was] particularly resentful of Adenauer's attitude and statements, [but] the impression he gave me was that there was room for successful negotiations with him. Indeed, the basic issues in regard to Germany and Berlin are limited, and there is probably already a measure of agreement about some of them.[77]

Macmillan believed that the imminent West German elections, and the Americans being 'very excited' about the Berlin Wall, made negotiations essential. The Prime Minister feared that the United States had been panicked[78] into wanting to issue a 'rather lunatic' declaration, which he had only managed to put off with French help.[79] Even though Macmillan had agreed to Kennedy's request to send more troops to Berlin, he regarded the idea as 'nonsense' militarily. In any case, Macmillan felt 'that from Kruschev's (*sic*) point of view, the eastern German internal situation was beginning to crumble & something had to be done'.[80] Macmillan believed that to react to the Wall as a threat would only create a dangerous situation.

Home reiterated his belief that negotiations should focus on the narrowest possible front – i.e. access to Berlin – with the negotiating positions he had already established in July.[81] The Foreign Secretary noted with satisfaction that 'We are now very close to the Americans on the whole problem', but, tactically, it was best to avoid negotiations before the West German elections of 19 September, as 'I believe that after they are safely elected a German Government will be less rigid in their approach to a settlement'.[82] Home saw that Rusk had impressed upon the Germans and the French in Paris the absolute necessity for negotiation. And, while the United States would go to war to defend Western rights in West Berlin, it would not do so over German reunification or theoretical issues related to the status of the GDR. This often boiled down to British officials dismissing the West German insistence on technicalities (or, as Macmillan termed it in his diary, 'Who stamped passports'[83]). Home commented that 'We naturally welcomed wholeheartedly the evolution of American thinking on the Berlin problem and supported it strongly'. The Foreign Secretary now saw an agreement over Berlin, however imperfect, as involving a compromise between Khrushchev's idea of 'free city' status and a continued Western presence in West Berlin.[84] To this end, the Cabinet decided that it was best not to inhibit negotiations on the narrow question of the Western presence in Berlin by discussing the even more difficult problems of the self-determination and reunification of Germany.[85] Macmillan impressed upon the American ambassador the crucial need for negotiation, stating that any French refusal to participate would only be exploited by Moscow.[86] Domestically, the Labour Party even mooted helping Macmillan out by moving a parliamentary motion to highlight 'the danger of allowing the French to hold up negotiations'.[87]

The weakened position of Adenauer and the advent of Schröder

In the period between the Wall's construction and the election of September 1961, Adenauer made a series of tactical misjudgements and gaffes.[88] This underlined the failure of his policy and further undermined his ability to thumb his nose at Anglo-American attempts at negotiation. The political damage done to Adenauer led Macmillan to conclude that, 'It seems doubtful whether Adenauer will be acceptable as Chancellor in a Coalition.'[89] In actual fact, while Adenauer remained as Chancellor, his position was significantly weakened as he lost his overall majority (see Table 4.1 and Figure 4.1).

Lord Home noted that until the construction of the Wall, Adenauer had looked like retaining his overall majority. That he did not do so was ascribed to the shock of the Berlin Wall, Western inaction in the wake of this, and Adenauer's behaviour in the latter part of the campaign.[90] However, the British embassy in Bonn cautioned that while 'The vote may have gone against Adenauer personally ... it was not a vote against his basic policies'.[91] Similarly, the Secretary of the *Deutsch–Englische Gesellschaft* advised Hugh Gaitskell (Labour Party leader, 1955–63) that 'Though the Socialists did not do as well as we expected or hoped, the main aim has been achieved, which was to break the absolute majority of the C.D.U. There is no doubt it was a plebiscite against Adenauer.'[92] Adenauer's *West-*

Table 4.1 Bundestag election results, 1957 and 1961

Party	1957 (%)	1961 (%)	1957 (seats)	1961 (seats)
CDU/CSU	50.2	45.2	270	241
SPD	31.8	36.3	160	190
FDP	7.5	12.7	41	66

Source: PRO: CAB 129/107, C (61) 154.

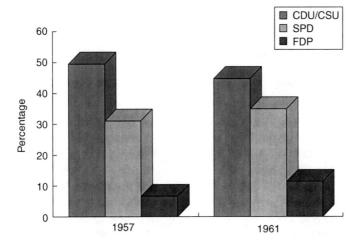

Figure 4.1 Bundestag election results, 1957 and 1961 (source: PRO: CAB 129/107, C (61) 154).

politik had been generally accepted across the political spectrum, while his personal autocratic style had proved unpopular with the electorate and the Berlin Wall revealed the paucity of the *Politik der Stärke.*

Of the rise of the FDP, the new coalition partners in government, Lord Home noted optimistically that 'On European questions they tended to blame Dr Adenauer for being too much of a little European, and they would like to see Britain [more closely involved]'.[93] Further satisfaction was gained by virtue of the fact that, because von Brentano was unacceptable to the FDP, Adenauer had to appoint Dr Gerhard Schröder as Foreign Minister in the new coalition. Very much less the creature of the Chancellor than Brentano, Schröder was from the Protestant progressive wing of the CDU and had some innovative ideas about the *Ostpolitik* (it has been argued that Adenauer's policies towards the East were so negative one can speak of Schröder as having initiated the 'first *Ostpolitik*' of the FRG).[94] Schröder's appointment was certainly a recognition that West Germany would have to modify its foreign policy in order to avoid isolation within the Western Alliance.[95] Schröder initiated a more flexible *Politik der Bewegung* ('Policy of Movement'), which sought to undermine Communist propaganda against Bonn whilst developing cultural, human and economic contacts with the Soviet bloc.[96] Departing from the notion that only Moscow's view mattered, Schröder sought to exploit the satellite aspirations for achieving a certain freedom of action.[97] Such political goals were to be achieved by primarily economic means, and Schröder asserted that Bonn would 'be constantly on the watch for any opportunities ... We should not set our sights too high to begin with but should try to move forward, patiently and step by step'.[98] Sir Christopher Steel saw Schröder as being the man who finally might get Bonn's Eastern policy to articulate something other than negativity.[99] It was a development that could only be welcome in London.

Pushing at an opening door: encouraging the Americans to talk

Harold Macmillan was convinced that Britain had been the source of inspiration for the American government's change of policy over Germany in the early 1960s. For Macmillan, Kennedy had 'now been convinced of the steady pressure of our diplomacy *and* . . . [re-appraised] the new strategic situation . . . [whilst realising] that the slogan "be tough on Berlin" is not, in itself, a policy'.[100] Ormsby Gore recalled that Kennedy had the feeling that Bonn was quite willing to 'allow the West to get into serious crisis with the Soviet Union over Berlin', proffering no solution and intent to rely on the United States to 'maintain its tough attitude'.[101] When Kennedy telephoned Macmillan for advice on how to deal with Adenauer on the subject of negotiations with the Soviet Union, Macmillan was forthright, recording his advice in his diary:

> I would suggest that you brought as much pressure as you can on Adenauer and made him understand that there is a possibility of a deal . . . The things which, since you ask me, I feel they ought to be prepared to accept, are first the Oder–Neisse Line, which is generally agreed; secondly, some formula which amounts to a considerable degree of *de facto* recognition of the D.D.R. . . . thirdly, I think, [Adenauer] must recognise that political ties between West Berlin and the Federal Republic ought to be given up, but that economic and financial ties could be even strengthened and increased; and fourthly . . . a declaration by the [West] Germans [renouncing] nuclear weapons.[102]

The need to secure a German pledge on nuclear weapons was heightened as Adenauer and Strauß began to infer strongly that if the United States was weakening in its commitment to West Germany, then Bonn might have recourse to acquiring nuclear weapons.[103] Keen to avoid Bonn's charges of a diminished Anglo-American willingness to defend the FRG, the British informed the State Department that there were four points on which the West should not compromise: *de jure* recognition of the GDR; the surrender of Western rights in Berlin; the acceptance of the presence of Soviet troops in West Berlin; and, finally, 'servitudes' (restrictions) on the Federal German government.[104] While Home made these conditions clear to Gromyko,[105] the downgrading of the issue of German reunification from the top of the negotiating agenda meant that it was now possible to focus on avenues more likely to bring East–West agreement.

In November 1961, Macmillan's Cabinet recognised that the Soviets would wish to address the issues of the GDR, the Oder–Neiße line, the political relationship between West Berlin and the Federal Republic, as well as the issue of nuclear weapons for West Germany.[106] Home was hopeful that the West Germans would agree to more contact with the GDR, and that something could be worked out with regard to the Oder–Neiße line.[107] Knowing that Bonn saw West Berlin, constitutionally, as part of their state, Home conceded that it would therefore resist particularly on this point. Consequently, there was a real need to impress upon the West Germans the necessity of abandoning practices such as their parliamentary meetings in West Berlin.[108] Reassuringly, Rusk told Ormsby Gore that the 'Anglo-Saxons had little time' for the 'continental attachment' to 'informal formalities' that characterised West German policy.[109]

The British government was now confident that the FRG would recognise the need for increased dealings with the GDR, and for some form of recognition of the present boundaries of Germany.[110] At Bermuda in December 1961, Home told Kennedy that the West might have to make four concessions in order to get a settlement with the East: de facto recognition of the GDR; the recognition of the Oder–Neiße line; concessions on Western occupation rights in Berlin; and diminished links between West Berlin and the FRG.[111] So far as occupation rights were concerned, the West had to retain them, but could present those rights in such a way as to appear as trustees for the people of the city: 'We might also strengthen our position by proving (by plebiscite or other means) that we were in West Berlin by consent of its people.' At the same time, Macmillan told Kennedy that it was entirely unrealistic not to recognise the GDR, arguing that not only was reunification out of the question but also the majority of West Germans did not even want it.[112] The Kennedy administration recognised that the USSR, too, was increasingly reconciled to a *modus vivendi* incorporating 'two Germanies', whilst paying lip service to reunification.[113] (Indeed, Gromyko confirmed this to Macmillan in October 1961.[114])

By the year's end, Steel reflected on the Wall as having been no bad thing in terms of stabilising the situation: 'By no means all the consequences of the Wall have been negative. Formally ... we must regret it ... [but] it has removed a great deal of Berlin's sting from the Soviet point of view and ... made negotiation easier.'[115] Under pressure from Washington to compromise,[116] Adenauer openly lamented the demise of John Foster Dulles, who had given Bonn a 'virtual veto over American policy'.[117] Yet Macmillan was not entirely triumphant, fearing that 'German psychology' might lead to an adverse reaction:

> For 15 years, Adenauer has been telling the German people that the western Powers w[oul]d, in the long run, secure for them the reunification of Germany. Now it is becoming clear ... that Germany is *not*

going to be re-united & that 'de facto' recognition of East Germany will be inevitable. This ... may be dangerous & another German myth may grow up of an Anglo-Saxon ... 'sell-out', (from wh[ich] France disassociated herself, getting 'Peace with Honour' at our expense) & this may, in years to come, lead to a sort of new NAZISM & [lead to] a neutral or pro-Russian Germany. For this reason, I hope that the Germans will now form an '*all Party*' front, to carry the burden of whatever finally [emerges] between them.[118]

Whatever its necessity, Macmillan feared that the acceptance of the status quo in Europe might impose undue pressure on the Federal Republic. The Prime Minister even anticipated the Grand Coalition (1966–9) that provided the necessary political base for the transition from the *Ostpolitik* of Adenauer to that of Brandt. In the meantime, Britain sought quietly to distance itself from the more intransigent elements of West German policy.

Trying to find a middle way

While Britain had endorsed the West German stance on the Oder–Neiße line from the early 1950s – notably in the Bonn Convention of 1952 and the Paris Accords of 1954 – backsliding on these commitments was prompted, in part, by de Gaulle's 'unofficial' recognition of the Polish western frontier line in March 1959. On 11 November 1959 the Foreign Office Minister John Profumo had, in reply to a parliamentary question, restated the British position as believing that 'the final delimitation of the boundary will be formalised by a final peace treaty'.[119] This was reiterated subsequently as official policy in what became known as the 'Profumo formula'. However, Profumo had used the word 'formalised' while omitting the term 'administered by Poland', which, the FO noted, 'was meant to betoken a shift in our position. The nuance however was scarcely noticed.'[120] Decreasing tolerance of the domestic situation in the FRG led the Foreign Office to advise Selwyn Lloyd that 'With a little courage Dr Adenauer could without damage to his electoral prospects afford to ignore the politically active "Association of Expellees". But it might nevertheless need all the resources of American diplomacy to persuade him to do this.'[121] Even before the construction of the Berlin Wall, Macmillan and the Foreign Office had settled upon a policy of 'accepting the stabilisation of Germany's eastern frontier and the Oder/Neiße line', and the effective abandonment of reunification as a prime policy except in the most official and legalistic manner.[122] The head of the Northern Department believed that 'since our general policy is to work towards the German acceptance of the Oder–Neisse line, we are storing up trouble for ourselves if we encourage the [West] Germans to press their demands'.[123]

In their desire to seek a modification in West German policy, the

British government found an increasingly sympathetic ear in Washington. Rusk informed the US embassy in Warsaw that he had told Bonn that the Oder–Neiße line was 'a card of only moderate value'. This information was immediately passed to the British legation in Warsaw.[124] Furthermore, the Soviet leadership was made aware of this. Gromyko told Khrushchev and Gomułka in October 1961 that Rusk, Home and Macmillan had recently adopted a conciliatory tone, as the Soviets concluded that the Americans and the British

> [W]ere trying to achieve an understanding on the question of Germany and West Berlin ... Rusk emphasised that we should guarantee free access to West Berlin ... [and] declared with Kennedy's approval that the government of the USA is prepared to recognize the borders of Germany de facto and de jure (the border on the Oder–Neisse). With regard to Czechoslovakia's borders, they are thinking over some form of commitment to recognize that country's borders. They were prepared to recognize the border between the GDR and West Germany de facto.[125]

The British took the opportunity to attempt to entrench the *status quo* by clandestine means and, so long as the Soviets did not increase the pressure on West Berlin, then achieve a *modus vivendi*. Khrushchev seemed to accept the logic of this new position. Upon hearing Gromyko's report of the new Anglo-Saxon orthodoxy, he told his Foreign Minister and Gomułka that 'Everything we say here must remain top secret because our position corresponds to their position', adding perceptively that 'The West Germans are afraid that the USA will say more than it should about Germany's borders ... Nobody supports West Germany in its desire for reunification'. In essence, the British and the Americans now accepted Khrushchev's statement that 'We cannot permit the reunification of Germany'[126] as a reasonable prerequisite for discussion. There now seemed a basis for agreement on the de facto recognition of the status quo: co-existence would have to rest on a far more solid premise than the fear of nuclear war;[127] namely, a decision to effectively accept the division of Germany in order to achieve a level of enduring mutual security.

Macmillan advised Kennedy that Khrushchev's restraint in not signing a peace treaty with the GDR could be taken as a sign of the Soviet leader's willingness to talk seriously. Macmillan believed that this was less out of his moderation and more

> from his unwillingness to entrust dangerous decisions to Mr Ulbricht ... we have been given a breathing space; and I know that it is your intention, in spite of the difficulties inside the western alliance, to make full use of it ... Adenauer ... seems to have come down ...

> [in favour] of narrowing any negotiation so as to deal only with access
> [to Berlin] and the minimum amount of recognition of the D.D.R.
> required for practical purposes, thus avoiding such larger issues as the
> Oder–Neisse line or the ultimate future of Germany.[128]

Adenauer's obduracy persisted, and when the Chancellor met Macmillan
in January 1962 he scoffed at the idea of 'chasing after' the Soviets.[129]
Kennedy informed Ormsby Gore that French and West German intransigence disappointed him, and Home concluded that Kennedy was unsure
of what to do, but 'This might suggest that [the President] is willing to
leave Dr Adenauer with the choice of peace or war; but ... [the] ultimate
choice must rest with the United States, and Dr Adenauer will be aware of
this'. At the same time, Home doubted that Kennedy could really get Adenauer to moderate his opposition to détente (despite some initial success
in November 1961 in Washington).[130] Adenauer's desperation stretched
even to the leaking of US proposals linking the Oder–Neiße line to a settlement on Berlin to the press. Macmillan's patience was running thin,
and he wondered how the United States managed to maintain theirs as
'[t]here is no such thing today as confidence between countries nominally
allied ... An occasional act of treachery like Bismarck's Ems telegram may
be defensible as an act of state, but this continuous chatter does not even
reach that high level of perfidy'.[131]

While Adenauer was doomed in his attempts to defy the United States
by relying on de Gaulle, continued Soviet intransigence prevented a compromise that would have included a guarantee of access rights to West
Berlin. Although Home had assured Gromyko that the West accepted the
authority of the GDR, and would never change frontiers by force, the
Soviet Foreign Minister demanded that the West grant the GDR de jure
recognition. The Foreign Secretary countered that while both sides
should strive for agreement, the Soviets should not try and squeeze the
Western Allies out of Berlin.[132] As the unreasonable nature of Soviet
demands ruled out the prospect of a settlement, Britain focused on its
own, more limited, method of alleviating tension.

The Oder–Neiße line and the secret guarantee to Poland

Sir George Clutton, British ambassador in Warsaw, believed that the
West's recognition of the Oder–Neiße line represented no real concession
at all. In December 1961, Clutton advised London that recognition of the
line would rid the West of an embarrassing 'academic and legal concept'
that became more obtuse with each passing year:

> Moreover, the Federal Government's retention of the shibboleths of
> self-determination and right to the homeland and their reluctance
> openly to recognise the inevitable does the western Germans ... incal-

culable damage ... the problem of the Oder–Neisse line in any negotiations is not that of making a concession, but rather of ridding ourselves of an albatross from around our necks.[133]

Conversely, following a series of meetings with West German notables, Henry Kissinger, acting as a foreign policy adviser to Kennedy, advised that the recognition of the Oder–Neiße line was out of the question until reunification. Furthermore, 'If it were offered in return for a Berlin settlement [for instance] it would look like paying ransom'.[134] In any case, the West German position remained perfectly legitimate under international law, and was restated in an official publication in 1961 thus: 'the eastern frontiers of Germany can be regulated only in a peace treaty with the legitimate Government of all Germany ... up to now the question of the German eastern territories has been regulated by no binding act on Germany.'[135] This position had been restated, along with a renunciation of force, by the CDU's Dr Carstens to the *Bundestag* as recently as 29 November 1961. It was concluded in the Foreign Office that it was unreasonable for Bonn to adopt any other policy. After all, it was hardly Bonn's fault that there had been no peace treaty. Furthermore, since the West German state held that Germany existed in its 1937 borders, there was no reason for it for it to recognise the Oder–Neiße line against strong domestic opposition. In any case, the fact that West Germany had renounced any forcible revision of borders was proof that Bonn was not 'demanding' any changes to the status quo.[136] It was therefore resolved that Britain should desist from pressurising Bonn over the frontier issue, and perhaps take the initiative itself. It was recognised, however, that any initiative would be limited in scope. Despite enlisting the agreement of the United States on the issue of German boundaries, and communicating dissatisfaction with the current impasse to Moscow, British concern that its relations with Eastern Europe were being damaged remained undiminished. Any approach from the East Europeans was therefore likely to receive a sympathetic hearing in London.

Count Stefan Zamoyski, of the Polish government-in-exile, advised the British government that no Polish government, regardless of political hue, could accept a revision of the Oder–Neiße line.[137] (Although the sensitivity of the subject meant that Home refused to see Zamoyski personally.[138]) Undaunted, the Polish President-in-exile, General Anders, wrote identical letters to Harold Macmillan and John F. Kennedy in February 1962 regarding the Oder–Neiße line. Anders believed that the border between Germany and Poland remained the conceivable subject of barter in negotiations on Berlin and Germany. Until such time there was no hope of the reunification of Germany and, furthermore, Poland would remain dependent upon the Soviet Union for its security. This question, Anders asserted, united all Poles, regardless of political affiliation, world-wide. Moreover, the continued non-recognition of the Oder–Neiße line tends to encourage a revival of the ambitious 'Ost-Politik' engendered by Bismarck and faithfully executed by Hitler, at a time when such a revival is as yet only advocated by ... [the] refugees ... Formal recognition ... would strengthen the more sober outlook prevailing among the West German population and incline the Government to endorse a situation impossible of change unless by force ... [The Polish case] is based on realities, although its moral grounds might appear even more convincing. Its settlement would remove one of the most bitter issues between the two principal nations of Central Europe and render possible a détente.[139]

Polish unanimity on the Oder–Neiße line was evident as the Communist government in Warsaw continued to make a virtually identical case to that made by Anders,[140] and Polish Prime Minister Józef Cyrankiewicz stated on 10 March 1962 that 'It is obvious that without the recognition of our frontier on the Odra and Nysa any diplomatic relations with the German Federal Republic are impossible'.[141] This, of course, made nonsense of the West German position that a future all-German government could come to an agreement with a 'free' Poland (Adenauer's policy being predicated on an insistence that that the problem was Communist rule in Poland). While it was clear that reconciliation between Bonn and Warsaw was dependent upon the recognition of Oder–Neiße line, both the Americans and the British gave non-committal answers to the Anders letter.[142] However, the long-standing British ambiguity over the Oder–Neiße line meant that the letter struck a chord in British governmental and Foreign Office circles. Clutton advised putting pressure on West Germany to recognise the Oder–Neiße frontier, but only in the event of an agreement with the Soviet Union regarding Berlin and Germany. This agreement would have to signal a détente that would be enduring and

> leaving aside the emotional element inherent in the problem, a concession on the Oder/Neisse line would in fact cost us nothing and the West Germans far less than any other concession that they might be called upon to make. In the second place, I cannot see how there can be a *détente* in Central Europe until there is some form of recognition of the ... Oder/Neisse line ... [As it is] there is now ... no possibility of any improvement in relations between the Federal Republic and Poland without this.[143]

It was clear that the Polish 'western territories' were now Polish for good, barring war. That was not to say one should alienate Bonn by declaring this publicly. The best safeguard against independent action by the FRG remained the continuation of the integration of that country into the Western Alliance. In any case, the recognition of the Oder–Neiße line would add nothing to the integration of the FRG into the West, nor add in substance to Bonn's pledges of the renunciation of force. These pledges, moreover, were seen as being of more value than any pressure on the FRG to modify policy, as any move towards the recognition of the line at this time would actually revive the old German aspirations in the East. The new, more sober, outlook was highlighted in the West German population:

> This development, though gradual, is encouraging. In default of a final peace settlement, a natural trend of this kind, on which we are sure we can rely without enforced pressure form outside, will much best serve to give the lie to Soviet propaganda about West German revanchist tendencies. It will also do more than any extraneous act of ours to strengthen the hand of the Federal Government in the cause of peace. We do not think that our interests in the matter are at odds. For both of us they lie in a definitive peace settlement in Europe, and for that we shall continue to strive.[144]

Clutton judged that the Poles were relatively uninterested in a British recognition of the Oder–Neiße line, seeking instead that London put pressure on West Germany to recognise the line.[145] Home's Assistant Private Secretary, J. Oliver Wright, who privately viewed Bonn's position as 'untenable' in the long run,[146] saw Anders' letter as being entirely reasonable.

> Her Majesty's Government regret that so long after the war this question still remains unsettled. [Furthermore] we recognise as a matter of fact that over the past decade and a half the areas in question have become thoroughly settled under Polish administration ... [and] we do not look upon this issue as a possible subject of barter: we are not so unrealistic as to suppose that it could be so treated.

Nevertheless, the current state of negotiations on Berlin precluded the British government doing as the General, and indeed the government in Warsaw, asked. Wright also believed it best not to put such an undertaking to Anders in writing, as the Warsaw government would hear of it and take offence. Thus, he advised communicating an oral assurance to Anders and the People's Republic of Poland in Warsaw simultaneously.[147] In April 1962, Clutton therefore assured Winiewicz, deputy Polish Foreign Minister, that 'In any negotiations that we might have on the subject of Germany or Berlin he could be quite certain that Her Majesty's Government did not regard Poland's western frontier as a subject of barter'. A 'delighted' Winiewicz commented that the priority now was to get Adenauer to adopt a similar position. Clutton replied that an extremely cautious policy would be required in the Federal Republic, as such statements could cause the small extremist fringe on the eastern territories to greatly enlarge their support.[148] A simultaneous assurance was given to the Polish government-in-exile in London. The British had made these assurances on the understanding that they would remain confidential. London had no intention of upsetting the West Germans unduly, simply to please the Poles. However, if an agreement could be reached with Moscow, Britain would be more tempted to be less sensitive to Bonn's feelings.

Common cause amongst the Anglo-Saxons

In October 1962, Home reported to the Cabinet that he had effectively offered to endorse the status quo in Europe – dependent on an initial agreement guaranteeing access to West Berlin – in discussion with Gromyko in New York. Home optimistically noted Khrushchev's interest in the expansion of East–West dialogue and asserted the possibility of an agreement between the two superpowers on disarmament and nuclear testing. If this were so, Home speculated, not only would the German question be shelved, but that of Berlin too.[149] US frustration with Bonn served to advance the British argument on the German Question in Washington. Kennedy told Ormsby Gore that the Cuban Missile Crisis reinforced his belief that negotiation was the way forward. This realisation only heightened the President's disappointment in Bonn's failure to face 'realities' in Europe.[150] While Christopher Steel wished to avoid a linkage of the issues of Berlin and Cuba, he believed that an American-inspired arrangement could perhaps involve some recognition of the GDR. However,

> Such a solution conflicts ... directly with the edifice of illusions and shibboleths constructed [by the FRG] ... Nevertheless, this is what [Kennedy] has in mind when he talks of 'realities'. [Privately one recognises] The fact ... that Germany is not divided by any legal or constitutional arrangements but by twenty-two Soviet divisions. There are very many Germans ... who fully realize this, but it will need some decisive shock to overcome the artificial inertia. Perhaps Adenauer's disappearance could begin it. Meanwhile, the United Kingdom must refrain very carefully from taking the lead.[151]

While Macmillan rejected any specific linkage between Cuba and Berlin, he did at least conclude that the neutralisation and demilitarisation of the two would lead to 'some degree of *détente* ... thus removing the Berlin situation from the arena of acute controversy'.[152] Macmillan did 'not think [Berlin and Cuba were] of equal value to us and I fear that to make an explicit link between them might even encourage Mr Khrushchev to feel that he might take Berlin at the risk not of nuclear war but only of the loss of Cuba'. As Len Scott remarks, 'Such judgements were vindicated, not least as Khrushchev's Cuban adventure marked his last attempt to force the Berlin issue'.[153] Certainly, the US Minister in Bonn later recounted that the Cuban Missile Crisis had caused Khrushchev to put Berlin on the back burner as an insoluble problem.[154] According to Sorenson, the events of October 1962 also fundamentally changed Kennedy's perspective on the German question. Ironically, Kennedy came to a conclusion not dissimilar to that reached by Macmillan after the Paris Summit:

> During 1961–1962 the President interested himself in a variety of negotiating proposals ... Most failed to survive copious Allied study and deliberate French and German leaks. The result, as ... Macmillan commented to him, was that he had little specific to offer the Russians, 'hardly the soup course and none of the fish' ... Our error, JFK later acknowledged, was in trying to push the Germans to accept ideas in which he could not interest Khrushchev anyway.[155]

By the end of 1962, Steel concluded that Adenauer, with de Gaulle's backing, continued successfully to obstruct Schröder's efforts to establish a common Western negotiating position on both Berlin and Germany with which to approach the USSR.[156] While the rhetoric had softened, the German Question seemed as intractable as ever.

A new goal: Macmillan and the EEC

The failure of Macmillan's diplomacy up to 1960 caused him to rethink his policy. The Free Trade area, which Macmillan had tried unsuccessfully to link to the German Question,[157] was long-since a dead duck. In its stead, Macmillan came up with his so-called 'Grand Design' over Christmas and New Year 1960–1.[158] This was revealed to the Cabinet in April 1961 and had, as its centrepiece, an application for British membership of the EEC.[159] De Gaulle was the implacable foe in all this, and Macmillan therefore realised that he required Bonn's support for British entry and resolved not to 'upset the Germans unduly.'[160] (All the more important as Macmillan noted that the economy was getting 'spectacularly worse'.[161]) On 31 July 1961, Macmillan announced to the Commons that Britain was applying for full membership of the EEC.[162] That same month, the US ambassador in London identified the three (inter-related) areas of primary British policy concern as being its economic difficulties, Berlin and entry into the EEC.[163] A State Department memorandum concluded that Macmillan was

> A man with a strong sense of history, he would like to have to his credit as Prime Minister a major historical achievement. He apparently felt that this achievement might have been in the field of East–West relations; despite his continued, sometimes almost frenetic, efforts along these lines, he now seems sanguine. Nonetheless, he has not, and in fact cannot, abandon the British quest for a contribution

to the solution of this problem as influential as the not-inconsiderable resources of Her Majesty's Government can devise. To many observers, Britain's successful entry into the Common Market would be a comparable achievement, and this may well be the answer to Macmillan's quest for a place in history.[164]

The Federal Republic could also help Britain by reducing its defence burden through increased offset costs for British forces in West Germany. Unfortunately, as Macmillan noted, the West Germans were fairly insistent on not paying the 'full amount' of offset.[165] Unhelpfully, this caused Macmillan to indulge his envy of a 'happy Germany, rich – incredibly rich – with no problems, exc[luding] Berlin'.[166] Fearing for the future, Macmillan confided to Home that:

> There is only one issue now which dominates everything for the next few months. Shall we or shall we not be able to bring off our entry into the Common Market? On that the fortunes and probably the life of the Government depend. It would perhaps be pompous to say that the fortunes of the country are at stake too, but many of us feel this to be the case.[167]

While Macmillan still objected to the intransigent foreign policy of Bonn, he would let the Americans pressurise Bonn so as to try and win West German support for EEC membership. In April 1962, the Prime Minister noted that 'The Germans are behaving in a foolish way & annoying the Americans ... [and any] move towards negotiation in Berlin is at once sabotaged by the Germans & the French. But, until the Common Market is settled, one way or the other, it is best for Britain to keep quiet.'[168] Hoping for Bonn's goodwill towards his EEC application, Macmillan now paid due deference to West German sensibilities. Sir Evelyn Shuckburgh informed Kennedy's National Security adviser, McGeorge Bundy, that while Macmillan favoured a summit, he could only endorse it after he was assured that Bonn was favourable to a Berlin–German settlement.[169] Fearing that Bonn would see British 'betrayal' over Berlin as a pretext to side with de Gaulle,[170] Macmillan requested that the United States make it clear to the French and Germans that the Anglo-Americans had not proposed any concessions to the Soviets.[171]

Unfortunately, the preceding years meant that Britain now faced a formidable obstacle to its ambitions in the shape of the Franco-German axis. Macmillan tried, unsuccessfully, to woo de Gaulle at a meeting at Champs in June 1962 in what he believed was the last opportunity for British EEC entry.[172] After lengthy discussions, Macmillan failed to persuade de Gaulle that the British enthusiasm for Europe was genuine.[173] Macmillan now feared that the application for EEC membership was doomed, and his diaries for the latter part of 1962 and the early part of

1963 are full of abuse for Adenauer and de Gaulle.[174] The Nassau Agreement of December 1962 provided the French President with an excellent pretext for vetoing Britain's application to join the EEC, allowing de Gaulle to point to the continued 'Atlantic' mindset of the British. The Nassau Agreement might have secured the future of Britain's strategic deterrent (by the sale of the Polaris missile system to Britain), but it also guaranteed exclusion from the EEC.[175]

De Gaulle's 'Non!' on British membership[176] was compounded by the conclusion of the Franco-German Treaty of January 1963. These two events left Britain isolated in Western Europe, and laid bare the problems of relying on the Special Relationship to bolster British policy towards Europe. It seemed as though Macmillan's 1958 prediction of a new 'Continental System' was fulfilled, as he had suffered a political blow commensurate with the 'Paris Summit'. The Prime Minister lamented that 'All our policies at home and abroad are in ruins'.[177] Macmillan saw the French veto as being born of a desire to dominate Europe, which 'So long as Adenauer-Petain remains . . . is easy'. The Nassau Agreement, in Macmillan's view, was just an excuse for this,[178] and the PM observed to Kennedy that 'By a curious paradox de Gaulle's attitude is cementing that very Anglo-Saxon Alliance which he professes to dislike'.[179] Kennedy and the State Department had long favoured British EEC entry, and the President was therefore amenable to Macmillan's pleas to intercede with Adenauer.[180] Knowing Adenauer's reputation for vanity, Macmillan even suggested that Kennedy

> [M]ight . . . refer to Adenauer's personal achievement as the man, who having saved Europe by the Franco-German reconciliation, could now put a crown on his life's work by saving the wider unity of Europe and the western Alliance. Pray forgive me for venturing to make this suggestion but of course it is a vital moment for us all.[181]

Kennedy duly advised Adenauer of his alarm at the seemingly anti-American stance of his axis with de Gaulle, and of the necessity for British EEC membership.[182] Yet there were some signs of hope. The Franco-German Treaty masked the fact that the West German government, with the very notable exception of Adenauer, was largely in favour of British entry into the EEC. In January 1963, the German delegation in Brussels stated that, 'For political and economic reasons . . . we regard it as necessary that Great Britain should be a full member of the European Community'.[183] Most notably, Schröder himself wrote a conciliatory letter to Edward Heath, the Minster responsible for the failed EEC negotiations.[184] Much was made in Britain of the fact that Adenauer's designated successor, the Anglophile Erhard, had remarked in Bonn that 'The day will dawn, when all six countries will realise we have made a mistake today'.[185] British policy-makers therefore resolved to bide their time, believing, as Sir Frank Roberts later wrote, that 'so long as

Dr Adenauer remained in office relations between the two countries could never have been really good'.[186]

Consolation prize: the PTB Treaty

Ironically, given his past attempts at détente, Macmillan was leaving the field to the United States precisely at a time when he recognised a new Soviet willingness to compromise. Macmillan wrote to Kennedy in March 1963 with regard to

> Khrushchev's concern with what he calls the German problem. Here again I wish we could get down to serious negotiation. It may well be that what the Russians want is in effect what we want – to put the whole matter of Berlin on ice. What we do not really know is what the Russians mean by 'recognising the facts as they are' in Germany. Undoubtedly the building of the Wall, although it emphasises the weakness of the East German regime in its power to hold the loyalty of its citizens, has removed a great deal of the pressure on East Germany and may make the Russians content to leave well alone.[187]

Détente seemed to have arrived in tangible form in 1963 in the guise of the Partial Test Ban (PTB) Treaty, and Macmillan noted the favourable press coverage with satisfaction.[188] In actual fact, the conclusion of the treaty gave a veneer of gloss to diminishing British status just prior to Harold Macmillan's resignation, and his replacement by Alec Douglas-Home, in October 1963. The new Foreign Secretary, R.A. ('Rab') Butler, recalled that Macmillan (like Churchill) suffered from a surfeit of enthusiasm for the possibilities afforded by 'Summitry', and Home had a better appreciation of the limited utility of détente for Britain.[189] The British Minister given special responsibility for the PTB Treaty, Quentin Hogg, later judged that the treaty would not have been concluded without British participation.[190] What Hogg omits to mention was that, in contrast to Macmillan's earlier initiatives, it was the new willingness of the super-powers to engage with each other in the aftermath of the Cuban Missile Crisis that allowed the British to play the role of facilitator.

The potential for Bonn to acquire nuclear weapons had been a cardinal concern of Moscow in signing the PTB Treaty.[191] Signally, Rusk agreed with Khrushchev that the US shared the view of having 'no desire whatsoever of [seeing] West Germany equipped with nuclear weapons', as there were enough nuclear-armed states in the world.[192] Marc Trachtenberg sees the PTB Treaty as a de facto solution to the German Question as the main issue of East–West tension. The agreement 'tie[d] both Germany and Russia into the status quo ... [as] a [Cold War] system was taking shape'.[193] The PTB Treaty was thus symptomatic of a tacit acceptance of the status quo, although, as Richard Crockatt has observed, it also spelled the end of real British influence on East–West détente.[194] Christof Münger's assertion that the PTB Treaty stabilised both the territorial and nuclear status quo of Europe is thus entirely accurate.[195] The so-called 'first' Cold War was ending, albeit slowly.

The German progressive: Schröder

Following the PTB Treaty, Macmillan fumed that the FRG expected support whilst obstructing détente at every turn – Bonn having only signed the treaty with great reluctance.[196] Macmillan comforted himself that the 'old man's days were numbered' and that Schröder would continue to support détente (although Macmillan feared that Adenauer and von Brentano would continue to exercise their influence from the sidelines).[197] Despite the perception by some British policy-makers and officials that Schröder was a politician 'on the make',[198] his 'Policy of Movement' received staunch support, and London took a keen interest in the furious attacks on it from the 'Adenauer-Strauß' wing of the CDU/CSU.[199] Following a WEU meeting, Rab Butler advised Rusk that

> Schroeder's attitude was particularly encouraging. On East/West relations he showed that he had no use for the French policy of immobilisme. He entered, of course, his usual caveats about the dangers of lulling the public into a state of false optimism and the need of not impairing the basic western positions on Berlin and Germany. Subject to that he thought it was right that you and we should continue to probe the Russian position and see if there were possibilities of reaching limited agreements on peripheral questions.[200]

The US government shared this favourable impression of Schröder and hoped that, once Adenauer was removed from the scene, the *Politik der Bewegung* could develop more fully.[201] This seemed likely when Adenauer's successor, Erhard, told the *Bundestag* that Bonn wished to 'increase and expand its economic exchanges with the East European states'. Henceforward, West German policy would aim to break down barriers in Europe, although the emphasis on reunification remained.[202] Despite signs of progress, Butler stressed that the question of Berlin continued to be the main obstacle to a general arrangement between East and West and that, if concluded, any non-aggression pact should be accompanied by some sort of declaration of intent on the 'German issue'.[203] Sir Frank Roberts later recalled the new urgency given to the development of Anglo-German understanding following his arrival as British ambassador in Bonn in February 1963. Roberts recognised that the UK had been unable to compete with American power and, unlike the French, had failed to participate in 'integrative mechanisms' with the West Germans. By 1964, Britain was, however, finally addressing the need to improve bilateral relations with Bonn.[204]

Economics and Cold War

Macmillan believed that military stalemate would cause economic warfare to move to the centre of Western Cold-War strategy. This view was shared by the Kennedy administration.[205] Certain bloc states, such as Romania, were identified as being suitable for economic inducement in the interest of 'promoting tendencies toward national autonomy and diversity'.[206] The West was increasingly aware that its economic muscle was superior to that of the Soviet Union[207] and Schröder, too, saw economics as the ideal medium in which to conduct his Eastern policy.[208] Since military measures were ruled out from the beginning, and diplomatic manoeuvrability was severely limited after the Wall, the economic option seemed Bonn's best. Unfortunately, the desire to avoid political concessions of any substance caused Bonn to over-play its economic hand, and the British perception that Poland had little desire to establish economic/political relations with Bonn, without the issues such as the Oder–Neiße line being addressed, were to prove accurate.[209]

In August 1962, an official American report by Roger Hilsman, head of research at the State Department, held that Schröder's policy would remain passive so long as Germany was divided. This meant that there was no possibility that the FRG would recognise the GDR. Schröder would therefore pursue an 'opportunistic' policy aimed at establishing influence in (non-political) areas with the satellites. Further, the Oder–Neiße line would only be considered as part of a deal on German reunification whilst the 'Hallstein Doctrine can probably still be considered useful, though not sacrosanct, for some years to come'.[210] Schröder confirmed this, telling Rusk that FRG policy would only advance when it did not enhance the status of the GDR[211] (although Fritz Erler, a senior SPD figure, was correct in his assessment that Bonn's policy had a leaden quality, as the GDR constantly urged its Warsaw Pact allies to rebuff Bonn's overtures).[212] In consequence, it took Schröder nearly two years to conclude an agreement for a trade mission with Warsaw (in March 1963), as this important first step had had to avoid violating the Hallstein Doctrine.[213] Trade missions were established in Romania, Hungary and Bulgaria in the succeeding year, but Czechoslovakia remained unmoved – due to the Bonn's attitude to the status of the Munich Pact.[214] (Indeed, the US ambassador in Czechoslovakia reported that President Novotný had decided in 1959 to reduce trade with West Germany because of what he described as the 'monopoly position' West Germany was achieving over Czechoslovak trade at that time.[215])

The explicit political goals of the *Osthandel*, such as the isolation of the GDR, meant that Bonn was sensitive to proposals emanating from its allies. A British proposal of long-term credits for the bloc prompted US Under Secretary of State Ball to comment that 'Erhard's obsession with using long-term credits for a political solution of the German problem ...

[means that] Bonn will certainly resist any British proposal for twenty-five year credits that do not provide a political *quid pro quo*'.[216] This demonstrated the difference in approach between the Federal Republic and Britain. British policy-makers and industry often saw Eastern Europe purely as a potential market. This was indicative of British insensitivity to the political dimension of the *Osthandel*. To Bonn's chagrin, Britain announced in late 1963 that it intended to upgrade the British missions in Bulgaria, Hungary and Rumania to embassy status.[217] Erhard informed Home early in 1964 that the satellites were beginning to show a greater degree of independence than hitherto, and that the inclusion of Berlin clauses in the trade agreements was particularly significant.[218] But Bonn's attempts to persuade the GDR, via economic inducements, to soften its attitude on a number of questions were largely unsuccessful.[219] The East European desk of the FO saw the logic in the cautious attitude of the GDR, as 'The East German régime realises that, over a long period, it is possible that the trade mission weapon could lead to the undermining of the "D.D.R."'.[220]

The limited success of Schröder's Eastern policy

The Foreign Office noted that the West German government increasingly found that its economic power was negated by insuperable political obstacles in Eastern Europe.[221] When it came to matters such as diplomatic relations, no amount of West German economic philanthropy would be able to draw the sting from the omnipresent perceived threat of (West) German revanchism in the Eastern bloc. The British ambassador in Warsaw pointed out to a CDU MdB who was attached to the West German trade mission that there was no hope of detaching Poland from the USSR by economic means 'Since . . . only the Soviet Union could guarantee Poland her borders'.[222] Sir Frank Roberts advised that the legalistic West German position on the Oder–Neiße line 'inhibits Federal politicians from doing anything to correct the impression left by speakers who talk of re-establishing Germany within her former frontiers'. Bonn's Eastern policy therefore opted to consolidate before moving any further forward, as, with elections in the offing in the FRG, room for manoeuvre was limited. In any case,

> The die-hards indeed have some arguments on their side. As you say, even though Germany gains nothing visible by refusing to recognize the Oder/Neisse line, it is very doubtful whether her relations with Poland would improve very much if she did. In other words recognition is a card which *may* turn out to be worth nothing at the eventual peace conference, but what is quite certain now is that it is worth little or nothing now – so why play it?[223]

At the heart of the failings of West German policy lay the continuing existence of the GDR. British officials in West Berlin were under no illusions that the Pankow regime was gaining in strength and confidence. An official in the British Military Government in Berlin later recalled that she 'certainly had no impression in E[ast] Berlin of a population actively seething with discontent. This picture, as painted by the Federal Republic, was quite false.'[224] Early in 1964 the British Commandant in Berlin, Major-General Peel Yates, reported that 1963 had been a year of transition between the era of tension 'to a policy of renewed attempts to solve these problems by contacts between Germans on both sides: in other words by the application to the German problem of the dogma of peaceful co-existence.'[225]

The fact was that the GDR was stabilising the situation by its persistence in defying Bonn.[226] From London's perspective this was no bad thing – the most any West German policy could be expected to achieve would be the undermining of the GDR to the extent that would create alarm in Moscow and instability in Europe. While British policy had the stated aim of German reunification, it did not see how dangerous levels of tension in Europe would further this goal. In this the Americans were increasingly on board, as when Rusk, for instance, cautioned Schröder that any real progress towards reunification must entail a discussion of the recognition of existing boundaries.[227] It was thus deemed preferable to have a stable GDR within the Communist bloc than one that threatened to collapse with uncertain consequences.

West German uncertainties over the viability of (previously rock-solid) principles underpinning their policy elicited gentle probing from the British government. In early 1964, Butler asked Erhard and Schröder why an official West German paper contained the word '*Heimatrecht*', as the British government envisaged reunification as being the union of the FRG and the 'Soviet Zone' (the GDR) only. Butler was thus openly refuting the idea that the Oder–Neiße territories would be included in a reunified Germany. Although this left open the possible revision of the border in talks between an 'all-German' government and Poland, it was clear that the British regarded any future 'unitary' Germany as being composed of the FRG and the GDR only. Home added that the West Germans should consider dropping the term '*Heimatrecht*' as it 'put off an awful lot of people, and not only in the East'.[228] However, despite clinging to the status of Germany within its 1937 borders, senior figures in the Federal Republic seemed to be softening their stance. Schröder had made it clear to Butler that he wanted to make some real progress on the German Question and, in that regard, he would like British help. Butler, echoing Macmillan's' assertion that the Americans should get used to being 'unpopular', pleaded that the United States take the lead with regard to any such initiative for two reasons: first, the Germans depended far more on the USA than on Britain; second, Britain had not been too successful in its dealings with the Federal Republic of late.[229]

The rhetoric of Schröder and his allies in the Bonn Republic was now intently studied in Washington and London for signs of progress. A major speech in Munich by Schröder on 4 April 1964 asserted that despite the wrongs done to the expellees, there was no wish for German vengeance. Furthermore, he was of the opinion that there was a long history of German co-operation with Eastern Europe that could now be resurrected.[230] The head of the FO's Western Department noted that Schröder, having established trade relations with the satellites, was preparing for another phase of his policy:

> Dr Schroeder's remarks about Germany's eastern frontiers strike me as unusually moderate in tone ... [Making] a distinct implication about accepting the *status quo*. Moreover, the statement [by Schröder] that 'the definitive position of the German eastern frontier should be determined peaceably and without the use of force in a peace treaty with the whole of Germany' ... sounds not very different from our standard formula.[231]

The British press also took notice of the manner in which Schröder was moving away from Adenauer's policies. The *Manchester Guardian*, for instance, wrote that 'No one should blame the West Germans for [taking so long to come] to this hard and bitter conclusion. The real miracle of post-war German history is the speed with which they have adjusted to the facts of international life, not the slowness.'[232] The US embassy in London noted how the Foreign Office had encouraged the trend toward sympathy with West Germany's problems in the press 'In recognition that the key to British policy towards France [and Europe] lies in Germany'.[233] In this the Foreign Office seemed to have been rather successful in raising the stock of Britain in Bonn. Rusk advised Butler he believed Erhard and Schröder were genuinely committed to a policy of reconciliation with Britain as part of their strategy of moving away from 'Gaullism'.[234] In June 1964, Sir Frank Roberts reported that the West Germans were no longer inherently suspicious of advice proffered to them on the Communist bloc or security questions.[235]

Bonn's willingness to place a lower priority on reunification reflected, in effect, a gradual acceptance of the status quo. This was mirrored in Soviet thinking, and Gromyko stated that it was for the two German states to agree on reunification and, in any case, Potsdam had said nothing about an obligation of the Four Powers to work for reunification.[236] Although Schröder made it clear that Bonn would prefer that the Four Powers continue to work for German reunification,[237] it seemed increasingly unlikely that they would – given the *modus vivendi* that was emerging between the superpowers. The concepts of 'Two Germanies' and 'Co-existence' now seemed increasingly synonymous.

Conclusion

In his dealings with Bonn, Macmillan often used unpleasant and ill-advised tactics of threat and blackmail – especially on the questions of European integration and Berlin.[238] De Gaulle, by contrast, backed Adenauer to the hilt.[239] De Gaulle therefore gained the gratitude of the Chancellor, but as the price the French president wanted became clear (namely, the formation of an anti-American axis in Western Europe), a schism emerged in the government in Bonn.[240] Furthermore, de Gaulle's Berlin policy was only the initial stage of his effort to assert his independence vis-à-vis Washington and negotiate bilaterally with Moscow.[241] This position was even more divorced from reality than Macmillan's had been (and was, eventually, to cause even greater consternation in Bonn).[242] Thus, John Gearson and Victor Mauer are correct in arguing that British policy on Berlin after 1958 was unpredictable, duplicitous and neglectful of Bonn's interests.[243] Yet this is to take too little account of the intransigent and highly provocative policy towards the East adopted by the Adenauer government after 1949. The Adenauer government successfully muddied the waters by their linkage of the legitimate case for West Berlin with a rejection of the territorial status quo in Europe and an indulgence of expellee aspirations. Successive British governments were correct in recognising the untenable (and indeed dangerous) nature of the situation created by West German policy in east–central Europe.

Macmillan's policy towards Germany had been misguided, but at least the farce of Paris in May 1960 left the Prime Minister with little option but to change direction. The decision to apply for EEC membership perhaps required such a shock in order to demonstrate the new role that Britain had to accustom itself to. In any case, it must be remembered that the economic arguments for European integration were not as overwhelming as has often been presented. Further, if the Conservative Party was hardly enthusiastic over British EEC membership, the Labour Party (and Hugh Gaitskell especially) was violently hostile. In September 1962, Gaitskell famously told the Labour Party Conference that if Britain joined the EEC 'It means the end of a thousand years of history … [to become] just a province of Europe'.[244] Even if Gaitskell was being rather dramatic, he was correct that EEC membership represented a momentous step for Britain to take.

Just as the US attitude had been instrumental in the accession of West Germany to NATO and the construction of Bonn's hard line, so it was again with the demise of the *Politik der Stärke* in the early 1960s. This, of course, had implications for the entire framework of West German policy on unification, the GDR and the 'lost territories'. By viewing Berlin as a Four-Power problem, rather than the capital of a future reunified Germany, London and Washington seemed to be closer to the Soviet position than the West German one. Khrushchev may well have been bluffing over Berlin, but Washington seemed eager to engage with the Soviet leader over what has recently been termed perceived 'actual [US] security interests'.[245] When the Wall went up on 13 August 1961, the line drawn in the sand over Berlin by the West was too far withdrawn for Bonn. Adenauer stated in 1956 that 'If [the Americans] face the possibility of war against Russia, they'll compromise on [the] division [of Europe and Germany]'.[246] As the Chancellor had feared, Bonn would not continue to enjoy US patronage of its hard-line policies if it risked a general war. This proved to be the case when the Berlin Wall was constructed in 1961. Willy Brandt later recalled:

> I wondered then, not for the first or last time, whether the two super-powers might not, with adamantine consistency, have been pursuing the same principle in Europe in 1945: that, whatever happened, they would respect the spheres of influence broadly agreed at Yalta . . . The basic principles governing the tacit arrangement and Washington remained in force during the construction of the Wall and thereafter.[247]

In London the undermining of Adenauer's position was welcomed, as any extension of his tenure as Chancellor seemed likely to perpetuate the anti-British Franco-German axis in Europe. The Wall signalled that a new approach was required and the British warmly welcomed this as it arrived in the person of the new Federal Foreign Minister, Dr Gerhard Schröder. Schröder's *Politik der Bewegung* was doubly welcome by the British government, accompanied as it was by a shift away from Adenauer's 'Gaullism'. A further corollary of the construction of the Wall was that, as Nigel Ashton notes, its creation was 'as effective in repairing a breach in Anglo-American relations as it had in shoring up the eastern bloc'.[248] Realising the weakened position of Adenauer, Macmillan sought to utilise the new American desire for détente by urging Kennedy to push Adenauer in the direction of conciliation. This approach was far more realistic than his earlier attempts at 'personal diplomacy', given the relative weakness of the British position. One unfortunate consequence of the demise of Adenauer's Eastern policy was the manner in which it reinforced divisions in the alliance with France and West Germany on one side and the United States and Britain on the other. This culminated in Nassau in December 1962, and in de Gaulle's 'Non' to British membership of the EEC one month later. Nassau made British exclusion from the EEC a certainty.[249] It also allowed Britain to enjoy an illusion of continued Great Power status. Ironically, this status was something that the United States had long sought to disabuse the British of, and was the rationale for Washington's support of the British application to the EEC.[250]

The early 1960s saw Macmillan's realisation that brokering détente was of limited utility in bolstering British power and prestige. In any case, only a modification of West German policy could achieve a real settlement in

Europe, and, in this, the new American desire for détente would be the crucial factor. This would work on the two contradictory levels of the ultimate guarantee of Western Europe by American power, and the prodding of the West German state in the direction of a new arrangement with the East. While Macmillan still disliked Bonn's policy, he avoided the mistakes of the 1950s when he had attempted to remedy the situation himself in a very public manner. In encouraging discussion, rather than seeking another 'Congress of Berlin' in every foray, the British interest was no longer seen as being synonymous with summitry. The secret guarantee to Poland is of such significance because it demonstrates the British acceptance of reality on a number of levels. First, détente was not going to provide Britain with anything like the prestige that Macmillan had originally believed. Second, the business of achieving a German settlement was in the gift of the superpowers and, to a lesser degree, the Germans themselves. Third, any hope of achieving British membership of the EEC was absolutely dependent upon Bonn's goodwill. And fourth, Britain could expand its influence in Eastern Europe by low-key bilateral diplomacy that would, at least, ascertain the degree to which the satellites desired to establish a degree of autonomy from Moscow. While British policy had suffered a series of sharp reverses over détente and European integration, it was now moving in the right direction. West German Eastern policy, by contrast, would have to make some hard choices in the years ahead.

Despite Schröder's modifications, the essential tenets of an intransigent Eastern policy remained in place as West Germany sought to isolate the GDR within the Eastern bloc by economic means. Although trade increased, the requisite political advantages did not accrue for the West German government. Despite extensive efforts by Bonn, the GDR was successfully consolidating itself. The emerging superpower *modus vivendi* included acknowledging each other's German client as being within their respective spheres of interest. In the absence of any more comprehensive agreement, the Partial Test Ban Treaty of 1963 substituted as a de facto peace settlement as the basis for what Trachtenberg describes as 'a relatively stable system'.[251] The modification of West German policy seemed sure to accelerate in the post-Adenauer era. In such a climate one could look forward to better Anglo-German relations whereby the previous misunderstandings would be much reduced. The Federal Republic would not be alienated to the extent that it had been in 1958–9. Britain recognised that the Federal Republic itself, and not just its territory, was the key to a settlement of outstanding questions in Europe. The belated acknowledgement that West Germany was a player in – and not simply the major source of tension of – the Cold War augured well for future relations between London and Bonn.

5 The Wilson government and the German Question

No government of which I am head will ever agree to a German finger on the nuclear trigger.

Harold Wilson

I wanted the Poles and Russians to know that we would never resort to force to alter the Oder–Neisse line or any other generally accepted territorial border.

Lyndon Baines Johnson

Soviet Russia has entered the ranks of people who want peace.

Konrad Adenauer

A new era? Labour and Germany

The Erhard government in Bonn was initially alarmed at the prospect of a Labour government following its victory in the election of October 1964. The Labour Party had a long history of antagonism towards the ruling CDU/CSU, and Aneurin Bevan, Shadow Foreign Secretary, cut to the heart of the matter when he denounced Bonn's 'Policy of Strength' in December 1958 because 'what we are seeking is ... to be strong enough to be peaceful. We are not seeking strength for its own sake'.[1] The Labour leadership, while keen proponents of a strong NATO,[2] disliked Bonn's Eastern policy because of the manner in which it linked Britain to an intransigent policy vis-à-vis the Soviet bloc. Furthermore, many figures in Labour's vocal left wing sympathised widely with the GDR and saw the Adenauer government as the very model of a capitalist state bent on an aggressive Cold War crusade.[3] The rank-and-file of the party, having opposed West German rearmament, remained hostile to Bonn. As Labour leader, Hugh Gaitskell had sought to prevail upon the West German state to adopt a more moderate Eastern policy, hoping that 'the Germans ... would feel that the renunciation of claims to the pre-1945 territories would be a price worth paying for reunification and the freedom of the satellite countries'.[4] Gaitskell's successor, Harold Wilson, had been a staunch opponent of Germany rearmament,[5] and his Private Secretary later recalled that Wilson had an affinity with the Russian people 'that was notably absent in his feelings towards the Germans'.[6] Bonn was hardly reassured when Wilson declared in Moscow in 1963 that 'We have no respect either for Adenauer or for Ulbricht'.[7] Despite this, the SPD Vice-Chair, Fritz Erler, was right when he observed in Washington that the Labour Party and Harold Wilson was gradually ridding itself of anti-German sentiment.[8] Such optimism was well founded, and Wilson's Moscow performance proved to be an isolated, if regrettable, gaffe.

On occasion, Wilson's propensity to engage in high-level diplomacy led him to try to play the role of 'honest broker' between East and West,[9] but he did not seek to use détente as an independent means of bolstering British power.[10] The head of the FO's Western Department approved of such restraint, as 'the West Germans are prone to interpret British willing-ness to seek ways and means of easing the situation in Germany as evid-ence of a desire to perpetuate the division of that country and to achieve a *détente* on that basis with the Russians'. Further, since French hints at the recognition of the GDR and the Oder–Neiße line meant that Bonn could no longer count on Paris as it had done previously,[11] an Anglo-German rapprochement was a central aim of the new Labour government.[12] The successful visit by Patrick Gordon Walker, Foreign Secretary until January 1965, to Bonn in November 1964 was a clear indication that both sides desired improved bilateral relations.[13] Refraining from attempts to negoti-ate with the USSR over the heads of West Germany was central to this, as Michael Stewart, Gordon Walker's successor, made clear to the Cabinet:

> We need to dispel long-standing German fears that we are trying to make a settlement with the Russians at the expense of the German claim to national unity. We must try and persuade them that progress towards reunification can only be made in an atmosphere of East/West *détente*, and that the arms control measures can contribute towards the creation of such an atmosphere, even if they are not linked with provi-sions for immediate progress towards German reunification.[14]

By late 1964 both the US administration of Lyndon B. Johnson, and the USSR, now led by Leonid Brezhnev, were moving towards a *modus vivendi* in Europe.[15] In such an atmosphere, the Foreign Office held that the Johnson administration had concluded that, since the Soviets demanded 'neither crisis nor serious negotiations' over Germany, it was best to let matters rest.[16] While the acceptance of the status quo would confirm a divided Germany, shorn of one-quarter of its territory, the weight of US influence would force a reluctant Bonn into tacitly agreeing to defer reunification.[17] Indeed, Roberts reported from Berlin that French attempts to undermine Bonn's links with the United States 'without offer-ing any prospect that France could replace the United States as Germany's "protecting power"' received little sympathy in Bonn.[18] Reassuringly, Erhard advised Wilson that while de Gaulle wanted to drive the Americans out of Europe – leaving France and the USSR as the dominant powers on the continent – West Germany would never accept this.[19]

The worldwide conflict: the US turns towards Asia

A long-standing admirer of the United States, Erhard's timing of his accession as Chancellor was unfortunate in that it coincided with increasing American involvement in Vietnam. It was ironic that a war in Asia undermined US interest in Europe[20] as, in the 1950s, the Korean War had focused attention on the Soviet threat to Germany and come to Adenauer's aid. Frank Roberts noted the Erhard government's fear that American involvement in Vietnam would lead to a willingness to deal with the USSR at West Germany's expense.[21] Ever impervious to the international situation, the stalwarts of the *Politik der Stärke* (the expellees, the right wing of the CDU/CSU etc.) desired a return to the days when the Soviet threat led the US government to underwrite West German intransigence. Accordingly, at a rally in Bonn in 1966, Wenzel Jacksch linked the question of the Oder–Neiße territories and the Sudetenland with the struggle of US-supported South Vietnam for freedom against Communist tyranny.[22] The analogy was lost on the Americans. In the 1950s, Korea had caused the US to see Germany as vulnerable; in the 1960s, Vietnam caused Washington to see Germany as a distraction. Given American flexibility over Germany, the question of recognition of the Oder–Neiße line was now bound to be raised 'whether the Germans like it or not'.[23] Worse for Bonn, Gromyko outlined the intractable nature of the Soviet attitude all too clearly, insisting on the acceptance of the current status of the GDR and the desirability of disarmament as a precondition for German unity.[24]

Clearly, détente was not going to happen overnight or in any manner resembling a diplomatic 'revolution'. The Johnson administration remained officially committed to German reunification, and Dean Rusk affirmed that a reunited Germany was an essential policy goal and one whose 'result could be expected to be a normalisation of relations between western and Eastern Europe'.[25] Yet the US goal was now 'to prevent World War III ... we learned the lessons of World War II, but no one is going to learn any lessons from World War III ... the problem is to prevent World War III before it comes about'.[26] Bonn could no longer be allowed to obstruct détente with its insistence on reunification as the priority goal. Rusk advised George C. McGhee that there was a 'serious conflict' between the needs of German electoral calculations and 'sober international realities'. The 'illusion' that Germany could be restored in its 1937 or 1938 dimensions was no longer one that the West could indulge. Rusk was 'deeply concerned' as to whether the Western Alliance could accept the 'historical responsibility' on this matter, now the subject of West Germany's unilateral demands. The problem, as Rusk saw it, was that Bonn's unwillingness to face up to these issues 'lends an air of unreality to their proposals ... [i]t is no concession for the Federal Republic to abandon what it does not have. I know of no other country in the world which would support the frontiers of 1937'.[27] A State Department Policy Planning Council paper from 1965 argued that the Federal Republic would need 'at some point ... to make a cleancut statement recognizing Poland's present western frontier ... It is fantasy to pretend that this 'concession' can be held out as a bargaining counter in some eventual negotiation on a final settlement'.[28] Nor was this simply private grumbling: Rusk warned Schröder that electoral manoeuvring over the eastern frontiers of Germany prior to the 1965 election was highly undesirable.[29] Rusk's position reveals the extent to which key American policy-makers now recognised that, in order to achieve a real lessening of tension in Europe, the West German government would have to modify its position.

Rusk told Michael Stewart that Bonn's desire for an initiative on reunification could go nowhere without movement on the issues of borders and security. Stewart stated bluntly that Bonn's policy was dictated by the impending national elections and the increasing success of the GDR's drive for recognition (notably with regard to the UAR). In response to Rusk's assertion that the West German elections would bring the question of the eastern frontiers to the fore, Stewart was absolutely emphatic in making the following points. First, there would be no reunification of Germany without Soviet assent; second, there was no chance of Germany recovering any of its territories and Bonn should be completely aware of that; and, third, what was required was a reunified Germany within present borders.[30] The British could now afford to be blunt, as it was clear that with American energies focused increasingly on the Cold War in Asia: the West German refusal to recognise the status quo could not be allowed to continue to destabilise Europe.

Implacable foe: the enduring rigidity of Soviet policy on Germany

The USSR now desired a settlement of matters in Europe because of worsening relations with China.[31] This was reflected in policy after the fall of Khrushchev in 1964,[32] as the USSR's primary objective had shifted from the neutralisation of all Germany to entrenching the status quo in Europe. Michael Stewart told his French counterpart that the Soviet Union desired the recognition of the intra-German border, effectively ensuring that the GDR and the FRG would now become responsible for reunification.[33] Erhard told Roberts in February 1965 that his government had no illusions about the prospects of persuading the Soviets to discuss German reunification seriously. Indeed, the Chancellor believed the Soviet position on Germany had hardened since

Khrushchev's fall, as the Soviet Union wished to strengthen the position of the GDR in uncommitted countries.[34] Faced with such deadlock in Europe, Wilson hoped that he could use his influence to soften Moscow's harsh attitude.[35]

Wilson was keen to continue his long-standing relationship with Moscow, although he was very aware of the Soviet obsession with Germany.[36] Gordon Walker confirmed this to be the case when a he received a Soviet delegation towards the end of 1964.[37] Michael Stewart similarly recalled that 'It was natural that ... the Russians should be suspicious of Germany, though they were inclined to use fear of Germany as an excuse for refusing to do anything they did not want to do'.[38] Gromyko told Wilson that Germany remained the first and most important question in European security, and that the Bonn government had a very 'unrealistic' view of the 'unsettled' business of the Second World War. Wilson retorted that there were many separate German questions, namely rearmament, Berlin, and German reunification. In stating that Britain had nothing to propose on reunification, Wilson effectively told Gromyko that the West was content to see the German Question removed from the agenda (although Stewart stressed that this would not mean the recognition of the GDR).[39] Soviet Premier Alexei Kosygin impressed again upon the British that, whatever Washington's interests, Germany, not Vietnam, remained the main bone of East–West contention. The Soviets thus proved duly unrelenting on the issue of Germany, and Stewart cautioned Wilson in October 1965 that his proposed visit to Moscow was likely to consist of a series of lectures on West German 'revanchism'.[40]

In Moscow, Wilson assured his hosts that Bonn regarded reunification as a long-term aspiration and was committed to peace in Europe. Furthermore, Britain was firmly against the West German possession of nuclear weapons. This did not satisfy the Soviets, and Wilson found himself facing demands that the FRG, if it genuinely required peace, must recognise the status quo and the GDR.[41] Yet there was little prospect of a rapprochement between Bonn and the East Europeans. Indeed, the satellites, alarmed that the Sino-Soviet dispute would cause Moscow to make an arrangement with Bonn, only stiffened their resistance to Schröder's overtures.[42]

The decision to allow Bonn to set the pace for détente

The Wilson government accepted that Schröder was at least attempting to ease tension with the Soviet bloc (and this sympathy was heightened by having encountered Soviet intransigence first-hand). Thus, West German caution was not dismissed out of hand in London[43] as Moscow continued to try and utilise bilateral diplomacy to highlight differences between Bonn and its allies on the German question.[44] The British government felt that it could neither desert Bonn nor force its hand, as Stewart made clear:

The position of the [West] German Government is crucial in any move towards ... *détente* in Europe because German territory is bound to be involved ... not even the United States, can now coerce the Germans into accepting arrangements that they do not want[45] ... Given German influence in Washington and NATO, any British initiative in the realm of European security is unlikely to prosper unless it has the support of the Government in Bonn ... therefore [we should take] the Germans more into our confidence on arms control and disarmament matters ... [Furthermore] our influence in Washington is bound to be affected to an important degree by our standing in Bonn.[46]

Of course, while the decision to move at the pace on détente dictated by Bonn was likely to reduce speed to that of the 'slowest ship in the convoy', at least now the convoy might reach its destination. This was the result of two factors. First, the British had little choice, given the weight of West German power vis-à-vis the UK.[47] Second, there was an earnest belief in London that the West Germans had irrevocably embarked upon a more moderate foreign policy.[48] Sir Frank Roberts asserted that 'most thinking Germans have surrendered any lingering thought of reunification as the precondition for better relations with the East, and now accept that the two processes must be concurrent and indeed that the latter might have to come first'. However, there were still fundamental obstacles in the path of West German reconciliation with the East. Of these, the Oder–Neiße line and the Hallstein Doctrine were the most notable. However, 'As things stand, it is unfortunately good electoral tactics here to feed the illusions on which informed opinion in Germany still partly subsists'.[49]

The German Question, the nuclear question

The ponderous nature of the West German acceptance of détente meant that Britain continued to rail against Bonn's policies when they impinged upon areas of vital British interest. For example, in continuing to place reunification before détente, the FRG was very uneasy about signing a non-proliferation agreement, because if the GDR did so too it would undermine Bonn's claim to 'sole legitimacy'.[50] Wilson told Rusk in January 1965 that the Germans must understand that reunification could only come about at the *end* of any process of détente,[51] and in July 1965 Wilson and Johnson agreed that the West German desire to link progress on reunification with proliferation was to be discouraged.[52] The whole issue of nuclear weapons remained a sensitive area in Anglo-German relations. The irritation in the Western Alliance caused by the concerted (and successful) British campaign against the Multilateral Force (MLF) was considerable.[53] In Bonn, this campaign looked to be motivated by anti-German sentiment, especially as Wilson had stated in 1963 'We are completely, utterly and unequivocally opposed now and in all circumstances, to any suggestion that Germany ... directly or indirectly, should have its finger on the nuclear trigger'.[54] In office, Wilson continued to be an active opponent of West German acquisition of nuclear weapons, confiding to de Gaulle his sympathy with the Soviet fear of the acquisition of nuclear weapons by Bonn.[55] On 22 February 1966, at a press conference in Moscow, Wilson went so far as to state: 'No government of which I am head will ever agree to a German finger on the nuclear trigger.' This, he hoped, would, 'shake [the Soviets of] their long-established and understandable German obsession'.[56] Of course, such statements did his image little good in Bonn.

British policy-makers remained wary of the 'Gaullist' faction in the West German government, which was particularly strong in the CSU. In 1965 Dr Jäger, Chairman of the *Bundestag* Defence Committee, 'saw no reason to declare any renunciation of nuclear weapons ... until and unless there was decisive progress over Germany's security or over the solution of the German problem'. Franz Josef Strauß criticised Western policy on Berlin and called for European political action to achieve German unity.[57] The West German government remained insistent on bringing the question of reunification into all areas of Western policy, and in November 1965 Erhard declared that 'If the Soviet Union would grant ... the reunification of our people, it would remove a decisive impediment to a lasting *détente* between East and West'.[58] At the CDU Conference that same month, Schröder stated that the Federal Republic must persuade Moscow that reunification was a requisite for détente, and in the meantime Eastern policy would be confined to trade and cultural exchanges.[59]

The perennial problem of the Hallstein Doctrine

From a British perspective, the Hallstein Doctrine was an increasingly unwieldy instrument of policy,[60] and Michael Stewart agreed with the Yugoslavs that the doctrine was an anachronism.[61] While viewing the doctrine as a global headache (as the FRG even resorted to economic 'bribes' to forestall states' recognition of the GDR),[62] the British could see no prospect, due to domestic and electoral pressures, of its modification.[63] Wilson recounts that in March 1965 Erhard was preoccupied with the problem of the status of the GDR as a number of Arab states, in retaliation for Bonn's establishment of relations with Israel, had recognised the GDR, 'with all that meant for Bonn under the inhibiting Hallstein Doctrine'.[64] In actual fact, Erhard told Wilson in strict confidence that the Federal Republic was considering a fresh diplomatic initiative towards the states of Eastern Europe. This would aim at undermining the dependence of the satellites upon the Soviet Union, although Wilson thought that the Soviets would be hostile and enquired as to the implications for the Hallstein Doctrine. Erhard stated that the Eastern bloc would be a special case, and the existence of two 'German' embassies side-by-side elsewhere in the world was simply not an option. Wilson was encouraging over the potential improvement in East–West relations, stating that these methods would be beneficial provided West Germany was to remain firmly in the NATO camp.[65] Schröder conceded the decreased utility of the Hallstein Doctrine to Wilson a year later, when the Foreign Minister admitted that the severing of relations with the Arab states had only allowed the Soviet Union to increase its influence. The West German government now desired to resurrect relations with these states before establishing relations with Eastern Europe. In tackling the latter, Schröder specifically asked if Britain could use its global influence to try and limit the amount of international recognition accorded the GDR, and George Brown (the new Foreign Secretary) and Wilson duly agreed.[66] This was a significant development. By recognising that the use of the Hallstein Doctrine against the Arab states had only aided the USSR, Bonn was placing its commitment to the Western Alliance above its desire for reunification.

The persistent irritant: the GDR

The Labour Party had advocated the de facto recognition of the GDR as policy since 1961, and subsequent events only seemed to confirm the necessity of this.[67] But, in government, the temptation to act was resisted, so as to avoid a major schism with Bonn,[68] and Wilson publicly affirmed the FRG's right to speak for all Germans in Berlin at the outset of 1965.[69] However, the ultra-defensive, near-paranoid attitude of the FRG on this issue was revealed by Bonn's reaction to the GDR's application to join the UN[70] (causing the American, British and French governments to issue a tripartite declaration affirming that they recognised the FRG as the sole legitimate government of Germany).[71] Yet, in petitioning its allies to keep the GDR out of the UN, the FRG allowed itself no prospect of membership either. Continued exclusion from the UN made West Germany aware that the 'political dwarf' status was increasingly disproportionate to the tag of 'economic giant'.[72] Surely, reasoned Bonn's allies, the West would benefit more than the East if both Germanies were represented at the UN?

Given Bonn's absolutist position, the GDR now saw that the international situation was moving in its direction, and the Olympic movement became the focus of its struggle.[73] Pankow, backed by the Soviet Union,[74] had long demanded two German teams, while Bonn made strenuous attempts to resist the drift towards the ending of a unitary German status in the Olympic movement. The prospects for the GDR's campaign for recognition in political, cultural and sporting spheres was becoming ever more propitious. Indicative of this, the International Olympic Committee announced on 8 October 1965 that from 1968 onwards two German teams would be allowed to compete at the Olympics. This was a slap in the face for Bonn, and was taken by Pankow and Moscow as a sign that the West was beginning to accept the need for the de facto recognition of the GDR.[75] The US embassy in Bonn noted that 'The FRG will not be able to disguise the setback which the Madrid decision represents ... acceptance of separate East German Olympic membership will seem a big step towards international recognition of the GDR, even though the decision has no legal significance'.[76] Willi Daume, the FRG's Olympic chief, warned the Federal government that they would be seen as the 'last cold warriors' if they demanded a continued boycott of the GDR. In the light of this, Bonn privately prepared 'retreat positions' for the eventuality of full East German representation in international sport.[77] The recognition of the GDR by the IOC was a bitter blow for the Federal Republic, and one that it had sought to fight to the bitter end by means of diplomacy.[78] From London's perspective, the GDR, for a 'non-existent' state, was absorbing an increasingly disproportionate amount of time in West German policy. This was hardly sustainable policy in the long run. *The Times* noted that 'until the two Germanies find some way of speaking to each other more freely and reducing the political, economic, and cultural gap between them, reunification is not only remote, but impossible'.[79]

British trade with Eastern Europe; Schröder's *Osthandel*

Germany had a long history of large-scale trade with the East, and it was therefore perhaps inevitable that trade was seen as affording the initial openings in any new German policy in that direction. In addition, prior to the expansion of East–West trade in the détente era, Britain's trade with Poland, for instance, compared favourably with that of other Western countries.[80] Ironically, therefore, British advocacy of East–West trade, if successful, meant that it was West Germany that stood to benefit most, by virtue of geography, history and economic strength. Trade with the Eastern bloc would hopefully facilitate détente whilst strengthening the British economy. In Opposition, Patrick Gordon Walker had advocated increasing economic and political links with Eastern Europe.[81] This was, Gordon Walker informed Rusk, one of the few areas in which Britain could take the initiative.[82] The perception of an explicitly political role for trade with Eastern Europe was shared by the Foreign Office.[83] Inevitably, British pursuit of trade with the Soviet bloc caused some disquiet in the FRG.[84] This was especially the case with regard to trade with the GDR.[85]

At the inception of the Wilson government, Britain maintained a discriminatory quota on imports from Eastern Europe (except Yugoslavia). However, quotas for certain industrial goods had been removed from Poland, Czechoslovakia and Hungary in 1964. It was also agreed that Poland could become an associate member during the Kennedy Round of 1967. Given that Yugoslavia was already an associate member of the General Agreement on Tariffs and Trade (GATT), and Czechoslovakia a dormant member, the Foreign Office saw little reason not to bring in

Bulgaria, Romania and Hungary as well.[86] Michael Stewart believed that 'The chief help we could give [the satellites] ... was to increase our trade, so that they would be less dependent on the eastern bloc'.[87] Consequently, great efforts were made by the Wilson government to expand trade and other contacts with Eastern Europe (though rather less so with the USSR).[88] Although the potential for trade with the Eastern bloc does seem to have been somewhat overstated,[89] the political advantages were deemed such so as to make the effort worthwhile.[90] Nevertheless, British trade with Eastern Europe lacked the inherently political dimension of its West German equivalent, as Bonn hoped to progress from questions of trade to a substantive political agenda.[91]

Erhard and Schröder had an inflated belief in the utility of the Mark as a political weapon (Brandt later recalled that Chancellor Erhard had repeatedly asked him how much the USSR would want for the GDR).[92] On occasion, it appeared to London that West German trade overtures were so overtly political as to virtually relegate their economic rationale to the incidental. When *Krupps* was discussing investment in Poland, it sought the views of the refugee organisations as to the best locations politically. The Poles sought to compel *Krupps* to invest in the place where they said labour was plentiful – i.e. western Poland. This was, of course, formerly German land, and so political a location as to be unacceptable to the West Germans.[93]

Similarly, the Soviet Union was willing to engage in trade with the FRG but determined not to allow Bonn to utilise it for political ends, and Khrushchev warned of Western trade 'policies ... trying to set some socialist countries against others'.[94] *Isvestiya* attacked Western attempts to expand contacts with Eastern Europe via 'bridge-building'[95] as one aspect of an aggressive NATO policy.[96] It was noted in London that 'This reflects the real Soviet concern about the cohesion of the bloc, a concern which outweighs the tactical need to speak approvingly of closer relations between bloc countries and the West'.[97] Julian Bullard, First Secretary in the Bonn embassy, noted that the USSR was willing to negotiate over trade 'while still continuing their very weighty criticisms of the Federal Republic in the foreign policy field'.[98] Berlin, as ever, was a seemingly insurmountable obstacle. Schröder confessed that the Soviets were indeed driving a hard bargain over trade and the issue of Berlin.[99] Yet intransigence was often mutual. The Head of Chancery in Bonn reported that the West Germans would rather forgo a

> Czech–German Agreement ... than [conclude] one that did not include Berlin; they would say that the disadvantage of concluding an agreement supporting the Communist 'three Germanies' theory would outweigh any possible gain from having a trade delegation in Prague, especially if it is unable to do no more towards improving relations than the existing trade delegations in other East European capitals.[100]

Since there were no real economic incentives for West German trade with the Soviet bloc, Bonn refused to make concessions on political matters in order to conclude commercial agreements. This, of course, was grist to the mill of those who had little interest in reconciliation with the East. The *BdV*'s Wenzel Jaksch stated in Munich that the FRG had no need to run after Czech trade, as 'It is more important for Germany's foreign policy to help Britain ... into the EEC than to support Romania's struggle for economic independence'.[101] Despite this, Schröder believed that it was important for the Western Alliance to aid the satellites to move away from Moscow. As early as June 1963, the FRG had tried (and failed) to get the NATO Economic Council to adopt a common restrictive stance on the question of long-term credits to the USSR. To Bonn's alarm, while refusing long-term credits for the USSR as being 'development assistance', British banks provided $278 million on fifteen-year terms in 1964. Bonn seemed powerless to prevent Western capital's collaboration with state planning, and in November 1964 a CDU statement recognised that if the FRG continued its credit policy, 'it would be the only [Western] state to lose its previous position in trade with the USSR. It would thereby expose itself to the Soviet Union in many ways which could be prejudicial to the political interests of the Federal Republic.'[102] Subsequently, the FRG began underwriting export contracts to the Soviet bloc for periods of up to eight years.[103] Nevertheless, Erhard expressed concern that certain of the allies had chosen to extend credits to the 'Soviet zone'.[104] Following his re-election in 1965, he told the *Bundestag* that 'Co-ordination of trade and credit policy towards the eastern *bloc* is a common interest of "peaceful political strategy" for western industrialised countries'.[105]

Yet Britain, like the FRG, was also vulnerable to its allies' actions regarding its areas of vital interest, and London was alarmed that Bonn seemed amongst the least enthusiastic of its allies in enforcing sanctions against Rhodesia.[106] Sir Frank Roberts highlighted the fact that the West Germans expected a *quid pro quo* on policy towards East Germany, given their support for British sanctions against the Smith regime in Rhodesia.[107] With such considerations in mind, Wilson personally assured Erhard that he accepted that inter-German trade was not regarded by Britain as international trade, but, rather, more like trade between England and Scotland.[108] This ensured West German co-operation on the issue of Rhodesian sanctions.[109] As ever, British co-operation with West German policy was at its best when London could measure the tangible benefit to itself.

While Bonn remained highly sensitive to Western trade with the GDR,[110] Gordon Walker asserted that the Wilson government regarded British trade with the GDR as a 'vital national interest'.[111] In any case, whatever Bonn's objections, Whitehall highlighted the fact that West Germany dominated Western trade with the GDR (see Table 5.1).

The Foreign Office's limited deference to West German sensibilities

Table 5.1 British trade with the GDR as compared with the FRG and France (£ million)[112]

	UK imports	UK exports	FRG imports	FRG exports	France imports	France exports
1962	6.6	7.2	82.4	76.9	3.1	5.7
1963	7.5	6.9	92.0	77.4	4.5	6.5
1964	10.3	5.0	92.6	103.3	5.1	9.5
1965	12.0	8.1	99.3	99.3	4.8	24.5

over the GDR was not shared by other government departments: on 3 January 1966, the Board of Trade advised the Foreign Office that it saw no need for the British to base their trade on any harmful de facto recognition of East Germany, which was viewed by the Board as a country no different from Czechoslovakia or Poland.[113] The Board of Trade harboured a 'grave suspicion that the Germans were using political arguments to justify a commercial end . . . We are not convinced by the German political arguments'.[114] The Foreign Office thus found itself caught between the Board of Trade and the demands of the West German government. The Board of Trade was told that to extend long-term credits to the GDR would be taken by the FRG as 'implying a very unwelcome change in our policy towards East Germany. Quite apart from broader considerations, it is not in our interest to antagonise the West Germans in this field at a time when we are resisting their demands to limit export credits to East Germany.'[115]

Against this, British industry was already complaining that it was at a disadvantage in trade with the GDR vis-à-vis the FRG.[116] Therefore, Bonn should be aware that any change in existing British policy would be blamed on the FRG leading 'to an increase in the number of those who favour a less restrictive British attitude to East Germany', thereby furthering Ulbricht's cause.[117] An uneasy Anglo-German compromise was reached, although in reality the issue could not be addressed until the FRG accepted the existence of the GDR.[118]

Wilson, West Germany and the EEC

The Wilson government's attitude towards the prospects for the second British application to join the EEC in 1966–7 relied heavily on the hope that the more sympathetic attitude of the post-Adenauer FRG could be utilised to good effect.[119] It was certainly true that the Federal government and the SPD leadership welcomed the announcement by Wilson in November 1966 that 'soundings' were to begin with a view to a second British application to join the EEC.[120] However, significant obstacles remained. These included disputes over trade with the GDR, and the omnipresent disagreements about offset payments for the BAOR (which only heightened West German awareness of Britain's economic plight).[121]

Again, the Germans insisted on quid pro quo. When George Brown met Schröder in November 1966, the latter stated that it should be understood that Bonn did not regard trade with the GDR as in any way important economically, but rather as a means of maintaining an internal link between the two parts of Germany. For Bonn, economic and trading relations with the GDR were therefore a political and not a commercial matter. Schröder proceeded to make it clear that if the United Kingdom desisted from extending five-year trade credits to the GDR (which the West Germans' EEC partners had already agreed to do), then Bonn would strongly press the British case for entry in to the EEC.[122] In his memoirs, Sir Frank Roberts makes explicit the link between the EEC, East–West relations and the development of Anglo-German relations:

> At [Anglo-German] Königswinter [Conference] meetings throughout the Sixties, the main thrust of the German participants was to press the British ... to maintain their determination to join the Community, while the main thrust of the British was that the Germans should ... repeat in the Soviet Union and Eastern Europe their successful policy of reconciliation in the West.[123]

The situation was hardly helped by the fact that Wilson's attitude to the EEC was initially vague in the extreme. In Paris in April 1965, he declared that 'Personally the Common Market is of no interest to me'.[124] Wilson's biographer, Philip Ziegler, asserts that the first two years of the Wilson government were part of the process of realising there could be no halfway house and that the British would be forced to join the EEC. Following the March 1966 election victory, Wilson seems to have favoured enhancing trade links between EFTA and the EEC.[125] Although, in May 1966, Erhard said that he did not think the time was right for British entry to the EEC, Wilson took this in his stride and calmly expressed a willingness to enter negotiations for entry if the chance presented itself.[126] Traumatic Commonwealth conferences and EFTA relations in 1966 caused Wilson to look more favourably on British links with the EEC[127] and, significantly, the staunch pro-European George Brown was appointed as Foreign Secretary in July 1966.[128] Brown held that only the unification of Europe could create the conditions for German reunification, as the USSR would never agree to reunify Germany if it retained the ability to strike out on its own: 'A politically united Europe ... [was] the only chance for the Eastern European countries to free themselves from close control by Russia'.[129] The Minister of Housing, Richard Crossman, seeing that Brown (and Stewart) had applied intense pressure on Wilson for EEC entry, noted that: 'As [Wilson] sees it, the difficulties of staying outside Europe and surviving as an independent power are very great compared with entering on the right conditions'.[130] By 1967, Wilson was arguing that he was 'convinced that if Britain is a member of a united European community our chance of achieving [East–West détente] will be immeasurably greater'.[131]

The enduring problem of the Oder–Neiße line

Any sign of Western policy shifts on the German Question were eagerly scrutinised in the Soviet bloc, and the Poles especially went to extreme lengths to encourage the West to accept the rectitude of their position.[132] The New York-based Polish–American Congress typically warned President Johnson that 'Reluctance on the part of the United States to acknowledge the Odra–Nysa border leaves the Polish people with only the Soviet Union as a major supporter of their present western boundaries'.[133] The unyielding demand for the recognition of the Oder–Neiße line was the Warsaw regime's ace in its deck of nationalist cards,[134] and Bonn's obstructionism was anathema to many in the US policy-making elite. The British hoped to take advantage of this. Having made the 1962 assurance to the Poles, London now aimed to encourage Washington to prevail upon Bonn to adopt a more 'realistic' attitude towards the Oder–Neiße line.[135]

By the mid-1960s, the United States, while loath to offend West German sensibilities, was equally averse to endorsing the continued validity of the *Reich* borders of 1937.[136] A brutally frank memo asserted that while the United States and Britain had originally named the Oder–Neiße line as being 'merely provisional' by 1950, two states *'were tacitly accepting the line for the purposes of negotiating the reunification of Germany'*. At Berlin in 1954, and Geneva in 1955 and 1959, in Western proposals for reunification 'no mention was made of territory east of the Oder–Neisse line'. Furthermore, since 1950 no official US statement had made reference to returning any of the lost territories to Germany

> At the time of Potsdam and Yalta, the intent of the United States was to give Poland *substantially* the German territory east of the Oder–Neisse line ... After 1950, due to the onset of the Cold War and our special relationship with the new Federal Republic we deliberately avoided mention in our public statements of our agreement to substantial Polish accession of territory in the West.

The memo admitted that '[d]espite the our bargaining position taken by the Germans on the borders of 1937 as well as [our] formal commitment' to the provisional nature of Polish administration of the territories, all parties 'know full well that the western frontiers of Poland will never be rolled back without involving the world in war'. To endorse the West German position on 'self-determination' would imply raise the 'fearsome hobgoblin' of nine million Germans wishing to return to their '*Heimat*'. Against this, a confirmation the status quo would damage the Federal Republic in 'one of its most sensitive political issues.' US policy had been duplicitous:

Thus we are currently engaged in trying to talk out of both sides of our mouth at the same time. Although we are irritated by occasional FRG references to the alleged sanctity of the German frontiers of December 31, 1937, we are most reluctant to set the matter straight by publicly reminding them of our commitment to the ultimate cession of large chunks of pre-war German territory which the Poles now occupy.

Secretary Rusk was advised to tell the West German government that, while the United States appreciated

[T]he political delicacy with which the territorial question must be handled in the forthcoming political campaign, repeated references to the 1937 German boundaries are beginning to cast doubt on our own post-war commitments with respect to the German–Polish frontier, and that we might be compelled to clarify our position by means of a public statement.[137]

Rusk endorsed this position, noting that the US must reaffirm its record on these matters since 1945 and 'not just that piece of it which gives encouragement to inflammatory German pretensions which it is not our policy to support'.[138] Thus, the Byrnes speech of 1946, the Western repudiation of the Görlitz Treaty in 1950, the final act of the London Conference of 1954, and the Allied positions at Geneva of 1955 and 1959 were, by the admission of the State Department itself, Cold War rhetorical devices. If Bonn had not been 'ground' between the 'millstones' of Potsdam as Adenauer had feared, it was now to be 'squeezed' by the American perception of the dictates of Alliance policy.

Sensitive to the changing (and increasingly disadvantageous) international climate, Bonn realised that it had to act to prevent its losing the initiative entirely. To this end, Schröder informed Gordon Walker in November 1964 that Bonn was thinking of a non-aggression pact with Poland, renouncing the forcible change of borders. However, the British knew (as did, in all likelihood, Schröder) that this was not enough for the Poles.[139] It was noted that 'suspicion and fear of West Germany in Poland was mainly the result of the Polish Government's policy of deliberately fostering these attitudes in order to distract attention away from the economic and political stagnation in Poland itself'.[140] Despite this, the British were exasperated when West German officials asserted that fear of Germany in Poland was an entirely Communist construct. The British embassy in Bonn reported that the negative attitude of the East Europeans meant that while West German policy was self-righteous, it was no less so than that of the Czechs and the Poles: 'I am not denying that the Germans are often thick-skinned and insensitive, or that this makes them blind to anti-German feeling in Eastern Europe; but their view that this feeling is deliberately fostered by the East European governments surely has much truth in it.'[141]

The logic in Bonn was simple: by portraying the Polish Communists as implacable enemies *per se*, their demands for the recognition of their western border could be dismissed as a tactical device designed to sow discord between Bonn and its allies. In reality, the issue of the Oder–Neiße line remained both the most emotive and the most intractable problem associated with Bonn's Eastern policy. The Polish ambassador told Sir Paul Gore-Booth that although he saw the logic in the German position, he rather wished that Bonn would recognise the Oder–Neiße line in advance of reunification – if only to enhance Polish security.[142] Despite the fact that the Labour Party had been a strong advocate of the recognition of the Oder–Neiße line prior to 1964,[143] it was unwilling to make the running itself. Nor had Polish hope on this matter appeared unfounded. The Labour Conference of 1961 had voted to recognise the line after Gaitskell made a speech identifying this as a necessity that 'most reasonable Germans themselves understand'.[144] Wilson endorsed this position at Warsaw airport in 1963, stating 'there is no difference on this matter between the attitude of the Polish government and the Labour Party'.[145]

It was widely recognised in London that Poland, in addition to security guarantees, sought to make trouble by trying to get the British publicly to disavow their adherence to Bonn's policy of non-recognition of the Oder–Neiße frontier. Yet, given the Labour Party's recent history, it was hardly surprising when, in September 1965, Polish Foreign Minister Adam Rapacki tried to get Michael Stewart to make public the 1962 assurance on the Oder–Neiße line. Stewart rebutted Rapacki's assertion that to do so would serve further to undermine the hope of 'revanchists' in the Federal Republic, warning that any publicity would only fuel the revanchists against the moderates.[146] The British had made the 1962 assurance on the Oder–Neiße line on the understanding that it would remain confidential, and this logic held true three years later.[147] The secret guarantee of 1962 was as far as the Wilson government intended to go on the matter. Indeed, it was the furthest they could go without causing an open rupture with Bonn. Since de Gaulle had already effectively recognised the Oder–Neiße line in 1959, British recognition would be a major blow to the West German government.[148] Indeed, the danger of Britain doing so was demonstrated when the French made a reference to the Oder–Neiße line in a communiqué following a visit to Paris by Cyrankiewicz.[149] The French had pressed ahead with the offending reference despite the pleadings of the government in Bonn and an outcry in the West German press.[150] In February 1966, de Gaulle stated unequivocally that German reunification 'can only take place on condition that the present borders, especially those with Poland as well as those with Czechoslovakia, are honoured'.[151] The Erhard government became increasingly exasperated at such statements that were, as they saw it, part-and-parcel of de Gaulle's unpredictable, knee-jerk, opportunist diplomacy.

British policy had achieved its aim of assuaging Polish fears while the West Germans prepared themselves to finally recognise the loss of the eastern territories. As it stood, Bonn's 'revisionist' position precluded a viable long-term European security system. In March 1966, Wilson's Private Secretary, J. Oliver Wright, bluntly informed the West German ambassador that 'I said I thought it was really for the Federal Republic to make up their minds where their true interest lay, choose, and then come to their allies for support'.[152] This was certainly true, and, for Bonn, difficult choices would have to be made sooner rather then later.[153] Fortunately, opinion within the Federal Republic was increasingly flexible. Encouragingly, from the British perspective, Blankenhorn conceded privately to Wright that Bonn's stance on the 1937 frontiers was too formalist and legalistic, and that it would be better to abandon it. This could only be done over time, and the German lamented Adenauer's failure to prepare opinion in the FRG for a new look at these questions. It would have been much easier in 1955 than it was 'today' (in 1966), although on a non-official level a number of organisations had taken up realistic positions with regard to the eastern territories.[154]

Blankenhorn's thinking was a recognition that the question of the 'eastern territories' was evolving to the disadvantage of West Germany. The Foreign Office Minister, Lord Lennox, saw the Polish assent for 42,000 West German exit visas as being motivated by unemployment and a desire to clear the Oder–Neiße territories of its remaining Germans. The fact that, constitutionally, the FRG was bound to accept ethnic Germans as resident citizens meant that 'one corollary is that the Germans are evidently acquiescing in this whittling away of their stake in the Oder–Neisse territories'.[155] This, combined with shifts in public opinion, caused George Brown to advise Gromyko in May 1966 that the West Germans were adopting a distinctly more relaxed attitude over both the Oder–Neiße territories and the GDR.[156] For their part, the Americans noted that parliamentary debates in Bonn concerning the Oder–Neiße question witnessed even SPD deputies backing the more moderate position of the Erhard government – to the evident consternation of the more right-wing CDU and CSU deputies.[157]

Shifting sands: the German people and the new flexibility

As time passed, the issue of the 'lost territories' slipped down the agenda as a new generation of Germans concerned themselves with matters of a more materialist nature. The Federal Republic now saw a spate of publications arguing that the issue of the eastern territories distracted from the real issues facing the West German state.[158] The new mood was reflected in the writings of prominent intellectuals who advocated a more conciliatory approach to Eastern Europe.[159] Although most of these figures were on the political left, the right was, at least, largely acquiescent in the move towards a new pragmatism. (The evolution of West German public opinion can be seen in the survey depicted in Table 5.2 and Figure 5.1.)

Although the essentials of the Adenauer's policy remained intact, the changing public mood subtly reflected by the Erhard government (following the 1965 election, for instance, Seebohm, the prominent expellee, was almost excluded from the new government).[161] In the FRG, the recognition of the significance of such steps led to fierce attacks by irreconcilable elements – most notably the expellee organisations – on any further dilution of what they saw as basic principles. The British embassy in Bonn noted that 'In particular they [the *BdV*] may be worried by the fact that the Federal Cabinet had … approved the Ministry of Foreign Affair's proposals to pursue its forward policy in Eastern Europe'.[162] When the *Bürgermeister* of Hamburg, Weichmann, visited the USSR, the British embassy in Bonn noted 'an interesting example of German/Soviet contact at a non-Governmental level … symptomatic of the extent to which the new, pragmatic approach to problems of E/W relations has popular support in Germany'.[163] Even Adenauer, now in retirement at the venerable age of ninety, declared at the CDU Congress in the spring of 1966 that: 'Soviet Russia has entered the ranks of people who want peace'.[164]

Table 5.2 'Do you believe we should reconcile ourselves to the present Polish frontier – the Oder–Neiße line – or not?'[160]

	1951	*1956*	*1962*	*1964*	*1967*	*1969*
Yes (%)	8	9	26	22	47	51
No (%)	80	73	50	59	34	32
No opinion (%)	12	19	24	19	19	17

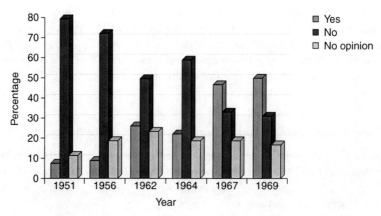

Figure 5.1 'Do you believe we should reconcile ourselves to the present Polish frontier – the Oder–Neiße line – or not?'

When press reports that Federal President Lübke had called for the recognition of the Oder–Neiße line proved to be much exaggerated, the British embassy in Bonn noted with satisfaction 'a welcome trend towards freer thinking even among conservative CDU figures'.[165]

The younger generation, particularly, had little sentiment for the Sudetenland, Danzig or Prussia. This increasingly freed the political parties from their subservience to history.[166] Thus, the FDP joined the SPD in calling for more trade with the GDR.[167] By 1966, the SPD was holding inter-party debates with the SED, calling for the permanent renunciation of the Munich Agreement and moving towards recognition of the Oder–Neiße line and diplomatic relations with Eastern Europe.[168] Public opinion increasingly favoured the removal of the Hallstein Doctrine and the establishment of diplomatic links with the Eastern bloc (tendencies especially strong in FDP and SPD voters).[169] In November 1966, a British despatch from Bonn highlighted the favourable attitude of the West German public to diplomatic relations with Eastern Europe (below).

Unsurprisingly, CDU supporters were more resistant to a change in policy than were those of the FDP/SPD. Significantly, however, it was noted that 'refugees' had a higher 'yes' rating than 'natives' did (65 per cent and 57 per cent respectively).[170] It was apparent to British policy-makers that West German public opinion was, if anything, moving ahead of the Erhard government in its thinking.

Table 5.3 'Should the FRG establish diplomatic relations with Poland, Czecho-slovakia and Hungary, even though those countries maintain relations with the GDR? i.e. Should West Germany abandon the Hallstein Doctrine?'

Yes (%)	59
No (%)	12
No opinion (%)	29

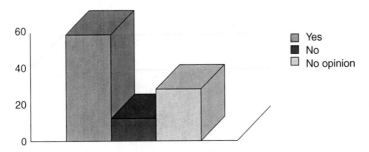

Figure 5.2 'Should the FRG establish diplomatic relations with Poland, Czechoslovakia and Hungary, even though those countries maintain relations with the GDR? i.e. Should West Germany abandon the Hallstein Doctrine?'

The limits of the *Politik der Bewegung*

The Erhard government unveiled a 'Peace Note' on 25 March 1966 which, whilst asserting that Germans should be allowed to decide freely their own political life (*Lebensform*), renounced any 'revisionist' agenda.[171] However, no mention was made of diplomatic relations, the Oder–Neiße line or the GDR. This seemed to many observers to be simply another Jacksch Resolution – a vacuous statement of good intention.[172] Of course, the failure to tackle specifics meant that the Soviet bloc was dismissive in its reaction.[173] Despite this, the note at least demonstrated that the FRG was willing to limit the scope of its activity in Eastern Europe in the interests of achieving a rapprochement, and Michael Stewart advised Wilson that the 'note was encouraging despite some shortcomings in the text'.[174]

On the anniversary of the German invasion of 1939, the Polish Deputy Foreign Minister laid down three pre-conditions for the normalisation of relations with Bonn: first, the recognition of Poland's western frontier; second, the absolute renunciation of direct and indirect access to nuclear arms by the Federal Republic; and third, the recognition of the 'incontrovertible fact of the GDR's existence'.[175] Such demands were recognised by the British embassy in Warsaw as being far beyond what Bonn could then accept.[176] In particular, the demand for the recognition of the GDR was seen as a 'wild hope but not one the Poles really expect [to be] fulfilled'. Furthermore, the Warsaw embassy felt that the Poles were demonstrating solidarity with the GDR, an ally 'to whom no Poles, not even Party members, feel close'. For Warsaw, this had the advantage of being relatively pain-free, whilst simultaneously keeping open the option of establishing diplomatic relations with Bonn.[177]

Poland was determined to keep up the pressure on Bonn, and George Brown was roundly abused in the Polish press for a speech in which he had defended West German foreign policy.[178] It was a familiar scenario as British policy-makers found themselves caught between loyalty to their ally and their attempts to reach out to the Eastern bloc. British relations with Poland, although improving, would be limited so long as West German policy remained in its essentials.[179] The fact of the matter was that the countries of Eastern Europe would not entertain diplomatic relations with Bonn without the latter's prior recognition of the Oder–Neiße line. In Moscow in October 1966, the Soviet bloc agreed upon a common position as the price of diplomatic relations with the Federal Republic. The demands were virtually identical to those made by the Polish Foreign Minister one month earlier, specifically asserting that the West German attempts to split the Communist states had failed.[180] Recognising this, the West German conservative daily *Die Welt* speculated that the Moscow decision was designed, in the immediate place, to prevent Romania from straying too far from the socialist fold in its dealings with Bonn.[181]

The British recognised that Schröder's Eastern policy had been far too overt an attempt to 'divide-and-rule' the satellites. Hence, the Poles and the Czechs, in particular, had adhered to a strong line on relations with Bonn, not least because they feared that Bonn would succeed in its goals if it dealt with the bloc piecemeal.[182] By 1966, the Johnson administration also viewed Bonn's policy as having reached what was termed the *Sackgasse* ('dead-end'). President Johnson, speaking in New York on 7 October 1966, identified three points on which NATO must move forward. These were the modernisation of the Western Alliance, further Western integration, and progress on East–West relations. The President called for the reunification of Germany within a larger European framework, as 'Our task is to achieve a reconciliation with the East – a shift from the narrow concept of coexistence to the broader vision of peaceful engagement'. In reference to the 'sensitive' issue of boundaries, the US government was unequivocally opposed to any changes. Johnson later recalled that, in making the speech,

> I was thinking ... of what was probably the most important unresolved border problem in Europe: the frontier between Poland and Germany ... Without offending our German allies, I wanted the Poles and the Russians to know that we would never resort to force to alter the Oder–Neisse line ... That was the meaning of the carefully chosen words I used in New York, and I was sure that every European from the Atlantic to Moscow understood them.

Signally, Johnson also declared that the US government was absolutely opposed to the spread of nuclear weapons.[183] Aside from the issue of the status of the GDR, Johnson now seemed to accept two of the essential Soviet demands on Germany. In the light of the speech of October 7 – 'particularly [concerning Johnson's] remarks on German reunification and European boundaries' – the US ambassador in Bonn advised Washington as to the best manner in which to realise these objectives. He thus proposed West German recognition of the Oder–Neiße line, the dropping of the concept of *Recht auf Heimat*, and West German acceptance of nuclear non-proliferation. Given the nature of these goals, the subsequent accession of the SPD to power as part of the 'Grand Coalition' (and the installation of Brandt as Foreign Minister in particular) was welcomed, given its 'more reasonable' attitudes to the frontier and nuclear questions.[184]

The fall of Erhard

The fall of Erhard was caused by the economic stagnation after 1965, growing discord within the CDU/CSU, and the disenchantment of his FDP coalition partners over the lack of progress on reunification and the Eastern policy. The FDP resigned from the government on 27 October 1966, and the Chancellor finally departed on 30 November 1966.[185]

The new Chancellor was the CDU's Kurt-Georg Kiesinger, in a CDU/CSU–SPD 'Grand Coalition', with Brandt as the new Foreign Minister. Although economic failings had been the predominant reason for Erhard's demise, Wolfram Hanrieder identifies the inherent inflexibility of the Erhard government's Eastern policy as being its downfall:

> Even a partial modification of Bonn's policy appeared risky ... Because Bonn's diplomacy toward the Soviet bloc held together with logical (although self-defeating) juridical consistency, compromising one part would have compromised the whole. And scrapping one of its essential tenets would have caused the collapse of Bonn's entire legal–political reunification strategy and perhaps entailed a revision of its other foreign policy programs as well.[186]

In Bonn, Roberts noted that 'there was little to show during 1966 for [Schröder's] policy ... of improving relations with Eastern Europe'.[187] Bonn's failure to convert assurances of good intent into concrete measures meant that the East Europeans focused on – and prioritised – the perceived revisionist dimensions of West German policy. The refusal to accept that both blocs accepted the status quo of territory as a starting point in détente meant that West Germany would never achieve any of its objectives peacefully. Since war was never an option, Bonn's objectives would have to change.

High hopes in London: the SPD enters power

Serious modification of West German policy would require an unprecedented domestic consensus. The very nature of the revolutionary changes required meant that, as the German ambassador to London had recognised, 'a 'Grand Coalition' would be a necessary prerequisite for 'significant adjustments' to the *Ostpolitik*.[188] This would involve, inevitably, the SPD – the Party that was making the most positive noises about Eastern policy – and, as early as July 1963, the SPD's Egon Bahr had spoken out in favour of a policy of *Wandel durch Annäherung* ('change through rapprochement').[189] Herbert Wehner, Deputy Co-Chair of SPD, had also predicted to Roberts a grand coalition in the FRG because of 'the realisation that matters of the greatest national importance would face Germany in the near future, which could only be faced by a coalition between the two leading parties'. However, Schröder would not be acceptable as foreign minister from the point of view of the SPD, as 'The foreign political issue on which Schroeder and the S.P.D. failed to agree was his [Schröder's] refusal to contemplate any form of move towards a Peace Treaty'.[190]

The Labour Party welcomed the prospect of SPD participation in government and, in common with the Foreign Office, welcomed the German party's progressive ideas on East–West relations. Indeed, Rusk went so far as to suggest that the Labour Party wanted Erhard to fail so as to pave the way for an SPD government.[191] In July 1965, Roberts reported Wehner's favourable remarks about the UK, his advocacy of close Anglo-German links 'and in particular with the British Labour Party' (as this would not 'do the S.P.D. any harm' in the *Bundestag* election of September 1965).[192] The traditionally excellent relations between the Labour Party and the SPD were in stark contrast to the businesslike, but cool, relations between the Wilson government and the CDU/CSU.[193] The Labour Party noted favourably the SPD's 'Eight Point Programme' of 8 November 1966, welcoming SPD support for British entry into the EEC, its anti-nuclear pledge and the intention to seek better relations with Eastern Europe. In the latter category the SPD had the stated aims of diplomatic relations, the renunciation of the Munich Agreement, and a desire to finalise matters via a peace treaty.[194] The prospect of such developments gave the British great hopes for the future. And while George Brown gave a written answer to a question on the Oder–Neiße line in the Commons in December 1966, stating that this question could only be settled by a peace treaty,[195] it was the first time in over a decade that a British Foreign Secretary could actually have some confidence that his answer on this issue was something other than a stonewalling exercise.

Brandt was certainly prepared to adopt a more radical *Ostpolitik* than Schröder ever had.[196] As early as 1962, Brandt had declared 'The crucial task of German foreign policy is of entering a new relationship with the Great Power in the East'.[197] Further, Brandt would face much less opposition on the *Ostpolitik* than had his predecessor from within his own government, as the 'Grand Coalition' had considerably weakened the position of the CSU.[198] Sir Frank Roberts reported on 1 January 1967 that 'the movement begun by Schröder towards more normal relations with Eastern Europe should be stimulated by the entry of the SPD into the Government'.[199] Brandt believed that the time had come for the FRG to play a more positive and flexible role in East–West relations. Brandt sought breakthroughs with Hungary, Czechoslovakia and Romania, as the current stalemate, he believed, profited only the GDR. Despite this, Brandt made it clear that the elimination of the GDR was not a pre-condition for Bonn's establishing diplomatic links with Eastern Europe.[200] Any such intention would have instantly condemned Brandt's policies to failure, and would have been inconsistent with his acceptance of the notion that reunification could not precede détente. In January 1967, Brandt stated that 'We will attempt to insert ourselves into the policy of détente. This is a precondition for progress on the German Question'.[201] This was a crucial point, and one that the British had long seen as a fundamental requirement for détente.

Coming to terms with 'the past that will not pass away'

Chancellor Kiesinger's speech to the *Bundestag* on 13 December 1966 heralded the beginning of a major departure in Bonn's policy. The West German government finally seemed to accept that it would have to make concessions in order to achieve substantive progress on political issues.

> The Federal Government condemns the policy of Hitler which aimed at the destruction of the Czechoslovak State. It subscribes to the view that the Munich Agreement, which came about under duress is no longer valid. At the same time, problems exist which still require a solution, as for example [the] question of nationality law.
>
> Where the initiation of contacts [between] authorities of the Federal Republic and the other part of Germany is necessary ... this does not mean any recognition of a second German State. We will handle these contacts in each case so that world opinion cannot gain the impression that we are abandoning our legal standpoint.

Roberts believed that, while it was impossible to forecast Soviet bloc reaction, the statement was particularly significant because

> *for the first time a Federal Government has stated without any qualification that the Munich agreement is no longer valid*[202] and no longer has any territorial significance ... [Furthermore] the Federal Government has at last included a direct condemnation of the Agreement, or at least of Hitler's motives and methods in concluding it.[203]

The Foreign Office advised Wilson that the Kiesinger statement represented a distinct step forward, and 'it is fair to say that this is, at least in part, due to the presence of the S.P.D. in the Federal Govt. This was one of the points in the policy programme [that] they declared before joining the coalition.'[204] Furthermore, the Kiesinger speech signalled 'a distinctly more forthcoming German policy. The Federal Government is readier than its predecessor to admit that reunification must be a long-term process resulting from *détente* rather than an essential pre-condition of *détente*.'[205]

Roberts reported at the start of 1967 that the coalition 'has introduced a new and more conciliatory tone into its foreign policy declarations towards western friends and eastern opponents alike'.[206] The Wilson government could now more easily defend the FRG from charges of revanchism (although the Nazi past of the new Chancellor provided yet more ammunition for the Soviet bloc).[207] When, in February 1967, Poland's Adam Rapacki complained to George Brown that West Germany still failed to recognise the Oder–Neiße line, the Foreign Secretary retorted that Poland already had the reality of that frontier. What more did the Poles want? Brown concluded that West Germany was uninterested in revision, and 'carp[ing]' would only undermine the good work that the Grand Coalition was just beginning.[208] Signally, the FRG undertook the revolutionary step of establishing diplomatic relations with Romania in January 1967,[209] a step Wilson later hailed as the effective renunciation of the Hallstein Doctrine and a great breakthrough.[210] Accepting that Germany disunity and the GDR would not go away were intensely difficult steps for the West German state to take,[211] but in establishing relations with a state that maintained relations with the GDR, Bonn was taking a major step towards its 'normalisation' internationally. It would be a slow process but, as Brandt recalled, 'The Federal Republic had been caught up in the ritual non-recognition of the other German state too long for it to free itself all at once'.[212] Nevertheless, West Germany was coming to terms with its past.

Conclusion

While Wilson was fond of playing the international statesman, he resolved that to try and take any kind of lead on the German Question would be futile. That is not to say he would not welcome détente, but, in specific regard to the German Question, he accepted that only Bonn could address the central issues. Unlike some of his predecessors, Wilson treated the Federal Republic in a manner more commensurate with its status and power.[213] Emulating the Macmillan and Home governments after 1960–1, Wilson let the United States take the lead in détente. British relations with West Germany thus, by-and-large, avoided the mistakes of the recent past. Furthermore, the fear of isolation in the FRG engendered by the emerging superpower consensus, combined with the Erhard government's suspicion of de Gaulle, meant that the Wilson government had a propitious opportunity for bettering relations with Bonn, albeit to a limited extent. This it took.

The crucial factor conducive to the achievement of an atmosphere for détente in Europe was, of course, the attitude of the US government. The ending of the ambiguous American stance on European frontiers resulted from two inter-related factors. First, whilst in the 1950s the USA regarded the indulgence of West German policy as essential to Western security policy, this was not the case by the 1960s. Indeed, Britain had realised this as long ago as the mid-1950s, with the Federal Republic accession to NATO. Churchill, in the eyes of many in the British Foreign Office, had not been wrong when proposing his 'eastern Locarno' – just a little premature. Second, by the 1960s the idea of a 'new Rapallo' was entirely inconceivable. In 1966, the wily Adenauer recognised that there was a sufficient coalition of interest between the superpowers for détente to have become irresistible. At the CDU Congress of March 1966, Adenauer declared that the 'Soviet Union has entered the ranks of the peoples who desire peace ... Soviet Russia needs peace, and peace in Europe. In the long run Russia is faced with the choice of subordination to Red China or hands off Europe.'[214] Although some commentators declared Adenauer to be senile (while Erhard was enraged),[215] the former Chancellor's position was perfectly consistent with his *Westpolitik*, his lack of interest in the 'Asia' beyond the Elbe, and his desire for a long-term American commitment to Europe. Furthermore, his reading of the desire of the USSR to achieve a settlement in Europe so as to deal with China was entirely accurate.

After 1964, Harold Wilson was reluctant to allow Bonn's Eastern policy to obstruct progress on specific issues. The non-proliferation negotiations were a notable example of this, and Wilson continued the post-Berlin Wall tactic of going through Washington to pressure Bonn. As a corollary of this, Wilson declared that the West Germans had to understand that reunification must await détente. However, Erhard and Schröder maintained the Adenauer formula and insisted that reunification was a precondition for détente. In reality, reunification was as distant as ever, despite the fact that the superpowers were moving towards an accommodating. Brandt, the British noted with satisfaction, accepted the premise that détente must precede reunification.

In contrast to its Conservative predecessor, the Wilson government undertook a more active policy towards Eastern Europe. This was aimed at improving the general atmosphere for negotiation, rather than trying to bypass Bonn in order to achieve a settlement of outstanding questions. This was a recognition of the fine line between Britain's pursuing its own agenda in Eastern Europe, and offending West Germany.[216] The Wilson government had to retain West German goodwill over Rhodesia, offset costs, the future direction of NATO strategy and proposed British entry into the EEC. The arrival of George Brown at the Foreign Office in 1966 signalled a real British commitment to the EEC. Wilson's assertion in 1967 that membership of the EEC would facilitate détente meant that British perspectives on the West German Eastern policy were converging with the British desire for a reversal of its economic decline. In short, if one views the EEC as a facilitator of détente, then the Wilson government's support of Brandt's *Ostpolitik* as part of that détente would intensify West German support for British EEC membership. The more active diplomacy adopted in Eastern Europe after 1964 did not, however, lead to any advance on the secret 1962 assurance to Poland over the Oder–Neiße line. There was no desire in London to alienate Bonn by emulating de Gaulle's attempted wooing of the Soviet bloc. The 1962 assurance, combined with the conciliatory visits of Labour Party politicians, was as far as the Wilson government was prepared to go, and even the extension of trade links was carefully marshalled so as to avoid giving undue offence to Bonn.

Whitehall noted that the Federal Republic was moving in the direction of coming to terms with the East. The peace note of March 1966 reflected this new mood in the Federal Republic. However, the Moscow declaration by the Warsaw Pact in October 1966 signalled that the Soviet bloc would never come to terms with the Erhard government's mix of conciliatory rhetoric and essentially unreformed policy stance. Johnson's speech in New York on 7 October 1966 signalled that the international situation also demanded a change of direction in the West German policy. Fortunately, Johnson managed this process well and was supportive of Bonn at this crucial juncture.[217] The NATO alliance became an indispensable base for Brandt's *Ostpolitik*, and the British, by virtue of their role in easing the shock to NATO administered by the French withdrawal from the integrated military structure in 1966, greatly smoothed the path for Brandt.[218] It was in such a role that Britain came to demonstrate that it had come to terms with its limitations, and was prepared to deploy its limited weight in support of broader Western initiatives that had a realistic prospect of success. London took careful note of the increasingly fierce debate in the Federal Republic as former 'heresies' such as the recognition of the Oder–Neiße line were openly advocated:

> It would take great courage even in the present political atmosphere ... for a party to base its foreign policy programme on the recognition of the Oder–Neisse Line and the acceptance of the DDR as a state ... But the present [situation] ... in the Federal Republic ... [means that] West German politicians ... have for the first time publicly called for an end to self-delusion and the acceptance of the Communist bloc's conditions for better relations between it and the Federal Republic.[219]

The ending of policy based on a German national 'self-delusion' had long been advocated by the British, who had been prone to such flights of fancy themselves. The arrival of this increasingly universal 'pragmatism' would herald the beginnings of a real détente in Europe. By 1967, the Wilson government had resolved to make the second application to the EEC. For its part, Bonn, however hesitantly, had embarked upon the path that was to lead to Helsinki in 1975.[220] That Britain could effectively stand by and support the Federal Republic in this signalled that London had found a role in Europe more commensurate with its place in the international system.

6 Conclusion

New roles in a new era

As Bevin, Eden and Churchill *et al.* had foreseen, the East–West conflict remained impervious to any détente so long as the German Question remained an active factor in diplomacy. In 1955, Harold Macmillan predicted that the priority accorded to reunification by West Germany would have a distorting effect upon Western policy:

> Whether or not Germany will eventually be unified is likely to depend on internal events in the Soviet Union. Desirable as it is on general grounds, German reunification cannot in itself be the sole object of policy. That policy surely is to defend Western Europe, or at any rate such portions of it as are in practice defensible.[1]

That the British government viewed the German Question as a serious obstacle to an understanding between East and West was in no small part due to the policies of its ally, the Federal Republic. This was particularly problematic because the United States of America seemed entirely content to endorse this situation. The dictates of alliance politics meant that Britain supported the West German claim to self-determination but disliked the manner in which, as practical policy, it militated against the British desire for détente. As Sir Frank Roberts recalled in 1992, 'people tended to forget' that Britain was obligated by treaty to work for German unity.[2]

Hans von Herwath reflected that the German problem was 'both a cohesive and divisive element in Anglo-German relations'. While Britain always recognised the Federal Republic's claim to be the successor to the German *Reich*, opinions on the importance of the German unity often clashed.[3] As the British ambassador to Bonn noted in 1960: 'Since we can no longer physically control Germany, the best hope of dealing with this latent risk remains in my opinion to assimilate the Federal Republic as closely as possible to Western Europe and to have it as an ally on our side.'[4] A Foreign Office official reflected the manner in which, broadly speaking, the integration of the Federal Republic into the West had been, from a British perspective, a success story:

It has not been necessary for the [FRG] to seize upon issues such as reunification or lost territories as *foci* of resentment against the allies. . . . I consider that we have been extraordinarily lucky over the course of internal development in the [FRG] when one remembers with what apprehension Sir Winston Churchill at Potsdam regarded the placing under Polish administration of all the territories to the east of the Oder and the western Neisse.[5]

Against this, the security obtained by the accession of West Germany to NATO meant that Western states were increasingly less inclined to subordinate national interests for the common good of the alliance.[6] From this point, the clash between West German and British policy can be traced. In actual fact, the hard-line position adopted by Bonn was untenable once Washington ceased to back it unreservedly in the early 1960s. For its part, it was obvious that the United States would continue to protect West Germany and to support the desire for unity (a promise which it kept in 1989–90). It would not, however, do so to the detriment of East–West dialogue in Europe. As has been recently observed 'Having devoted himself to bringing the Federal Republic into the West, Adenauer learned that the West was a more complex place than he had imagined'.[7]

By 1966, there was little real objection in London and Washington to the Eastern bloc demand that 'One of the main requisites of guaranteeing European security is the inviolability of the existing frontiers between the European states, inclusive of the frontiers of the . . . [GDR], Poland and Czechoslovakia'.[8] British policy-makers had long seen this as a necessity, but their attempt to ensure that this be the case had caused many headaches in Anglo-German relations. Why was this so?

In order to answer this question we must recall that, in addition to the pursuit of discrete national goals, British policy-makers saw differences of opinion as being derived from different analytical approaches in Bonn and London.[9] British policy-makers ascribed a legalistic mindset to their opposite numbers in West Germany. The head of Chancery in Bonn noted in 1966 that 'We [the British] tend to look for what is "realistic" i.e. practical and likely to be obtainable, whereas the Germans always begin by trying to identify what is "right". This is partly a consequence of the legalistic bias in . . . [the] education . . . of German officials, but it is also partly a conceptual matter.'[10] Assumptions (or stereotypes) about German legalism were an essential component of British interpretations of the FRG's policy.[11] This is understandable. In attempting to make sense of the external policies of other states, statesmen have long sought to identify national characteristics that might provide insight into the behaviour of decision-makers.[12]

A comparison of the British and West German positions based on this assumption illustrates how this tendency in British thinking operated. The perception was that Bonn favoured legalism because it suited national interest rather than any inherent disposition to the observation of international law. Elizabeth Wiskemann noted in 1956 that West Germany's neighbours couldn't have helped noticing that the pre-1945 amoral pursuit of power in the name of 'national interest' had been replaced by an insistent, almost pedantic, adherence to the letter of international law.[13] British positions on the German Question were self-serving mechanisms based on hardheaded political considerations. The USSR was appeased during the Second World War, just as Hitler's Germany had been prior to 1939. When that policy failed to deliver British security (or at least security for Western Europe), British policy-makers were happy to ally with an increasingly anti-Communist United States and to resurrect a German state by, amongst other devices, the effective negation of allied wartime conference decisions. By 1955, the British found that they had created an immovable (German) object in Europe on two fronts: first, against the Soviet bloc (the desired goal), and second, against elements in Britain and the West who sought compromise with Moscow. British policy-makers failed to realise that the FRG was capable of defying their attempts to compromise German interests in order to achieve a settlement with Moscow. (For the divergent approaches of London and Bonn, see Table 6.1).

The fact that the inspiration for Bonn's *Ostpolitik* was alien to British officials was compounded by the formulaic legal manner in which it was articulated. British policy-makers were often bemused by what they saw as the West German attachment to democratic legalism. For instance, the 'blood' conception of German citizenship (*Abstammung*) meant that Bonn felt it could speak for the German diaspora in countries that Germany had occupied in the Second World War. The manner in which the West Germans upheld the principle of *Recht auf Heimat* was also rather bewildering to British policy-makers. To assert that this principle was simply a matter of allowing, for instance, Sudeten Germans to return home as private citizens was incredible to British eyes, and attempts to legitimise the *Recht auf Heimat* with the language of self-determination were doomed to failure. *Ostpolitik* therefore rested on a fallacy. West German policy seemed to imply that its morality was of a universal nature. Bonn's assertion of rectitude in no way assured the success of its policy: the East Europeans would never accept Bonn's moral authority.

Of utility on an analytical level for contrasting Anglo-German attitudes is Wolfers' distinction between 'possession' and 'milieu' aims. West Germany accorded its relations with Eastern Europe a far higher priority than did Britain. This, of course, was derived from differences in the geography and history. The status of the GDR after 1949 is a case in point. For the FRG, the GDR represented an immediate threat to the legitimacy and unity of the German nation. There was little appreciation in Britain for this line of reasoning, or for the assiduousness with which West German policy insisted on non-recognition of both the GDR and the Oder–Neiße

Table 6.1 British and West German Eastern policies compared

	British perspective (pragmatic)	West German policy (legal)
I	Germany is divided. The GDR exists. This will continue to be the case as the USSR has 22 divisions there.	Bonn is the only legitimate German government and the sole successor state to the German *Reich* (the principle of *Alleinvertretungsrecht*). According to international law, Germany exists within its 1937 borders. The GDR is illegitimate.
II	The Oder–Neiße territories are forever lost to Germany. As Macmillan stated, 'possession is nine tenths of the law'.	The Oder–Neiße territories are provisionally administered by Poland and the USSR. This will continue to be the case until a final peace treaty with an *all* German government.
III	Britain renounced the Munich Pact in August 1942 (this was later endorsed by the wartime allies).	The Munich Pact is not null and void *ab initio*. The Munich Pact was only invalidated by Hitler's occupation of Bohemia-Moravia in 1939.
IV	The expulsion of Germans from Eastern Europe is a fact of history. The expelled Germans will never be allowed to return by the East Europeans.	The expulsions were a crime. The FRG asserts that the principle of self-determination means that the expellees should be allowed the right of return (*Recht auf Heimat*).
V	The states of Eastern Europe should have absolute national sovereignty. Citizens within their borders are subject to their jurisdiction.	West Germany, as the sole successor state, has the right to speak for the *Volksdeutsche* in Eastern Europe. According to the blood principle of (West) German nationality (*Abstammung*), they are entitled to German citizenship.
VI	The territorial status quo will not be changed outside of war.	The territorial status quo is provisional pending a final peace settlement.

line. For Britain, the GDR was an unpleasant, anti-democratic Soviet satellite – although no worse than many other regimes. However, from a British perspective, the FRG was obsessed by the GDR and expended excessive time and effort in trying to isolate it via mechanisms such as the Hallstein Doctrine. For Bonn, on the other hand, this doctrine was an effort to prevent the 'deepening of the division of Germany', and therefore a vital national interest.[14]

British policy-makers believed that if Bonn recognised East European fears and made suitable adjustments in policy, the German Question would cease to be a source of tension in East–West relations. The Adenauer and Erhard governments, by contrast, saw the issue of Germany as an excuse for the Soviet Union to make trouble in the West so as to expand Communism. From the German perspective, Soviet Communism was a form of Muscovite imperialism – a feeling heightened by resentment over Soviet policy in Germany since 1945.[15]

Thus, while the British asserted that 'One must negotiate with people one does not like', Adenauer saw the Communist threat very differently. The *Politik der Stärke* was predicated on the belief that a strong and prosperous West Germany – within a strong and prosperous West – would act as a 'magnet' to the peoples of the Soviet bloc. Many commentators thus saw Adenauer as vindicated when the Berlin Wall fell, Communism collapsed and Germany reunified.[16] British policy-makers too often failed to appreciate that Moscow looked more malign to nearly all Germans, and not just to those of Adenauer's political hue. Even Willy Brandt – whose name will forever be associated with the *neue Ostpolitik*, conciliation and reason – did not like or trust the Soviets, having been the Mayor of embattled West Berlin. Brandt's belief in détente was founded on hard-headed calculation of West German interests and not, as British proponents of détente often supposed, on a predisposition to achieve peace at any price. Indicative of the differing Anglo-German perspective, Hugh Gaitskell's book of his Harvard speeches was entitled *The Challenge of Co-existence*, while Brandt's was entitled *The Ordeal of Co-existence*.[17] West Germany did, however, accept the 'ordeal' as a necessary fact of life. On 17 June 1967, the 'Day of German Unity', Chancellor Kiesinger stated that: 'Germany, a reunified Germany, has a critical size ... too big to play no rôle in the balance of power and too small to keep its surrounding powers in balance ... For this reason the growing together of the divided parts of Germany can only be seen as embedded in the process of overcoming the East/West conflict in Europe.'[18]

This meant that, for practical purposes, Bonn was abandoning its insistence that reunification must precede a European settlement, as Kiesinger conceded that the division of his country was unlikely to be overcome in the immediate future. German unity was evolving from the demand of the 1950s into the long-term goal of the 1970s and 1980s. This opened the way for détente in Europe, something British policy-makers had been advocating since the 1950s. Brandt's *neue Ostpolitik* was institutionalised in the final act by the Helsinki process of the 1970s. In reality, this process confirmed what Britain had accepted during the Second World War: the USSR would dominate Eastern Europe. Might such an arrangement have been achieved earlier if Britain had possessed more influence? In 1944, E.H. Carr had argued, in effect, for a pan-European framework to ensure peace:

> [T]here can be no security in Western Europe unless there is also security in Eastern Europe, and security in Eastern Europe is unattainable unless it is buttressed by the military power of Russia ... A case so clear and cogent for close co-operation between Russia and Britain after the war cannot fail to carry conviction to any open and impartial

mind ... If Britain's frontier is on the Rhine, it might just as perti-
nently be said ... that Russia's frontier is on the Oder.[19]

Bonn's refusal to accept Soviet dominance of Europe up to the Elbe had
obstructed this vision but, by shelving the 'dream' of reunification, West
Germany could pave the way for the 'realistic' goal of East–West détente.
British policy-makers saw the departure in West German policy after 1967
as a vindication of their views.[20] But to make such a policy shift ten years
earlier, at the behest of the British, would have been impossible. The
necessary popular consensus in West Germany did not exist.

Independence, sovereignty and membership of NATO permitted West
Germany to pursue distinct national goals. Its aspirations to reunification
and revision of its eastern borders were not unusual aims for any democracy pursuing its national interests. As George Kennan put it in 1952,
'German recovery must be measured ... in [terms of] self-confidence,
hope, initiative, and will to act'.[21] The Adenauer government successfully
played on Western fears of a 'new Rapallo' and, as Rapallo had brought
Britain and France to the bargaining table at Locarno in 1925, so the
'Rapallo factor' helped cause the Western Alliance to defer the implementation of Potsdam after 1949. As a result, the Western Alliance endorsed a
West German Eastern policy that refused to accept the status quo and thus
challenged Soviet dominance in Eastern Europe.

The West German desire for reunification was no less real simply
because it seemed unlikely to be achieved. But in regarding reunification
as a foreign policy goal, rather than as a deeply felt national aspiration,
British observers concluded that Bonn was acting according to established
rules of diplomacy. Thus, when the Adenauer government began to make
policy based on 'unrealistic' principles, the British were somewhat
affronted. The view in London was that Bonn should be grateful as a
defeated nation to have been saved from Henry Morgenthau and Joseph
Stalin by British fairmindedness. Unrealistic aspirations, dreams wrapped
in legalisms, were hardly a substitute for a policy that accorded with the
international situation, as it existed in the 1950s and 1960s. The blind
adherence to the principles of the 1937 boundaries and *Recht auf Heimat*
did not change the fact that twenty-two Soviet divisions were stationed in
the GDR.

British observers too often chose to ignore the domestic roots of West
Germany's Eastern policies. It was no accident, for example, that the
leader of the CSU, Franz Josef Strauß, was amongst the most vociferous
supporters of the *Sudetendeutsche*. This was because Bavaria had received a
very high proportion of ethnic Germans from the Sudetenland after 1945.
While British officials did concede the electoral pressures acting upon the
Federal Republic, they misunderstood the depth of West German bitterness over the expulsions after 1945. The British perspective thus ignored
the interaction of foreign and domestic policy. In Britain, of course, the

issue of the Oder–Neiße line was not one that would elicit passion from the general public. At best, it was a cause for newspapers to censure West German 'intransigence'. In the Federal Republic, however, the *Ostpolitik* had a function that transcended the stated goal of restoring Germany in its 1937 frontiers. If this had been the sole objective of the Eastern policy, then British analysts would have been correct in considering it unrealistic. The *Ostpolitik*, however, was more complex than this. It served as a unifying force in a fragile new democracy, it strengthened Bonn's claim to be the legitimate successor of the *Reich*, and it speeded the integration of the refugees by allowing them to identify with the new state. All of these were largely lost on Britain – a country that, whatever its economic decline, was confident in its identity and in its history.

Many British policy-makers believed that 'professional' diplomats in the *AA* had always wanted to recognise the Oder–Neiße line and had only been obstructed by Adenauer and the expellee organisations. Macmillan was particularly prone to such thinking. This was to ignore the fact that these 'professionals' were Germans as well as diplomats. The fact that the British were 'observers' and the West Germans were 'participants' meant, in London's view, that the former had always viewed the situation more 'rationally'. This was to confuse 'dispassionate' for 'rational'.

By 1955 Britain had achieved much by its adroit diplomacy, playing a crucial role in the formation of the Western Alliance. Unfortunately, this gave a misleading impression of the ability of Britain to continue on the world stage as an independent actor. In 1956, an inter-departmental working group advocated closer links with Western Europe. This, it was held, would prevent West German domination whilst strengthening the Western European leg of the NATO alliance.[22] However, concerns about the Commonwealth, the 'Special Relationship' and a lack of vision at the highest levels put paid to any such scheme. The commonality of language and history was thus mistaken for a commonality of interest. For much of the post-war era there was, in Oliver Wright's words, 'No chance of Britain joining the EEC, the League of defeated Nations'.[23] But as another former FO official put it, 'The British decision to stay out of Europe was tragic, all the more tragic for it having been inevitable'.[24]

The British effort to stay at the 'top table' by attempting to broker détente did not add substance to the illusion of British power. British efforts in this direction remind one of a man who arrives at a poker game with a group of millionaires. The man assures the other players that, although he is relatively poor, he would nevertheless like to play in order to accumulate sufficient stake money by his winnings to be regarded as a major player. Adenauer likened Britain to 'a rich man who has lost all his property but does not realise it'.[25]

The self-perception of Britain as a great power was particularly detrimental to policy towards Europe. Julian Amery, a Minister in several Conservative cabinets of the 1950s and 1960s, identifies this belief as fundamental to Macmillan's misunderstanding of West Germany: 'I think at this stage he really didn't look upon full partners in the arena. And they sensed this ... not surprisingly, this was a difficulty.'[26] The mistaken belief that Britain could facilitate détente was the other side of the coin of the refusal to participate in European integration. It is interesting to speculate that had Britain joined the EEC *before* attempting to broker détente, the former may have facilitated the latter. While Britain felt that it could achieve a settlement with Moscow over the heads of the West Germans, to pursue détente to the detriment of West German interests was a mistake. West Germany had to be a partner in any such process. But there was more to British policy than simply a misreading of the situation in Central Europe. There existed a genuine concern about the prospect of nuclear war amongst British policy-makers. And British analysts were essentially correct in their diagnosis of what was required in order to achieve an enduring security arrangement in Europe. Consequently, a balance must be struck between condemning the apparent British inability to empathise with the West German position and an appreciation of the material and psychological factors shaping the British point of view.

The stress upon the end product of negotiation was therefore the key to British policy. Whatever the rights and wrongs of the (West) German case, to challenge the status quo risked nuclear war, and charges of 'appeasement' therefore left the British somewhat bewildered. In November 1959 Harold Macmillan recorded in his diary: 'Poor old H.M.G. Whether it's Germany, or Europe, or Africa, or Cyprus, we are always trying to conciliate both antagonists, and getting nothing but suspicion and abuse from both sides.'[27] Yet, Macmillan too often seemed to forget that, for all its faults, West Germany was an important ally. De Gaulle understood this. In backing German national interest, French policy was in fact advancing that of France. British policy seems to have been based on assumption that, once created, the Western Alliance was cast in stone. Therefore, the next step was to negotiate with Moscow. The problem was that such negotiations, unless conducted with alliance solidarity, would undermine the Western bloc. As the British ambassador in Moscow noted in 1973, '[the] Russians use ... "détente" ... to embrace a series of objectives which in fact are not necessarily conducive to a genuine relaxation of tension at all ... [and] these objectives include ... the perpetuation of the division of Germany'.[28]

Following the failure of the Paris Summit, British policy aimed at securing accession to the EEC. It was thus resolved to woo West Germany and leave the business of pressuring Bonn to Washington. However, West German bitterness at Macmillan's policies in 1958–60 was slow to dissipate. This was particularly true in the case of Adenauer. It is true that Adenauer was often strongly anti-British, but this sentiment was not inherent in his worldview. It can be traced to British policy over issues such as détente, disengagement and Berlin during the 1950s and early 1960s.

Although Frank Roberts constantly stressed the Chancellor's Anglophobia in his despatches from Bonn, he was afterwards more balanced in his judgement: 'We had good relations with Adenauer before Macmillan ... Macmillan was, I think, to put it bluntly, anti-German and certainly anti-Adenauer.'[29]

Yet British policy did eventually adjust itself to realities, and the secret undertaking to Poland concerning the Oder–Neiße line in 1962 demonstrated a desire to ease Warsaw's fears without alienating the FRG by openly flouting its stated position. In any case, following the Kennedy administration's decision actively to pursue a rapprochement with the USSR, Britain could see that it was only a matter of time before Bonn came to terms with the loss of the eastern territories. Legitimate aspiration would replace political imperative, as Kiesinger made clear in 1968: 'Whenever people from the two parts of Germany meet up with each other ... it becomes evident that people of one language, one history [and] one culture feel they belong together ... Germans perceive themselves as one nation.'[30]

In this new era of political pragmatism, American pressure on Bonn would relieve Britain of its self-appointed role as mediator and open the way for Britain's European policy. The United States would broker détente, West Germany would reconcile itself to giving up its claim to the boundaries of 1937, and Britain would join the EEC. Despite the new enthusiasm for Europe and the pursuit of more limited diplomatic objectives, great power illusions persisted in British policy. Nassau may have secured British strategic nuclear status, but it also gave de Gaulle the perfect excuse he needed to veto the first British EEC application. At the same time, however, it is clear that when Macmillan behaved as if Britain was a great power, he enjoyed widespread support within the British public. Signally, however, two of Macmillan's greatest foreign policy coups – Moscow in 1959 and Nassau in 1962 – are nowadays seldom considered to have represented great advances in the British interest.

By 1964, the fiction of British great power status was eroding in appearance as well as in substance. Pressure on West German foreign policy would only be applied when it directly impinged upon the British interest. Such was the case with the quest for a non-proliferation treaty. Wilson accepted that West Germany must address the issues arising from its *Ostpolitik* with the proviso that détente must precede reunification. When Brandt enacted into Federal policy his own long-held belief that détente could only precede reunification, Anglo-German relations could, for the first time since 1955, enjoy a real commonality of interest with regard to the *Ost-* and *Deutschlandpolitik*. Thus, when Brandt concluded an agreement with Poland in 1970, the British Cabinet could be fully supportive and welcome the effective recognition of the Oder–Neiße line as a 'contribution towards removing a long-standing source of tension'.[31] From 1969 onwards, Bonn exchanged its support of British membership of the EEC with London's support for the Brandt's *neue Ostpolitik.*[32] This meant that, as Roger Morgan has written, 'when the two governments faced the new challenges of the Helsinki process in the mid-Seventies, they did so with attitudes and expectations which, although not identical, were much more compatible than British and [West] German attitudes had been a decade earlier.'[33]

By 1967 it was clear that Britain was at last beginning to formulate policies that were more commensurate with its status. Phil Williams has argued that because Britain played a secondary role in détente in the 1960s and 1970s, British policy had lost direction sometime early in the 1960s.[34] In fact, Britain actually found a direction in the mid-1960s, a role more suited to British capabilities and needs. Henry Kissinger later identified a fundamental lack of confidence amongst British statesman from the mid-1960s onwards. Kissinger believed that Britain was still possessed of the experience of a great power, but that British leaders were increasingly reluctant to act as if their decisions mattered: 'British statesmen were content to act as honoured consultants to our deliberations.'[35] It would be more accurate to argue that this perceived lack of confidence actually reflected an adjustment to a more proportionate view of British influence. In diplomacy, it is just as important to recognise one's weaknesses as it is to recognise one's strengths. By 1967, it was clear that Britain's true interests lay in Western Europe. Signally, the manner in which Britain stopped trying to achieve a solution to the German Question reveals a new realism in British policy. George Brown articulated this in 1971: 'Geographically, historically and in every other way the British are among the leading nations of Western Europe. I have always quarrelled with Dean Acheson's much-repeated remark about Britain's having lost an Empire and not found a role. We *have* a role: our role is to lead Europe.'[36] Britain's opportunity to lead Europe had passed, but Brown was pointing the way forward.

Notes

Introduction: Britain, Germany and Europe in the Cold War

1 Carolyn Eisenberg, *Drawing the Line: The American Decision to Divide Germany, 1944–1949* (Cambridge: Cambridge University Press, 1996). 'It was the Americans and their British partners who had opted for [German] partition' (Eisenberg, 1996: 495).

2 On this and the British role in the partition of Germany, see Anne Deighton, *The Impossible Peace: Britain, the Division of Germany and the Origins of the Cold War* (Oxford: Oxford University Press, 1990). Sir Orme Sargent, Permanent Under-Secretary of State at the Foreign Office, stressed the necessity of establishing a separate West German state as, 'the only alternative to [partition] was Communism on the Rhine' (Deighton, 1990: 73).

3 While the term *Ostpolitik* has become virtually synonymous with Brandt's Chancellorship (1969–74), Sir David Goodall (former Permanent Secretary at the FO) pointed out that 'I suppose that the FRG always had an *Ostpolitik* from the word go' (letter to the author, 14 May 2000).

4 For instance, Wilfried Loth, *Overcoming the Cold War: A History of Détente, 1950–1991* (Basingstoke: Palgrave, 2002).

5 F.S. Northedge and A. Wells, *Britain and Soviet Communism* (London: Macmillan, 1982), 124.

6 Brian White, *Britain, Détente, and Changing East–West Relations* (London: Routledge, 1992); Elizabeth Barker, *Britain in a Divided Europe 1945–70* (London: Weidenfeld & Nicolson, 1971); Elizabeth Barker, *The British Between the Superpowers 1945–50* (London: Macmillan, 1983); Anne Deighton (ed.), *Britain and the First Cold War* (London: Macmillan, 1990); F.S. Northedge, *Descent from Power: British Foreign Policy 1945–1973* (London: Allen & Unwin, 1974); David Sanders, *Losing an Empire, Finding a Role: British Foreign Policy Since 1945* (London: Macmillan, 1990); S. Smith, M. Smith and B. White (eds), *British Foreign Policy: Tradition, Change and Transformation* (London: Unwin Hyman, 1988).

7 Roger Morgan, 'The British View', in Edwina Moreton (ed.), *Germany Between East and West*, (Cambridge: Cambridge University Press/RIIA, 1987); Sabine Lee, *An Uneasy Relationship: British–German Relations between 1955 and 1961* (Brockmeyer: Bochum, 1996), 198–204. On German Eastern policy, Rudolf Morsey and Konrad Repgen (eds), *Untersunungen und Dokumente zur Ostpolitik und Biographie*, Adenauer-Studien III (Mainz: Mattias Grünewald, 1974); Carl G. Anthon, 'Adenauer's Ostpolitik 1955–1963', *World Affairs* (Washington), 139/2 (1976), 112–24; Michael Freund, *From Cold War to Ostpolitik* (London: Oswald Wolff, 1972); Renata Fritsch-Bournatzel, *Confronting the German Question: Germans on the East–West Divide* (Oxford: Berg, 1988); William E. Griffith,

The Ostpolitik of the Federal Republic of Germany (Colorado: Westview Press, 1978); Angela Stent, *From Embargo to Ostpolitik: The Political Economy of West German-Soviet Relations 1955–1980* (Cambridge University Press, 1980); Walter F. Hahn, *Between Westpolitik and Ostpolitik: Changing West German Security Views*, (London: Sage, 1975); Karl Kaiser, *German Foreign Policy in Transition: Bonn between East and West* (London: RIIA/Oxford University Press), 1968; Karl Kaiser and Roger Morgan (eds), *Britain and West Germany: Changing Societies and the Future of Foreign Policy* (London: RIIA/Oxford University Press, 1971); Edwina Moreton (ed.), *Germany Between East and West* (Cambridge University Press/RIIA, 1987); J.K. Sowden, *The German Question 1945–1973: Continuity in Change* (Bradford: Bradford University Press, 1975); Michael Stürmer, '*Ostpolitik, Deutschlandpolitik* and the Western Alliance: German perspectives on détente' in Keith Dyson (ed.), *European Détente: Case Studies of the Politics of East–West Relations* (London: Frances Pinter, 1986).

8 For British policy on, and towards, West Germany and the German question see Klaus Larres, *Politik der Illusionen: Churchill, Eisenhower und die deutsche Frage, 1945–1955* (Göttingen: Vandenhoeck and Ruprecht, 1995); Sabine Lee, *An Uneasy Relationship: British–German Relations between 1955 and 1961* (Brockmeyer: Bochum, 1996); Daniel Gossel, *Briten, Deutsche und Europa: die Deutsche Frage in der britischen Außenpolitik, 1945–1962* (Stuttgart: Steiner, 1999); Yvonne Kipp, *Eden, Adenauer und die Deutsche Frage: Britische Deutschlandpolitik im internationalen Spannungsfeld 1951–1957* (Paderborn: Ferdinand Schöningh Verlag, 2002).

9 Roger Morgan, 'Willy Brandt's "Neue Ostpolitik": British Perceptions and Positions, 1969–1975', in A.M. Birke, M. Brechtken and A. Searle, *An Anglo-German Dialogue* (Munich: K.G. Saur, 2000); Gottfried Niedhart, 'The British Reaction towards Ostpolitik: Anglo-West German Relations in the Era of Détente, 1967–1971', in Christian Haase and Daniel Gossel (eds), *Debating Foreign Affairs: the Public Dimension of British Foreign Policy* (Berlin: Philo, 2003).

10 The German question, the question of how to fit Germany into a European state system, was at the very heart of the Cold War in Europe. On this, see John Lewis Gaddis, *We Now Know: Rethinking Cold War History* (Oxford: Oxford University Press, 1997), 113–51; Marc Trachtenberg, *A Constructed Peace: the Making of a European Settlement 1945–1963* (Princeton, NJ: Princeton University Press, 1999); Wilfried Loth, 'Germany in the Cold War: Strategies and Decisions' in Odd Arne Westad (ed.), *Reviewing the Cold War: Approaches, Interpretations, Theory* (London: Frank Cass, 2000), 242–57; W.R. Smyser, *From Yalta to Berlin: the Cold War Struggle Over Germany* (London: Palgrave, 1999); Charles R. Planck, *The Changing Status of German Reunification in Western Diplomacy, 1955–1966* (Baltimore: Johns Hopkins University, 1967); Timothy Garton Ash, *In Europe's Name: Germany and the Divided Continent* (London: Vintage, 1994); Wolfram F. Hanrieder, *Germany, America, Europe: Forty Years of West German Foreign Policy* (New Haven, CT: Yale University Press, 1989). On the question historically, see Wolf D. Gruner, *Die Deutsche Frage: ein Problem der europäischen Geschichte seit 1800* (Munich: Beck, 1985); Stefan Wolff, *The German Question since 1919: An Analysis with Key Documents* (London: Praeger, 2003).

11 On this see, R. Gerald Hughes, ' "Possession is nine tenths of the law": Britain and the boundaries of Eastern Europe since 1945', *Diplomacy and Statecraft*, 16/4 (2005), 723–47.

12 Trachtenberg, *A Constructed Peace*, 1999: 3.

13 As argued over a generation by Konrad Adenauer in 'The German Problem, a World Problem', *Foreign Affairs*, 41/1 (1962), 59–65, and Eberhard Schulz, 'Unfinished Business: the German National Question and the Future of Europe', *International Affairs*, 60/3 (1984), 391–402.

14 Eisenberg, *Drawing the Line*, 1996: 460.

15 John F. Kennedy Library (hereafter JFKL): NSF Box 170, Bruce to Rusk, no. 229, 17 July 1961.

16 For a survey of the literature see, R. Gerald Hughes, ' "Don't let's be beastly to the Germans": Britain and the German Affair in History', *Twentieth Century British History*, 17/2 (2006), 257–83. See also Thomas Kielinger, *Crossroads and Roundabouts: Junctions in German–British Relations* (London: Foreign and Commonwealth Office, 1997).

17 For instance, Jeremy Noakes, Peter Wende and Jonathan Wright (eds), *Britain and Germany in Europe* (German Historical Institute, London/Oxford: Oxford University Press, 2002); Klaus Larres and Elizabeth Meehan (eds), *Uneasy Allies: British–German Relations and European Integration Since 1945* (Oxford: Oxford University Press, 2000); A.M. Birke, M. Brechtken and A. Searle (eds), *An Anglo-German Dialogue: the Munich Lectures on the History of International Relations* (Munich: K.G. Saur, 2000); Sabine Lee, *Victory in Europe: Britain and Germany since 1945* (London: Longman, 2001); Adolf M. Birke, *Britain and Germany: Historical Patterns of a Relationship* (German Historical Institute, London, 1987); Saki Dockrill, *Britain's Policy for West German Rearmament* (Cambridge: Cambridge University Press, 1991); Karl Kaiser and John Roper (eds), *British–German Defence Co-operation* (London: Jane's/RIIA, 1988); Klaus Larres, 'Reunification or Integration with the West? Britain and the Federal Republic of Germany in the Early 1950s', in Richard Aldrich and Michael Hopkins (eds), *Intelligence, Defence and Diplomacy in the Post-War World* (London: Frank Cass, 1994); Sabine Lee, *An Uneasy Relationship: British–German Relations between 1955 and 1961* (Brockmeyer: Bochum, 1996); Sabine Lee, 'Pragmatism versus Principle? Macmillan and Germany', in Richard Aldous and Sabine Lee (eds), *Harold Macmillan: Aspects of a Political Life* (London: Macmillan, 1999); Spencer Mawby, *Containing Germany: Britain and the Arming of the Federal Republic* (London: Macmillan, 1999); Roger Morgan, *Britain and Germany since 1945: Two Societies and Two Foreign Policies* (London: German Historical Institute, 1988); Roger Morgan and Colin Bray (eds), *Partners and Rivals in Western Europe: Britain, France and Germany* (London: Gower, 1986); Neil Thomas, *A Compromised Policy: Britain, Germany and the Soviet Threat 1945–6* (London: Minerva Press, 1994); Donald Cameron Watt, *Britain Looks to Germany* (London: Oswald Wolff, 1965); Jonathan Wright, 'The Role of Britain in West German Foreign Policy since 1949', *German Politics*, 5/1 (1996), 2–26.

18 Christopher Coker, 'The New Barbarians', *Parliamentary Brief*, July 1993, 27.

19 Dockrill, *Britain's Policy for West German Rearmament*, 1991: 175. John Foster Dulles (Secretary of State 1953–9) was a particularly staunch ally of Adenauer. On this, see Hans-Jürgen Grabbe, 'Konrad Adenauer, John Foster Dulles, and West German–American Relations', in Richard H. Immerman (ed.), *John Foster Dulles and the Diplomacy of the Cold War* (Princeton, NJ: Princeton University Press, 1992). On European conservatives and the US see Wolfram Kaiser, 'Trigger-happy Protestant Materialists? The European Christian Democrats and the United States', in Marc Trachtenberg (ed.), *Between Empire and Alliance: America and Europe during the Cold War* (Lanham: Rowman & Littlefield, 2003), 63–82.

20 Morgan, 'The British View', 1987: 85.

21 National Archives, Public Record Office, Kew (hereafter PRO): FO 371/145739 [WG 1019/12] Foreign Minister Heinrich von Brentano, Bonn, 28 June 1956.

22 Giles, Frank (ed.), *Forty Years On: Four Decades of Koenigswinter Conferences* (Blackpool: BPCC, 1989: 1). Oliver Wright, Private Secretary to the Prime Ministers Home and Wilson in the 1960s, believed that, 'The Germans, like all of us, but perhaps more so than most, attach enormous importance to legality.' Interview: Sir J. Oliver Wright.

23 Article two of the Paris Agreements of September 1954 stipulated that the three Western allies 'in view of the international situation, reserved the rights and responsibilities hitherto possessed and exercised by them in connection with Berlin and Germany as a whole, including the reunification of Germany and a peace settlement.' Anthon, 'Adenauer's Ostpolitik 1955–1963', 1976: 113.

24 Rajendra K. Jain, *Germany, the Soviet Union and Eastern Europe 1949–1991* (London: Sangam, 1993), 16.

25 Edwina Moreton, 'The View from London' in *Eroding Empire: Western Relations with Eastern Europe*, Lincoln Gordon with J.F. Brown, Pierre Hassner, Josef Joffe and Edwina Moreton (Washington: Brookings Institution, 1987), 242.

26 On this see, John Baylis, *Anglo-American Defence Relations* (London: Macmillan, 1984).

27 Moreton, 'The View from London', 1987: 238.

28 Arnold Wolfers, *Discord and Collaboration: Essays on International Politics* (Baltimore: Johns Hopkins University Press, 1962), 74.

29 Roger Morgan, *Britain and Germany since 1945*, 1988: 5–6.

30 For an discussion of this, see Günther Gillessen, 'Germany's Position in the Centre of Europe: The Significance of Germany's Position and Misunderstandings about German Interests', in Arnulf Baring (ed.), *Germany's New Position in Europe: Problems and Perspectives* (Providence, RI: Berg, 1994), 21–33.

31 Eberhard Schulz, 'Berlin, the German Question and the Future of Europe: Long-Term Perspectives', in Keith Dyson (ed.), *European Détente: Case Studies of the Politics of East–West Relations* (London: Frances Pinter, 1986), 128.

32 On this see, Pertti Ahonen, 'Domestic Constraints on West German Ostpolitik: the role of the Expellee Organizations in the Adenauer Era', *Central European History*, 98/1 (1998), 31–63; Pertti Ahonen, *After the Expulsion: West Germany and Eastern Europe 1945–1990* (Oxford: Oxford University Press, 2003).

33 Gustav Schmidt, 'European Security: Anglo-German Relationships 1949–1956', in Noakes, Wende and Wright (eds), *Britain and Germany in Europe*, 2002: 118. On this theme, see also Martin A.L. Longden, 'From "Hot War" to "Cold War": Western Europe in British Grand Strategy, 1945–1948', in Michael F. Hopkins, Michael D. Kandiah and Gillian Staerck (eds), *Cold War Britain, 1945–1964: New Perspectives* (Basingstoke: Palgrave, 2003), 97–110. On the underlying assumptions of British foreign policy, Paul Kennedy, *The Realities behind Diplomacy: Background Influences on British External Policy, 1865–1980* (London: Fontana, 1981); Wolfram Kaiser, 'Against Napoleon and Hitler: Background Influences on British Diplomacy' in Wolfram Kaiser and Gillian Staerck (eds), *British Foreign Policy 1955–64: Contracting Options* (Basingstoke: Macmillan, 2000), 110–31.

34 Wolfram Kaiser, *Using Europe, Abusing the Europeans: Britain and European Integration 1945–63* (London: Macmillan, 1996); Martin P.C. Schaad, *Bullying Bonn: Anglo-German Diplomacy on European Integration* (London: Macmillan, 2000).

35 John P.S. Gearson, *Harold Macmillan and the Berlin Wall Crisis, 1958–1962: The Limits of Interest and Force* (Basingstoke: Macmillan, 1998); Sabine Lee, 'Anglo-German Relations 1958–59: The Postwar Turning Point?', *Diplomacy and Statecraft*, 6/3 (1995), 787–808. For a rather moralistic condemnation of Macmillan and British policy generally, see Ann Tusa, *The Last Division: Berlin and the Wall* (London: Hodder & Stoughton, 1996). On the West and the Berlin Wall Crisis, see Rolf Steininger, *Der Mauerbau: Die Westmächte und Adenauer in der Berlinkrise 1958–1963* (Munich: Olzog, 2001); John Gearson and Kori Schake (eds), *The Berlin Wall Crisis: Perspectives on Cold War Alliances* (Basingstoke: Palgrave Macmillan, 2002).

36 On this see, R. Gerald Hughes, 'Unfinished Business from Potsdam: Britain, West Germany, and the Oder–Neiße line, 1945–1962', *International History Review*, 27/2 (2005), 259–94.

1 *Stunde null* to *Deutschlandvertrag*

1 'If the German people [surrender] ... the Soviets, according to the agreement between Roosevelt, Churchill and Stalin, would occupy all of East and SouthEast Europe along with the greater part of the Reich. An *iron curtain* would fall over this enormous territory controlled by the Soviet Union, behind which nations would be slaughtered ... One day those in the USA will curse the day in which a long-forgotten American president released a communiqué at a conference at Yalta, which will long since have sunk into legend.' Josef Goebbels, 'Das Jahr 2000', *Das Reich*, 25 February 1945, 1–2.

2 J.H. Backer, *The Decision to Divide Germany* (NC: Duke University Press, 1978), 25–6.

3 Tom Bower, *Blind Eye to Murder: Britain, America and the Purging of Nazi Germany – A Pledge Betrayed* (London: Warner Books, 1997), 144.

4 Churchill, 25 October 1942. Ibid., 5. Six years later Churchill had shifted his position somewhat, believing that 'There can be no revival of Europe, without the active and loyal aid of all the German tribes'.

5 *Documents on Germany Under Occupation 1945–1954*, selected and edited by Beate Ruhm von Oppen (London: RIIA/Oxford: Oxford University Press, 1955), 2–3.

6 Wolfgang Wagner, *The Genesis of the Oder–Neisse Line: A Study in Diplomatic Negotiations During World War II* (Stuttgart: Brentano, 1957), 92.

7 PRO: FO 371/163594, [CG 1081/1] FO memo, 19 January 1962.

8 Diary entry for 7 March 1945, John Colville, *The Fringes of Power: Downing Street Diaries*, Volume II, *1941–April 1955* (London: Sceptre, 1987), 211.

9 On the genesis of post-1945 hostility, see Erik Goldstein, 'Britain and the Origins of the Cold War 1917–1925', in M.F. Hopkins, M.D. Kandiah and G. Staerck, *Cold War Britain, 1945–1964*, 7–16.

10 On this see, for instance, Keith Salisbury, *Churchill and Roosevelt at War: the War they Fought and the Peace they Hoped to Make* (London: Macmillan, 1994), 78–88. On British apprehension of the USSR and the USA, see Wagner, *The Genesis of the Oder–Neisse Line*, 65–9.

11 Avon papers: AP 20/1/25, diary entry, 3 July 1945.

12 Diary entry for 20 March 1945, *The Fringes of Power*, 215.

13 On this see, Geoffrey Warner, 'From Ally to Enemy: Britain's Relations with the Soviet Union, 1941–1948', in Michael Dockrill and Brian McKercher (eds), *Diplomacy and World Power: Studies in British Foreign Policy, 1890–1950* (Cambridge: Cambridge University Press, 1996), 221–43.

14 *The Times*, 10 March 1944.

15 Robert Rhodes James, *Anthony Eden* (London: Papermac, 1987), 281.

16 H. Thomas, *Armed Truce: The Beginnings of the Cold War, 1945–6* (London: Heinemann, 1987), 209.

17 See P.G.H. Holdich, 'A Policy of Percentages? British Policy in the Balkans After the Moscow Conference of October 1944', *International History Review*, 9/1 (1987), 28–47.

18 Stuart Croft, 'British Policy Towards Western Europe: 1945–1951', in Peter M.R. Stirk and David Willis (eds), *Shaping Postwar Europe: European Unity and Disunity 1945–1957* (London: Pinter Publishers, 1991), 78.

19 Sir A. Clark Kerr, Moscow to Eden, 10 July 1945, *DBPO, Series I: Volume 1: The Conference at Potsdam, July–August 1945* (London: HMSO, 1984), 147.

20 Churchill to Sir Alexander Cadogan, 19 April 1944. Winston S. Churchill, *The Second World War*, Volume V, *Closing the Ring* (London: Cassell, 1952), 543.

21 Brian White, 'Britain and East–West Relations', in Michael Smith, Steve Smith and Brian White (eds), *British Foreign Policy: Tradition, Change and Transformation* (London: Unwin Hyman, 1988), 152–4.

22 On this see, Wolfgang Wagner, *The Genesis of the Oder–Neisse Line: A Study in Diplomatic Negotiations During World War II* (Stuttgart: Brentano, 1957); Gotthold Rhode and Wolfgang Wagner (eds), *The Genesis of the Oder–Neisse Line: A Study in Diplomatic Negotiations During World War II: Sources and Documents*, Stuttgart: Brentano, 1959). For the Polish perspective, see Edward J. Rozek, *Allied War Diplomacy: A Pattern in Poland* (New York: John Wiley, 1958); W.M. Drzewieniecki, *The German–Polish Frontier* (Chicago: Polish Western Association of America, 1959).

23 That is, the loss of Poland's own 'eastern territories' to the Soviet Union. On this see, Jacek Tebinka, 'British Memoranda on Changing the Curzon Line in 1944', *Acta Poloniae Historica*, 80 (1999), 167–94. US sympathy for the Soviet claim that the boundaries of Poland had been pushed too far to the East after 1918 was widespread. Harry S. Truman Library: Oral History (HSTL: OH): Elbridge Durbrow, online, available at: www.trumanlibrary.org/oralhist/durbrow.htm.

24 J. Ciechanowski, *Victory in Defeat* (London: Doubleday, 1947), 269. Ciechanowski was the Polish wartime ambassador in Washington DC.

25 Speech in the House of Commons, 15 December 1944. Winston S. Churchill, *The Dawn of Liberation: War Speeches by the Rt. Hon. Winston S. Churchill, 1944*, complied by Charles Eade, (London: Cassell, 1945), 295.

26 *The Times*, 16 December 1944.

27 'Declaration Regarding the Unconditional Surrender of Germany and the Assumption of Supreme Authority by the Allies', 11 February 1945, Cmd. 1552, *Selected Documents on Germany and the Question of Berlin 1944–1961*, 38.

28 Article IX (b) of Potsdam Declaration, 2 August 1945, see von Oppen, *Documents on Germany Under Occupation*, 49.

29 Ingo von Münch (ed.), *Dokumente des geteilten Deutschland* (Stuttgart: Ernst Klett, 1976), 42.

30 PRO: FO 371/46990, [C 5694/5333/18] Sir A. Clark Kerr, 7 September 1945 to Molotov requesting ambassadorial Four-Power representation to the Polish Government in Warsaw. See also PRO: FO 371 46993–7.

31 *Hansard*, HC Deb, vol. 413, col. 317, 20 August 1945. See also Sir Anthony Eden, *Full Circle* (London: Cassell, 1960), 4–5.

32 Harold Macmillan, *Tides of Fortune 1945–55* (London: Macmillan, 1969), 101.

33 *Hansard*, vol. 413, col. 293, 16 August 1945. See also Winston S. Churchill, *The Second World War*, Volume VI, *Triumph and Tragedy* (London: Cassell, 1952), 573.

34 Alan Bullock, *Ernest Bevin: Foreign Secretary 1945–1951* (Oxford: Oxford University Press, 1985), 27.

35 Even the sympathetic Douglas Hurd sees Churchill's position as being unrealistic here. Douglas Hurd, *The Search for Peace: A Century of Peace Diplomacy* (London: Warner Books, 1997), 52–4.

36 Permanent Under-Secretary of State for Foreign Affairs.

37 Prime Minister to Cadogan, 19 April 1944, Churchill, *The Second World War*, Volume V, 543.

38 PRO: FO 371/177943, Research Department Memorandum LR2/30, Cadogan, 2 November 1944.

39 On Moscow's original rationale see, R.C. Raack, 'Stalin Fixes the Oder–Neisse Line' *Journal of Contemporary History*, 25/4 (1990), 467–88.

40 PRO: FO 371/103714 [C 1083/10] UKHComm, Wahnerheide, TelNo. 543 Saving to FO, 16 July 1953.

41 Gladwyn Jebb, *The Memoirs of Lord Gladwyn* (London: Weidenfeld & Nicolson,

1972), 113–15. On the division of Germany and its immediate consequences, see R. Harrison Wagner, 'The Decision to Divide Germany and the Origins of the Cold War', *International Studies Quarterly*, 49/4 (1978), 446–56; *Documents on British Policy Overseas (DPBO), Series I Volume V: Germany and Western Europe 11 August–31 December 1945* (London: HMSO, 1990), 307.

42 Frank Roberts quoted in Morgan, 'The British View', 88.

43 May 1946, memorandum by Oliver Harvey, 'Future Policy Towards Germany' quoted in ibid., 89.

44 PRO: CAB 129/9, CP (46) 156, Gen. 121/1, memorandum by 'The Future of Germany and the Ruhr', Ernest Bevin, 11 March 1946.

45 Bower, *Blind Eye to Murder*, 185. See also Denis Healey, *The Time of My Life* (London: Michael Joseph, 1989), 101–2; Sean Greenwood, *Britain and the Cold War, 1945–1991* (London: Macmillan, 2000), 20.

46 *Hansard*, HC Deb, vol. 446, col. 405, 22 January 1948.

47 Labour Party Archive, Manchester (hereafter LPA): International Department, Proceedings of international Socialist Conference, Bournemouth 10 November 1946.

48 *Hansard*, HC Deb, vol. 446, col. 404, 12 May 1947.

49 PRO: FO 371/46990, [C 5694/5333/18] Sir A. Clark Kerr to Molotov, 7 September 1945.

50 Hans-Åke Persson, *Rhetorik und Realpolitik: Grossbritannien, die Oder–Neisse Grenze und die Vertreibung der Deutschen nach dem Zweiten Weltkrieg* (Berlin: Berliner Wissenschafts-Verlag, 2001), 147–51, 169–74, 185–7.

51 Truman to Byrnes (unsent), 5 January 1946. Trachtenberg, *A Constructed Peace*, 38. Truman later stressed his unhappiness with the agreement on Germany's eastern frontiers reached at Potsdam. Harry S. Truman, *Year of Decisions*, Memoirs: Volume One (New York: Doubleday, 1955), 367–70. On US attitudes to the expulsion of Germans from the Oder–Neiße territories, see Persson, *Rhetorik und Realpolitik*, 174–7.

52 Digest of a meeting with Allen W. Dulles at the Council on Foreign Relations, 3 December 1945. 'That Was Then: Allen W. Dulles on the Occupation of Germany' *Foreign Affairs*, November/December 2003, online, available at: foreignaffairs.org.

53 Vladimir O. Petchatov, ' "The Allies are Pressing on you to Break your Will …": Foreign Policy Correspondence between Stalin and Molotov and other Politburo Members, September 1945–December 1946' (Washington DC: Cold War International History Project, 1999).

54 PRO: CAB 129/9, CP (46) 156, Gen. 121/1, memorandum 'The Future of Germany and the Ruhr', Ernest Bevin, 11 March 1946; Rolf Steininger (ed.), *Die Ruhrfrage 1945–6 und die Entstehung des Landes Nordrhein Westfalen: Britische, Französische und Amerikanische Akten* (Düsseldorf: Droste, 1988), 725.

55 Byrnes speech, 6 September 1946, online, available at: www.lpb.bwue.de/publikat/byrnes3.htm, Die Landeszentrale für politische Bildung Baden-Württemberg. There are very good grounds for regarding Byrnes' speech with some cynicism. Byrnes, signalling early US disillusion with the idea that Germany could be run on a Four-Power basis, had actually offered to recognise the Oder–Neiße line at Potsdam whilst effectively breaking Germany up into distinct economic units. See Trachtenberg, *A Constructed Peace*, 26.

56 H. Bodensieck (ed.), *Die Deutsche Frage seit dem Zweiten Welt Krieg* (Stuttgart: Ernst Klett, 3rd edn, 1985), 29–30.

57 Eisenberg, *Drawing the Line*, esp. 363–410.

58 Ahonen, *After the Expulsion*, 26–7.

59 National Archives (College Park, Washington DC) RG 59 Lot Files 87 D 236 Box 1, memorandum State Department's Office of Public Affairs 50/10

'American Responsibility for the Expulsion of Germans from Eastern Europe' (nd, *c.*1947).

60 Debra J. Allen, *The Oder–Neisse Line: The United States, Poland, and Germany in the Cold War* (London: Praeger, 2003), 72–80.

61 Eisenberg, *Drawing the Line*, 278.

62 *Foreign Relations of the United States* (*FRUS*), 1947, Volume II, 789.

63 HSTL: OH: Elbridge Durbrow, 68–9, online, available at: www.truman-library.org/oralhist/durbrow.htm.

64 Eisenberg, *Drawing the Line*, 355.

65 Hugh Gaitskell Archives, UCL, Box C21 Frank Pakenham to Bevin, 24 November 1948.

66 PRO: FO 953/380, [30/30/965] Report of UNESCO meeting (New York), Christopher Mayhew, Under Secretary for Foreign Affairs, BISME, Cairo to MEID, 10 February 1948.

67 Gaddis, *We Now Know*, 150–1. On 2 April 1945, Hitler predicted 'it is … certain that both these Powers will sooner or later find it desirable to seek the support of the sole surviving great nation in Europe, the German people.' Gaddis, *We Now Know*, 1.

68 Morgan, 'The British View', 89.

69 HSTL: OH: Elbridge Durbrow, 73, online, available at: www.trumanlibrary.org/oralhist/durbrow.htm. In this the British were in solid agreement with the United States. A State Department Memorandum concluded that 'the West [must] develop West Germany politically and economically as part of the Western European system under the … protection of the western allies.' State Department Memorandum, 6 September 1948 (Jacques J. Rubenstein, Special Assistant Secretary of State for Economic Affairs, to Willard Thorp, Assistant Secretary of State). *FRUS*, 1948, Volume II, 1287–9.

70 Dean Acheson, 12 October 1949. Wolfgang Heidelmeye and Guenter Hindrichs (eds), *Documents on Berlin 1943–1963* (Munich: Oldenbourg, 1963), 159–60; *FRUS*, 1949, Volume III, 532.

71 Klaus Larres, 'Britain and the GDR: Political and Economic Relations, 1949–1989', in Larres and Meehan, *Uneasy Allies*, 66–7.

72 Chester Wilmot, 'Britain's Strategic Relationship to Europe', *International Affairs*, 29/3 (1953), 414.

73 For the full text, see von Oppen, *Documents on Germany Under Occupation*, 517–20. On the manner in which West German policy was strengthened by this, see PRO: FO 371/154093, [WG 1076/21] 'Germany's position under international law', German Embassy Paper, 4 July 1960. The similarity to the actually declared aims of the Federal Republic's founding fathers is obvious. The West German *Grundgesetz* (Basic Law), signed on May 23 1949, declared in the Preamble that 'They [the German people in the three western zones] have also acted on behalf of those Germans to whom participation was denied [i.e. those in the Soviet zone and beyond the Oder–Neiße line]. The entire German people are called upon to achieve in free self-determination the unity and freedom of Germany.' From *Democracy in Germany: History and Perspectives, Federal Republic of Germany* (Bonn: Press and Information Office of the Federal Government, 1983), 97.

74 PRO: FO 371/177917, [RG 103155/3] R.G. Sheridan, 14 August 1964.

75 For the full text of the 10 March note, see Bodensieck, *Die Deutsche Frage seit dem Zweiten Weltkrieg*, 51. For discussion of the note, see Gaddis, *We Now Know*, 124–9; Melvyn P. Leffler, *A Preponderance of Power: National Security, the Truman Administration, and the Cold War* (Stanford: Stanford University Press, 1992), 457–63.

76 On the debate, see Hannes Adomeit, *Imperial Overstretch: Germany in Soviet Policy from Stalin to Gorbachev* (Baden-Baden: Nomos, 1998), 87–92; Ruud van

Dojk, *The 1952 Stalin Note Debate: Myth or Missed Opportunity?*, Cold War International History Project Working Paper Number 14, May 1996. For a provocative statement of a more anti-Western view see, for example, Wilfried Loth, 'Das Ende der Legende: Hermann Graml und die Stalin-Note: Eine Entgegnung', *Vierteljahrshefte für Zeitgeschichte*, 50/4 (2002), 653–64.

77 PRO: PREM 11/172, [C. (52) 137] 'The Oder Neisse Line. A Memorandum by the Secretary of State for Foreign Affairs [Eden]' May 1952.

78 Andreas Hillgruber, 'Adenauer und die Stalin-Note' in Dieter Blumenwitz (ed.), *Konrad Adenauer und seine Zeit*, vol. 2 (Stuttgart: Deutsche-Verlags Anstalt, 1976), 113–15.

79 Kipp, *Eden, Adenauer und die deutsche Frage*, 89.

80 PRO: FO 371/103665, [C 1073/43] BBC Monitoring report of North-West German radio interview with Adenauer, 11 June 1953. See also Josef Joffe, 'The View from Bonn', in Lincoln Gordon *et al.*, *Eroding Empire*, 140–1.

81 Ahonen, 'Domestic Constraints on West German Ostpolitik', 40.

82 Adenauer to the *Bundestag*, 11 July 1953. Quoted in the pamphlet *The Wall and Humanity* (Berlin (Ost): GDR Information Office, 1962), 9.

83 FDP Wahlprogramm 1953; Schumacher statement: Hamburg-Bergedorf, 1946 (repeated in numerous SPD statements and publications for the next dozen or so years). Ahonen, 'Domestic Constraints on West German Ostpolitik', 41.

84 PRO: FO 371/103664, FO Research Department, LR 8/2 (GER/215/53), 'Political factors relating to the reunification of Germany', no exact date, *c.* June 1953.

85 PRO: FO 371/103699, [C 1071/935] Discussion between Adenauer and Eden, Paris, 12 December 1953.

86 John W. Young, 'Cold War and Détente with Moscow', in John W. Young (ed.), *The Foreign Policy of Churchill's Peacetime Administration 1951–55* (Leicester University Press, 1988), 64–5.

87 PRO: FO 371/103665, [C 1071/56] Lloyd to Churchill, 22 June 1953.

88 Young, 'Cold War and Détente with Moscow', 64.

89 Christopher Andrew, 'Anglo-American-Soviet Intelligence Relations' in A. Lane and H. Temperley (eds), *The Rise and Fall of the Grand Alliance 1941–45* (London: Macmillan, 1995), 127–8.

90 Greenwood, *Britain and the Cold War*, 10. See also Bower, *A Pledge Betrayed*, 408.

91 Drew Middleton, 'Adenauer: Germany Reborn', in New York Times (ed.), *Portraits of Power* (London: Octopus, 1979), 138.

92 PRO: DEFE 4/10, Ernest Bevin from the Minutes, C-O-S meeting, 10 Downing Street, 4 February 1948.

93 Bevin paper written for the US Department of State, January 1948; Christopher Bluth, 'British–German Defence Relations, 1950–80: A Survey', Karl Kaiser and John Roper (eds), *British–German Defence Co-operation* (London: Jane's/RIIA, 1988), 3.

94 The debate in the French National Assembly on the NATO alliance in 1949 was marked by a succession of anti-German outbursts. F. Roy Willis, 'Germany, France and Europe', in Wolfgang F. Hanrieder (ed.), *West German Foreign Policy: 1949–1979* (Colorado: Westview Press, 1980), 97.

95 Harry Pollitt, *In Defence of Peace: the Case Against Rearming the Nazis* (London: Communist Party, 1954), 1.

96 Aneurin Bevan, Barbara. Castle, Tom Driberg, Ian Mikardo and Harold Wilson, *It Need Not Happen*, (London: Tribune, 1954), 13.

97 See Memorandum des Bundeskanzlers [Geh. 91/50] 29 August 1950, document 113, Auftrag des Auswärtigen Amts vom Institut für Zeitgeschichte (ed.), *Akten zur Auswärtigen Politik der Bundesrepublik Deutschland 1949/50: September 1949 bis Dezember 1950* (Munich: Oldenbourg, 1997).

98 Ivone Kirkpatrick, *The Inner Circle* (London; Macmillan, 1959), 238. Eisenhower stated in a report to Congress on the first six months of 1955 that the 'war scare' of Korea had been a catalyst for German rearmament. Jain, *Germany, the Soviet Union and Eastern Europe 1949–1991*, 4, 285 (n).

99 Spencer Mawby, 'Détente deferred: The Attlee Government, German rearmament and Anglo-Soviet Rapprochement 1950–51', *Contemporary British History*, 12/2 (1998), 1–21.

100 Spencer Mawby, *Containing Germany: Britain and the Arming of the Federal Republic*, (Basingstoke: Macmillan, 1999), 3–4. Denis Healey specifically proposed using German rearmament as a bargaining chip in discussion with the Foreign Minister Herbert Morrison. LPA: Meeting of Dalton, Healey and Morrison, Foreign Office, 12 April 1951.

101 PRO: PREM 8/1203, Attlee to Bevin, 5 September 1950.

102 Mawby, *Containing Germany*, 2.

103 Beatrice Heuser, *NATO, Britain, France and the FRG: Nuclear Strategies and Forces for Europe, 1949–2000* (London: Macmillan, 1997), 22.

104 PRO: T 234/24, A. Mackay, HM Treasury, note on German support costs, 26 November 1955. See also Kirkpatrick, *The Inner Circle*, 242. Khrushchev recognised this: 'for ... western politicians the development of the West German economy – while West Germany is being dragged into NATO and participating in the arms race – is almost beneficial.' JFKL: POF Box 125, Notes, Soviet Affairs, Number 241, 18 May 1960, 'The Quotable Khrushchev April 1959–March 1960'. Speech to Supreme Soviet, 14 January 1960.

105 Konrad Adenauer, 'Germany and Europe', *Foreign Affairs*, April 1953, 366.

106 Lloyd later specifically warned against the Soviet desire to break up NATO, in which Moscow saw the SPD as potential allies, PRO: CAB 129/86 C 57 (53), 4 March 1957.

107 For instance, on 8 June 1953 the *Evening Standard* asserted that while Adenauer was genuinely committed to Western integration and democracy, the same could not be assured of his successors. Furthermore, it must be remembered that any restitution of territory to Germany would be at the expense of Poland, Czechoslovakia and France!

108 PRO: CAB 129/74, C (55) 83, 'Talks with the Soviet Union', note by the Foreign Secretary, 25 March 1955. A belief in the fragility of West German democratic culture persisted and Selwyn Lloyd informed Macmillan in 1958 that 'We must be under no illusions as to the tremendous influence which Dr Adenauer personally exercises on German thought. As soon as he is gone, the scene could change rapidly.' PRO: FO 371/137398, Lloyd in a brief to Macmillan, 10 January 1958. Adenauer was similarly pessimistic about the prospects for Germany reverting to nationalism after him, hence his messianic zeal to submerge Germany in Europe, and often invoked Louis XVs famous quote: 'After me; the deluge.' During a late-night conversation at Claridge's in London in 1954, Adenauer stated 'Once I am gone I don't know what is to become of Germany'. Rudolf Augstein, *Konrad Adenauer* (London: Secker & Warburg, 1964), 173.

109 Bodleian: COB 12, (1: CDU 1954–56), meetings with CDU at Freidrichsruh, 10–13 October 1955.

110 Claus Arndt, 'Legal Problems of the German Eastern Territories', *American Journal of International Law*, 74/1 (1980), 126–8.

111 FRG government memorandum submitted to the *Bundesrat* in 1954 (*Bundesrat-Drucksache* No. 400/54). Krzysztof Skubiszewski, 'Poland's Western Frontiers and the 1970 Treaties', *American Journal of International Law*, 67/1 (1973), 25.

112 Von Brentano interview, Südwestfunk Baden-Baden, 2 May *1956. The Bulletin:*

A Weekly Survey of German Affairs (Bonn: Press and Information Office of the German Federal Government, 4 May 1956).

113 Keesing's Research Report Number 8, *Germany and Eastern Europe Since 1945: From the Potsdam Agreement to Chancellor Brandt's 'Ostpolitik'* (New York: Scribner, 1973), 60. The GDR believed the treaty 'represented a radical break with the aggressive policies former German governments had practiced against their Polish neighbour.' See GDR Academy of Sciences, *Information GDR* (Oxford: Pergamon, 1989), 174.

114 SED Abteilung Massenorganisation, *Warum ist die Oder–Neiße-Linie eine Freidensgrenze?* (East Berlin, 1950), 1.

115 Enno Meyer, *Deutschland und Polen: 1914–1970* (Stuttgart: Ernst Klett, 1971), 92.

116 Rechtsverwahrung des Deutschen Bundestages zur Warschauer Deklaration, 13 June 1950. Ingo von Münch (ed.), *Dokumente des geteilen Deutschland* (Stuttgart: Brentano, 1968), 496.

117 Ludwik Gelberg, 'The Warsaw Treaty of 1970 and the western Boundary of Poland', *American Journal of International Law*, 76/1 (1982), 123.

118 R.W. Piotrowicz, 'The Polish–German Frontier in International Law: the Final Solution', *British Year Book of International Law 1992* (Oxford: Oxford University Press, 1992), 371.

119 See the letter of Adenauer to the Chairman of the Allied High Commission, John C. McCloy [231–11 II/6646/50] 24 August 1950, document 112, *Akten zur Auswärtigen Politik der Bundesrepublik Deutschland 1949/50: September 1949 bis Dezember 1950* (Munich: Oldenbourg, 1997).

120 PRO: FO 1008/2, Control Commission for Germany (British Element), Tel. No. 29, Wahnerheide, 12 January 1951. Discussion of draft Adenauer statement to be delivered on 15 January 1951.

121 'Homeland across the Oder–Neisse: Herr Kaiser's demands', *Manchester Guardian*, 25 August 1951. A note on the FO file containing this described the speech as 'understandable but regrettable', PRO: FO 371/93471, [C 1083/13].

122 PRO: FO 371/93471, [C 1083/23] Sir Ivone Kirkpatrick, Control Commission for Germany (British element), Wahnerheide, Tel. no. 1111, 20 November 1951.

123 PRO: PREM 11/172, 15 November 1951, Sir Ivone Kirkpatrick telegram to FO, meeting between Kirkpatrick, McCloy, François-Poncet and Adenauer.

124 Federal statement, 9 June 1950 upon the announcement of the intention to sign a GDR–Polish [the Treaty of Görlitz] agreement on 6 July 1950, Keesing's, *Germany and Eastern Europe Since 1945*, 59. Adenauer told the three western High Commissioners on 17 March 1952 that no German government could accept the Oder–Neiße line. Adenauer said that the only line he could take was that Germany would reach agreement with some future free Polish government. Acting High Commissioner Hays to Secretary of State Acheson, 17 March 1952. *FRUS*, 1951–2, Volume VII, 182–3.

125 PRO: PREM 11/172, 15 November 1951, Sir Ivone Kirkpatrick telegram to FO, meeting between Kirkpatrick, McCloy, François-Poncet and Adenauer.

126 Willy Brandt, *My Life In Politics* (London: Hamish Hamilton, 1992), 35.

127 Kirkpatrick termed Adenauer a 'redoubtable ... adversary ... always quick to detect any weakness in his opponent's armour and to drive his weapon through the chink.' Kirkpatrick, *The Inner Circle*, 230.

128 PRO: PREM 11/172, Eden to Churchill, nd [1951].

129 PRO: PREM 11/172, 16 November 1951, Churchill minute, M 58c/51.

130 PRO: FO 371/103714, [C 1083/5] FO Minute, Anthony Nutting MP (Parliamentary Under-Secretary of State for Foreign Affairs), 14 May 1953.

Report on conversation with Wolfgang Schutz, PR adviser to the Ministry of All-German Affairs on the question of the eastern territories.

131 PRO: FO 371/109638, [CW 1194/42] Gladwyn Jebb, Paris to G.W. Harrison, FO, 10 November 1954.

132 PRO: FO 371/103714, [C 1083/14] P.F. Hancock minute, 9 October 1953.

133 For a recent study, see Sabine Lee, 'CDU Refugee Policies and the Landesverband Oder/Neiße: Electoral Tool or Instrument of Integration?', *German Politics*, 8/1 (1999), 131–49.

134 Ian Clark and Nicholas J. Wheeler, *The British Origins of Nuclear Strategy, 1945–55* (Oxford: Clarendon, 1995), 42.

135 Bullock, *Bevin, 1945–1951*, 82.

136 Barker, *The British Between the Superpowers 1945–50*, 185.

137 LPA: NEC International Sub-Committee, Memo on 'Questions of International Policy', 1951.

138 PRO: FO 371/85052, [C 5541/27/18] Bevin to Harvey, Paris, 5 September 1950.

139 See *FRUS*, 1952–4, volume VII, 29.

140 PRO: FO 371/98127, British embassy, 26 May 1952 and 28 May 1952, records of conversations at the Quai d' Orsay.

141 Valur Ingimundarson, 'The Eisenhower, the Adenauer Government, and the Political Uses of the East German Uprising in 1953', *Diplomatic History*, 20/3 (1996), 384. On Anglo-American reactions to the East German Rising of June 1953, see Klaus Larres, 'Preserving Law and Order; Britain, the United States and the East German Uprising of 1953', *Twentieth Century British History*, 5/3 (1994), 320–50.

142 Adenauer speech in Berne, 25 March 1949. Paul Weymar, *Konrad Adenauer: the Authorised Biography*, trans. Peter de Mendelssohn (London: Andre Deutsch, 1957), 240. Adenauer later denounced the Oder–Neiße line as being restrictive of Germany 'both economically and as a people', *Manchester Guardian*, 9 September 1949.

143 Konrad Adenauer, *Erinnerungen, 1955–1959* (Stuttgart: DVA, 1967), 453.

144 *The Times*, 21 September 1949 (Adenauer speech to the Bundestag, 20 September 1949).

145 Memorandum of meeting between de Gaulle and Adenauer, 21 January 1963, document 37, *Akten zur Auswärtigen Politik der Bundesrepublik Deutschland 1963: Band I* (Munich: Oldenbourg, 1994).

146 Rudolf Walter Leonhardt, *This Germany: the Story Since the Third Reich*, trans. Catherine Hutter, (London: Penguin, 1966), 36.

147 W. Benz (ed.), 'Introduction', in *Die Vertreibung der Deutschen aus dem Osten: Ursachen, Erignisse, Folgen* (Frankfurt: Fischer 1985), 10.

148 *Charta der deutschen Heimatvertreibenen* (Bonn: Bundesministerium für Vertriebene, Flüchtlinge und Kriegsgeschädigte, 1950). This is still available at the official CDU web page at: www.cdu.de/omv/charta.htm.

149 Sabine Lee, 'Perception and Reality: Anglo-German Relations during the Berlin Crisis, 1958–1959', *German History*, 13/1 (1995), 47–69.

150 *Hansard*, HC Deb, vol. 518, cols. 230–1, 21 July 1953.

151 Klaus Larres, *Churchill's Cold War: The Politics of Personal Diplomacy* (London: Yale University Press, 2002), 190–2.

152 *Hansard*, HC Deb, vol. 515, col. 897.

153 *Hansard*, HC Deb, vol. 515, col. 896. See also Bodensieck, *Die Deutsche Frage seit dem Zweiten Weltkrieg*, 57.

154 PRO: FO 371/103705, [C 1074/7] Adenauer Press Conference, London, 16 May 1953.

155 See *FRUS*, 1952–4, volume VI, 964–75.

156 President Dwight D. Eisenhower letter and draft resolution to Vice-President

Richard M. Nixon and the Speaker of the House of Representatives, Joseph W. Martin Jr, 20 February 1953. Zygmunt C. Szkopiak (ed.), *The Yalta Agreements: the White Book: Documents prior to, during and after the Crimea Conference 1945* (London: Polish Government in Exile, 1986), 152.

157 Konrad Adenauer, *Erinnerungen 1953–1955* (Stuttgart: DVA, 1966), 243.

158 Bulletin of the Press and Information Bureau of the Federal Government, 31 July 1953.

159 Ernest R. May, 'The American Commitment to Germany 1949–55', *Diplomatic History*, 13/4 (1989), 459.

160 Avon Papers: AP 20/1/30, diary entry, 27 November 1954.

161 Churchill to Eisenhower, 8 August 1953, Peter G. Boyle (ed.), *The Churchill–Eisenhower Correspondence* (University of North Carolina, 1990), 166.

162 Larres, *Churchill's Cold War*, 217–18.

163 Despite its stillborn appearance, Coral Bell later heralded this moment as the birth of détente as a 'western aspiration'. Coral Bell, *The Diplomacy of Détente* (London: Martin Robertson, 1977), 6ff.

164 Eden was always far closer to the professionals in the Foreign Office than was his more impetuous chief. Kipp, *Eden, Adenauer und die Deutsche Frage*, 394.

165 See PRO: PREM 11/428; PRO: PREM 11/449; PRO: PREM 11/905.

166 Kipp, *Eden, Adenauer und die Deutsche Frage*, 155, 197.

167 Adenauer sent Blankenhorn to Washington in June 1953 in order to forestall a deal over his head by the three Western Allies at the planned Bermuda summit, *The Times*, 3 June 1953.

168 *Manchester Guardian*, 8 June 1953.

169 Larres, *Politik der Illusionen*, 194–6.

170 Sir William Hayter, *The Kremlin and the Embassy* (London: Hodder & Stoughton, 1966), 107. Jebb himself was very suspicious of the moderate stance of Malenkov, possibly suspecting the hand of Burgess and Maclean. Thus, Jebb was relieved when Khrushchev and Bulganin initiated a tougher foreign policy line as Jebb himself suggested in a letter to Hayter. See *The Memoirs of Lord Gladwyn*, 277.

171 *The Memoirs of Lord Gladwyn*, 277–8.

172 Brian White, *Britain, Détente and Changing East–West Relations* (London: Routledge, 1992), 50.

173 Klaus Larres, 'Germany and the West: the "Rapallo factor" in German Foreign Policy from the 1950s to the 1990s', in Klaus Larres and Panikos Panayi, *The Federal Republic of Germany Since 1949: Politics, Society and Economy Before and Since Reunification* (London: Longman, 1996), n. 55, 290. On Britain and the 'Rapallo factor', see Spencer Mawby, 'Revisiting Rapallo: Britain, Germany and the Cold War, 1945–1955' in Hopkins *et al.* (2003), 81–94

174 Konrad Adenauer, *World Indivisible* (London: George Allen & Unwin, 1956), 36. Dean Rusk later recalled that Adenauer was the ultimate 'Cold Warrior', someone who was forever giving him books on the expansionist tendencies of the Slavs. JFKL Oral History Program (JFK: OHP): Dean Rusk, interview number four, 177.

175 Stiftung Bundeskanzler Adenauer Haus (StBKAH): KAA/02.14/28, Adenauer speech, 77th German 'Katholikentag', Cologne, 2 September 1956.

176 JFKL: POF Box 117, Adenauer to Kennedy, 4 October 1961.

177 Cmd. 8571, *Convention on Relations Between the Three Western Powers and the Federal Republic*, London: HMSO, 26 May 1952.

178 See, for instance, *White Book on the Bonn War Treaty*, Information Office of the GDR, 1952.

179 *Hansard*, HC Deb, vol. 520, cols. 315–16, 5 November 1953.

180 Adenauer, *World Indivisible*, 51.

181 Churchill to Eisenhower, 18 September 1954 in Boyle, *The Churchill–Eisenhower Correspondence*, 175. On Britain and the EDC, see Kevin Ruane, *The Rise and Fall of the European Defence Community: Anglo-American Relations and the Crisis of European Defence, 1950–55* (London: Macmillan, 2000).

182 Eden, *Full Circle*, 149–53, 154.

183 Rhodes James, *Anthony Eden*, 388.

184 For full text, see von Oppen, *Documents on Germany Under Occupation*, 614–49.

185 Jain, *Germany, the Soviet Union and Eastern Europe*, 9–10.

186 PRO: 472/7, [N 1071/6] 'Meeting of the Political Consultative Committee of the Warsaw Pact', Prague, [P 10133/12 G] 19 May 1955.

187 The official government bulletin stressed the historic significance of the regaining of (West) German sovereignty, 'Im Besitz der Souveränität', *Bulletin des Presse- und Informationsamtes der Bundesregierung*, 5 May 1955, no. 84, 695–6.

188 Ronald J. Granieri, *The Ambivalent Alliance: Konrad Adenauer, the CDU/CSU, and the West, 1949–1966* (Oxford: Berghahn, 2003), 73.

189 UCL: Gaitskell Papers, (Box G 166): *The Berlin Conference*, published by *Soviet News*, London, 1954.

190 General Treaty on Germany (*Deutschlandvertrag*), 23 October 1954. Stefan Wolff, *The German Question since 1919: An Analysis with Key Documents*, Perspectives on the Twentieth Century Series (London: Praeger, 2003), 195.

191 Andreas Hillgruber, *Europa in der Weltpolitik der Nachkriegszeit (1945–1963)* (Munich: Oldenbourg, 1981), 70.

192 Paul Wedermeyer, *Konrad Adenauer: The Authorised Autobiography* (London: Heinemann, 1957), 458.

193 StBKAH: KAA/02.13/54, Adenauer quoted in the *Bulletin*, 240, 22 December 1955, 2057.

194 *Documents on Canadian External Affairs*, High Commissioner in United Kingdom to Secretary of State for External Affairs, 2 February 1955, Report of the second plenary session of Commonwealth Prime Ministers, London, online, available at: www.dfait-maeci.gc.ca/department/history/dcer.

195 *Hansard*, HC Deb, vol. 557, col. 248, 24 July 1955.

196 Alan Watson, *The Germans: Who are they now?* (London: Thames Methuen, 1992), 229.

197 Konrad Adenauer, *Erinnerungen 1945–53* (Stuttgart: DVA, 1965), 282.

198 Quoted in speech by the British Defence Secretary, George Robertson, 'NATO at 50' Conference, 10 March 1999. British embassy in Washington DC, online, available at: www.britainusa.com.

199 Clemens A. Wurm, 'Britain and West European Integration, 1948–9 to 1955: Politics and Economics', in Noakes, Wende and Wright, *Britain and Germany in Europe*, 27–48.

200 Prittie, *Adenauer*, 26.

201 Terence Prittie, 'The Statesman: Historical Perspective', in Horst Osterheld, Terence Prittie and François Seydoux, *Konrad Adenauer* (Bonn: Aktuell, 1983), 26. For a discussion of Bevin and European integration see, Hugo Young, *This Blessed Plot: Britain and Europe from Churchill to Blair* (London: Papermac, 1999), 26–70.

202 Churchill made this plea in a speech in Zurich in September 1946. Prittie, *Adenauer*, 25.

203 On this, John W. Young, 'Churchill's "No" to Europe: the "Rejection" of European Union by Churchill's Post-War Government, 1951–1952', *Historical Journal*, 28/4 (1985), 923–37; Kaiser, *Using Europe, Abusing the Europeans*, 11–2.

204 Rhodes James, *Anthony Eden*, 350–1.

205 PRO: FO 371/103699, [C 1071/935] Adenauer–Eden meeting, British embassy Paris, 12 December 1953.

206 Adenauer, *Erinnerungen 1953–1955*, 386–9.

207 Adenauer, *World Indivisible*, 52; 53–4.

208 Lee, 'Anglo-German Relations 1958–59', 789.

209 Adenauer, *World Indivisible*, 47–8.

210 'Statement by the Four Powers on Control Machinery in Germany', 5 June 1945 in Cmd. 1552, *Selected Documents on Germany and the Question of Berlin 1944–1961* (London: HMSO, 1961).

211 Duff Cooper, *Old Men Forget* (London: Readers Union, Rupert Hart-Davis, 1955), 337.

212 *New York Times*, 18 August 1950.

213 Northedge and Wells, *Britain and Soviet Communism*, 133.

214 D. Wilson, 'Anglo-Soviet Relations: the Effect on Ideas and Reality', *International Affairs*, 50/3 (1974), 391.

215 Lord Strang, *Britain in World Affairs* (Westport: Greenwood Press, 1961), 359–60.

216 Harold Nicolson, *Diplomacy* (London: Thornton Butterworth, 1939), 54.

217 Churchill, 14 February 1950. R.R. James (ed.), *Winston Churchill: His Complete Speeches 1897–1963*, Volume VIII, *1950–63* (London: Heinemann, 1974), 736–44.

218 Coral Bell, *Negotiation from Strength* (London: Chatto & Windus, 1962).

219 Morgan, 'The British View', 87.

220 John L. Gaddis, *Strategies of Containment: A Critical Appraisal of Postwar American National Security Policy* (New York: Oxford University Press, 1982), 71; George F. Kennan, *The Nuclear Delusion* (New York: Pantheon, 1982), xii–xiii.

221 By 1948, the British intelligence community had no doubt as to whom their political masters regarded as the enemy. See, for instance, JIC (48) 19 (0). 'Sigint Intelligence Requirements – 1948'. Draft report by the Joint Intelligence Committee, 11 May 1948, L/WS/1/1196/, IOLR. Richard J. Aldrich, *Espionage, Security and Intelligence in Britain 1945–1970* (Manchester: Manchester University Press, 1998), 39–43.

222 On this so-called *Zweckpessimismus* ('calculated pessimism'), see Roland G. Foerster, 'Innenpolitik Aspekte der Sicherheit Westdeutschlands (1947–1950)' in MGFA (ed.), *Anfänge westdeutscher Sicherheitspolitik, 1945–1956: Band 1: Von der Kapitulation bis zum Pleven-Plan* (Munich: Oldenbourg, 1982), 510–11.

223 Pyotr Abrasimov, *West Berlin: Yesterday and Today* (Dresden: Zeit in Bild, 1981), 36.

2 Détente or *Politik der Stärke?*

1 *Documents on Germany under Occupation 1945–1954*, selected and edited by Beate Ruhm von Oppen (RIIA/Oxford: Oxford University Press, 1955), 600–9. The London statement was endorsed in October 1954 by the full NATO council and again in September 1955 by the three Western foreign ministers. Bonn reminded the British of this in subsequent years. See, for instance, PRO: FO 371/154093, [WG 1076/21] 'Germany's position under international law', German embassy Paper, 4 July 1960.

2 Caroline Kennedy-Pipe, *Stalin's Cold War: Soviet Strategies in Europe, 1943–56* (Manchester: Manchester University Press, 1995), 196.

3 Adomeit, *Imperial Overstretch*, 71–2.

4 In 1950, the Foreign Office noted that Moscow saw Germany's eastern frontiers as permanent. PRO: FO 371/86156 [Ger/157/50] Changes in German frontier since 1945, FO minute Research Department, 4 July 1950.

5 PRO: FO 975/93 [B. 273] Soviet Note to the Western Powers, 9 April 1950.

6 Joffe, 'The View from Bonn', 141.

7 Ahonen, *After the Expulsion*, 114–15.

8 Eisenhower, diary entry, 8 October 1953. Trachtenberg, *A Constructed Peace*, 132.

9 There was much contemporary speculation over historical precedents for this, often referring to the centuries-old *Drang nach Osten* ('drive to the East'). With regard to eastward-looking events and understandings with Russian, one might point to the four partitions of Poland (1772, 1793, 1795 and 1939); the Holy Alliance (1815); the *Dreikaiserbund* (1873); the Soviet–German Treaties of Rapallo (1922) and Berlin (1926); and the Nazi-Soviet Pact (1939). These events all featured in commentaries on West German policy toward the East after 1949.

10 In her recent study on Eden and Germany, Yvonne Kipp asserts that British fears on Rapallo were based less on historical realities than on a myth of 'German–Russian complicity'. Kipp, *Eden, Adenauer und die Deutsche Frage*, 83.

11 'Politics of swing' or 'pendulum politics' – that is, a Germany that would incline towards the East or the West, dependent upon circumstances.

12 Kipp, *Eden, Adenauer und die Deutsche Frage*, 393.

13 StBKAH: KKA/02.14, Adenauer speech to 'Grandes Conférences Catholiques', Brussels, 25 September 1956.

14 NSC 162/2, 3 October 1953. John Lewis Gaddis, *Strategies of Containment: A Critical Appraisal of Postwar American National Security Policy* (Oxford: Oxford University Press, 1982), 155. For the limits of 'roll-back', see Valur Ingimundarson, 'The Eisenhower, the Adenauer Government, and the Political Uses of the East German Uprising in 1953', *Diplomatic History*, 20/3 (1996), 326–8.

15 NATO document MC (FINAL) of 22 November 1954: 'The most effective pattern of NATO military strength for the next few years'. Heuser, *NATO, Britain, France and the FRG*, 1.

16 *The Policy of the Renunciation of Force: Documents on German and Soviet Declarations of the Renunciation of Force* (Bonn: Federal Press and Information Office, 1968), 5.

17 *Handbook of German Affairs* (Washington DC: German Mission, 1954), 84.

18 Lawrence L. Whetten, *Germany's Ostpolitik: Relations between the Federal Republic and the Warsaw Pact. Countries* (Oxford: Oxford University Press/RIIA, 1971), 11–12.

19 Planck, *The Changing Status of German Reunification in Western Diplomacy, 1955–1966*, 6.

20 PRO: FO 371/103664, FO Research Department, LR 8/2 (GER/215/53), 'Political factors relating to the reunification of Germany', no exact date, *c.* June 1953.

21 Karl Kaiser, *German Foreign Policy in Transition: Bonn between East and West* (Oxford: Oxford University Press, 1968), 1–2.

22 Planck, *The Changing Status of German Reunification in Western Diplomacy*, 4.

23 PRO: CAB 129/74, C (55), 25 March 1955.

24 See, for instance, PRO: CAB 128/31, CC (57), 16 (7), 7 March 1957.

25 StBKAH: KAA/02.14/21, Adenauer press conference, Washington DC, 13 June 1956.

26 Antonio Varsori, 'Britain as a Bridge Between East and West', in Wilfred Loth (ed.), *Europe, Cold War and Coexistence, 1953–1965* (London: Frank Cass, 2004), 18.

27 PRO: CAB 129/79, C 83 (55), 25 March 1955.

28 Vladislav Zubok, CWIHP, Working paper 6: 'Khrushchev and the Berlin Crisis (1958–62)'.

29 JFKL: POF Box 125, Notes, Soviet Affairs, number 215, 14 October 1957, 'The

Quotable Khrushchev 1934–1957'. Speech in Rangoon, *Pravda*, 7 December 1955.

30 PRO: PRO: CAB 128/29, CC (55) 31 (9), 15 September 1955.

31 StBKAH: KAA/02.13/40, Adenauer speech, 9 September 1955, Moscow.

32 Heinrich von Siegler, *The Reunification and Security of Germany: A Documentary Basis for Discussion* (Munich: Siegler & Co. K. G. Verlag für Zeitarchive, 1957), 59; Anthon, 'Adenauer's Ostpolitik', 116.

33 Jain, *Germany, the Soviet Union and Eastern Europe 1949–1991*, 12.

34 Gordon A. Craig, *The Germans* (London: Pelican Books, 1984), 47

35 'Ollenhauer on Diplomatic Relations between Bonn and Moscow', *News from Germany* [SPD newspaper] 9/10, October 1955.

36 PRO: PRO: CAB 128/29, CC (55) 31 (9), 15 September 1955.

37 Macmillan, *Tides of Fortune*, 649.

38 Adenauer, *World Indivisible*, 19.

39 Macmillan, *Tides of Fortune*, 648.

40 PRO: CAB 128/29, CC (55) 23 (5), 14 July 1955.

41 UCL: Gaitskell Papers, (Box C68): Foreign Affairs Group of the PLP. Denis Healey, 'The Problem of the E.D.C.' [nd 1953].

42 PRO: CAB 129/74, C (55) 83, 25 March 1955. This was reiterated constantly e.g. PRO: PREM 11/1365, Hoyer Miller (ambassador to Bonn 1955–7) to FO, 16 March 1956.

43 PRO: FO 371/137398, [WG 1052/11] 17 December 1957, Macmillan to Lloyd.

44 PRO: PREM 11/2876, Macmillan–Dulles meeting, Downing Street, 4 February 1959.

45 PRO: CAB 128/29, CM (55) 36 (5), 20 October 1955. See also Lloyd to Cabinet, PRO: CAB 128/31 C (57) 16 (7), 7 March 1957.

46 Stephanie C. Salzmann, *Great Britain, Germany and the Soviet Union: Rapallo and After, 1922–1934* (London: Boydell, 2003), 1.

47 PRO: CAB 129/81 C (56) 112, 2 May 1956 'The Future of NATO', note by Secretary to the Cabinet, Norman Brook. For similar, see PRO: CAB 128/31 C (57) 16 (7), 7 March 1957. In 1955 Macmillan noted in Cabinet the alarm in the United States and France over Adenauer's visit to Moscow, PRO: CAB 128/29 CC (55) 31 (9), 15 September 1955.

48 PRO: CAB 129/81, C 112 (56), 2 May 1956.

49 PRO: CAB 129/86, C (57) 53, 4 March 1957.

50 PRO: PREM 11/2347, 17 December 1958.

51 PRO: FO 371/137398, [WG 1081/3] P.A. Wilkinson (Bonn) to P.F. Hancock (Head of the Western Department), 31 December 1957.

52 StBKAH: KAA/02.14/8, extract from Adenauer's electoral campaign broadcast of 2 March 1956.

53 Anthon, 'Adenauer's Ostpolitik', 114–15.

54 PRO: CAB 129/9, CP (46) 156, Gen. 121/1, memorandum by 'The Future of Germany and the Ruhr', Ernest Bevin, 11 March 1946.

55 PRO: FO 371/118254 [WG 1071/1374] Conversation between Sir Ivone Kirkpatrick and the West German ambassador Hans von Herwarth, 15 December 1955.

56 Adenauer, *World Indivisible*, 19.

57 Excerpt from von Brentano speech to the Bundestag, 31 January 1957. Siegler, *The Reunification and Security of Germany*, 147.

58 Northedge and Wells, *Britain and Soviet Communism*, 115–16.

59 Michael Stürmer, '*Ostpolitik, Deutschlandpolitik* and the Western Alliance: German perspectives on détente' in Dyson, *European Détente*, 135.

60 PRO: FO 371/103664, FO Research Department, LR 8/2 (GER/215/53),

'Political factors relating to the reunification of Germany', no exact date, *c.* June 1953.

61 Alec Douglas-Home, *The Way the Wind Blows* (New York: Quadrangle, 1976), 149.

62 PRO: CAB 129/74, C (55) 83, 'Talks with the Soviet Union', note by the Foreign Secretary (Eden), 25 March 1955.

63 *Documents Relating to the Meeting of Heads of Government of France, the United Kingdom, the Soviet Union, and the United States of America,* [Geneva 18–23 July 1955] (London: HMSO, 1955), 22–3.

64 *News Chronicle,* 25 July 1955.

65 On this, Antonio Varsori, 'British Policy Aims at Geneva', in Gunther Bischof and Saki Dockrill (eds), *Cold War Respite: the Geneva Summit of 1955* (Louisiana: Louisiana University Press, 2000), 75–96.

66 Planck, *The Changing Status of German Reunification in Western Diplomacy,* 11–12.

67 *Documents Relating to the Meeting of Heads of Government of France, the United Kingdom, the Soviet Union, and the United States of America,* Cmd. 8081 (London: HMSO, 1955), 7–8.

68 Dwight D. Eisenhower, *Mandate for Change: The White House Years 1953–1956* (London: Heinemann, 1963), 523.

69 Northedge and Wells, *Britain and Soviet Communism,* 115.

70 Gladwyn Jebb (ambassador to Paris 1954–60), *The Memoirs of Lord Gladwyn* (London: Weidenfeld & Nicolson, 1972), 277.

71 See PRO: FO 371/137335 [WG 10113/100] for a fairly typical example of this in the frank exchange of notes between Sir Frederick Hoyer Miller (Permanent Under Secretary of State) and A. Rumbold (Assistant Under-Secretary of State), 14 November 1958 and 18 November 1958. Rumbold informed Hoyer Millar (14 November 1958) that 'The issues raised by Khrushchev's speech provide us with a golden opportunity for embarking on the kind of tripartite consultations for which the French government have been pressing.' Hoyer Millar replied (18 November 1958) that we 'will have to recognise the DDR sooner or later and that the SPD and FDP realise this, even if the CDU/CSU don't'.

72 *The Economist,* 17 December 1955.

73 See, for instance, PRO: CAB 128/33, CC (59) 32 (4), 28 May 1959.

74 For a discussion of this, see Henry A. Kissinger, *The Troubled Partnership: A Reappraisal of the Atlantic Alliance* (Council on Foreign Relations, 1965), 65ff.

75 PRO: FO 371/137398, [WG 1071/2] Macmillan to Lloyd, 17 December 1957.

76 PRO: PREM 11/2676. Meeting between Macmillan, Lloyd, Adenauer and von Brentano, Palais Schaumberg, Bonn, 12 March 1959.

77 Eric Roll, quoted in George Peden, *The Treasury and British Public Policy 1906–1959* (Oxford: Oxford University Press, 2000), 421.

78 PRO: T 234/19, [234/87/01] W. Strath to L. Petch (Under-Secretary HM Treasury), HM Treasury, 13 June 1955.

79 Alastair Horne, *Macmillan 1894–1956* (London: Macmillan, 1988), 381.

80 On this see Wolfram Kaiser, 'Money, Money, Money: the Economics and Politics of the Stationing Costs 1955–1965', in Gustav Schmidt (ed.), *Zwischen Bündnissicherung und privilegierter Partnerschaft: Die deutsch-britischen Beziehungen und die Vereinigten Staaten von Amerika, 1955–1963* (Bochum: N. Brockmeyer, 1995), 1–31.

81 NATO Ministerial meeting, December 1955. Saki Dockrill, 'Retreat from the Continent? Britain's Motives for Troop Reductions in West Germany 1955–1958', *Journal of Strategic Studies,* 20/3 (1997), 57.

82 Macmillan to Eden, 10 July 1956. Horne, *Macmillan 1894–1956,* 382.

83 JFKL: POF Box 127, Macmillan to Kennedy, 23 February 1962.

84 G. Wyn Rees, *Anglo-American Approaches to Security, 1955–60* (London: Macmillan, 1996), 48. The British official in Bonn responsible for matters relating to the BAOR in 1965 concurred with this view. Interview: D.A.S. Gladstone.

85 On the Hallstein Doctrine, see Ruediger M. Booz, *'Hallsteinzeit': Deutsche Aussenpolitik 1955–1972* (Bonn: Bouvier, 1995); Werner Kilian, *Die Hallstein Doktrin: der diplomatische Krieg zwischen der BRD und der DDR 1955–1973* (Berlin: Duncker and Humblot, 2001). The West Germans meant to carry their struggle into every areas of political and social life – including sport. On this, see Martin H. Geyer, 'Der Kampf um nationale Repräsentation: Deutsche-deutsche Sportsbeziehungen und die 'Hallstein-Doktrin'', *Vierteljahrshefte für Zeitgeschichte*, 44/1 (1996), 55–86.

86 Keesing's *Germany and Eastern Europe Since 1945*, 129.

87 Federal Government Declaration, 28 June 1956. Heinrich von Siegler, *Wiedervereinigung und Sicherheit Deutschland: zweite erweiterte Auflage* (Bonn: Verlag für Zeit Achiv, 1957), 141–2. On the roots of the Hallstein Doctrine, see Wilhelm Grewe, *Rückblenden: 1951–1976* (Frankfurt aM: Propyläen, 1979), 250–62.

88 Sir Christopher Steel, 'Anglo-German Relations: II. A British View', *International Affairs*, 39/4 (1963), 528.

89 PRO: FO 371/103691 [C 1071/700] *The Times*, 10 November 1953, Adenauer interview in Washington DC.

90 Lee, *An Uneasy Relationship*, 198–204.

91 Garton Ash, *In Europe's Name*, 225.

92 PRO: FO 371/154098, [WG 1081/41] Sir C. Steel, Bonn to C.D.W. O'Neill, 25 October 1960.

93 Elizabeth Wiskemann, *Germany's Eastern Neighbours: Problems Relating to the Oder–Neisse Line and the Czech Frontier Regions* (Oxford: Oxford University Press/RIIA, 1956), 112.

94 Ethnic Germans were scattered throughout Central and Eastern Europe due to recurrent emigrations (*Drang Nach Osten*) down the centuries. Prior to 1941 there was even an autonomous German 'Republic' on the Volga in the Soviet Union.

95 PRO: FO 371/103714, [C 1083/7] C.H. Johnstone, UKHComm, Wahnerheide to FO, 11 June 1953. Johnstone is commenting on the prominent Sudeten German and Deutsche Partei deputy, Christoph Seebohm, and his recent assertion that it would be wrong to return to the German borders of borders of 1937 as this would exclude the Sudetenland.

96 'The Atlantic Charter', 14 August 1941. Quoted here, for instance, from an expellee publication from the late 1970s. Kulturstiftung der deutschen Vertreibenen, *Materialien zu Oder–Neisse-Fragen: Eine Dokumentation* (Bonn: 1979), 25.

97 Cmd. 6739, *Policy of His Majesty's Government in the United Kingdom in Regard to Czechoslovakia*, 5 August 1942.

98 Literally 'transfer', although often translated as 'expulsion'.

99 See Timothy Burcher, *The Sudeten German Question and Czechoslovak–German Relations Since 1989* (London: RUSI, 1996), 1–12.

100 StBKAH: KAA/02.14/21, Adenauer to Bundestag, 8 November 1956.

101 This being the idea of lowering East–West tension by means of agreements to withdraw armed forces a specified distance from the borders on which NATO faced the Warsaw Pact.

102 Klaus Larres, 'Britain and the GDR: Political and Economic Relations, 1949–1989', in J. Noakes *et al.* (eds), *Uneasy Allies*, 72–3; Terence Prittie, *Adenauer: A Study in Fortitude* (London: Tom Stacey, 1972), 247.

103 PRO: CAB 129/86, C (57) 53, 4 March 1957.

104 Relations with the Soviet Union, Memorandum by the Foreign Secretary to Cabinet, PRO: CAB 129 C. (58) 9, 21 January 1958 (emphasis in original).

105 Rees, *Anglo-American Approaches to Security, 1955–60*, 48.

106 Bernard Ledwidge in John P.S. Gearson, Witness Seminar, 'British Policy and the Berlin Wall Crisis 1958–61', *Contemporary Record*, 6/1 (1992), 142.

107 PRO: PREM 11/1337, Eden to Belgian Foreign Minister Spaak, 28 May 1956.

108 By contrast, in 1959 Adenauer lectured Macmillan that by virtue of history the Germans knew the Russians best of all and were therefore best placed to deal with Moscow. See PRO: PREM 11/2676, meeting between Adenauer and Macmillan, Bonn, 12 March 1959.

109 PRO: FO 371/137398, [WG 1071/2] D.A. Logan (Assistant Private Secretary to Selwyn Lloyd) to Philip de Zuleta (Private Secretary to Macmillan), 10 January 1958.

110 PRO: FO 371/154044, [WG 10338/14] Chancery, Bonn, 3 May 1960. Article written by Adenauer expressing his philosophy, published in the Bulletin of the Federal Press and Information Office, 30 April 1960.

111 Bodleian: Harold Macmillan Diaries (hereafter HMD), 18 November 1958.

112 HMD: 19 November 1958.

113 PRO: FO 371/137357, [WG 1022/1] Clive M. Rose, 3 January 1958.

114 PRO: FO 371/137357, [WG 1022/12] J.K. Drinkall (Western Department), 26 February 1958.

115 PRO: FO 371/130746, [WG 1082/6] Sir Christopher Steel, Bonn to FO, report of von Brentano speech at Frankfurt a.M, 8 April 1957. Von Brentano was moderate in comparison to some his political colleagues. On 6 April 1957 Herr Seiboth, deputy chair of the *BHE*, asserted that the Sudetenland and Memel were still part of Germany (i.e. Germany's 1939 boundaries). PRO: FO 371/130746, [WG 1072/6] Sir Christopher Steel, Bonn to FO, 8 April 1957.

116 PRO: FO 371/124533, [WG 1041/1] S. J. Barrett (Counsellor), Bonn, 16 August 1956.

117 *Daily Telegraph*, 25 September 1957 [headline] 'Frontier Change means war, says Mr Gomułka'.

118 PRO: FO 371/128833, [NP 1081/2] 1 August 1957, E. Berthoud to T. Brimelow (Head of the Northern Department), FO. Indeed, many of the Polish settlers in the German 'eastern territories' had themselves been uprooted from the portion of eastern Poland assigned to the USSR in 1945! (i.e. east of the Curzon line). See PRO: PREM 11/172, [C. (52) 137] 'The Oder Neisse Line. A Memorandum by the Secretary of State for Foreign Affairs [Eden]' May 1952.

119 PRO: FO 371/145738, [WG 1019/10] Sir Christopher Steel, Bonn. Detailed report on Nazism and Anti-Semitism in FRG, 9 March 1959.

120 *Dokumente zur Deutschlandpolitik III/3:1 Januar bis 31 Dezember 1957* (München, 1997), 1597.

121 *The Economist*, 14 September 1957. See also the *Manchester Guardian*, 30 November 1960, 'Poland and Germany', 'Diplomatic Commentary' by Richard Scott.

122 For a collection of rumours, suggestions and innuendo on this subject, see PRO: FO 371/137415, [WG 1083/4] FO Minute, P.S. Falla (Deputy Director of Research FO), 5 November 1958.

123 PRO: FO 371/130746, [WG 1082/18] B.H.C. Sykes (Western Department), 3 January 1958. Comments on the file reveal that Sykes enjoyed 'excellent' relations with the *AA's Ostabteilung* when stationed in Bonn between 1953 and 1957 (and was First Secretary from 1955).

124 PRO: FO 137357, [WG 1022/17] C.M. Rose, comment on the *Bundestag* foreign affairs debate of 25 March 1958, 21 April 1958.

125 PRO: CAB 129 C. (58) 9, 21 January 1958, Relations with the Soviet Union (section D), 'Definition of our attitude to satellite countries', Memorandum by the Foreign Secretary to Cabinet, emphasis in original.

126 Jonathan Steele (complier and editor), *Eastern Europe Since Stalin: Sources for Contemporary History* (New York: Crane Russak, 1974), 33–127.

127 PRO: FO 371/145863, [WG 1078/44] FO Brief, 'Relations between the Federal Republic and Eastern Europe' (n.d. brief prepared for the visit of Adenauer in October 1959).

128 'Problems of Germany's East European Policy', speech to Upper Silesian expellees, Bochum, 1 July 1956. Heinrich von Brentano, *Germany and Europe: Reflections on German Foreign Policy*, trans. Edward Fitzgerald (New York: Praeger, 1964), 104.

129 PRO: PREM 11/2175, FO Minute, *c.* July 1958.

130 Walter Laqueur, *Europe Since Hitler* (London: Pelican Books, 1972), 410.

131 On this, see Richard Blanke, 'The German Minority in inter-war Poland and German foreign policy: some reconsiderations' in *Journal of Contemporary History*, 25/1 (1990), 87–102.

132 V. Gransow and K. Jarausch (eds), *Die Deutsche Vereinigung* (Cologne: Wissenschaft und Politik, 1991), 30.

133 On the 1913 law, see Roger Brubaker, *Citizenship and Nationhood in France and Germany* (Cambridge, MA: Harvard University Press, 1992), esp. p. 115.

134 PRO: FO 371/130867, [WG 1821/1] Chancery, Bonn to FO, 14 March 1957. At this time, German emigration from Hungary [WG/1821/3] and Romania [WG 1821/2; WG 1821/5; WG 1821/6] was also being stepped up. By 1967 the *Volksdeutsche* in Eastern Europe had virtually completely disappeared from Eastern Europe. PRO: FCO 51/10 Research paper 'Ethnic Germans in Eastern Europe'.

135 Adenauer, quoted in Garton Ash, *In Europe's Name*, 225. Brandt quotes Adenauer on the eastern territories as stating 'They're gone' as early as August 1953. Brandt, *My Life in Politics*, 35.

136 Brandt in Berlin, 17 January 1958. Wolfgang Schmidt, *Kalter Krieg, Koexistenz und kleine Schritte: Willy Brandt und die Deutschlandpolitik 1948–1963* (Wiesbaden: Westdeutscher, 2001), 219.

137 PRO: FO 371/130746, [WG 1082/3] FO Minute, C.M. Rose (Western Department), discussion of Oder–Neiße line with Herr Sikora (German embassy) and Italian counsellor, 18 December 1956.

138 PRO: FO 371/130746, [WG 1082/18] Paul F. Grey (ambassador), Prague, 20 December 1957, discussion with French ambassador on the latter's meeting with von Brentano. The substance of the 'obstacle' von Brentano had in mind was the domestic lobby within the Federal Republic.

139 PRO: FO 371/145693, [WG 1015/124] Sir Gladwyn Jebb, Paris to Sir Frederick Hoyer Millar (Permanent Under Secretary of State), 31 January 1959. Report on a conversation with the Polish ambassador to Paris 31 January 1959, emphasis in original.

140 PRO: FO 371/145863, [WG 1078/44] FO Brief, 'Relations between the Federal Republic and Eastern Europe', undated 1959.

141 PRO: PREM 11/2876, Macmillan–Dulles meeting, Downing Street, 4 February 1959. Previously, even Dulles had encouraged von Brentano to adopt a more 'realistic and progressive' policy. PRO: FO 371/137378, [WG 1022/19] Paul F. Grey to Sir A. Rumbold (Under Secretary of State), 17 June 1958.

142 PRO: FO 371/130746, [WG 1072/4] Grotewohl quoted on GDR radio, BBC monitoring report, 16 January 1957.

143 PRO: FO 371/145863, [WG 1078/44] FO Brief, 'Relations between the Federal Republic and Eastern Europe', undated [1959].

144 PRO: FO 371/154098, [WG 1081/37] G.L. Clutton Warsaw to C.D.W. O' Neill (Assistant Under Secretary of State), FO, 27 September 1960.

145 PRO: FO 371/154090, [WG 1075/1] Main report to Congress by Vice-Chairman M. Izydorczyk. Chancery, Warsaw to Northern Department, 2 February 1960.

146 When, for instance, Liberal Party leader Clement Davies visited the Leipzig Trade Fair in 1958, the West German government complained that its policy of 'non-contact' was being undermined. PRO: FO 371/137398, [WG 1071/7] BBC Monitoring Report, 4 March 1958.

147 Jain, *Germany, the Soviet Union and Eastern Europe 1949–1991*, n. 65 *p.* 287.

148 This view was shared by many contemporary observers, e.g. Heinrich End, *Zweimal deutsche Aussenpolitik: Internationale Dimensionen des innerdeutschen Konflikts 1949–1972* (Cologne: Wissenschaft und Politik, 1973), 43–4.

149 In 1960, for example, of sixteen newly independent African countries not one recognised the GDR. William Glenn Gray, *Germany's Cold War: The Global Campaign to Isolate East Germany, 1949–1969* (University of North Carolina Press, 2003), 227.

150 On this, Beate Ihme-Tuchel, 'Das Bemühen der SED um die diplomatische Anerkennung durch Jugoslawien 1956/57', *Zeitschrift für Geschichtswissenschaft*, 42/8 (1994), 695–702.

151 PRO: FO 371/130746, [WG 1082/11] D.M. Gordon (Foreign Service Officer), 20 September 1957.

152 PRO: FO 371/137357, [WG 1022/10] P.S. Falla, FO, 18 March 1958.

153 PRO: FO 371/160570, [CG 1072/14] Chancery, Cairo to FO, 20 May 1961.

154 HMD: 28 August 1961. Specifically, Macmillan was referring here to the impending conference of the Non-aligned Movement to be held in Belgrade.

155 Willi Daume to Gerhard Schröder, 29 January 1956. Geyer, 'Der Kampf um nationale Repräsentation', 58.

156 The East Berlin suburb in which the government of the GDR was located.

157 Baltruschat letter to the GDR journal *Deutsche Aussenpolitik*, PRO: FO 371/160570 [CG 1072/22] IRD research paper B. 536, 'Prestige or Security? East German plans to exploit International Conferences', November 1958, emphasis in the original. Comment by W.J. Wilberforce, FO, n.d. [1961].

158 *Neues Deutschland*, 14 March 1960.

159 Bodleian: COB 86 (1: Lady Emmet Papers 1960). Königswater Conference, 25–27 March 1960, Report by Sir William Hayter (ambassador to Moscow 1953–7, Deputy Under Secretary at the Foreign Office 1957–8).

160 Hans von Herwarth, 'Anglo-German Relations: I. A German View', *International Affairs*, 39/4 (1963), 518.

161 PRO: FO 371/154093, [WG 1076/21] Selwyn Lloyd quoted in 'Germany's position under international law', German embassy Paper, 4 July 1960.

162 PRO: PREM 11/2717, Lloyd to Macmillan, 21 May 1959. Khrushchev said virtually the same to Eisenhower, JFKL: POF Box 126: Eisenhower–Khrushchev meeting, Washington, 26 September 1959.

163 See, for instance, PRO: PREM 11/2876, Macmillan–Dulles meeting, Downing Street, 4 February 1959.

3 Macmillan and the search for détente

1 Macmillan, *Tides of Fortune*, 101.

2 HMD: 6 March 1951.

3 Evelyn Shuckburgh, *Descent to Suez: Diaries, 1951–56* (London: Weidenfeld & Nicolson, 1986), 274. Emphasis in the original.

4 D.R. Thorpe, *Selwyn Lloyd* (London: Jonathan Cape, 1989), 287. One of Lloyd's successors, R.A. Butler (Foreign Secretary, 1963–4), concurred. R.A. Butler, *The Art of the Possible* (London: Hamish Hamilton, 1971), 257–8.

5 White, *Britain, Détente and Changing East–West Relations*, 59.

6 Commons, 20 February 1946; Macmillan, *Tides of Fortune*, 120–1.

7 HMD: 24 March 1963.

8 PRO: CAB 129/113, C (63) 61, 'Nuclear Tests: Exchange of Messages', Annex A: Letter from Macmillan to President Kennedy, 16 March 1963.

9 Anatoly Dobrynin, *In Confidence: Moscow's ambassador to America's Six Cold War Presidents* (New York: Times, 1995), 63.

10 PRO: FO 371/188477, [N 103118/1] A.A. Stark, Bonn to H.F.T. Smith, Northern Department, 22 February 1966. As well as memories of Soviet atrocities in 1944–5, Smith noted 'an ineradicable feeling of superiority' of the Germans towards the Russians. The latter tendency was manifested by the 'surprising number of Germans' ready to attribute the Soviet victory in the Second World War to Anglo-American aid.

11 Sir Curtis Keeble, 'Macmillan and the Soviet Union', in Richard Aldous and Sabine Lee (eds), *Harold Macmillan: Aspects of a Political Life*, 215.

12 P.M.H. Bell, *France and Britain 1940–1994: The Long Separation* (London: Longman, 1997), 150–5.

13 Harold Macmillan, *Riding the Storm 1956–1959* (London: Macmillan, 1971), 330ff. Macmillan entitles this chapter 'Honeymoon at Washington'.

14 White, *Britain, Détente and Changing East–West Relations*, 60. At this meeting, Macmillan took the lead on a 'dual track' approach. The military 'track' was to agree on stationing US IRBMs in Europe whilst the political 'track' was to be the offer of a meeting to address differences. In the final event, the final communiqué offered the USSR a meeting at foreign minister level.

15 Macmillan remarked to Richard Crossman in French North Africa in 1944: 'We ... are Greeks in this American Empire ... We must run the Allied forces HQ as the Greeks ran the operations of the Emperor Claudius.' *Daily Telegraph*, 9 February 1964.

16 Thomas Kielinger, *Crossroads and Roundabouts: Junctions in German–British Relations* (London: FCO and Bonn: Press and Information Office of the Federal Government, 1997), 199–200, 203.

17 Macmillan, *Riding the Storm*, 296.

18 Alastair Horne, *Macmillan 1957–1986* (London: Macmillan, 1989), 33.

19 Macmillan, *Tides of Fortune*, 606.

20 Sabine Lee, 'Pragmatism Versus Principle? Macmillan and Germany', in Richard Aldous and Sabine Lee (eds), *Harold Macmillan: Aspects of a Political Life* (London: Macmillan, 1999), 117.

21 The British Minister in Bonn added, however, that the ageing Adenauer was prone to agreeing with the last opinion given to him. PRO: FO 371/137358, [WG 1022/13] M.S. Williams, Bonn to Sir A. Rumbold, 19 May 1958.

22 Lee, 'Pragmatism Versus Principle? Macmillan and Germany', 120–1.

23 Adenauer, as Churchill had, increasingly gave the impression of clinging to power at any price. There was particular disquiet over the Chancellor's decision (and subsequent retraction) to run for president in 1959. Adenauer disliked the fact that the presidency was a largely ceremonial post and that his erstwhile successor, Ludwig Erhard, was, in his eyes, not capable enough a politician. Daniel Koerfer, *Kampf und Kanzleramt* (Stuttgart: Deutsche Verlagsanstalt, 1987), 188–277.

24 For an interesting contemporary account of this aspect of British policy, see O. Harries, 'Faith in the Summit: Some British Attitudes', *Foreign Affairs*, 40/1 (1961), 59.

25 PRO: FO 371/137357, [WG 1022/1] Steel to FO, tel. no. 2 saving, 2 January 1958.
26 JFKL: NSF Box 74, L.M. Scott (Munich) to Rusk, report on Strauß speech of 8 July 1961, 9 July 1961. The following day Adenauer, too, dismissed proposals for a '52-Nation "Super Conference"'.
27 PRO: FO 371/145773, [WG 1073/51] Steel to FO, 14 February 1959.
28 *Defence: Outline of Future Policy*, Cmd. 124, HMSO, 1957.
29 Horne, *Macmillan 1957–1986*, 32–3.
30 HMD: 7 April 1957. See also Bodleian: COB 12 (3: Germany 1956–7), Conservative Research Department, Ursula Branston, Report on the Königswater Conference, 4–10 April 1957.
31 For a discussion of the 'personal' in Anglo-German relations, see Magnus Brechtken, 'Personality, Image and Perception: Patterns and Problems of Anglo–German Relations in the 19th and 20th Centuries', in Adolf M. Birke, Magnus Brechtken and Alaric Searle, *An Anglo-German Dialogue: The Munich Lectures on the History of International Relations*, Prince Albert Studies vol. 17 (Munich: K.G. Saur, 2000).
32 See Arnulf Baring, 'The institutions of German Foreign Policy', in Kaiser and Morgan, *Britain and West Germany*, 162–4.
33 Willy Brandt, *People and Politics: The Years 1960–1975*, trans. by J. Maxwell Brownjohn (Boston: Little, Brown & Company, 1978), 19.
34 Alastair Horne, *Harold Macmillan 1894–1956* (London: Macmillan, 1988), 351.
35 Interview: Michael Palliser. Macmillan's official biographer gives a slightly different version, Horne, *Macmillan 1957–1986*, 36.
36 For a description of Macmillan's Great War, see Simon Ball, *The Guardsmen: Harold Macmillan, Three Friends, and the World They Made* (London: Harper, 2005), 27–75.
37 John P.S. Gearson, *Harold Macmillan and the Berlin Wall Crisis, 1958–1962* (London: Macmillan, 1998), 16.
38 HMD: 5 August 1961.
39 Interview: Sir J. Oliver Wright.
40 Horne, *Macmillan, 1957–1986*, 136.
41 Terence Prittie, 'The Statesman: Historical Perspective', in Horst Osterheld, Terence Prittie and François Seydoux, *Konrad Adenauer* (Bonn: Aktuell, 1983), 27. Adenauer's view of the press as a destructive force culminated in the notorious '*Spiegel* Affair' of 1962. On this see, Ronald F. Bunn, *German Politics and the Spiegel Affair: a Case Study of the Bonn System* (Baton Rouge: Louisiana University Press, 1968). On 12 November 1962, *BILD-Zeitung* concluded of the '*Spiegel* Affair', 'The federal government has disgraced itself'. For a British perspective (largely delighting in the discomfort of Adenauer, Strauß *et al.*) see PRO: FO 371/163694.
42 Dr Ritter, German embassy, at lunch with Philip de Zuleta (Private Secretary to the Prime Minister and First Secretary), PRO: FO 371/137374, [WG 1072/1] 11 April 1958. See also Adenauer to Cabinet, 11 March 1959. Kabinettsprotokolle 1959, 'Die Kabinettsprotokolle der Bundesregeirungung' online, Cabinet meeting, 9 November 1956, online, available at: www.bundesarchiv.de/kabinettsprotokolle/web/index.jsp.
43 Bunn, *German Politics and the Spiegel Affair*, 121.
44 See, for instance, the meeting between Adenauer and Macmillan, Palais Schaumberg, Bonn, 13 March 1959, PRO: PREM 11/2676.
45 Frank Roberts, *Dealing with Dictators: The Destruction and Revival of Europe 1930–70* (London: Weidenfeld & Nicolson, 1991), 244.
46 *Daily Telegraph*, 4 April 1959. On the roots of such attitudes, see Keith Robbins, *Present and Past: British Images of Germany in the First Half of the Twentieth Century and their Historical Legacy* (Göttingen: Wallstein Verlag, 1999).

47 PRO: FO 371/145738, [WG 1019/6] FO Brief for PM's talk with (Federal ambassador) Herr von Herwarth, 11 February 1959.

48 E.g. 'Adenauer's Aides: The Guilty Men', *Daily Express*, 12 February 1959.

49 PRO FO 371/145738, [WG 1019] K.R.C. Pridam (First Secretary, Western Department), 18 March 1959. The Labour Party was only too aware of the anti-(West) German sentiment in its ranks. See LPA: LPID memo 'Mis-use of Delegation Visits by SED Propaganda', *c.* July 1960.

50 PRO FO 371/145738, [WG 1019] A. Rumbold, minute, 21 April 1959.

51 Lee, 'Pragmatism Versus Principle? Macmillan and Germany', p. 115.

52 For instance, Steel reported that Adenauer had made insulting remarks about Britain at a CDU party meeting. See PRO: FO 371/145773 [WG 1072/10], Steel, Bonn to FO, 14 February 1959.

53 Noel Annan, *Changing Enemies: The Defeat and Regeneration of Germany* (London: HarperCollins, 1996), 218; Adenauer also stated this at interview with Terence Prittie for the *Manchester Guardian* in 1949, quoted in Prittie, *Adenauer*, 27.

54 In 1946, the Secretary of the International Department of the Labour Party, Denis Healey, wrote to advise John Hynd MP (Control Commission for Germany) of the growing relationship between the Labour Party and the SPD, LPA: LPID Box 2, 2 August 1946. Morgan Phillips, Labour's General Secretary, sent his good wishes to the first post-war SPD Congress in Hanover, *Daily Herald*, 9 May 1946. On 16 October 1947 the Labour Party's General Purposes and Finance Sub-Committee agreed to lend the SPD £500 (after a request by Erich Ollenhauer on 19 August 1947), LPA: LPID Box 7.

55 Annan, *Changing Enemies*, 218.

56 Herwarth, quoted in Kielinger, *Crossroads and Roundabouts*, 202.

57 Ivone Kirkpatrick, *The Inner Circle* (London: Macmillan, 1959), 231; Jonathan Wright, 'The Role of Britain in West German Foreign Policy since 1949', *German Politics*, 5/1 (1996), 32.

58 Adenauer, *Erinnerungen 1945–53*, 382–99.

59 Sabine Lee, *An Uneasy Relationship: British–German Relations Between 1955 and 1961* (Bochum: Brockmeyer, 1961), 65–70; Martin C. Schaad, 'Bonn between London and Paris?' in Noakes, Wende and Wright, *Britain and Germany in Europe 1949–1990*, 67–93.

60 PRO: PREM 11/2676. Meeting between Adenauer and Macmillan, Bonn, 13 March 1959.

61 PRO: FO 371/103664, FO Research Department, LR 8/2 (GER/215/53), 'Political factors relating to the reunification of Germany', no exact date, *c.* June 1953.

62 HMD: 15 March 1958.

63 PRO: FO 371/130732, [WG 1062/3] Sir Christopher Steel, Bonn to FO, 11 October 1957. The FTA was a British-sponsored scheme to abolish tariffs between EFTA and EEC states. However, there would be no common external tariff and the Europeans (rightly) saw it as a British attempt to keep their Commonwealth links undiminished. For a very comprehensive account of this, see Kaiser, *Using Europe, Abusing the Europeans*, 61–107. On its defeat resulting from French opposition and poor British tactics, see James Ellison, *Threatening Europe: Britain and the Creation of the European Community, 1955–58* (London: Palgrave Macmillan, 2000), 125–8.

64 Gladwyn Jebb, *The Memoirs of Lord Gladwyn* (London: Weidenfeld & Nicolson, 1972), 285.

65 John P.S. Gearson, 'British Policy and the Berlin Wall Crisis 1958–61', *Contemporary Record*, 6/1 (1992), 110; Lee, 'Anglo-German Relations 1958–59' p. 787; Victor Mauer, 'Harold Macmillan and the Deadline Crisis Over Berlin 1958–9', *Twentieth Century British History*, 9/1 (1998), 56.

66 William Taubman, *Khrushchev: the Man and his Era* (New York: W.W. Norton, 2003), 396–7.
67 Khrushchev claimed later he was only trying to gain recognition for the GDR. *Khrushchev Remembers*, trans. Strobe Talbott (London: Andre Deutsch, 1971), 453.
68 Gearson, 'British Policy and the Berlin Wall Crisis 1958–61', 108.
69 Khrushchev speech, Leipzig 7 March 1959, *Soviet News* (published by the Press Department of the Soviet embassy in London), no. 4033, Wed. 1 April 1959.
70 For the peak of West German success, see Gray, *Germany's Cold War*, 162–73.
71 Garton Ash, *In Europe's Name*, 51.
72 Adenauer, *Erinnerungen, 1955–1959*, 468–71; Gossel, *Briten, Deutsche und Europa*, 189–202; Henning Köhler, *Adenauer: Eine Politische Biographie* (Frankfurt aM: Propyläen, 1994), 1015, 1022.
73 PRO: FO 371/137358, [WG 1022/20] Chancery, Bonn to Western Department, 23 June 1958.
74 PRO: FO 371/137337, [WG 10713/159] A. Rumbold, FO submission, 20 November 1958.
75 PRO: FO 371/137336, [WG 1072/12] Lloyd minute, 14 November 1958.
76 Christian Bremen, *Die Eisenhower-Administration und die zweite Berlin-Krise, 1958–1961* (Berlin: de Gruyter, 1998), 124.
77 Dwight D. Eisenhower, *Waging Peace: The White House Years 1956–61* (London: Heinemann, 1966), 333.
78 PRO: FO 371/137335, [WG 10713/76] tel. No 525, Jebb, Paris, 17 November 1958.
79 PRO: FO 371/137411, [WG 1074/20] I.M. Sinclair (FO Assistant legal adviser), 29 November 1958.
80 Harold Davies, *The Meaning of Berlin: A Reply to Lord Home's Yellow Book* (London: Gladiator, 1963), 10.
81 *The Times*, 1 September 1960.
82 Interview: D.A.S. Gladstone.
83 FO 371/160474, [CG 1015/30] W.J.A. Wilberforce (Northern Department), written comments on report by Sir Frank Roberts, Moscow, 25 May 1961, Soviet protests on *Bundesrat* meeting in Berlin.
84 HMD: 16 January 1959. Macmillan–Steel meeting.
85 HMD: 16 January 1959. Macmillan, meeting with Sir Norman Brook (Cabinet Secretary) and Sir Frederick Hoyer Millar.
86 Dwight D. Eisenhower Library (DDEL): NSC Box 9, NSC meeting, 6 February 1959.
87 HMD: 4 February 1959.
88 PRO: FO 371/145818, [WG 1073/58] Sir Frank Roberts, UKDel, Paris to Sir F. Hoyer-Millar, 6 February 1959, conversation with Federal ambassador Blankenhorn about Adenauer's views on reunification. This was reaffirmed in Washington by the West Germans. PRO: FO 371/145818, [WG 1073/70] FO submission, P.F. Hancock. 16 February 1959, 'Four-Power working group on German reunification and European security', Washington DC.
89 PRO: PREM 11/2876, Macmillan to Dulles, Downing Street, 5 February 1959. The West German insistence on the non-recognition of the GDR meant that the Western Allies refused to allow GDR personnel to man checkpoints.
90 HMD: 9 March 1959.
91 HMD: 10 March 1959. Macmillan meeting with de Gaulle in Paris; Jebb concurred with this (*Memoirs*, 318).
92 HMD: 4 March 1959.
93 PRO: PREM 11/2315, Macmillan to Lloyd and Heathcoat-Amory, 24 June 1958; Kaiser, *Using Europe, Abusing the Europeans*, 151–2.

94 Charles de Gaulle, *Memoirs of Hope: Renewal and Endeavour*, trans. Terence Kilmartin (New York: Simon & Schuster, 1971), 188. The 'Continental System' was Napoleon's mechanism for attempting to strangle British commerce by closing the continent off to Britain from 1807. It failed. In March 1960 Macmillan even cast the EEC in a tradition running from Philip II to Hitler: a continental menace that Britain would fight. PRO: PREM 11/3132, Macmillan memo, *c.* March 1960.

95 PRO: PREM 11/2676, meeting between Adenauer and Macmillan, Palais Schaumberg, Bonn, 13 March 1959. Despite the worsening agreement the official West German bulletin headlined with 'Macmillan and Adenauer in Complete Unanimity', *The Bulletin*, Federal Press and Information Office, 7/1, 17 March 1959.

96 PRO: PREM 11/2679, Macmillan to Lloyd, 'The organisation of Europe', 20 November 1959.

97 PRO: FO 371/145818, [WG 1071/67G] 'Berlin and Germany', memo by Sir Gladwyn Jebb, 18 January 1959.

98 Andrei Gromyko, *Memories*, trans. Harold Shukman (London: Hutchison, 1989), 156–7.

99 PRO: CAB 133/293, Top Secret Annex of the trip to Moscow, 21 February 1959–3 March 1959. Lloyd had actually brokered this in Kiev.

100 *Hansard*, vol. 601, col. 450, 4 March 1959.

101 PRO: PREM 11/2676, Meeting between Macmillan, Lloyd, Adenauer and von Brentano, Palais Schaumberg, Bonn, 12 March 1959. Lloyd pointed out that he had not used the word 'disengagement' and stressed the fact that British were, in fact, opposed to the idea. On 'disengagement', Macmillan was caught between a rock and a hard place. In addition to Adenauer's opposition, the Labour Party attacked him from the other extreme. In 1962, Harold Wilson pointed out that Macmillan's 'encouraging proposals' on 'disengagement' in Moscow were 'later dropped owing to unfortunate pressures from West Germany.' *Hansard*, HC Deb, vol. 662, col. 789, 5 July 1962.

102 PRO: PREM 11/2676, von Brentano–Lloyd meeting, Bonn, 13 March 1959.

103 Lee, 'Pragmatism Versus Principle? Macmillan and Germany', 123.

104 Adenauer, *Erinnerungen 1955–1959*, 469.

105 PRO: FO 370/2756/56082, 'Anglo-German Relations 1945–64' [nd, 1964].

106 Eisenhower, *Waging Peace*, 337.

107 HMD: 5 January 1959.

108 PRO: PREM 11/2876, Meeting between Dulles and Macmillan, Downing Street, 5 February 1959.

109 US National Archives, Washington DC (hereafter USNA): RG 59 Central Files, MEMCON: Eisenhower/Dulles–Macmillan/Lloyd, Walter Reed Hospital, 20 March 1959. Dulles dictated the memorandum from his perspective on (and contributions to) the conversation.

110 John P.S. Gearson, 'Britain and the Berlin Wall Crisis', in John Gearson and Kori Schake (eds), *The Berlin Wall Crisis: Perspectives on Cold War Alliances* (Basingstoke: Palgrave Macmillan, 2002), 55.

111 HMD: 21 March 1959. Although this had been accepted by Moscow on 30 March 1959, the USSR expressed disappointment about the exclusion of the FRG and the GDR. PRO: FO 371/145808, [WG 1081/11] Chancery, Moscow 30 March 1959.

112 PRO: FO 371/145693, [WG 1051/1] Steel to FO, 31 March 1959.

113 HMD: 9 April 1959.

114 HMD: 28 May 1959. For similar, 17 June and 15 July 1959.

115 HMD: 18 June 1959.

116 HMD: 22 June 1959.

117 JFKL: POF Box 126, Summary of Conversation between Nixon and Khrushchev, 20 July 1959, Moscow.

118 HMD: 2 July 1959.

119 HMD: 26 July 1959.

120 Stephen Ambrose, *Eisenhower: The President* (New York: Simon & Schuster, 1984), 534.

121 Dulles, 21 April 1959. Trachtenberg, *A Constructed Peace*, 267. As it was, the September visit to the United States yielded little of consequence. See JFKL: POF Box 126, Eisenhower–Khrushchev meeting, Washington, 26 September 1959.

122 Lloyd directed a memo that set out the reasons for the disillusionment of the Germans, describing their attitude towards Britain as 'bitter'. Franco-German differences were also highlighted as scant consolation. PRO: PREM 11/2714, Lloyd Memo to Macmillan, 4 December 1959.

123 Konrad Adenauer, *Erinnerungen 1959–1963* (Stuttgart: DVA, 1968), 27.

124 PRO: PREM 11/2991, Adenauer–de Gaulle–Eisenhower–Macmillan meeting, 20 December 1959.

125 Henning Köhler, *Adenauer: Eine politische Biographie* (Berlin: Ullstein, 1994), 1015–16. Just how desperate Adenauer was to sabotage Macmillan's personal diplomacy is shown by his visit to 'Red' Berlin and Brandt. During the visit, the best the Chancellor could say of the West Berlin government was that it made 'sound use ... [of the] very large Federal subsidy', PRO: FO 371/154008, [WG 1072/2] British High Command Berlin, 13 January 1960. The Berliners reciprocated this dislike, and when Adenauer had a street named after him following his death the street-sign was repeatedly vandalised – e.g. with the painted slogan '*Was hast du jemals für uns getan, du alte Sau?*' ['What did you ever do for us, you old bastard?'] Interview: Anne E. Stoddart.

126 For a review of the trip from the British perspective, see PRO: FO 371/153725.

127 PRO: FO 371/153791, 13 January 1960, S.J. Barrett (Second Secretary, Berlin) to W.J.A. Wilberforce (Western Department).

128 Tusa, *The Last Division*, 191.

129 HMD: 7 February 1960.

130 HMD: 29 March 1960.

131 PRO: PREM 11/2890, Macmillan–de Gaulle meeting, Downing Street, 24 April 1960.

132 Harold Macmillan, *Pointing the Way 1959–1961* (London: Macmillan, 1972), 195.

133 'Summit Casualty – Macmillan', *New York Times*, 22 May 1960.

134 Horne, *Macmillan 1957–1986*, 323.

135 HMD: 21 May 1960.

136 HMD: 6 August 1960; Macmillan, *Pointing the Way*, 317–18.

137 Hans von Herwarth, *Von Adenauer zu Brandt* (Munich: Propyläen, 1990), 279–80.

138 HMD: 10 August 1960. Having once remarked that 'A thick skin is a gift from God' (*New York Times*, 30 December 1959), Adenauer was perhaps better equipped to deal with failure than the sensitive Macmillan.

139 PRO: PREM 11/2993, Adenauer–Macmillan meeting, Bonn, 10 August 1960.

140 HMD: 10 August 1960.

141 PRO: PREM 11/3164, excerpt passed to Macmillan, 30 March 1960.

142 Von Brentano, 25 April 1957. Vladislav Zubok and Constantine Pleshakov, *Inside the Kremlin's Cold War: From Stalin to Khrushchev* (Cambridge, MA: Harvard University Press, 1996), 196.

143 Tom Bower, *Blind Eye to Murder*, 430–3.

144 On the prominence of ex-Nazis, see T.H. Tetens, *The New Germany and the Old Nazis* (London: Secker & Warburg, 1961); Peter Reichel, *Vergangenheitsbewaeltigung in Deutschland: Die Auseinandersetzung mit der NS-Diktatur von 1945 bis heute* (Munich: Beck, 2001); Norbert Frei, *Adenauer's Germany and the Politics of Amnesty and Integration* (New York: Columbia University Press, 2002).

145 Daniel E. Rogers, 'The Chancellors of the Federal Republic and the Political Legacy of the Holocaust', in Alan E. Steinweis and Daniel E. Rogers (eds), *The Impact of Nazism: New Perspectives on the Third Reich and Its Legacy* (London: University of Nebraska Press, 2003), 235. Adenauer stated that to distance himself from Globke would be 'mean' and 'disloyal', *Süddeutsche Zeitung*, 21 March 1956.

146 This included the widow of SS Obergruppenführer Reinhard Heydrich, one of the chief architects of the 'Final Solution'. *News from Germany*, 12/10, October 1958. On the whole issue of pensions for former members of the NSDAP, SS etc., see Bernd Karsten, 'Pensionen für NS-Verbrecher in der Bundesrepublik 1949–1963', *Historische Mitteilungen*, 7/2 (1994), 262–82.

147 The anomaly of 'successor' status sat rather uneasily with de-Nazification pledges after the Second World War. The Berlin Conference of 1947, for instance, resolved to eliminate Nazism in the education system and organise the judicial system in accordance with 'the principles of democracy'. Cmd. 7087, *Protocol of the Proceedings of the Berlin Conference*, HMSO: 1947, 7.

148 Margarete Myers Feinstein, *State Symbols: The Quest for Legitimacy in the Federal Republic of Germany and the German Democratic Republic, 1949–1959* (Boston: Brill, 2001), 86.

149 For the definitive 'Brown Book' (*Braunbuch*) on prominent Nazis in the FRG, see Nationalrat der Nationalen Front des Demokratischen Deutschland, *Braunbuch: Kriegs- und Nazi Verbrecher in der Bundesrepublik*, (East Berlin: Dokumentationszentrum der Staatlichen Archivverwaltung der DDR, 1965). On ex-Nazis in the GDR see, Olaf Kappelt, *Braunbuch DDR. Nazis in der DDR* (West Berlin: Reichmann Verlag, 1981).

150 As a British defector, Peet exercised considerable influence on like-minded persons in Britain. Stefan Berger and Norman LaPorte 'John Peet (1915–1988): An Englishman in the GDR', *History*, 89/1 (2004), 49–69.

151 Christopher Andrew and Vasili Mitrokhin, *The Mitrokhin Archive: the KGB in Europe and the West* (London: Penguin, 2000), 573. Globke was eventually brought down in early 1963 after a sustained campaign by the GDR. On this campaign, see Michael Lemke, 'Kampagnen gegen Bonn: Die Systemkrise der DDR und die West-Propaganda der SED 1960–1963' in *Vierteljahrshefte für Zeitgeschichte*, 41/1 (1993), 153–74. On Globke, see Klaus Gotto (ed.), *Der Staatssekretär Adenauers: Persönlichkeit und politisches Wirken Hans Globkes* (Stuttgart: Klett-Cotta, 1980). Despite GDR propaganda to the contrary, a recent study has highlighted the failure of the GDR's own de-Nazification programme; see Timothy R. Vogt, *Denazification in Soviet-Occupied Germany: Brandenburg, 1945–1948* (Cambridge, MA: Harvard University Press, 2000).

152 *News from Germany*, 14/1, January 1960.

153 Rogers, 'The Chancellors of the Federal Republic and the Political Legacy of the Holocaust', 236. See also Daniel E. Rogers, *Politics After Hitler: the Western Allies and the German Party System* (London: Macmillan, 1995), 107–11.

154 PRO: FO 371/145738 [WG 1019/6] FO Brief on ex-Nazis and war criminals for PM's talk with Herr Herwarth, 11 February 1959. On the question of compensation, nothing was paid to victims in the Eastern bloc satellite states as the FRG did not maintain diplomatic relations with any of them.

155 *Hansard*, HC Deb, vol. 618, cols. 829–30, 29 February 1960. There were many Commons questions on the issue of ex-Nazis in the FRG at this time.

Examples include: PQ, 24 February 1959 to Foreign Secretary Sir F. Medlicott (Conservative) on possible resurgence of Nazism in Germany; PQ from Mr Swingler (Labour), 19 February 1959, PQs Mr Arthur Lewis (Labour), 17 and 24 February, 4 May, 11 May 1959; PQ Mr Zillacus (Labour), 23 April 1959. Conversely, Mr J.B. Hynd (Labour) asked a PQ 15 April 1959 concerning ex-Nazis in the service of Pankow.

156 LPA: Int/1959–60/12, 'Germany – Former Nazis', March 1960.

157 See, for instance, *White Book on the Bonn War Treaty* (East Berlin: Nationales Druckhaus, 1952), 33ff; Rudi Goguel and Heinz Pohl (eds), *Oder–Neisse: Eine Dokumentation* (East Berlin: Kongress, 1956); *Jahrbuch der Deutschen Demokratischen Republik 1961* (East Berlin: Verlag die Wirtschaft, 1961), 77ff.

158 See, for instance, PRO: FO 371/154090, [WG 1075/2] Chancery, Bonn to Western Department, FO, 16 February 1960.

159 Control Commission for Germany (British Element), *Background Letter: January–December 1950* (Vol. III), Wahnerheide, 1950, 85.

160 Kurt P. Tauber, *Beyond Eagle and Swastika: German Nationalism Since 1945*, vol. 1 (Middletown, CO: Wesleyan, 1967), 917–18.

161 On a more positive note, great strides had been made in the economic and social assimilation of the expellees. See Barbara Marshall, *The New Germany and Migration in Europe* (Manchester: Manchester University Press, 2000), 1–26. On the flight of refugees from the GDR to the FRG, see Helge Heidemeyer, *Flucht und Zuwanderung aus der SBZ/DDR 1945/1949–1961: die Fluechtlingspolitik der Bundesrepublik Deutschland bis zum Bau der Berliner Mauer* (Düsseldorf: Droste, 1994). Heidemeyer argues that Bonn had no 'consistent refugee policy but reacted to emergencies and demands from the political sphere seldom showing initiative itself' (p. 333).

162 'Under Polish administration' and 'Under Soviet administration' respectively; see, for instance, Walter Hubatsch (with Johanna Schomerus and Werner John), *Die Deutsche Frage* (Würzburg: A.G. Ploetz, 1961), 164–74.

163 Gesamtdeutsches Bewesstein (ed.), *Deutschland im Europäischen Spannungsfeld* (Leer: Gerhard Rautenberg, 1963), 5.

164 Michael Burleigh, *Germany turns Eastwards: A study of Ostforschung in the Third Reich* (Cambridge: Cambridge University Press, 1988), 314. The Poles defined *Ostforschung* as 'the "scientific" elaboration of political ideas of revisionism.' The Poles themselves countered with organisations such as the Silesian Institute in Opole, which was established in 1957 and used by the Communists to legitimise post-war territorial acquisitions on a historical basis. Jan Herman Brinks, 'Polish-Germans in Poland', Centre for German–Jewish Studies, 1999, online, available at: www.sussex.ac.uk/Units/cgjs/publications/hbpolgerpol.html.

165 Wiskemann, *Germany's Eastern Neighbours*, 112.

166 The *Bund der Vertriebenen*, created as the expellee umbrella organisation in 1958, still exists today (although its influence has dwindled massively since the 1950s), articulating its grievances online, available at: www.bund-der-vertriebenen.de.

167 Theodor Schieder (ed.), *Dokumentation der Vertreibung der Deutschen aus Ost-Mitteleuropa*, vols I–V (Bonn: Bundesministerium für Vertriebene, Flüchtlinge und Kriegsgeschädigte, 1953–60).

168 Siegfried Schütt, *Theodor Oberländer: Eine dokumentarische Untersuchung* (Munich: Langen Müller, 1995) is typical of attempts to portray Oberländer as a decent conservative who sought to ameliorate the worst aspects of Nazi rule. Oberländer typified the expellee satisfaction with the West German state policy by joining the CDU in 1958. On the sullying of the name of the Bonn Republic by the presence of Theodor Oberländer see, Norbert Muhlen, 'The Survivors', *Commentary*, 36/5, November 1963, 23.

169 Thomas Etzemüller, *Sozialgeschichte als politische Geschichte: Werner Conze und die Neuorientierung der westdeutschen Geschichtwissenschaft nach 1945* (Munich: Oldenbourg, 2001), 319–20. In May 1960, Oberländer was forced to resign from the Adenauer government because of his Nazi past (specifically with regard to his activities in wartime Lvov). For a GDR indictment of Oberländer, of the sort that eventually toppled him, see Committee for German Unity (eds), *The Truth about Oberländer: the Brown Book on the Criminal Fascist Past of Adenauer's Minister* (East Berlin, 1960).

170 Jakob Kaiser at the *Deutsche Heimat in Osten* Exposition in November 1950. Quoted in Zoltan M. Szar, *Germany's Eastern Frontiers* (Chicago: Henry Regnery, 1960), ix.

171 PRO: FO 371/154047, [WG 10355/1] Chancery, Warsaw to FO, 13 January 1960.

172 'The Right of Germans to Self-Determination', speech delivered on 22 July 1956 in Königstein to the Ackermann Society (an association of the Sudeten German Catholics). Heinrich von Brentano, *Germany and Europe: Reflections on German Foreign Policy*, foreword by Ludwig Erhard (New York: Praeger, 1964), 105.

173 Speech in Cologne, 28 June 1959. Hans-Peter Schwarz (ed.), *Konrad Adenauer: Reden 1917–1967: Eine Auswahl* (Stuttgart: DVA, 1975), 405.

174 Adenauer in the CDU's *Bundesvorstand*, 16 September 1959. Gunter Buchstab (ed.), *Protokolle des CDU-Bundesvorstandes 1953–1957*, (Düsseldorf: Droste, 1990), 392–3.

175 PRO: FO 371/154090, [WG 0175/10] F.W. Marten, Bonn to E.E. Tomkins (Head, Western Department), 30 August 1960.

176 *The Times*, 29 August 1960. Erhard speech to Upper Silesian *Landsmannschaft*, 28 September 1960.

177 PRO: FO 371/154090, [WG 1075/11] Chancery, Bonn, 22 September 1960.

178 *The Times*, 29 August 1960.

179 PRO: FO 371/154090, [WG 1075/10] F.W. Marten, Bonn to E.E. Tomkins, 30 August 1960. Rally of Upper Silesians, 28 August 1960.

180 PRO: FO 371/154097, [WG 1081/29] Chancery, Bonn, 10 July 1960. Adenauer speech in Düsseldorf, 10 July 1960.

181 PRO: PRO: FO 371/154095, [WG 1081/12] R.H. Mason, 20 July 1960.

182 PRO: FO 371/154097, [WG 1081/29] Polish communication to John Profumo, MP, regarding HMG stance on the FRG's *Ostpolitik*, 20 July 1960.

183 PRO: FO 371/154097, [WG 1081/33] Sir Christopher Steel, Bonn to C.D.W. O'Neill (Assistant Under-Secretary of State), FO, 19 August 1960. On the roots of the expellee organisations and their influence in the FRG, see Ahonen, *After the Expulsion*, 24–53.

184 It was with an eye to such elements that Adenauer had declared in the *Bundestag* in December 1952 that the German soldier had fought honourably in the Second World War. Volker Berghahn, *Modern Germany: Society, Economy and Politics in the Twentieth Century* (Cambridge: Cambridge University Press, 1982), 212.

185 Ahonen, *After the Expulsion*, 115.

186 The *BdV* was very active, with thirty-three separate mass meetings held between 27 April and 11 September 1960 alone. The *BdV* was formed by the amalgamation of *Bund der vertreiben Deutschen* and *Verband der Landsmannschaften*. There was a plethora of organisations under the *BdV* umbrella. These included the *Landsmannschaften* of the Silesians, East Prussians, Danzigers and Pomeranians, and the *Deutsche Jugend des Ostens* (*DJO*). The DJO was an organisation with *c.*150,000 members that proclaimed its mission as imbuing the youth with zeal for the lost 'eastern territories' '[In order that

the spirit will] persist and liberate the Fatherland East of the Oder–Neisse.'
PRO: FO 371/154090, [WG 1075/2] Chancery, Bonn to W. Dept, 16 February
1960.

187 Jaksch was a Sudeten German and an SPD *Bundestag* deputy. As leader of
the *BdV* from 1964–6 he typified the expellee as victim, as he had been an
anti-Nazi in-exile between 1938 and 1945. Alfred Grosser, *Germany in Our
Time: A Political History of the Postwar Years* (London: Pelican Books, 1974),
296–7.

188 PRO: FO 371/154090, [WG1075/4] Chancery, Bonn to FO, 5 April 1960.
Sudetendeutsche   Landmannschaft   Federal   Assembly   [*Bundesversammlung*]
Munich, 3 April 1960.

189 PRO: FO 371/154097, [WG 1081/33] R.H. Mason, *c.* September 1960.

190 PRO: FO 371/154047, [WG 10335/6] *Aide mémoire* from the Polish ambassador to Lord Privy Seal, 30 September 1960.

191 *Hansard*, HC Deb, volume 621, col. 1234, 13 April 1960. Of course, John
Profumo was later to find out for himself that 'private' activity could lead to
repercussions for public figures.

192 PRO: FO 371/154090, [WG 1075/6] Chancery, Bonn 13 May 1960. Report of
meetings between Welbourne-Ker, First Secretary (Information) and Communist diplomats and correspondents.

193 PRO: FO 371/154090, [WG 1075/2] Chancery, Bonn to W. Dept, 16 February
1960 (*Bund der Vertreiben* 'Federal Assembly' [104 representatives for claimed
membership of 2.5 m] Bonn, 14 February 1960 – detailed comment on proceedings).

194 PRO: FO 371/154097, [WG 1081/33] J.E. Killick (Western Department), 6
September 1960.

195 The Ministries of All-German Affairs and Refugees represented two departments of government perhaps peculiar and somewhat incomprehensible in
role and function to many in London. Brandt's abolition of the Ministry for
Refugees in October 1969 was an unmistakable early sign of the acceptance of
the demise of the concept of *Recht auf Heimat*; Grosser, *Germany in Our Time*,
298.

196 PRO: FO 371/154098, [WG 1081/41] Sir C. Steel, Bonn to C.D.W. O'Neill, 25
October 1960.

197 Lee, 'Pragmatism Versus Principle? Macmillan and Germany', 121–2.

198 Horne, *Macmillan 1957–1986*, 278. Despite his use of the New York platform,
Macmillan had written in his diary in 1957 that 'The United Nations seems to
be turning out an institution for causing the maximum of international
trouble'. Bodleian: HMD: 18 February 1957.

199 PRO: FO 371/154047, [WG 10355/3] Sir George Clutton, Warsaw to FO, 8
September 1960. Gomułka asserted that West German militarism and revisionism was one of the greatest problems before the UN.

200 Gromyko, *Memories*, 157.

201 PRO: FO 331/154047, [WG 10355/6] Macmillan's speech to the UN General
Assembly, 29 September 1960.

202 Macmillan, *Pointing the Way*, 278.

203 HMD: 29 September 1960.

204 PRO: FO 371/154089, [WG 1074/74] Sir Evelyn Shuckburgh, Moscow to
Home, 9 November 1960.

205 PRO: FO 371/154047, [WG 10355/5] Clutton, Warsaw, 5 October 1960 to
FO.

206 PRO: FO 371/154097, [WG 10355/6] Conversation between Edward Heath
MP (Lord Privy Seal) and the Polish ambassador, Dr Rodzinski, 30 September
1960.

207 PRO: FO 371/154097, [WG 10355/6] W.J.A. Wilberforce, Northern Department, 11 October 1960.

208 PRO: FO 371/154097, [WG 10355/6] R.H. Mason minute on 'Anglo-Polish relations', 19 October 1960.

209 *The German View* (Bonn: Federal Press and Information Office, 1960).

210 PRO: FO 371/154091, [WG 1075/17] Heath to Longden, 14 November 1960.

211 PRO: FO 371/154047, [WG 10355/8] Sir George Clutton, Warsaw 8 October 1960, report of Gomułka speech.

212 PRO: FO 371/154091, [WG 1075/13] C.C. Parrott, ambassador, Prague, 8 October 1960.

213 For a recent study, see Niklas Perzi, *Die Beneš-Dekrete: Eine europäische Tragödie* (Vienna/Linz: Niederösterreichisches Pressehaus, St Pölten, 2003).

214 PRO: FO 371/154091, [WG 1075/14] Parrott to R.H. Mason (Head, Northern Department), 7 October 1960.

215 PRO: FO 371/154090, [WG 1075/12] Parrott to Mason, 13 October 1960.

216 LPA: Int/1960–1/3, notes on a visit to Czechoslovakia, 2–9 October 1960, James Callaghan MP.

217 PRO: FO 371/70682 [C 8168] Pierson Dixon, Prague embassy to R.M.A. Hankey, Northern Department, FO, 30 September 1948.

218 See, for instance, PRO: FO 371/70682 [c 7533/3701/18] R.M.A. Hankey to Pierson Dixon, Prague embassy, 14 September 1948.

219 PRO: FCO 28/961 [C3/8] Roger Jackling, Bonn to T. Brimelow, FCO, 26 October 1970.

220 PRO: FO 371/154098, [WG 1981/37] W.J.A. Wilberforce (Western Department), 19 December 1960.

221 PRO: FO 371/154047, [WG 10335/10] Chancery, Warsaw to Northern Department, 19 October 1960. Discussion, Clutton on the Polish *aide-mémoire* of 30. September 1960 with Mr Beam, US ambassador in Warsaw on 14 October 1960.

222 PRO: FO 371/154047, [WG 10335/10] Western Department, FO to Warsaw, 16 November 1960.

223 PRO: FO 371/154047, [WG 10335/10] Clutton, Warsaw to Western Department, 30 November 1960.

224 Gomułka had told the US broadcaster CBC that Herter had been 'more reasonable' than Macmillan.

225 PRO: FO 371/154047, [WG 10335/10] P.W.J. Buxton (Northern Department), 27 October 1960.

226 PRO: FO 371/154047, [WG 10335/10] B. Cartledge, 31 October 1960. On 1 November, A.D.C. McAlpine doubted the use of following the US line, as Britain could really do nothing to stop the consolidation of the Western territories.

227 PRO: FO 371/154047, [WG 10335/10] Heath Mason, note on file, n.d. [October 1960]. Mason is referring to the fact that, on 17 October 1960, the Republican presidential candidate, Richard Nixon, told a Polish–American audience that 'all Poles in Poland as well as abroad are united in their determination to defend the new western frontier', PRO: FO 371/154098, [WG 1081/39] Nixon speech in Buffalo, 17 October 1960.

228 PRO: FO 371/161134, [WG 1081/1] J.E. Killick (Deputy in Western Department) to Sir E. Shuckburgh (Deputy Under Secretary of State), 23 January 1961.

229 PRO: FO 371/161134, [WG 1081/1] Sir E. Shuckburgh, 23 January 1961.

230 PRO: FO 371/154095, [WG 1081/1] E. Berthoud, Warsaw to E.E. Tomkins (Head of the Western Department), 29 December 1959. Berthoud report on discussion with French ambassador to Poland, Burin des Roziers, on recent Adenauer–de Gaulle talks (Paris, 1–2 December 1959).

231 HMD: 10 June 1958.

232 PRO: PREM 11/3345, Macmillan–Adenauer meeting, Admiralty House, 22 February 1961.

233 See David Sanders, *Losing an Empire, Finding a Role: British Foreign Policy Since 1945* (London: Macmillan, 1990), 141–2.

234 PRO: FCO 51/18, LR 5/5, Joint Research Department Memorandum, 'Reunification as a factor in West German foreign policy, 1955–1965', 5 April 1967.

235 *OdW* – Eastern Committee of German Industry.

236 Robert Mark Spaulding, *Osthandel and Ostpolitik: German Foreign Trade Policies in Eastern Europe from Bismarck to Adenauer* (Oxford: Berghahn Books, 1997), 442–3.

237 Garton Ash, *In Europe's Name*, 51.

238 Jain, *Germany, the Soviet Union and Eastern Europe 1949–1991*, 11.

239 Anthon, 'Adenauer's Ostpolitik 1955–1963', 117.

240 PRO: FO 371/145863, [WG 1078/44] FO Brief, 'Relations between the Federal Republic and Eastern Europe' [nd, 1959].

241 R.W. Dean, *West German Trade with the East: The Political Dimension* (New York: Praeger, 1974), 121.

242 Spaulding, *Osthandel and Ostpolitik*, 455–6. Adenauer realised the departure when telling Soviet ambassador Smirnov that he 'risked being stoned' if this was to become public knowledge, (n) p. 469.

243 JFKL: POF Box 125, Notes, Soviet Affairs, Number 241, 18 May 1960, 'The Quotable Khrushchev April 1959–March 1960'. Letter from Khrushchev to Adenauer, 18 August 1959.

244 Hélène Seppain, *Contrasting US and German Attitudes to Soviet Trade, 1917–91: Politics by Economic Means* (London: St Martin's Press, 1992), 161–2. The head of the *OdW*, Otto Wolff von Amerongen, called for the de-politicisation of trade and by 1960 was even speculating that trade would be the area in which the first signs of an East–West understanding would arise (Seppain, 163).

245 Spaulding, *Osthandel and Ostpolitik*, 422–3.

246 PRO: FO 371/137358, [WG 1022/23] J.K. Drinkall, 16 July 1958.

247 PRO: FO 371/163552, [CG 103155/5] R.G. Braithwaite (Northern Department), 3 October 1962.

248 Seppain, *Contrasting US and German Attitudes to Soviet Trade*, 157–8.

249 On British policy, see Klaus Larres, 'Britain and the GDR in the 1960s: the Politics of Trade and Recognition by Stealth' in Noakes, Wende and Wright, *Britain and Germany in Europe*, 189–96.

250 West German officials were ultra-sensitive on this point. Sloppy language could cause the West Germans major offence. In 1962, the Foreign Office issued the Conservative Party with a 'Dictionary of terms' for a CDU delegation visit. It was advised, for instance, to avoid referring to the 'GDR' or the 'DDR' and to add the words 'in freedom' or 'self-determination for the whole German people' when making any reference to German reunification. Bodleian: COB 64 (3), (P 10010/180), 14 March 1962.

251 Tusa, *The Last Division*, 73. For an account of the diplomatic intricacies involved with the status of the GDR, see Geoffrey McDermott, *Berlin: Success of a Mission?* (London: Andre Deutsch, 1963).

252 Tusa, *The Last Division*, 63.

253 PRO: 371/137462, [WG 1152/16] Macmillan memo, 15 April 1958. Cited in Klaus Larres, 'Britain and the GDR: Political and Economic Relations, 1949–1989', 78.

254 See, for instance, PRO: FO 371/137398, [WG 1071/7] BBC Monitoring Report, 4 March 1958.

255 PRO: FO 371/160605, [CG 1154/1]; *Sunday Telegraph*, 5 February 1961.

A controversial figure, Boothby became something of a focal point for anti-West German sentiment. On 5 August 1963, the editor of the *Statesman's Year Book*, Sigrid H. Steinberg, wrote to Boothby advising that 'In view of [his] interest in promoting better relations with the eastern countries' Boothby should be aware that the West German postal authorities regularly 'intercept letters clearly directed to East German addresses and ... re-direct them to West Germany.' Steinberg expressed the hope that 'an experienced politician like yourself can use this knowledge to some advantage in combating the grotesque arrogance of the Adenauer regime'. Archiv der Hansestadt Lübeck: Hansischer Geschichtsverein VII 13.1 (Sigrid H. Steinberg Papers).

256 *The Times*, 13 March 1961.
257 Seppain, *Contrasting US and German Attitudes to Soviet Trade*, (n) pp. 297–8.
258 PRO: PREM 11/3805, Sir Evelyn Shuckburgh to Lord Home, 20 June 1962.
259 PRO: CAB 129/112, C (63) 13, 'East–West Trade Differences with the Americans', memo by Lord Home, 4 March 1963.
260 von Herwarth, 'Anglo-German Relations', 518.
261 PRO: CAB 129/112, C (63) 15, 'Policy for East–West Trade', memo by the President of the Board of Trade, 8 February 1963. The memo laid out the objectives of British trade with the bloc in the preceding 'five or six years'. First, excessive dependency upon bloc supplies must be avoided; second, these imports must not disrupt British industry; and third, the strategic embargo must not be violated.
262 See, for instance, PRO: FO 371/160605, [CG 1154/1].
263 Seppain, *Contrasting US and German Attitudes to Soviet Trade*, 188–9.
264 *Newsweek*, 30 April 1956.
265 Adenauer likened Britain to 'a rich man who has lost all his property but does not realise it'. Quoted in John W. Young, *Britain and European Unity 1945–1992* (London: Macmillan, 1993), 69.
266 PRO: PREM 11/2347, Chancery, Bonn to FO, 16 April 1958.
267 Donald Cameron Watt, *Succeeding John Bull: America in Britain's Place 1900–1975* (Cambridge: Cambridge University Press, 1984), 135.
268 Jebb, *Memoirs*, 318.
269 PRO: FO 371/154098, [WG 1081/38] G.L. Clutton, Warsaw to C.D.W. O'Neill FO, 14 September 1960.

4 The fall of the *Politik der Stärke* and rise of the Anglo-Saxon consensus

1 DDEL: NSC meeting, 6 February 1958.
2 PRO: FO 371/145688, [WG 1015/42] Sir H. Caccia, ambassador, Washington to FO, 13 January 1959.
3 HMD: 5–7 January 1961.
4 HMD: 23 February 1961.
5 On the reluctance of the United States to back Adenauer to the hilt over Berlin, see William Burr, 'Avoiding the Slippery Slope: the Eisenhower Administration and the Berlin Crisis: November 1958–January 1959', *Diplomatic History*, 18/2 (1994), 177–205; Kara Stibora Fulcher, 'A Sustainable Position? The United States, the Federal Republic, and the Ossification of Allied Policy on Germany, 1958–1962', *Diplomatic History*, 26/2 (2002), 283–307.
6 DDEL: President Dwight D. Eisenhower to Revd. Billy Graham, 22 March 1956.
7 Bremen, *Die Eisenhower-Administration und die zweite Berlin-Krise, 1958–1961*, 425. See also Trachtenberg, *A Constructed Peace*, 260.
8 On this see, Kori Schake, 'US Policy in the 1958 and 1961 Berlin Crises', in J. Gearson and K. Schake, *The Berlin Wall Crisis*, 22–42.

9 John Gearson, 'Britain and the Berlin Wall Crisis', in ibid., 61–5.

10 For the link between the EEC, Britain and US policy at this time, see Miriam Camps, 'Britain, the Six and American Policy', *Foreign Affairs*, 39/1 (1960), 112–22.

11 Bodleian: Harold Macmillan Diary (HMD), 2 November 1960.

12 JFKL: OHP: David Bruce, 6.

13 HMD: 31 December 1960.

14 PRO: PREM 11/3778, Macmillan to Home, 15 April 1962.

15 JFKL: OHP: Senator Mike Mansfied, 10; Martin Hillenbrand, 6; Dean Rusk, interview four, 161.

16 JFKL: OHP: Dr Wilhelm Grewe, 2.

17 JFKL: OHP: Lord Harlech (David Ormsby Gore), 2–3.

18 A. Paul Kubricht, 'Politics and Foreign Policy: A brief Look at the Kennedy Administration's Eastern European Diplomacy', *Diplomatic History*, 11/1 (1987), 55; Theodore C. Sorenson, *Kennedy* (London: Pan Books, 1966), 645.

19 For assessments of the Eisenhower administration's policies towards Eastern Europe, see Jim Marchio, 'Resistance Potential and Rollback: US Intelligence and the Eisenhower Administration's Policies Towards Eastern Europe, 1953–56', *Intelligence and National Security*, 10/2 (1995), 219–41; Ronald R. Krebs, 'Liberation à la Finland: Reexamining Eisenhower Administration Objectives in Eastern Europe', *Journal of Strategic Studies*, 20/3 (1997), 1–26.

20 John F. Kennedy, 'A Democrat looks at Foreign Policy', *Foreign Affairs*, 36/1 (1957), 49.

21 JFKL: OHP: Theodore C. Sorenson, interviews 3 and 4, 108. Adenauer was 41 when Kennedy was born.

22 *The Times*, 25 October 1960.

23 PRO: FO 371/154098, [WG 1081/39] Nixon speech in Buffalo, 17 October 1960. Buxton, FO, written comments, 31 October 1960.

24 PRO: FO 371/177943, [WG 1081/9/1960] Brief for Lloyd's trip to Washington, 12–14 April 1960.

25 PRO: FO 371/177943, [RG 1081/1] R.B.J. Ledwidge (Head of Western Department), 23 December 1963.

26 JFKL: OHP: Dr Wilhelm Grewe, 3. Grewe concedes that this accounted for a heightened desire for a Nixon win in Bonn.

27 See, for instance, Zbigniew Brzezinski, 'The Challenge of Change in the Soviet Bloc', *Foreign Affairs*, 39/3 (1961), 430–43; Zbigniew Brzezinski and William E. Griffith, 'Peaceful Engagement in Eastern Europe', *Foreign Affairs*, 39/4 (1961), 642–54. On Britain and Germany, see Henry A. Kissinger, *The Troubled Partnership: A Re-appraisal of the Atlantic Alliance* (Council on Foreign Relations, 1965), 65–88.

28 Heinrich von Brentano, 'Goals and Means of the Western Alliance', *Foreign Affairs*, 39/3 (1961), 416–29.

29 Trachtenberg, *A Constructed Peace*, 283–6.

30 Garton Ash, *In Europe's Name*, 53.

31 PRO: FO 371/160571, [WG 1022/2] Chancery, Bonn, 6 July 1961. In reality no moves were made in this direction until Dr Gerhard Schröder succeeded Dr Heinrich von Brentano after the September 1961 elections.

32 Sorenson, *Kennedy*, 644.

33 On this, see Christof Münger, 'Ich bin ein West-Berliner: der Wandel der amerikanischen Berlinpolitik während der Präsidentschaft John F. Kennedys', *Zürcher Beiträge zur Sicherheitspolitik und Konfliktforschung*, No. 49, Zürich 1999. URL:http://cms.isn.ch/public/docs/doc_223_290_de.pdf.

34 Walt Rostow, *The Diffusion of Power: An Essay in Recent History* (New York: Macmillan, 1992), 224.

35 JFKL: POF Box 127, Memo 'Berlin', Dean Acheson to Kennedy, 3 April 1961.
36 Sorenson, *Kennedy*, 645.
37 JFKL: POF Box 127, Bundy to Kennedy, 4 April 1961.
38 Frank A. Mayer, *Adenauer and Kennedy: A Study in German–American Relations, 1961–1963*, (London: Macmillan: 1996), 32.
39 JFK–Macmillan meeting, Washington, April 5, 1961. *FRUS*, 1961–2, Volume XIV, 40.
40 HMD: 1 June 1961. Talk between Macmillan and Lord Beaverbrook.
41 HMD: 11 June 1961. Kennedy visit to the UK, JFKL: OHP: Lord Harlech, 61–3.
42 JFKL: OHP: Couve de Murville, 5.
43 HMD: 15 June 1961.
44 JFKL: OHP: Lord Harlech, 63.
45 Home was very vulnerable to this charge, even from his own side. Geoffrey McDermott, Deputy Commandant in Berlin (a civilian post), regarded Home as 'a great one for appeasement, really enthusiastic running ahead of Chamberlain, whose Private Secretary he was.' JFKL: OHP: Geoffrey McDermott, 17. For Home's close association with, and admiration of, Chamberlain, see D.R. Thorpe, *Alec Douglas-Home* (London: Sinclair-Stevenson, 1996), 63–107. The point that Home was intimately involved with giving Germany a free hand in the east at Munich was made by many in the Labour Party. See, for instance, Gordon Schaffer, *Do You Want War over Berlin?* (London: Gladiator, 1961), 6–7.
46 PRO: CAB 129/106, C (61) 116, 'Berlin', memorandum by Lord Home, 26 July 1961.
47 Ibid.
48 This had long been advocated by the USSR and the GDR. It was not at all popular with Adenauer. In January 1959, for instance, Adenauer had told a group of journalists that the West Germans would not even consider the possibility of such an arrangement. PRO: FO 371/145692, [WG 1015/101] Steel, Bonn, 30 January 1959, report on confidential talk given by Adenauer to small group of foreign journalists.
49 PRO: CAB 129/106, C (61) 116, 'Berlin', memorandum by Lord Home, 26 July 1961. Despite this, Home denied at interview in 1974 that he had pushed for a deal involving the recognition of the GDR and the Oder–Neiße line, JFKL: OHP: Alec Douglas-Home, 2.
50 Arthur M. Schlesinger, *A Thousand Days: John F. Kennedy in the White House* (London: André Deutsch, 1965), 356.
51 McGeorge Bundy, *Danger and Survival* (New York: Random House, 1988), 366–71.
52 HMD: 8 August 1961, lunch between Macmillan, Home and Schuckburgh.
53 JFKL: NSF Box 74, Walter C. Dowling to Rusk, telegram 1218, 8 February 1961.
54 JFKL: POF Box 116, Kennedy–von Brentano MemCon, 17 February 1961.
55 JFKL: NSF Box 74, George C. McGhee, memo for Walt Rostow, 1 June 61.
56 Mayer, *Adenauer and Kennedy*, 36, 41.
57 HMD: 9 August 1961.
58 For the evolution of British thinking, see Richard Griffiths, 'A Slow One Hundred and Eighty Degree Turn: British Policy towards the Common Market. 1955–60', in George Wilkes (ed.), *Britain's Failure to Enter the European Community 1961–63: The Enlargement Negotiations and Crises in European, Atlantic and Commonwealth Relations* (London: Frank Cass, 1997).
59 HMD: 9 August 1961.
60 That is, the notion that a Soviet ballistic missile capability against the United

States would undermine the willingness of the USA to defend Western Europe. This was sometimes boiled down to the question 'Would the USA sacrifice Chicago to save Hamburg?'

61 Trachtenberg, *A Constructed Peace*, 274–83.
62 On West German reactions to the Wall, see Hope Harrison, 'The Berlin Wall, Ostpolitik and Détente', in David C. Geyer and Bernd Schaefer (eds), *American Détente and German Ostpolitik 1969–1972* (Washington DC: German Historical Institute, 2004), 13–5.
63 Jain, *Germany, the Soviet Union and Eastern Europe 1949–1991*, 12, 18.
64 Gromyko, *Memories*, 196.
65 Adenauer speech to the *Bundestag*, 18 August 1961. Wolfgang Heidelmeye and Guenter Hindrichs (eds), *Documents on Berlin 1943–1963* (Munich: Oldenbourg, 1963), 281–8.
66 Garton Ash, *In Europe's Name*, 51; Ash notes that Adenauer did not exactly lead the West by example.
67 Literally, 'shut gate panic'. In times past a term applied to women who were afraid of not marrying and being 'left on the shelf', nowadays it is occasionally applied to career women who have delayed having children.
68 JFKL: OHP: Martin Hillenbrand, 17.
69 Dean Rusk, *As I Saw It* (London: I.B. Tauris, 1991), 195.
70 Schlesinger, *A Thousand Days*, 359; Michael Beschloss, *The Crisis Years: Kennedy and Khruschchev 1960–1963* (New York: Random House, 1991), 278.
71 Anne E. Stoddart, letter to author, 25 May 2000.
72 PRO: FO 371/160509, [WG 1052/1] Steel to FO, 14 August 1961.
73 Schlesinger, *A Thousand Days*, 356. Rostow recounts Kennedy's words thus: 'He will have to do something to stop the flow of refugees – perhaps a wall. And we won't be able to prevent it. I can hold the Alliance together to defend West Berlin but I cannot act to keep East Berlin open.' Walt W. Rostow, *The Diffusion of Power: An Essay in Recent History* (New York: IISS 1972), 231.
74 PRO: FO 371/160505, [CG 1019/15] J.C.C. Bennett, Bonn to P.W.J. Buxton (Central Department), 18 August 1961. Not all the Germans were so surprised. In November 1958, anticipating the construction of the Berlin Wall, Willy Brandt told Sir Christopher Steel that he believed that the East would eventually turn the Western Sector boundaries into a *de facto* international boundary. In Brandt's opinion, although the West would protest it would acquiesce. PRO: FO 371/137355, [WG 1015/3] Steel, Berlin, 17 November 1958, to FO.
75 JFKL: NSF Box 212, USIA, R-9-62, 16 February 1962. British newspapers reflected this (e.g. *Daily Telegraph*, 19 August 1961, *Daily Mail*, 21 August 1961, *Daily Mirror*, 23 August 1961).
76 PRO: FO 371/160571, [CG 1081/8] B.C. Cartledge (Northern Department), 10 October 1961.
77 Nehru letter to Macmillan, 12 September 1961. Macmillan, *Pointing the Way*, 398–9.
78 The US administration was certainly aware of the 'marked uneasiness' about western policy in the FRG. JFKL: NSF Box 212, USIA, R-9-62, 16 February 1962.
79 HMD: 19 August 1961.
80 HMD: 19 August 1961. See also HMD: 25 August 1961.
81 See above PRO: CAB 129/106, C (61) 116, 'Berlin', memorandum by Lord Home, 26 July 1961.
82 PRO: CAB 129/106, C (61) 132, 'Berlin' memorandum by Lord Home, 1 September 1961; Caccia advised Rusk of Home's opinion of this on 18 August 1961, JFKL: NSF Box 170.

83 HMD: 22 September 1961.
84 PRO: CAB 129/106, C (61) 132, 'Berlin' memorandum by Lord Home, 1 September 1961.
85 PRO: CAB 128/35, CC (61), 49 (3), 5 September 1961.
86 JFKL: NSF Box 170, ambassador Bruce to Rusk, 6 September 1961.
87 LPA: LPID, David Ennals to Lord Alexander, 16 October 1961.
88 Steininger, *Der Mauerbau*, 277–80.
89 HMD: 19 September 1961.
90 PRO: CAB 129/107, C (61) 154, 'Political Situation After the West German Elections', memo by Lord Home, 6 October 1961. Adenauer, for instance, made a speech in Regensburg mentioning Brandt's illegitimacy (making references to the SPD man as 'Fromm'). Mayer, *Adenauer and Kennedy*, 45. Brandt himself recalls that Strauß was particularly keen to encourage such attacks on his origins. Willy Brandt, *People and Politics* (London: Hamish Hamilton), 1992, 268–9.
91 PRO: FO 371/160506, [CG 1019/21] E. M. Rose (Minister in Bonn) to Home, 29 September 1961.
92 UCL: Gaitskell Papers, (Box F23): Lilo Milchsack, to Gaitskell, 20 September 1961.
93 PRO: CAB 129/107, C (61) 154, 'Political Situation After the West German Elections', memo by Lord Home, 6 October 1961.
94 For example, Torsten Oppelland, 'Gerhard Schröder and the First "*Ostpolitik*"', in Wilfried Loth (ed.), *Europe, Cold War and Coexistence, 1953–1965* (London: Frank Cass, 2004), 274–84.
95 Lazlo Gorgey, *Bonn's Eastern Policy, 1964–1971* (Connecticut: Hamden, 1972), 2–4.
96 Gerhard Schröder, *Decision for Europe* (London: Thames & Hudson, 1964), 62–4. On the 'Policy of Movement', see Franz Eibl, *Politik der Bewegung: Gerhard Schröder als Außenminister 1961–1966* (Munich: Oldenbourg, 2001); for a biography of Schröder, see Torsten Oppelland, *Gerhard Schröder 1910–1989: Politik Zwischen Staat, Partei und Konfession* (Düsseldorf: Droste, 2002).
97 Gerhard Schroeder, 'Germany Looks at Eastern Europe', *Foreign Affairs*, 44/1 (1965), 15–25.
98 Schröder, *Decision for Europe*, 198.
99 PRO: FO 371/163527, [G1011/1] Annual Reviews of events in the F.R.G. for 1961, Sir Christopher Steel, Bonn to FO 2 January 1962.
100 HMD: 26 September 1961. Macmillan fretted that Kennedy could be vulnerable to charges of following a 'Chamberlain policy.'
101 JFKL: OHP: Lord Harlech, 61.
102 HMD: 9 November 1961. Home informed the Cabinet that much turned on Kennedy's ability to talk Adenauer around to the Anglo-Saxon way of thinking in the Chancellor's visit to Washington 19–21 November 1961. PRO: CAB 129/107, C (61) 184, 'Berlin', memo by Lord Home, 21 November 1961.
103 Adenauer asserted that Dulles' 1954 commitment to defend the FRG as if it were the USA was gravely undermined. Trachtenberg, *A Constructed Peace*, 234–5.
104 JFKL: NSF Box 88, MemCon, Foy D. Kohler (Assistant Secretary of State for European Affairs) and Lord Hood (British Minister in Washington), 14 October 1961.
105 Rusk, *As I Saw It*, 197–8.
106 PRO: CAB 128/35, CC (61), 65 (3), 23 November 1961. Home had recognised these as the points on which the Soviets would press hardest, see PRO: CAB 129/107, C (61) 184, 'Berlin', memo by Lord Home, 21 November 1961.
107 The Western ambassadorial meeting in Washington (USA, UK, France, FRG)

agreed that the undertaking given in the Paris Treaties of 1954 ('never to have recourse to force to achieve the reunification of Germany or the modification of the present boundaries') could be broadened to include the Oder–Neiße line. PRO: CAB 129/107, C (61) 184, 'Berlin', memo by Lord Home, 21 November 1961, Annex A, 'Paper on the Western ambassadorial Meeting in Washington', 14 November 1961.

108 PRO: CAB 129/107, C (61) 184, 'Berlin', memo by Lord Home, 21 November 1961. West Berlin's relationship with the FRG meant that it was often referred to as the 'twelfth Land'. West Berlin had (non-voting) deputies in the *Bundestag* and West German parties ran its city government. The British in Berlin and Bonn regarded the parliamentary meetings in West Berlin as 'highly inflammatory'. Interview: D.A.S. Gladstone.
109 JFKL: NSF Box 84, MemCon, Rusk-Ormsby Gore, 5 January 1962.
110 PRO: CAB 128/35, CC (61), 65 (3), 23 November 1961.
111 Thorpe, *Alec Douglas-Home*, 228.
112 PRO: PREM 11/3782, Bermuda Conference, 20–23 December 1961. See also JKL: POF Box 117.
113 JFKL: NSF Box 74, 'Soviet Position on Germany 1952-3', MM-RSB-61-240, 15 December 1961.
114 JFKL: NSF Box 88, Macmillan, Home and Gromyko meeting, Admiralty House, London, 10 October 1961.
115 PRO: FO 371/163527, [G1011/1] Annual Reviews of events in the F.R.G. for 1961. Sir Christopher Steel, Bonn to FO 2 January 1962.
116 Jain, *Germany, the Soviet Union and Eastern Europe 1949–1991*, 15.
117 Schlesinger, *A Thousand Days*, 363.
118 HMD: 26 September 1961.
119 *Hansard*, HC Deb, vol. 613, col. 394, 11 November 1959.
120 PRO: FO 371/177943, [WG 1081/9/1960] Brief for Lloyd's trip to Washington, 12–14 April 1960.
121 Ibid.
122 PRO: FO 371/160480, [CG 1018/42] Sir E. Shuckburgh to Sir H. Caccia, Washington, 26 July 1961.
123 PRO: FO 371/160571, [CG 1081/16] R.H. Mason to A.D. Wilson (Head of Central Department), 12 December 1961.
124 PRO: 371/160571, [CG 1081/17/61] Sir George Clutton (British ambassador), Warsaw to A.D. Wilson, 13 December 1961.
125 Cold War International History Project, Woodrow Wilson International Center for Scholars (hereafter CWIHP). Rough notes from a conversation (Gromyko, Khrushchev and Gomułk) on the international situation, n.d. (October 1961). URL: http//:www.cwihp.si.edu.
126 Ibid.
127 Nikita S. Khrushchev, 'On Peaceful Coexistence', *Foreign Affairs*, 38/1 (1959), 1–18.
128 JFKL: POF Box 127, Macmillan to Kennedy, 5 January 1962.
129 PRO: PREM 11/3776, meeting between Adenauer and Macmillan, Bonn, 9 January 1962; JFKL: POF Box 127, Macmillan to Kennedy, 15 January 1962.
130 PRO: CAB 129/108 C (62) 31, 'Berlin', memo by Lord Home, 23 February 1962.
131 PRO: PREM 11/3778, Macmillan to Home, 15 April 1962. Kennedy shared such feelings, JFKL: OHP: Martin Hillenbrand, 25. The Ems telegram had been skilfully used by Bismarck to engineer the outbreak of the Franco-Prussian War in 1870.
132 PRO: PREM 11/3805, [IAD 410/614] meeting between Gromyko and Home, Soviet Trade Delegation HQ, Geneva, 21 March 1962.

133 PRO; FO 371/160571, [CG 1081/17/61] Clutton to A.D. Wilson, 13 December 1961.
134 JFKL: NSF Box 75, Henry A. Kissinger to Carl Kaysen, 21 February 1962.
135 *Germany Reports*, Press and Information Office of the FRG, 1961, 188–9. This was derived under the legal concept of the 'continuity of the Reich' that had been effectively recognised at Potsdam (pp. 95–104).
136 PRO: FO 371/160571, [CG 1081/17] Memo 'Germany's eastern Frontiers', 15 December 1961, E.E. Tomkins.
137 PRO: PREM 11/3921, P.F. de Zuleta to A.C. I. Samuel, FO, 19 October 1961.
138 Ibid.
139 PRO: PREM 11/3921, Anders to Macmillan, 23 February 1962; JFKL: NSF Box 170, Anders to Kennedy, 23 February 1962.
140 It was noted by Home's Private Secretary, J. Oliver Wright, that the Polish government-in-exile and the Communists in Warsaw had the exact same opinion on this matter. PRO: PREM 11/3921, Wright to Macmillan, 12 March 1962.
141 PRO: FO 371/163594, [CG 1081/10] 18 May 1962, Mr Lottiniere, Canada House, passed on telegram of 21 March 1962 from ambassador of Canada to Poland, G.D. Southam. Southam quoted Polish PM (Cyrankiewicz) speech of 10 March 1962.
142 JFKL: NSF Box 170, McGeorge Bundy to Anders, 24 February 1962; PRO: PREM 11/3291, Macmillan to Anders, 15 March 1962.
143 PRO: FO 371/163594, (1081/14/2G), [CG 1081/2] Sir George Clutton, Warsaw to A.D. Wilson, 14 February 1962, emphasis in original.
144 PRO: PREM 11/3921, FO Confidential Memorandum, 'British attitude towards the Oder–Neisse line', 12 March 1962.
145 PRO: FO 371/166119, [NP 1051/2] Clutton to Mason, 27 January 1962. The Poles would, however, have greatly valued US recognition of the Oder–Neiße due to the enormous pressure this would place on the FRG. Brzezinski to Kennedy, JFKL: NSF Box 106, 12 April 1963.
146 Interview: Sir J. Oliver Wright.
147 PRO: PREM 11/3921, Wright to Macmillan (reply to de Zuleta letter of 25 February 1962), 12 March 1962. Interview: Sir J. Oliver Wright.
148 PRO: FO 371/163594, (1081/12/4), [CG 1081/9] Sir George Clutton,Warsaw to R.H. Mason (Head of Northern Department), 12 April 1962. Three years later the Poles were told that going public with this as it would disrupt Schröder's policies, PRO: FO 371/182671, [NP 1053/48] FO Minute, 16 September 1965.
149 PRO: CAB 128/39, CC (62), 59 (1), 9 October 1962.
150 PRO: PREM 11/3689, Sir David Ormsby Gore to Macmillan, No. 2036, 23 October 1962.
151 PRO: PREM 11/3691, Steel to FO, No. 898, 30 October 1962.
152 PRO: PREM 11/3691, [M 298/62] Macmillan personal minute to Home, 29 October 1962.
153 Macmillan to Home, 29 October 1962. L.V. Scott, *Macmillan, Kennedy and the Cuban Missile Crisis: Political, Military and Intelligence Aspects* (London: Palgrave Macmillan, 1999), 179–80.
154 JFKL: OHP: Martin Hillenbrand, 29–30.
155 Sorenson, *Kennedy*, 663.
156 PRO: FO 371/169160, [G 1011/1] Steel annual review for the FRG (1962), 4 January 1963.
157 Kaiser, *Using Europe, Abusing the Europeans*, 151–5.
158 Richard Crossman acknowledged Macmillan's 'sense of history' and saw the decision to seek EEC membership (specifically ruled out in the 1959 election

manifesto) as being intrinsically linked with Macmillan's 'Winds of Change' 1960 speech. Furthermore, the Labour Party believed that the cumulative crises of 'trying to go it alone' after Suez in 1956 had led to Macmillan being more amenable to Kennedy's pressure on Britain to join the EEC. R.H.S. Crossman, 'British Labor Looks at Europe', *Foreign Affairs*, 41/4 (1963), 733–5.

159 HMD: 26 April 1961.
160 See, for instance, HMD: 2 November 1960, 22 November 1960, 5 December 1960.
161 HMD: 8 July 1961.
162 *Hansard*, HC Deb, vol. 645, col. 928.
163 JFKL: NSF Box 170, David Bruce to Rusk, No. 229, 17 July 1961.
164 JFKL: NSF Box 175, Background paper, 'Current political scene in the United Kingdom', drafted by Mr Bergesen (EUR: BNA) for Macmillan's visit to Washington, 27–29 April 1962.
165 See, for instance, HMD: 10 January 1962, 21 February 1962, 15 March 1962.
166 HMD: 26 January 1962. Visit of Erhard to Britain.
167 PRO: PREM 11/3778, Macmillan to Home, 15 April 1962.
168 HMD: 16 April 1962.
169 JFKL: NSF Box 175, 26 April 1962.
170 HMD: 6 May 1962.
171 JFKL: NSF Box 175, Department of State circular 1896, 4 May 1962.
172 PRO: PREM 11/3775, 16 May 1962. Macmillan to Home.
173 On this, see Constantine A. Pagedas, 'Harold Macmillan and the 1962 Champs Meeting', *Diplomacy and Statecraft*, 9/1 (1998), 225–42.
174 HMD: 4 August 1962, 22 August 1962, 9 February 1962, Adenauer was 'false' and a 'de Gaulle tool'. 5 December 1962, 16 December 1962, 28 January 1963, de Gaulle was 'anti-European' and compared to Louis XIV and Napoleon.
175 On this, see Donette Murray, *Kennedy, Macmillan and Nuclear Weapons* (London: Macmillan, 2000), esp. pp. 94–104.
176 PRO: FO 371/171445, [111092/50] 'General de Gaulle, Press Conference', FO Memo, 19 January 1963.
177 Horne, *Macmillan 1957–86*, 487.
178 HMD: 4 February 1963. Dean Rusk concurred with this view. Rusk, *As I Saw It*, 239–40.
179 JFKL: NSF Box 173, [T. 24/63] 15 January 1963.
180 See, for instance, JFKL: OHP: Senator Mike Mansfield, 13.
181 JFKL: NSF Box 173, Macmillan to Kennedy, 19 January 1963.
182 Mayer, *Adenauer and Kennedy*, 92.
183 Rolf Steininger, 'Great Britain's first EEC failure in January 1963', *Diplomacy and Statecraft*, 7/2 (1996), 408. Text of statements in PRO: FO 371/171, [443/M 1092/13].
184 Schröder to Heath, 31 January 1963, document 67, *Akten zur Auswärtigen Politik der Bundesrepublik Deutschland 1963: Band I* (Munich: Oldenbourg, 1994), here p. 232.
185 *Manchester Guardian*, 30 January 1963.
186 PRO: FO 371/177903, [RG 1022/27] Sir Frank Roberts to R.A. Butler, 23 June 1964.
187 JFKL: NSF Box 127, Macmillan to Kennedy, 19 March 1963.
188 HMD: 26 July 1963.
189 Butler, *The Art of the Possible*, 257–8.
190 Lord Hailsham [Quentin Hogg] *The Door Wherein I Went* (London: Collins, 1975), 217.
191 Zubok and Pleshakov, *Inside the Kremlin's Cold War*, 159–60, 195–6.
192 Meeting Khrushchev–Rusk, Pitsunda (nr. Moscow), 9 August 1963. *FRUS*,

1961–63, Volume XV, online available at: www.state.gov/r/pa/ho/frus/kennedyjf/xv/46005.htm. Home assured Soviet Premier Anastas Mikoyan, during a meeting at the British embassy in Washington, that Britain was of the same opinion as the US, PRO: PREM 11/4818, 26 November 1963.

193 Trachtenberg, *A Constructed Peace*, 390. For a similar view see, Christof Münger, *Die Berliner Mauer, Kennedy und die Kubakrise: Die westliche Allianz in der Zerreißprobe 1961–1963* (Paderborn: Schöningh, 2003), 309–15.

194 Richard Crockatt, *The Fifty Years War: The United States and the Soviet Union, 1941–1991*, (London: Routledge, 1995), 157.

195 Münger, *Die Berliner Mauer, Kennedy und die Kubakrise*, 357.

196 HMD: 16 August 1963. The West German government was reluctant to sign the treaty as, since it was open to any state, they might find themselves co-signatories with the GDR. This would undermine the West German claim to be the sole representative of the German people.

197 HMD: 7 October 1963.

198 Interview: Sir Michael Palliser.

199 PRO: FO 371/177903, [RG 1022/29] Cabinet brief, 16 July 1964.

200 JFKL: NSF Box 171. Report from a 'recent' WEU meeting at The Hague from R.A. Butler, Foreign Secretary to US Secretary of State Dean Rusk, 28 October 1963. For Butler's report on the WEU meeting to Cabinet, see PRO: CAB 128/36, CC (63) 3 (2), 31 October 1963.

201 JFKL: POF Box 117, Bundy to Kennedy, 23 June 1963.

202 Erhard speech to the *Bundestag*, 18 October 1963. Jain, *Germany, the Soviet Union and Eastern Europe 1949–1991*, n. pp. 289–90.

203 PRO: CAB 128/36, CC (63), 3 (2), 31 October 1963. Butler was reporting on a WEU meeting (at which French opposition to negotiations with the USSR continued to be expressed). The West Germans remained opposed to the idea of a non-aggression pact as it would perpetuate the division of Germany, see, for instance, PRO: CAB 128/38, CC (63), 12 (2), 12 December 1963.

204 Roberts, *Dealing with Dictators*, 237–41. Roberts states that such was the level of relations between Adenauer and the British in early 1963, the Chancellor virtually ignored him after his appointment.

205 Macmillan, *Riding the Storm 1956–1959*, 491–2.

206 JFKL: NSF Box 155, William A. Crawford, Minister, US Legation, Bucharest to D of S, Airgram A-322, 29 June 1963, 'US policy and Rumanian–Soviet Economic Differences'.

207 In 1963 a CIA report was unambiguous regarding the limited nature of Soviet economic coercive potential, as 'neither in Yugoslavia, nor more recently Albania, did Soviet economic sanctions have the intended effect of bending the governments of these countries to the will of the Soviet regime.' JFKL: NSF Box 155, Central Intelligence Agency, Economic Intelligence Memorandum, July 1963, CIA/RR EM 63-22, 'Rumania's vulnerability of economic pressure'.

208 Schröder, *Decision for Europe*, 148–64.

209 PRO: FO 371/163552, [CG 103155/5] R.G. Braithwaite, 3 October 1962.

210 JFKL: NSF Box 75, Roger Hilsman, INR Research memo (REU-59), 3 August 1962.

211 JFKL: NSF Box 76, MemCon Rusk–Schröder, 14 October 1962, Washington.

212 JFKL: NSF Box 77, MemCon Rusk–Erler, 24 April 1963, Washington.

213 Schröder, *Decision for Europe*, 212.

214 William E. Griffith, *The Ostpolitik of the Federal Republic of Germany* (Colorado: Westview, 1978), 119.

215 JFKL: NSF Box 65. MemCon, Luther M. Hodges, Secretary of Commerce, Outerbridge Horsey, US ambassador and President Novotny, 9 September 1963, Prague Castle.

216 JFKL: NSF Box 171, Memo, Ball to Rusk, 18 September 1963, emphasis in original.
217 JFKL: NSF Box 171, Bruce to Rusk, telegram 2252, 7 November 1963.
218 PRO: PREM 11/4817, Meeting Home/Butler–Erhard/Schröder, Downing Street, 15 January 1964.
219 Jain, *Germany, the Soviet Union and Eastern Europe 1949–1991*, 21–2.
220 PRO: FO 371/177903, [RG 1022/10] D.N. Beevor, 17 April 1964.
221 PRO: FO 371/177943, [RG 1081/1] R.B.J. Ledwidge, 23 December 1963.
222 PRO: FO 371/177917, [RG 103155/3] Clutton-Blumenfeld meeting, 1 June 1964.
223 PRO: FO 371/177917, [RG 103155/3] Sir Frank Roberts to Sir George Clutton, 30 June 1964. Schröder said as much to Butler in November 1963, PRO: FO 371/177943, [RG 1081/1] R.B.J. Ledwidge, 23 December 1963.
224 Interview: Anne E. Stoddart.
225 PRO: FO 371/177893, [RG 1011/1] GDR events 1963, Major-General D. Peel Yates (Berlin) to Sir Frank Roberts, 30 January 1964.
226 Anne E. Stoddart, letter to author, 25 May 2000.
227 USNA: RG 59 Central Files, MEMCON: Lord Harlech–Rusk, State Department, Washington DC, 9 March 1964.
228 PRO: PREM 11/4817, Home/Butler–Erhard/Schröder meeting, Downing Street, 15 January 1964.
229 USNA: RG 59 Central Files, MEMCON: Lord Harlech–Rusk, Washington DC, 9 March 1964.
230 PRO: FO 371/177903, [RG 1022/7] Sir Frank Roberts, Tel. No. 104 Saving, 4 April 1964.
231 PRO: FO 371/177903, [RG 1022/7] R.B.J. Ledwidge to Lord Hood, 6 April 1964.
232 *Manchester Guardian*, 16 April 1964.
233 JFKL: NSF BOX 171 & POF Box 127, 'Current British thinking about France', Edward T. Lampson, US embassy, London, 15 October 1963.
234 JFKL: NSF Box 171, Rusk to Butler, telegram no. 2994, 9 November 1963.
235 PRO: FO 371/177927, [RG 1051/33] 'Anglo-German Relations', Sir Frank Roberts to R.A. Butler, 24 June 1964.
236 PRO: FO 371/177938, [N 1051/2] Sir H. Trevelyan, Moscow to FO 29 July 1964.
237 PRO: PREM 11/4817, Meeting Home/Butler–Erhard/Schröder, Downing Street, 15 January 1964.
238 Schaad, *Bullying Bonn*, 135–61.
239 Cyril Buffet, 'De Gaulle, the Bomb and Berlin: How to Use a Political Weapon', in Gearson and Schake, *The Berlin Wall Crisis*, 73–95.
240 On this, see Eckart Conze, 'Staatsräson und nationale Interessen: Die "Atlantiker-Gaullisten"-Debatte in der westdeutschen Politik- und Gesellschaftsgeschichte der 1960er Jahre', in Ursula Lehmkuhl, Clemens A. Wurm and Hubert Zimmermann (eds), *Deutschland, Großbritannien, Amerika: Politik, Gesellschaft und Internationale Geschichte im 20. Jahrhundert* (Stuttgart: Steiner, 2003), 197–226.
241 On this, see Marie-Pierre Rey, *La tentation du rapprochement: France et URSS à l'heure de la détente, 1964–1974* (Paris: Sorbonne, 1991).
242 On the failure of de Gaulle's vision see the chapter entitled 'Limitations of a Grand Design', Jean Lacoutre, *De Gaulle: The Ruler 1945–1970*, trans. Alan Sheridan (London: Harvill, 1993), 467–82.
243 Gearson, *Harold Macmillan and the Berlin Wall Crisis, 1958–1962*, 1–6, 199–204; Mauer, 'Harold Macmillan and the Deadline Crisis Over Berlin 1958–9', 54–85.

244 Philip Williams, *Hugh Gaitskell: A Political Biography* (London: Jonathan Cape, 1979), 729.
245 Münger, *Die Berliner Mauer, Kennedy und die Kubakrise*, 80. Münger credits the restraint shown by de Gaulle and Adenauer as having averted a more damaging rift in the Western Alliance.
246 Kabinettsprotokolle 1956, 'Die Kabinettsprotokolle der Bundesregeirungung' online, Cabinet meeting, 9 November 1956, online available at: www.bundesarchiv.de/kabinettsprotokolle/web/index.jsp.
247 Brandt, *People and Politics*, 29. On the origins of Brandt's *Ostpolitik* from his time as Mayor of West Berlin, see Gottfried Niedhart, 'The East–West Problem as Seen from Berlin: Willy Brandt's Early *Ostpolitik*', in Wilfried Loth (ed.), *Europe, Cold War and Coexistence, 1953–1965* (London: Frank Cass, 2004), 285–96.
248 Nigel Ashton, *Kennedy, Macmillan and the Cold War: the Irony of Interdependence* (London: Palgrave Macmillan, 2002), 63.
249 Under Secretary of State George Ball later regarded Nassau as 'a mistake', as it divided Western Europe. Mayer, *Adenauer and Kennedy*, 97.
250 Murray, *Kennedy, Macmillan and Nuclear Weapons*, 97–104.
251 Trachtenberg, *A Constructed Peace*, 398.

5 The Wilson government and the German Question

1 Bevan in the Commons, 4 December 1958. R. Gerald Hughes '"We are not seeking strength for its own sake": the Labour Party and West Germany, 1951–64', *Cold War History*, 3/1 (2002), 69.
2 Jeremy Black, '"The Bitterest Enemies of Communism": Labour Revisionists, Atlanticism and the Cold War', *Contemporary British History*, 15/3 (2001), 26–62.
3 Stefan Berger and Darren Lilleker, 'The British Labour Party and the German Democratic Republic during the era of non-recognition, 1949–1973', *Historical Journal*, 45/2 (2002), 433–58; Hughes '"We are not seeking strength for its own sake"', 69–72, 77–8.
4 Hugh Gaitskell, *The Challenge of Co-existence* (London: Methuen, 1957), 58.
5 Philip Ziegler, *Wilson: The Authorised Life* (London: Weidenfeld & Nicolson, 1993), 82–3, 98, 101.
6 Interview: Sir Michael Palliser. Quoted in Hughes, '"We are not seeking strength for its own sake"', 85. Gromyko later recalled that Wilson was well disposed towards the Russian people and desired a good working relationship. Gromyko, *Memories*, 161–2.
7 Ziegler, *Wilson*, 149.
8 JFKL: NSF Box 76, Coburn Kidd, Counsellor for US embassy, Bonn, memo of lunch with Fritz Erler, German embassy, Washington DC, 24 April 1963.
9 Over, for instance, Vietnam, when he met Soviet Premier Kosygin in London in 1967, Gerald Segal, *The Great Power Triangle* (London: St Martin's Press, 1982), 110–13.
10 For instance, Wilson assured de Gaulle that he had no desire to mediate between Bonn and Moscow on the German question. PRO: PREM 13/343, Meeting of Wilson and de Gaulle, Elysee Palace, 3 April 1965.
11 PRO: PREM 13/343, R.B.J. Ledwidge, 'Review of Germany and Berlin', 27 October 1964.
12 Michael Stewart, *Life and Labour: An Autobiography* (London: Sedgwick & Jackson, 1980), 163.
13 PRO: FO 371/182999, [RG 1015/13] A.A. Stark (Head of Chancery), Bonn to R.B.J. Ledwidge, 24 February 1965, enclosing copy of Aubrey Halford-MacLeod dispatch on Bavarian situation for the previous six months.

14 PRO: CAB 129/122 [*c.* (65) 119] Memorandum by Michael Stewart to Cabinet, 9 August 1965, 'Policy towards Germany'. Richard Crossman's anti-German sentiments remained undiminished and, commenting on Stewart's paper, he wrote to Wilson that 'Every time in the past when we have been felt by the Germans to be appeasing their worse instincts out of a desire to get their help, they have responded not with gratitude but with contempt. This was the lesson of Munich. I believe that in this respect the Germans have not changed.' PRO: PREM 13/343, Crossman to Wilson, 23 August 1965.

15 A.W. DePorte, *Europe between the Superpowers: The Enduring Balance* (New Haven, CT: Yale University Press, 1986), 184; Hanreider, *Germany, America, Europe,* 171–3.

16 PREM 13/341, Rusk–Butler meeting, Washington, 9 August 1964.

17 See Dennis L. Bark and David R. Gress, *A History of West Germany: Democracy and Discontent 1963–1991,* 2nd edn (London: Blackwell, 1993), 14–28; Hanreider, *Germany, America, Europe,* 170–6; Henry Kissinger, *The White House Years* (Boston: Little & Brown, 1979), 409–10.

18 PRO: FO 371/183006, [RG 1022/18] 'The Federal Republic of Germany's Position within the Western Alliance', Sir Frank Roberts to Stewart, 5 July 1965. De Gaulle was not averse to resurrecting the spectre of a French under-standing with the Soviet Union, while Erhard was 'aghast and terrified' at de Gaulle's recognition of Red China in 1964. Frank Roberts, *Dealing with Dicta-tors: The Destruction and Revival of Europe 1930–70* (London: Weidenfeld & Nicolson, 1991), 247. Wilson told Erhard that the USSR wanted to deal with Germany, the USA and Britain, not de Gaulle, when arranging détente. PRO: PREM 13/933, 23 May 1966.

19 PRO: PREM 13/902; PRO: PREM 13/933, meeting Wilson–Erhard, Downing Street, 23 May 1966. At the Hanover Fair, FRG Economics Minister, Schumüker, told Roberts that without British membership of the EEC the Community might break up due to Franco-German rivalry. PRO: FO 371/189210, [RG 1052/1] Sir Frank Roberts, Bonn to FO, 2 May 1966.

20 On this, Thomas Alan Schwartz, *Lyndon Johnson and Europe: In the Shadow of Vietnam* (London: Harvard University Press, 2003).

21 PRO: FO 371/183006, [RG 1022/18] 'The Federal Republic of Germany's Position within the Western Alliance', Sir Frank Roberts to Michael Stewart, 5 July 1965.

22 PRO: FO 371/189306, [RG 1821/4] Chancery, Bonn to FO, 16 May 1966.

23 PRO: FO 371/177943, [RG 1081/15] R.G. Sheridan (Western Department) to Gordon Walker, 26 November 1964.

24 USNA: RG 59 Central Files, MEMCON: Gromyko-Rusk ('Germany'), Soviet embassy, Washington DC, 9 December 1964.

25 Rusk to the US embassy, Bonn, 14 January 1965. *FRUS,* 1964–68, Volume XV, online, available at: www.state_gov/www/about_ state/history/vol_xv/t.html.

26 Lyndon B. Johnson Library Oral History Program (LBJL: OHP): Dean Rusk (tape 2), 22.

27 Rusk to McGhee, US embassy, Bonn, 14 January 1965. *FRUS,* 1964–8, Volume XV, online, available at: www.state.gov/www/about_state/history/vol_xv/ i.html. Rusk later stated that while German reunification disappeared from the East–West agenda for discussion, the US still believed in the reunification of Germany 'although ... neither the West nor the East had any intention of using force to achieve it.' Dean Rusk interviewed by G.R. Urban, 'Co-existence without sanctimony', in G.R. Urban (ed.), *Détente* (London: Temple Smith, 1976), 251.

28 Quoted in Allen, *The Oder–Neisse Line,* 255.

29 USNA: RG 59 Central Files, POL 32-4 GER. Telegram (of 24 November 1965)

from Washington DC to Bonn embassy concerning Rusk–Schröder meeting of 23 November 1965. In 1964, Thomas J. Dunnigan (First Secretary of the embassy in Bonn) noted that SPD Vice-Chairman Herbert Wehner had made a speech on *Heimatrecht* that was damaging to the chances of peace in Europe. Dunnigan concluded that 'Wehner would agree that such statements do not improve Germany's reputation abroad and contribute nothing towards improving chance of reunification; yet he is too sensitive to political factors before a crucial national election to ignore any segment of the voting public. This is the dilemma with which the "Tag der Heimat" confronts all politicians.' USNA: RG 59 Central Files, AIRGRAM A-503, 10 September 1964.

30 USNA: RG 59 Central Files, MEMCON on 'German Reunification' British embassy, Washington DC, 22 March 1965.

31 Adenauer had told Macmillan that when he visited Moscow in 1955, Khrushchev had said that the Soviet Union could not deal with the USA and China simultaneously, PRO: PREM 11/3776, meeting between Macmillan and Adenauer, Palais Schaumberg, 9 January 1962. By 1967, Wilson found that Soviet Premier Alexei Kosygin was obsessed with China. PRO: PREM 13/1471, Wilson meeting with Kosygin, 15 February 1967.

32 PRO: PREM 13/343, R.B.J. Ledwidge, 'Review of Germany and Berlin', 27 October 1964. For the Soviet perspective, see Adomeit, *Imperial Overstretch*, 103–4.

33 PRO: PREM 13/342. Meeting between Michael Stewart and Couve de Murville, French Foreign Minister, Quai d'Orsay, 2 April 1965.

34 PRO: PREM 13/343, meeting with Erhard, Sir Frank Roberts to FO, 24 February 1965.

35 Interview: Michael Palliser.

36 Wilson told de Gaulle in April 1965 that, having visited the USSR some twelve times since 1945, the attitude of the Soviets had become considerably more 'pragmatic', except with regard to the question of Germany. Indeed, Wilson asserted, the Soviets were unduly obsessed with Germany in a curious mixture of deference and fear. PRO: PREM 13/343, Meeting of Wilson and de Gaulle, Elysée Palace, 3 April 1965.

37 PRO: FO 371/177971, [N 1072/1] Patrick Gordon Walker (Foreign Secretary) to Lord Harlech [Ormsby Gore] Washington, No. 4053, 9 December 1964. Although keen to promote détente, Harold Wilson told de Gaulle that he had no intention of playing the role of mediator over Germany between Washington and Moscow.

38 Stewart, *Life and Labour*, 158. Stewart saw Gromyko seemed '100% orthodox' and only much later did he detect a tendency to reflect, particularly over Germany.

39 PRO: PREM 13/343, Wilson–Stewart–Gromyko meeting, Downing Street, 18 March 1965.

40 PRO: PREM 13/1081, [PM/65/145] 1 October 1965. Michael Stewart to Wilson, 1 October 1965. Kosygin made the remark to Lord Thomson.

41 PRO: PREM 13/1081. Wilson–Kosygin meeting, Moscow, 23 February 1966.

42 PRO: FO 371/183008, [RG 103138] A.D. Loehnis, Northern Department, 1 October 1965.

43 PRO: FO 371/177928, [RG 1051/66] Schröder–Gordon Walker meeting, Bonn, 15 November 1964.

44 After a meeting with Couve de Murville in April 1965, Gromyko declared that 'France starts from the fact that two German states exist'. This prompted Schröder to warn against the 'Europeanization of the German question' in the *Bundestag*, John van Oudenaren, *Détente in Europe: the Soviet Union and the West since 1953* (London: Duke University Press, 1991), 75.

45 One of Lyndon B. Johnson's senior policy advisers, Walt Rostow, stressed in a memo in early 1965 that to force Bonn into premature concessions on the *Ostpolitik* would serve no purpose and risk reigniting nationalism in Germany, as had been the case in the Weimar Republic. Memorandum on German Unity from Chairman of Policy Planning Council (Rostow) to Secretary of State Dean Rusk, Washington, 7 January 1965. *FRUS*, 1964–8, volume 15, online, available at: www.state_gov/www/about_ state/history/vol_xv/t.html.

46 PRO: CAB 129/122 [*c.* (65) 119] Memorandum by Michael Stewart to Cabinet, 9 August 1965, 'Policy towards Germany'. A keen opponent of what he perceived as the destabilising influence of West German policy, Richard Crossman disagreed strongly with Michael Stewart. Crossman therefore asserted that, in his opinion, 'More and more Germans are realising ... that the Ulbricht regime [in the GDR] is [only] strengthened by West German attempts to overthrow it, and [the East German state] can [in fact] only be "killed by kindness".' PRO: PREM 13/343, Crossman to Wilson, 23 August 1965.

47 PRO: FO 371/183006, [RG 1022/11] G. Holhner (Northern Department), 19 May 1965.

48 PRO: FO 371/183006, [RG 1022/12] J.C.C. Bennett (Western Department), 27 May 1965.

49 PRO: PREM 13/329, Sir Frank Roberts to FO, 'The Political Scene in the Federal Republic', 1 March 1965.

50 Christoph Bluth, *Britain, Germany and Western Nuclear Strategy* (Oxford: Oxford University Press, 1995), 152.

51 PRO: PREM 13/343, Wilson–Rusk meeting, 29 January 1965.

52 PRO: PREM 13/343, Johnson–Wilson meeting, White House, 30 July 1965. In 1969 the Wilson Government put a great deal of pressure on Bonn to accept the Non-Proliferation Treaty, Harold Wilson, *The Labour Government 1964–70: A Personal Record* (London: Weidenfeld & Nicolson/Michael Joseph, 1971), 612.

53 The MLF was a scheme that proposed a multinational NATO deterrent force. For West Germany, it was not just a question of acquiring nuclear weapons but rather the desire for 'equality of treatment'. On this, see Bluth, *Britain, Germany and Western Nuclear Strategy*, 52–104. Lyndon Johnson remarked, with characteristic bluntness, 'If Europe isn't for it, then the hell with it.' Granieri, *The Ambivalent Alliance*, 204.

54 Richard Crossman, *Back-bench Diaries* (London: Weidenfeld & Nicolson, 1969), 973; Ziegler, *Wilson*, 141.

55 PRO: PREM 13/343, meeting de Gaulle–Wilson, Elysée Palace, 3 April 1965.

56 Wilson, *The Labour Government 1964–70*, 214.

57 PRO: FO 371/183000, [RG 1015/47] Hywel I. Duck, Bonn to R.G. Sheridan, Western Department, 5 August 1965. Report on CSU Congress in Nuremburg, 5–7 July 1965. *Pravda* was quick to criticise such West German thinking. In an article in August 1965, it claimed that the leaders of the CDU/CSU had resorted to a policy of chauvinism. It sneered that Bonn asserted that 'Nuclear weapons are an attribute of every sovereign state' in order to pose as a 'true patriot' who spares no effort in the struggle against 'discrimination in armaments'. A. Mikhailov, *Pravda*, 14 August 1965.

58 PRO: FO 371/183016, [RG 103138/31] Chancery, Bonn, 11 December 1965. Erhard declaration of 10 November 1965, emphasis in original.

59 PRO: FO 371/183016, [RG 103138/30] Sir Frank Roberts, Bonn, 29 November 1965. Schröder speech to CDU Conference of 26–7 November 1965.

60 PRO: 371/183006, [RG 1022/13] Jock L. Taylor, Bonn to P.C. Holmer, Western Department, 3 June 1965; Interview: D.A.S. Gladstone.

61 PRO: FO 371/182498, [N 1051/38] Stewart–Popovic meeting, Belgrade, 19 April 1965.

62 Early in 1965, for instance, an Indonesian threat to open a Consulate General in East Berlin was only headed off by the extension of DM 100m credit to Indonesia. PRO: FO 371/183061, [RG 1078/9] J.L. Taylor (Deputy Head of Chancery), Bonn to James Cable, 5 July 1965.

63 PRO: PREM 13/329, Sir Frank Roberts to FO, 1 March 1965: 'The Political Scene in the Federal Republic'.

64 Wilson, *The Labour Government, 1964–70*, 82.

65 PRO: PREM 13/329. Meeting between Wilson and Erhard, Bonn, 8 March 1965.

66 PRO: PREM 13/933. Meeting between Wilson/Brown–Erhard/Schröder, Downing Street, 23 May 1966.

67 On this, see Klaus Larres, 'Britain, East Germany and Détente: British Policy Toward the GDR and West Germany's Policy of Movement, 1955–1965', in Wilfred Loth (ed.), *Europe, Cold War and Coexistence, 1953–1965* (London: Frank Cass, 2004), 111–31.

68 PRO: FO 371/183061, [RG 1078/14] FO Minute, H.F.T. Smith to A.A. Stark, Bonn, 3 November 1965. Meeting of Anglo-German discussion group on the Soviet Union and Eastern Europe, London, 21–2 October 1965. See also Klaus Larres, 'Britain and the GDR: Political and Economic Relations, 1949–1989', 87.

69 Larres, 'Britain and the GDR', 87.

70 PRO: FO 371/189318, 'DDR application for UN membership', [G 2251/1 and G2251/2], comment by R.W.H. du Boulay, FO, UN (Pol.) Dept., 26 January 1966.

71 PRO: FO 371/189318, [G 2251/2] British UN mission to London, 2 March 1966.

72 For an examination of this oft-cited maxim, see W.R. Smyser, *The German Economy* (London: St Martin's Press, 1993), 17–25.

73 Geyer, 'Der Kampf um nationale Repräsentation', 56.

74 On this, see G.A. Carr, 'The Involvement of Politics in the Sporting Relationships of East and West Germany 1945–1972', *Journal of Sport History*, 7/1 (1980), 40–50.

75 Larres, 'Britain and the GDR', 86–7; Gray, *Germany's Cold War*, 190.

76 USNA: RG 59, Central files, US embassy, Bonn to Department of State, October 8, 1965.

77 Discussion at the *Auswärtiges Amt*, 4 November 1965; Geyer, 'Der Kampf um nationale Repräsentation', 86.

78 Gray, *Germany's Cold War*, 312 (n. 106).

79 *The Times*, 6 May 1966, cited in E.D. Johns, Jnr, *British Foreign Policy on the German* Question, MA Thesis (University of Virginia, 1990), 15.

80 Edwina Moreton, 'The View From London', 233–4.

81 Patrick Gordon Walker, August 1964, 'Thoughts on Foreign Policy', in Robert Pearce (ed.), *Political Diaries 1932–71* (London: The Historians' Press, 1991), 301.

82 PRO: PREM 13/902, Gordon Walker–Rusk meeting, Washington DC, 27 October 1964.

83 PRO: FO 371/188509, [N 1151/47] Perry A. Rhodes, Research Officer FO, 15 November 1966.

84 A notable example of this was the wide-diameter pipes export affair. The FRG had secured a Soviet contract, but withdrawn in the face of US pressure over the strategic embargo only to have the British take over the contract. Philip Hanson, *Western Economic Statecraft in East–West Relations: Embargoes, Sanctions, Linkage, Economic Warfare, and Détente* (London/Routledge & Kegan Paul Ltd, 1988), 28. Dean Rusk recalled that the British government was prone to

ignoring the Cold War when trade beckoned (notably over Cuba). LBJL: OHP: Dean Rusk, 7.

85 On British policy in the 1960s, see Klaus Larres, 'Britain and the GDR in the 1960s: the Politics of Trade and Recognition by Stealth', 197–215.

86 PRO: FO 371/189498, [N 1051/9] FO Minute, H.F.T. Smith, 6 January 1965, Policy towards Eastern Europe: General Review. For a discussion of the political nature of trade, see Gerard Curzon, *Multilateral Commercial Diplomacy: The General Agreement on Tariffs and Trade and its Impact on National and Commercial Policies and Techniques* (New York: Praeger, 1966).

87 Stewart, *Life and Labour*, 223. See also PRO: FO 371/188509, [N 1151/46], P.H. Gore-Booth (Permanent Under Secretary), memo, 15 November 1966.

88 Barker, *Britain in a Divided Europe 1945–70*, 263–70.

89 In 1965, UK trade with Eastern Europe constituted only 3 per cent of total foreign trade.

90 PRO: FO 371/182513, [N 1151/1] Trade with Eastern Europe, FO Draft Minute, Mr West, 1 January 1965.

91 PRO: FO 371/183006, [RG 1022/5] Sheridan comments on file, 23 March 1965. Sir Frank Roberts reported that Herr Mende told the FDP Congress recently that the Hallstein Doctrine should be ditched and that Bonn should establish diplomatic relations with Eastern Europe. The SPD said that Mende was 'vote catching' whilst the CDU defended the Hallstein Doctrine. PRO: FO 371/183006, [RG 1022/6] 25 March 1965.

92 1984 *Der Spiegel* interview with Brandt; Hanreider, *Germany, America, Europe*, 446 n. 29.

93 PRO: FO 371/183085, [RG 113155/2] Sir Frank Roberts, Bonn to FO, 22 April 1965.

94 PRO: FO 371/182498, [N 1051/10] Khrushchev quoted speaking in Hungary, 6 April 1964, S. Murrell (East European Research Department), 9 March 1965.

95 The phrase used by President Lyndon Johnson as early as May 1964; Larres, 'Britain and the GDR', 85.

96 *Isvestiya*, 10 February 1965, PRO: FO 371/182498, [N 1051/10] N.H. Marshall, Moscow to M.J.E. Fretwell, Northern Department, 19 February 1965.

97 PRO: FO 371/182498, [N 1051/10] signature illegible, undated (*c*.19 February 1965).

98 PRO: FO 371/189182, [RG 103138/11] Julian L. Bullard (First Secretary), Bonn to J.C.C. Bennett (Western Department), 1 April 1966. In Bonn, Soviet ambassador Smirnov informed Schröder that it was willing to conclude a commercial treaty provided it avoided irrelevant subjects – 'presumably Berlin'. PRO: FO 371/189182, [RG 103138/7] A.A. Stark, Bonn to A.H. Campbell, 18 February 1966. Report of meeting between Smirnov and Schröder, 11 February 1966.

99 PRO: FO 371/189209, [RG 1051/52] Record of Conversation at the Ministry of Foreign Affairs, Bonn, between Brown and Schröder, 4 November 1966.

100 PRO: FO 371/188477, [N 103118/1] A.A. Stark, Bonn to H.F.T. Smith, Northern Department, 22 February 1966.

101 PRO: FO 371/189306, [RG 1821/7] A.W. Rhodes, Bonn, 28 February 1966, citing G. Baker (Munich Consulate) to A.D.S. Goodall (Western Department).

102 Seppain, *Contrasting US and German Attitudes to Soviet Trade, 1917–91*, 191.

103 Angela Stent, *From Embargo to Ostpolitik: The Political Economy of West German-Soviet Relations, 1955–1980* (Cambridge: Cambridge University Press, 1982).

104 See, for instance, PRO: FO 371/183000, [RG 1015/77]; FO 371/183006, [RG 1032/14].

105 PRO: FO 371/183000, [RG 1015/83] Chancery, Bonn, 11 November 1965 (Erhard statement to the *Bundestag*, 10 November 1965).

106 PRO: FO 371/182044, [JR 1121/62] FO Minute, C.M. Le Quesne, 2 December 1965.

107 PRO: FO 371/189250, [G 1154/33] Sir Frank Roberts, Bonn to London, 31 March 1966; Interview: D.A.S. Gladstone. Rhodesia was 'the Wilson government's number one priority at this juncture'. Interview: J. Oliver Wright.

108 PRO: PREM 13/329, Erhard–Wilson meeting, Palais Schaumburg, Bonn, 8 March 1965.

109 West German co-operation on Rhodesia was acknowledged by George Brown in conversation with Schröder in November 1966; PRO: FO 371/189209, [RG 1051/52] Schröder–Brown meeting, Bonn, 4 November 1966.

110 McGhee to Rusk, 11 January 1965. *FRUS*, 1964–8, Volume XV, online, available at: www.state.gov/www/about_state/history/vol_xv/i.html.

111 PRO: FO 371/177928, [RG 1051/66] Schröder–Gordon Walker meeting, Bonn, 15 November 1964.

112 PRO: FO 371/189250, [RG 1154/10] Foreign Office/Board of Trade brief on trade with the GDR for the German Economic Committee, 16–18 February 1966.

113 PRO: FO 371/189250, R.L. Davies (Board of Trade) to A.H. Campbell, FO, 3 January 1966, [G 1154/1].

114 PRO: FO 371/189250, [G 1154/29] R.L. Davies to J.C.C. Bennett, 16 May 1966. See also PRO: FO 371/189250, [G 1154/26] D. O' Connell (BOT) to Veronica Beckett (Economic Relations FO), 20 April 1966.

115 PRO: FO 371/189250 [G 1154/27] Beckett to O'Connell to 12 May 1966.

116 PRO: FO 371/189250 [G 1154/10] Defensive brief of 9 February 1966 in advance of the visit by the German Economic Committee, 16–18 February 1966.

117 PRO: FO 371/189250 [G 1154/29] FO Brief on credits for the GDR, 1966.

118 This issue rumbled on, however, and Quadripartite talks in Bonn on 24 May 1966 witnessed considerable Anglo-German disagreement over the issue of trade credits to the GDR. PRO: FO 371/189250, [RG 1154/35] Mr Galsworthy (Minister in charge of economic affairs), Bonn to A.H. Campbell, 7 June 1966. The US position was that it didn't grant credits anyway; the French position was that it would desist if that were to be the position adopted by NATO, whilst the UK pointed to the insignificance of any potential credits to the GDR. See FO brief in FO 371/189250, [G1154/46].

119 On this see, Philip Alexander; 'We too mean business': Germany and the second British application to the EEC in 1966–67', in Oliver Daddow (ed.), *Harold Wilson and European Integration: Britain's Second Application to Join the EEC* (London: Frank Cass, 2003), 211–26.

120 N. Piers Ludlow, 'Germany, Britain, and the EEC, 1956–1972', in Noakes *et al.*, *Britain and Germany in Europe*, 102.

121 Wilson, *The Labour Government*, 112–13. Increasing British frustration with West German intransigence over offset costs led to George Brown telling Erhard that British forces in Germany might have to be reduced due to the pressure of having forces globally deployed in defence of the Free World. The Chancellor was unimpressed, and pointed out that if Britain wanted to be a World power it would have to pay for it. PRO: FO 371/189209, [RG 1051/53] Brown–Erhard meeting, 4 November 1966.

122 PRO: FO 371/189209, [RG 1051/52] Record of Conversation at the Ministry of Foreign Affairs, Bonn, 4 November 1966.

123 Roberts, *Dealing with Dictators*, 246.

124 Lacoutre, *De Gaulle: The Ruler 1945–1970*, 360. De Gaulle told Brandt that

Wilson's EEC application would be made '*à l'anglaise*', that is, by combining his 'candidacy' with so many provisos so as that the vote would go against him. Brandt, *People and Politics*, 135.

125 Ziegler, *Wilson*, 240. This conclusion was tentatively reached in an internal Labour Party memo, LPA: OV/GE/1, 'Britain and Europe', *c.* May 1966.

126 Ziegler, *Wilson*, 240. The British did themselves no favours in Bonn when Wilson and Brown had suggested to de Gaulle that British entry was required to help contain the Germans. Paris, of course, promptly leaked this information to Bonn. Ben Pimlott, *Harold Wilson* (London: HarperCollins, 1993), 441.

127 Ziegler, *Wilson*, 240; Roy Denman, *Missed Chances: Britain & Europe in the Twentieth Century* (London: Indigo, 1997), 227–8.

128 Denman, *Missed Chances*, 228.

129 George Brown, *In My Way* (London: Victor Gollancz, 1971), 207–8.

130 Diary entry, 19 February 1966, Richard Crossman, *The Diaries of a Cabinet Minister: Volume One Minister of Housing* (London: Book Club Associates, 1976), 461.

131 Barker, *Britain in a Divided Europe 1945–70*, 264–5.

132 The Polish ambassador in Brussels (Jan Wasilewski) went so far as to suggest to his US counterpart that a Western recognition of the frontier 'might even go so far as to mean the withdrawal of Soviet forces from eastern Germany'. USNA: RG 59 Central Files, AIRGRAM A-331, US embassy, Brussels to the State Department, 19 November 1965.

133 USNA: RG 59 Central Files, Francis J. Wazeter, President of the Polish–American Congress to President Johnson, 7 April 1965.

134 PRO: FO 371/188475, [N 1015/9] Mr Marsden, Paris to Perry Rhodes, FO, 15 March 1966. Marsden had been in conversation with the Polish ambassador to France. The Communist Party also attacked the Roman Catholic Church, its strongest challenger for the loyalty of the people, on this issue. Jonathan Luxmoore and Jolante Babiuch, *The Vatican and the Red Flag: The Struggle for the Soul of Eastern Europe* (London: Chapman, 2000), 203–95.

135 The British ambassador in Warsaw stressed to his American counterpart the fact that the Poles were happy with the British stance on the Oder–Neiße line. Furthermore, the Briton added that the British 'commitment to the Oder–Neisse line was almost as strong as [the] French' one. USNA: RG 59 Central Files, telegram 2376, Warsaw to Rusk, 4 November 1964.

136 Allen, *The Oder–Neisse Line*, 155–6.

137 USNA: RG 59 Central Files [POL 32-3 GER-POL] William R. Tyler (Assistant Secretary of State for European Affairs) to Rusk, 'Germany's eastern Frontiers', 2 November 1964.

138 USNA: RG 59 Central Files [POL 32-3 GER-POL] Rusk to Tyler, 3 November 1964.

139 PRO: FO 371/183020, [RG 103155/1] Schröder had confided this in December 1964. FO Minute, J.A. Henderson, 18 January 1965.

140 PRO: FO 371/183061, [RG 1078/14] H.F.T. Smith, Northern Department to A.A. Stark, Bonn, 3 November 1965. Meeting of Anglo-German discussion group on the Soviet Union and Eastern Europe, London, 21–2 October 1965.

141 PRO: FO 371/188477, [N 103118/1] Stark to Smith, 22 February 1966.

142 PRO: FO 371/182673, [NP 1054/7] FO Minute, P.H. Gore-Booth, 12 August 1965.

143 Hughes 'We are not seeking strength for its own sake', 78–84.

144 LPA: Gaitskell speech, 4 October 1961.

145 Hughes 'We are not seeking strength for its own sake', 86.

146 PRO: PREM 13/1699; PRO: FO 371/182672, Stewart–Rapacki meeting, Warsaw, 17 September 1965.

147 PRO: FO 371/182671, [NP 1053/48] FO Minute, 16 September 1965.

148 FO 371/182675, [WG 1072/3] Sir Frank Roberts to Michael Stewart, 1 October 1965.

149 FRG embassy, Paris to *Auswärtiges Amt*, 3 May 1965, document 342, *Akten zur Auswärtigen Politik der Bundesrepublik Deutschland 1965: Band II* (Munich: Oldenbourg, 1996).

150 Horst Osterheld, *Aussenpolitik unter Bundeskanzler Ludwig Erhard, 1963–1966: Ein dokumentarischer Bericht aus dem Kanzleramt* (Düsseldorf: Droste, 1992), 234.

151 Wilfred Pabst, *Das Jahrhundert der deutsch-französischen Konfrontation* (Hannover: Niedersächsische Landeszentrale für Politische Bildung, 1983), 119.

152 PRO: PREM 13/929. J. Oliver Wright report of conversation with German ambassador Herr Blankenhorn regarding Wilson's recent visit to Moscow, 7 March 1966.

153 Interview: J. Oliver Wright.

154 Blankenhorn added, however, that any modification of the Hallstein Doctrine was not possible at this time. PRO: PREM 13/928, J. Oliver Wright, FO to Bonn, 28 March 1966. The idea of effecting reconciliation with Poland, so as to isolate the GDR, was entirely consistent with the West German thinking since 1949. Interview: Sir J. Oliver Wright.

155 PRO: FO 371/189306, [RG 1821/1] A.D.S. Goodall, 12 April 1966, comment on the file.

156 PRO: PREM 13/1471, Brown–Gromyko meeting, 25 May 1966. Publicly, however, the Wilson government stuck to the Profumo formula over the Oder–Neiße line. Edwin Brooks, a Labour backbencher, asked in the Commons whether the time had not come to recognise the line. After being pressed by Michael Foot, Manny Shinwell and others, the Minister, Walter Padley, simply quoted Britain's treaty obligations at the House. *Hansard*, HC Deb, vol. 727, cols 1227–8.

157 USNA: RG 59 Central Files, AIRGRAM A-1343, Peter Rutter (First Secretary, Bonn) to the State Department, 4 March 1966.

158 For example, Georg Bluhm, *Die Oder–Neisse-Linie in der deutschen Aussenpolitik* (Freiburg: Rombach, 1963).

159 For instance, Karl Jaspers, *The Future of Germany* (Chicago: University of Chicago Press, 1967); Ralf Dahrendorf, *Society and Democracy in Germany* (London: Hamish Hamilton), 1967.

160 *Stern*, 21 December 1969.

161 World Survey, *The West German Federal Republic and the Ostpolitik in Election Year*, number 50, February 1973 (London: Atlantic Education Trust), 6. On Seebohm's thinking on the German Question (and that of many of his political associates), see the East German attack issued by the Institut für Zeitgeschichte (ed.), *Materialien zur revanchistischen Politik des Bonner Staates und der Landsmannschaften* (East Berlin: Redaktion Informationsdienste, 1964).

162 PRO: FO 371/189306, [RG 1821/8] A.N. Rhodes, Bonn, comments to A.D.S. Goodall, Western Department concerning the report of Anne E. Stoddart, Berlin to A.N. Rhodes, Bonn, 3 September 1966.

163 PRO: FO 371/189182, [RG 10318/20] Comment on file by A.D.S. Goodall, 28 September 1966.

164 Garton Ash, *In Europe's Name*, 53.

165 PRO: FO 371/189230, [RG 1018/10] D.A.S. Gladstone (British Representative on the Quadripartite Committee), Bonn to Bennett, FO, 28 October 1966. Gladstone recalls that intransigent statements were increasingly confined to the margins of the West German political scene. Interview: D.A.S. Gladstone.

166 PRO: PREM 13/1417, Sir Frank Roberts, Bonn, 19 September 1966. Interview: J. Oliver Wright.

167 *New York Times*, 16 June 1966.
168 Alfred Grosser, *Germany in Our Time: A Political History of the Postwar Years* (London: Pelican Books, 1974), 494–5.
169 See, for instance, PRO: FO 371/188473 [RG 1720/2] Sir Frank Roberts to George Brown; PRO: FO 371/188477, [N 103118/5] D.A.S. Gladstone, Bonn to P.A. Rhodes, 25 November 1966.
170 PRO: FO 371/188477, [N 103118/5] D.A.S. Gladstone, Bonn to P.A. Rhodes (western Department), 25 November 1966. Gladstone noted in the despatch that the complexity of the Hallstein Doctrine was now working against it. Gladstone later stated that such polls were reflected in everyday political life in West Germany. Interview: D.A.S. Gladstone.
171 Keesing's *Germany and Eastern Europe Since 1945*, 199–200. For Soviet, Czech and Polish responses, see 200–6.
172 Theo Sommer called it a 'one-shot operation'; Theo Sommer, 'Bonn Changes Course', *Foreign Affairs*, 45/4 (1967), 477–91.
173 Jain, *Germany, the Soviet Union and Eastern Europe 1949–1991*, 23–4.
174 PRO: PREM 13/902, Stewart to Wilson, 20 June 1966. See also, Philip Windsor, *Germany and the Management of Détente* (London: Chatto & Windus, 1971), 138–9.
175 PRO: FO 371/189187 [RG 103155/6] H.W. King to H.F.T. Smith. King reported that the British ambassador has been informed by Mr Kmiecik (ex-Counsellor in Polish Diplomatic Service) that many Poles feared that Poland could be left out in the cold with all its conditions as the FRG normalised its relations with Eastern Europe.
176 PRO: FO 371/189187, [RG 103155/4] Derek Tonkin (Head of Chancery), Warsaw to P.A. Rhodes, 2 September 1966.
177 PRO: FO 371/188477, [NP 103118/3] Chancery, Warsaw to FO, 7 October 1966.
178 PRO: FO 371/188483, [N 1052/9] Derek Tonkin, Warsaw to R. Clift, East European Department FO, 24 November 1966. Report in Polish newspaper *Trybuna Ludu*, 24 November 1966 referring to Brown speech to International Editors Conference on 21 November 1966.
179 PRO: FO 371/188483, [N 1052/8] FO Minute, notes for C.A. Johnson, MP, for a meeting with journalists from Eastern Europe, 23 November 1966.
180 PRO: 371/188477, [N 103118/4] FO Minute, Brian L. Crowe (Northern Department), 23 November 1966. Discussion with M. Lucet, French embassy.
181 PRO; FO 371/188477, [N 103118/4] S. Teichfeld, (E/E Sect., Joint Research Department) FO, 28 November 1966.
182 PRO: FO 371/189187, [RG 103155/6] H.W. King (First Secretary), Warsaw to H.F.T. Smith, FO, 15 December 1966.
183 Lyndon B. Johnson, *The Vantage Point: Perspectives of the Presidency 1963–69* (London: Weidenfeld & Nicolson, 1972), 474–5.
184 McGhee, Bonn to Johnson, 14 December 1966. *FRUS*, 1964–8, Volume XV, online, available at: www.state.gov/www/about_state/history/vol_xv/t.html. McGhee dismissed the Oder–Neiße line as an issue, writing that 'There are no Germans east of the Oder–Neisse line. Germany does not need *Lebensraum* – it has a deficit in workers'. Quoted in Allen, *The Oder–Neisse Line*, 256.
185 Volker Berghahn, *Modern Germany: Society, Economy and Politics in the Twentieth Century* (Cambridge: Cambridge University Press, 1982), 240–1; Bark and Gress, *A History of West Germany* vol. 2, 56–7; Torsten Opelland, 'Domestic Political Developments I: 1949–69', in Larres and Panayi, *The Federal Republic Since 1949*, 93–5. One of the final nails in Erhard's coffin had been provided by Johnson's refusal not to be deflected in his pursuit of the issue of offset costs despite protests of German economic difficulties. See Lyndon B.

Johnson, *The Vantage Point*, 307; Deborah Shapley, *Promise and Power: The Life and Times of Robert McNamara* (Boston: Little, Brown & Company, 1993), 399. The former West German ambassador to Washington, Dr Wilhelm Grewe, contrasted the brutal approach of Johnson with that of Kennedy in this matter. JFKL: OHP: Wilhelm Grewe, 5.

186 Hanreider, *Germany, America, Europe*, 181.

187 PRO: FCO 33/91, Sir Frank Roberts to George Brown, no. 1012, Annual Review of the FRG in 1966, 1 January 1967.

188 PRO: FO 371/183000, [RG 1015/46] R.B.J. Ledwidge to Sir Frank Roberts, Bonn, 3 August 1965. Blankenhorn, Federal ambassador to London to Walter Padley MP, 2 August 1965. In 1961 Harold Macmillan had predicted in his diary that, for West Germany to make the painful substantive changes required, there would have to be a coalition between the major parties. HMD: 26 September 1961.

189 William E. Paterson, 'The German Social Democratic Party', in William E. Paterson and Alastair H. Thomas (eds), *Social Democratic Parties in Western Europe* (Oxford: Oxford University Press, 1977), 198; Seppain, *Contrasting US and German Attitudes to Soviet Trade, 1917–91*, 190.

190 PRO: FO 371/183000, [RG 1015/46] Sir Frank Roberts, Bonn, 30 July 1965 to R.B.J. Ledwidge (Head of the Western Department). Brandt actually told the SPD Congress in June 1966 that 'Many people act as though we have the territories east of the Oder–Neisse. They also act as though friendly states had committed themselves to mere legal reservations, when in fact some had not done that ... therefore our demand for working out the basic peace treaty'. PRO: PREM 13/982.

191 Dean Rusk to the US embassy, Bonn, 14 January 1965. *FRUS*, 1964–8, Volume XV, online, available at: www.state.gov/www/about_state/history/vol_xv/i.html.

192 PRO: FO 371/183000, [RG 1015/45] Sir Frank Roberts, Bonn, to FO, 30 July 1965.

193 Michael Stewart, for instance, recorded his dislike for Erhard in his autobiography. See Stewart, *Life and Labour*, 140. Conversely, Erhard, like Adenauer, disliked socialists, and this extended to the Labour Party. In an election speech in August 1965, Erhard proceeded to use the economic policy failings of the Wilson government to beat the SPD. (Sir Frank Roberts, Bonn, to FO, 10 August 1965). J. Oliver Wright informed Sir Edward Tomkins of Wilson's ire at the CDU/CSU over this issue (8 September 1965). PRO: PREM 13/1530. Disparaging remarks about the British economy under Labour were hardly isolated, however, and the Conservative Party also noted that unfavourable references to Wilson's 'follies' were made by several leading CDU/CSU figures during the 1965 campaign. Bodleian: CCO4/9/176, Report of Susan Walker trip to observe 1965 *Bundestag* election.

194 LPA: OV/1966–67/14, 'The New German Government and S.P.D. Programme'.

195 *Hansard*, HC Deb, vol. 738, col. 14, 12 December 1966.

196 PRO: FCO 33/102, [RG 2/3] 'FRG foreign policy', FO to Prague, Bucharest, Budapest, 7 January 1967.

197 Gearson, *Harold Macmillan and the Berlin Wall Crisis, 1958–1962*, 117.

198 PRO: FCO 33/102, [RG 2/3] FRG foreign policy, FO to Prague, Bucharest, Budapest, 7 January 1967.

199 PRO: FCO 33/91, Sir Frank Roberts to George Brown, no. 1012, Annual Review of the FRG in 1966, 1 January 1967. The enthusiasm for Brandt and the SPD was shared by the Johnson administration. See, for instance, McGhee to Johnson, 14 December 1966. *FRUS*, 1964–8, Volume XV, online, available at: www.state_gov/www/about_ state/history/vol_xv/t.html.

200 PRO: FO 371/188477, [N 103118/8] Extract taken from a US telegram (Berlin–Washington), 11 December 1966.

201 PRO: FCO 33/102, [RG 2/3] Brandt interview in *Welt am Sonntag*, 8 January 1967.

202 (Emphasis in the original.) Harold Wilson scribbled in the margin 'Is this right? I am often asked off the cuff about it in the House. Can I say this?' (16 December 1966). A Foreign Office note responding to this enquiry indeed confirmed that, indeed, Wilson could 'say this' (19 December 1966), PRO: PREM 13/1530.

203 PRO: PREM 13/1530, Sir Frank Roberts to FO, 14 December 1966.

204 PRO: PREM 13/1530, C.D.W. to Wilson, 19 December 1966.

205 PRO: FCO 33/223, [RGS 2/2] FCO Brief for the visit of Alexei Kosygin, 26 January 1967, emphasis in original.

206 PRO: FCO 33/91, Sir Frank Roberts to George Brown, no. 1012, Annual Review of the FRG in 1966, 1 January 1967.

207 Kiesinger had actually been a member of the Nazi party and had worked a middle-level official in the propaganda section of the Foreign Ministry. Rogers, 'The Chancellors of the Federal Republic and the Political Legacy of the Holocaust', 236–7.

208 PRO: PREM 13/1699, Brown–Rapacki meeting, London, 21 February 1967.

209 For the text of the 31 January Communiqué, see Boris Meissner (ed.), *Die Deutsche Ostpolitik 1961–1970: Kontinuität und Wandel: Dokumentation* (Cologne: Wissenschaft und Politik, 1970), 181.

210 Wilson, *The Labour Government*, 82.

211 On this, see Mary Sarotte, *Dealing with the Devil: East Germany, Détente and Ostpolitik, 1969–1973* (Durham, NC: University of North Carolina Press, 2001).

212 Brandt, *My Life in Politics*, 220.

213 Larres, 'Britain, East Germany and Détente', 127.

214 For the text of Adenauer's speech to the CDU Congress, Bonn, 21 March 1966, see *Konrad Adenauer: Reden 1917–1967*, 473–82.

215 Erhard stated that despite 'talk of a change in the political attitude of the Soviet leadership. But it cannot be overlooked that the Soviet Union still threatens us with the possibility of military attack, and that its enormous military power is still directed against Western Europe.' PRO: FO 371/189182 [RG 10318/1–27] Sir Frank Roberts to Stewart, 23 March 1966.

216 This was made clear to Bonn. See, for instance, PRO: PREM 13/329, Erhard–Wilson meeting, Bonn, 8 March 1965.

217 Thomas Alan Schwartz recently noted that while historians have traditionally focused on Johnson's Vietnam policies, his policy toward Europe was 'one of the most important achievements of his presidency'. Schwartz, *Lyndon Johnson and Europe*, 225.

218 Barker, *Britain in a Divided Europe 1945–70*, 261. Michael Stewart's speech at the WEU on 15 March 1966 called for a 'calm and dignified' approach to Bonn's relations with East. On this see M.M. Harrison, *The Reluctant Ally: France and Atlantic Security* (Baltimore: Johns Hopkins University, 1981), 145–7.

219 PRO: FCO 33/223, [RGS 2/2] (1036), Hywel I. Duck (Chancery, Internal Affairs), Bonn to A.D.S. Goodall, German Desk FCO, 17 March 1967.

220 On this, see Hughes, 'Possession is nine tenths of the law', 735–7.

6 Conclusion: new roles in a new era

1 PRO: FO 800/673, Harold Macmillan, Memorandum written in Paris, July 1955.

2 Frank Roberts, quoted in John P.S. Gearson, Witness Seminar: 'British Policy and the Berlin Wall Crisis 1958–61', *Contemporary Record*, 6/1 (1992), 132.

3 Herwarth, 'Anglo-German Relations', 518.

4 PRO: 371/145738 [WG 1019/10] Sir Christopher Steel, Bonn, report on Nazism and Anti-Semitism in FRG, 9 March 1959.

5 PRO: 371/15409, [WG 1075/20] J.E. Killick minute, 20 December 1960.

6 Hans J. Morgenthau, 'Alliances in Theory and Practice' in Arnold Wolfers (ed.), *Alliance Theory in the Cold War* (London: Johns Hopkins, 1959), 195.

7 Granieri, *The Ambivalent Alliance*, 223.

8 PRO: PREM 13/902, Brash, Bucharest, Warsaw Treaty Organisation Declaration on European Security, 8 July 1966.

9 Therefore, policy-making is seen as having objective and subjective components. For example, from the perspective of the Foreign Office, the West German government refused to recognise the Oder–Neiße line because it was against the 'national interest'. Subjectively, one might say that the recognition of the Oder–Neiße line was withheld because, according to international agreement, this was to be left in abeyance until the final peace settlement. In the eyes of the British, the 'legal' dimension was used to support and strengthen the 'national interest' of West Germany. For a typical exposition of the West German case, see Peter Habel and Helmut Kistler, *Kontorvers: Die Grenze zwischen Deutschen und Polen* (Bonn: Herausgegeben von der Bundeszentrale Politische Bildung, 1970).

10 PRO: FO 371/188477, [N 103118/1] A.A. Stark, Bonn to H.F.T. Smith, Northern Department, 22 February 1966.

11 On stereotypes in Anglo-German relations, see Rainier Erwig, *Stereotypes in Contemporary Anglo-German Relations* (London: Macmillan, 2000); Kielinger, *Crossroads and Roundabouts*, 1–23; H. Husemann (ed.), *As Others See Us: Anglo-German Perceptions* (Frankfurt aM: Peter Lang, 1988); C. Cullingford and H. Husemann (eds), *Anglo-German Attitudes* (Aldershot: Avebury, 1995).

12 At the policy-making level, the most notorious example of the attempt to try and establish it was the notorious Chequers seminar on the 'Germans' held by Thatcher in 1990. The agenda at the seminar set out questions of concern to Thatcher: 'What does history tell us about the character and behaviour of the German-speaking people of Europe? Are there enduring national characteristics? Have the Germans changed in the last 40 (or 80 or 150 years)? Is it better psychologically to "stand up to Germany"? Or to pursue a friendly approach?' Hugo Young, *This Blessed Plot: Britain and Europe from Churchill to Blair* (London: Papermac), 361.

13 Wiskemann, *Germany's Eastern Neighbours*, 112.

14 In 1965 when the British required West German co-operation over Rhodesian sanctions, however, they were keen to please Bonn over the issue of GDR. The British could perhaps have reflected that just as the GDR was of vital national interest to Bonn, so was Rhodesian UDI to London in 1965.

15 On this, see Norman M. Naimark, *The Russians in Germany: a History of the Soviet Zone of Occupation, 1945–1949* (Cambridge, MA: Harvard University Press, 1995).

16 For instance, Karl Kaiser, 'Germany's Unification', *Foreign Affairs*, 79/1 (1990–1), 179–205.

17 Hugh Gaitskell, *The Challenge of Co-existence* (London: Methuen, 1957); Willy Brandt, *The Ordeal of Co-existence* (Cambridge, MA: Harvard University Press, 1963).

18 PRO: FCO 33/223, Sir Frank Roberts, Bonn to FO, Telegram number 96, 21 June 1967, 'The Day of German Unity' commemorated the 1953 rising in the GDR.

19 *The Times*, 10 March 1944. As it turned out, the impracticality of a neutral Germany meant that Britain, or at least the West, and the Soviet Union met on the Elbe.

20 Frank Roberts, 'The German–Soviet Treaty and its Effects on European and Atlantic Policies: A British View', *The Atlantic Community Quarterly*, 9/2 (1971), 184.

21 Kennan to Secretary of State Acheson, 5 September 1951, *FRUS*, 1951, Volume III, 1328.

22 PRO: FO 371/122075, report of working group of the FO, Treasury, Board of Trade and Commonwealth Relations Office, 20 April 1956. Sean Greenwood, *Britain and European Integration Since the Second World War* (Manchester: Manchester University Press, 1996), 82–3.

23 Interview: J. Oliver Wright.

24 Interview: D.A.S. Gladstone.

25 John W. Young, *Britain and European Unity 1945–1992* (London: Macmillan, 1993), 69.

26 Julian Amery, quoted in Gearson, 'British Policy and the Berlin Wall Crisis 1958–61', 139. Klaus Larres asserts that Britain did not perceive West Germany as an equal until after accession to the EEC in 1973. Klaus Larres, 'Introduction' in Larres and Meehan (eds), *Uneasy Allies*, 1.

27 HMD: 25 November 1959.

28 Sir John Killick despatch, 4 January 1973 (WRG 3/303/1), *Documents on British Policy Overseas*, series III, volume III, *Détente in Europe, 1972–1976* (London: Whitehall Publishing, 2001), 191 (n. 24).

29 Gearson, 'British Policy and the Berlin Wall Crisis 1958–61', 131.

30 Report on the State of the Nation, 11 March 1968. F.J. Schmidt (ed.), *Im deutschen Bundestag: Deutschland und Ostpolitik*, vol. II (Bonn: Bertlesmann, 1973), 116.

31 PRO: CAB 128/47 CM 39 (70), 19 November 1970.

32 Edward Heath, *The Course of My Life: My Autobiography* (London: Hodder & Stoughton, 1998), 361, 606.

33 Roger Morgan, 'Willy Brandt's "Neue Ostpolitik": British Perceptions and Positions, 1969–1975', in Birke, Brechtken and Searle, *An Anglo-German Dialogue*, 200.

34 Philip Williams, 'Britain, détente and the Conference on Security and Cooperation in Europe', in Dyson, *European Détente*, 224–5.

35 Kissinger, *The White House Years*, 421. Kissinger also notes that Wilson told President Nixon that British membership of the EEC would restrain any 'nationalist ambitions' on the part of the Germans (p. 416).

36 Brown, *In My Way*, 209.

Bibliography

Primary sources

Archives

National Archives, Public Record Office, Kew

Selected classes
CAB 128: Cabinet Meetings
CAB 129: Cabinet Memoranda
DEFE 4: Ministry of Defence, Chiefs-of-Staff Committee minutes
FO 371: Foreign Office general correspondence since 1906
FO 800: Private papers
FO 975: Foreign Office Information Research Department
FCO 33: Foreign and Commonwealth Office Western Department
FCO 51: Foreign and Commonwealth Office Research Department
PREM 8: Prime Minister's Office (Attlee, 1945–51)
PREM 11: Prime Minister's Office (Churchill, Eden, Macmillan and Home, 1951–64)
PREM 13: Prime Minister's Office (Wilson, 1964–70)
T 234: Treasury Home and Overseas Planning Division

US National Archives, Washington, DC

RG 59 State Department Central Files/Lot Files
RG 263 CIA Files
RG 306 USIA Files

John F. Kennedy Library, Boston, MA

National Security Files (NSF)
Presidential Office Files (POF)
White House Staff Files (WHSF)

JFKL Oral History Program
Interviews: David K.E. Bruce; McGeorge Bundy; Maurice Couve de Murville; Sir Alec Douglas-Home; Wilhelm Grewe; Lord Harlech; Martin Hillenbrand; Foy D.

Kohler; Geoffrey McDermott; George C. McGhee; Robert S. McNamara; Mike Mansfield; Dean Rusk; Arthur Schlesinger Jr; Drexel A. Sprecher; Theodore Sorenson; Llewellyn Thompson; Peter Thorneycroft; Sir Humphrey Trevelyan; William R. Tyler.

Dwight D. Eisenhower Library, Abilene, KS

NSC Papers
White House Central Files
White House Office Files
John Foster Dulles Papers

Lyndon B. Johnson Library, Austin, TX

Oral History Transcript: Dean Rusk interviews, 8 July 1969 and 26 September 1969.

Truman Presidential Library, Independence, MO

Oral History Transcript: Elbridge Durbrow interview, 31 May 1973.

Bodleian Library, Oxford

Harold Macmillan Diaries (HMD)
Conservative Party Archive: Conservative Overseas Branch (COB); Special subjects (CC04); Conservative Research Department (COB 12); Lady Emmet Papers (COB 86)

University of Birmingham

Lord Avon Papers

Labour Party Archive, Manchester

Labour Party International Department (LPID) Papers
Labour Party Overseas Department (OV) Papers
National Executive Committee (NEC) Papers
International Sub-Committee of the National Executive Committee Papers
H.N. Brailsford Papers
Pamphlets Collection

University College London

Hugh Gaitskell Papers

Stiftung Bundeskanzler Adenauer Haus (StBKAH), Archiv, Rhöndorf

Serie Reden, Informationsgespräche, Interviews.
02.13: 1 January 1955–31 December 1955
02.14: 1 January 1956–31 December 1956
02.15, Vol. I: 1 January 1957–30 June 1957
02.16, Vol. I: 1 July 1957–31 December 1957
02.16, Vol. II: 1 July 1957–31 December 1957

Archiv der Hansestadt Lübeck

Hansischer Geschichtsverein VII 13.1: Sigrid H. Steinberg Papers

Interviews

• Sir J. Oliver Wright: Assistant Private Secretary to Lord Home, 1960–3; Private
  Secretary to Prime Ministers Alec Douglas-Home and Harold Wilson, 1963–6.
  Interview conducted 29 June 2000.
• D.A.S. Gladstone: Bonn Embassy, 1965–9. Interview conducted 18 July 2000.
• Sir Michael Palliser: Head of FO Planning Staff, 1964; Private Secretary to
  Prime Minister Harold Wilson, 1966–9. Interview conducted 25 July 2000.
• Anne E. Stoddart: Political Desk Officer, Berlin Military Government, 1963–7.
  Interview conducted 30 June 2000.
• Sir David Goodall: Bonn Embassy, 1961–3. Letter to author, 14 May 2000.

Unpublished dissertations

Huth, Sabine, *Anglo-German Relations 1955–61*, PhD thesis, University of Cam-
    bridge, 1990.
Johns, Jnr, E.D., *British Foreign Policy on the German Question*, MA thesis, University
    of Virginia, 1990.
Lewis, B.C., *The Ostpolitik of the Grand Coalition 1966–1969*, MSc (Econ) thesis, Uni-
    versity of Wales, Aberystwyth, 1977.

Published sources

Parliamentary debates

Hansard, HC Deb, Series 5c

Diplomatic Documents

Documents on British Policy Overseas (DBPO)

Series I:
Vol. 1: *The Conference at Potsdam, July–August 1945*, London: HMSO, 1984.
Vol. 5: *Germany and Western Europe, 11 August–31 December 1945*, London: HMSO,
    1990.

Vol. 6: *Eastern Europe, August 1945–April 1946*, London: HMSO, 1991.

Series II:
Vol. 3: *German Rearmament, September–December 1950*, London: HMSO, 1989.

Series III:
Volume 3: *Détente in Europe, 1972–1976*, London: Whitehall Publishing, 2001.

Miscellaneous

Cmd. 6739, *Policy of His Majesty's Government in the United Kingdom in Regard to Czechoslovakia*, HMSO, 1942.
Cmd. 7087, *Protocol of the Proceedings of the Berlin Conference*, HMSO, 1947.
Cmd. 8571, *Convention on Relations Between the Three Western Powers and the Federal Republic*, HMSO, 1952.
Cmd. 8081, *Documents Relating to the Meeting of Heads of Government of France, the United Kingdom, the Soviet Union, and the United States of America*, HMSO, 1955.
Cmd. 124, *Defence: Outline of Future Policy*, HMSO, 1957.
Documents on Germany Under Occupation 1945–1954, selected and edited by Beate Ruhm von Oppen, RIIA/Oxford: Oxford University Press, 1955.
Documents Relating to the Meeting of Heads of Government of France, the United Kingdom, the Soviet Union, and the United States of America [Geneva 18–23 July 1955], London: HMSO, 1955.
Cmd. 1552: *Selected Documents on Germany and the Question of Berlin 1944–1961*, HMSO, 1961.

Federal Republic of Germany

Akten zur Auswärtigen Politik der Bundesrepublik Deutschland, Auftrag des Auswärtigen Amts vom Institut für Zeitgeschichte, ed. (Munich: Oldenbourg).

- 1949/50 (1997)
- 1951 (1999)
- 1952 (2000)
- 1953, I–II (2001)
- 1963, I–III (1994)

Die Kabinettsprotokolle der Bundesregierung Online version, available at: www.bundesarchiv.de/kabinettsprotokolle/web/index.jsp
FRG, Press and Information Office, *Documentation Relating to the Federal Government's Policy of Detente*, Bonn, 1978.
Protokolle des CDU-Bundesvorstandes 1953–1957, Gunter Buchstab, ed., Düsseldorf: Droste, 1990.
Efforts of the German Government and its Allies in the Cause of German Unity, 1955–1966, n.p., 1966.

Foreign Relations of the United States (FRUS)

1945
The Conference of Berlin (The Potsdam Conference), 1945. 2 vols. Washington, DC: GPO, 1960.

1947

Vol. 2: *Council of Foreign Ministers; Germany and Austria.* Washington, DC: GPO, 1970.

1948

Vol. 2: *Germany and Austria.* Washington, DC: GPO, 1973.

Vol. 3: *Council of Foreign Ministers; Germany and Austria.* Washington, DC: GPO, 1974.

1951

Vol. 3 (2 parts): *European Security and the German Question.* Washington, DC: GPO, 1982.

1955–7

Vol. 4: *Western European Security and Integration.* Washington, DC: GPO, 1986.

1958–60

Vol. 7, Pt 1: *Western European Integration and Security.* Washington, DC: GPO, 1993.

Vol. 7, Pt 2: *Western Europe.* Washington, DC: GPO, 1993.

Vol. 8: *Berlin Crisis, 1958–1959.* Washington, DC: GPO, 1993.

Vol. 9: *Berlin Crisis, 1959–1960; Germany; Austria.* Washington, DC: GPO, 1993.

1961–3

Vol. 14: *Berlin Crisis, 1961–62.* Washington, DC: GPO, 1994.

Vol. 15: *Berlin Crisis, 1962–1963.* Washington, DC: GPO, 1994.

1964–8

Vol. 15: *Germany and Berlin.* Washington, DC: GPO, 1999.

Newspapers and periodicals

Daily Express
Daily Herald
Daily Mail
Daily Mirror
Daily Telegraph
Daily Worker
Die Welt
The Economist
Manchester Guardian
Neues Deutschland
New Statesman and Society
New York Times
Observer
Stern
Süddeutsche Zeitung
Sunday Pictorial
Sunday Times
The Times

Books (including memoirs)

Abrasimov, Pyotr, *West Berlin: Yesterday and Today,* Dresden: Zeitim Bild, 1981.

Acheson, Dean, *Present at the Creation: My Years in the State Department,* New York: Norton, 1987.

Adenauer, Konrad, *World Indivisible,* London: George Allen & Unwin, 1956.

——, *Memoirs 1945–1953,* London: Weidenfeld & Nicolson, 1965.

——, *Erinnerungen 1953–1955*, Stuttgart: DVA, 1966.

——, *Erinnerungen 1955–1959*, Stuttgart: DVA, 1967.

——, *Erinnerungen 1959–1963: Fragmente*, Stuttgart: DVA, 1968.

Adomeit, Hannes, *Imperial Overstretch: Germany in Soviet Policy from Stalin to Gorbachev*, Baden-Baden: Nomos, 1998.

Ahonen, Pertti, *After the Expulsion: West Germany and Eastern Europe 1945–1990*, Oxford: Oxford University Press, 2003.

Aldrich, Richard J., *Espionage, Security and Intelligence in Britain 1945–1970*, Documents in Contemporary History, Manchester University Press, 1998.

Aldrich, Richard J. and Hopkins, Michael F. (eds), *Intelligence, Defence and Diplomacy*, Ilford; Frank Cass, 1994.

Allen, Debra J., *The Oder–Neisse Line: The United States, Poland, and Germany in the Cold War*, London: Praeger, 2003.

Ambrose, Stephen, *Eisenhower Volume Two: The President*, New York: Simon & Schuster, 1984.

Andrew, Christopher and Mitrokhin, Vasili, *The Mitrokhin Archive: the KGB in Europe and the West*, London: Penguin Books, 2000.

Annan, Noel, *Changing Enemies: The Defeat and Regeneration of Germany*, London: HarperCollins, 1996.

Ashton, Nigel, *Kennedy, Macmillan and the Cold War: the Irony of Interdependence*, London: Palgrave Macmillan, 2002.

Augstein, Rudolf, *Konrad Adenauer*, London: Secker & Warburg, 1964.

Backer, J.H., *The Decision to Divide Germany*, Duke, NC: Duke University Press, 1978.

Ball, Simon, *The Guardsmen: Harold Macmillan, Three Friends, and the World They Made*, London: Harper, 2005.

Bark, Dennis L. and Gress, David R., *A History of West Germany: Democracy and its Discontents 1963–1991*, 2nd edn, Oxford: Blackwell, 1993.

Barker, E., *Britain in a Divided Europe 1945–70*, London: Weidenfeld & Nicolson, 1971.

——, *The British Between the Superpowers 1945–50*, London: Macmillan, 1983.

Barnett, Corelli, *The Audit of War: The Illusion and Reality of Britain as a Great Nation*, London: Macmillan, 1986.

Bartlett, C.J., *The Global Conflict: The International Rivalry of the Great Powers, 1880–1970*, London: Longman, 1984.

Baylis, John, *Anglo-American Defence Relations, 1939–1984*, London: Macmillan, 1984.

Bell, Coral, *Negotiation from Strength*, London: Chatto and Windus, 1962.

——, *The Diplomacy of Détente*, London: Martin Robertson, 1977.

Bell, P.M.H., *France and Britain 1940–1994: The Long Separation*, London: Longman, 1997.

Benn, Tony, *Years of Hope: Diaries 1940–1962*, Ruth Winstone (ed.), London: Hutchison, 1994.

Benz, W. (ed.), *Die Vertreibung der Deutschen aus dem Osten: Ursachen, Erignisse, Folgen*, Frankfurt aM: Fischer, 1985.

Berghahn, Volker, *Modern Germany: Society, Economy and Politics in the Twentieth Century*, Cambridge: Cambridge University Press, 1982.

Beschloss, Michael, *The Crisis Years: Kennedy and Khruschev 1960–1963*, New York, Random House, 1991.

Bevan, Aneurin, Castle, Barbara, Driberg, Tom, Mikardo, Ian and Wilson, Harold, *It Need Not Happen*, London: Tribune, 1954.

Birke, Adolf M., *Britain and Germany: Historical Patterns of a Relationship*, London: German Historical Institute, 1987.

Bluhm, Georg, *Die Oder–Neisse-Linie in der deutschen Aussenpolitik*, Freiburg: Rombach, 1963.

Bluth, Christoph, *Britain, Germany and Western Nuclear Strategy*, Oxford: Oxford University Press, 1995.

Bodensieck, H. (ed.), *Die Deutsche Frage seit dem Zweiten Welt Krieg*, 3rd edn, Stuttgart: Ernst Klett, 1985.

Booz, Ruediger M., *'Hallsteinzeit': Deutsche Aussenpolitik 1955–1972*, Bonn: Bouvier, 1995.

Bower, Tom, *Blind Eye to Murder: Britain, America and the Purging of Nazi Germany – A Pledge Betrayed*, London: Warner Books, 1997.

Boyle, Peter G. (ed.), *The Churchill–Eisenhower Correspondence*, University of North Carolina, 1990.

Brady, John S., Crawford, Beverly and Wiliarty, Sarah Elise, *The Postwar Transformation of Germany: Democracy, Prosperity, and Nationhood*, University of Michigan Press, 1999.

Brandt, Willy, *The Ordeal of Co-existence*, Cambridge, MA: Harvard University Press, 1963.

——, *A Peace Policy for Europe*, New York: Simon & Schuster, 1969.

——, *People and Politics: The Years 1960–1975*, (trans. J. Maxwell Brownjohn), Boston: Little, Brown & Company, 1978.

——, *My Life In Politics*, London: Hamish Hamilton, 1992.

Bremen, Christian, *Die Eisenhower-Administration und die zweite Berlin-Krise, 1958–1961*, Berlin: de Gruyter, 1998.

Brentano, Heinrich von, *Germany and Europe: Reflections on German Foreign Policy*, trans. Edward Fitzgerald, New York: Frederick Praeger, 1964.

Brivati, Brian, *Hugh Gaitskell*, London: Richard Cohen Books, 1997.

Brown, George, *In My Way*, London: Victor Gollancz, 1971.

Brubaker, Roger, *Citizenship and Nationhood in France and Germany*, Cambridge, MA: Harvard University Press, 1992.

Buchstab, Gunter (ed.), *Protokolle des CDU-Bundesvorstandes 1953–1957*, Düsseldorf: Droste, 1990.

Bullock, Alan, *Ernest Bevin: Foreign Secretary 1945–1951*, Oxford: Oxford University Press, 1985.

Bundy, McGeorge, *Danger and Survival*, New York: Random House, 1988.

Bunn, Ronald F., *German Politics and the Spiegel Affair: A Case Study of the Bonn System*, Baton Rouge: Louisiana University Press, 1968.

Burcher, Timothy, *The Sudeten German Question and Czechoslovak–German Relations Since 1989*, London: RUSI Whitehall Paper Series, 1996.

Burleigh, Michael, *Germany turns Eastwards: A Study of Ostforschung in the Third Reich*, Cambridge: Cambridge University Press, 1988.

Butler, R.A., *The Art of the Possible*, London: Hamish Hamilton, 1971.

Cadogan, Sir Alexander, *The Diaries of Sir Alexander Cadogan 1938–45*, David Dilks (ed.), London: Cassell, 1971.

Callaghan, James, *Time and Chance*, London: Collins, 1987.

Camps, Miriam, *Britain and the European Community 1955–1963*, Oxford: Oxford University Press, 1964.

Cate, Curtis, *The Ides of August: The Berlin Wall Crisis 1961*, London: Weidenfeld & Nicolson, 1978.

Charta der deutschen Heimatvertriebenen, Bonn: Bundesministerium für Vertriebene, Flüchtlinge und Kriegsgeschädigte, 1950.

Childs, David, *Britain since 1945: A Political History*, London: Routledge, 1992

Churchill, Winston S., *The Dawn of Liberation: War Speeches by the Rt. Hon. Winston S. Churchill, 1944*, complied by Charles Eade, London: Cassell, 1945.

——, *The Second World War: Volume V: Closing the Ring*, London: Cassell & Co., 1952.

——, *The Second World War: Volume VI: Triumph and Tragedy*, London: Cassell & Co., 1952.

Ciechanowski, J., *Victory in Defeat*, London: Doubleday, 1947.

Clark, Ian and Wheeler, Nicholas J., *The British Origins of Nuclear Strategy, 1945–55*, Oxford: Clarendon, 1995.

Coates, W.P. and Z.K., *A History of Anglo-Soviet Relations 1943–1950*, Volume 2, London: Lawrence and Wishart, 1958.

Colville, John, *The Fringes of Power: Downing Street Diaries Volume II: 1941–April 1955*, London: Sceptre, 1987.

Committee for German Unity (eds), *The Truth about Oberländer: the Brown Book on the Criminal Fascist Past of Adenauer's Minister*, East Berlin, 1960.

Control Commission for Germany (British Element), *Background Letter: January–December 1950* (Vols II and III), Wahnerheide, 1950.

Cooper, Duff, *Old Men Forget*, London: Readers Union, Rupert Hart-Davis, 1955.

Coopey, R., Fielding, S. and Tiratsoo, N., (eds), *The Wilson Governments 1964–1970*, London: Pinter, 1995.

Cosgrave, Patrick, *R.A. Butler: An English Life*, London: Quartet Books, 1981.

Craig, Gordon A., *The Germans*, London: Pelican Books, 1984.

Crockatt, Richard, *The Fifty Years War: the United States and the Soviet Union in World Politics, 1941–1991*, London: Routledge, 1995.

Crossman, Richard, *Back-bench Diaries*, London: Weidenfeld & Nicolson, 1969.

——, *The Diaries of a Cabinet Minister: Volume One Minister of Housing*, London: Book Club Associates, 1976.

Cullingford, C. and Husemann, H. (eds), *Anglo-German Attitudes*, Aldershot: Avebury.

Curzon, Gerard, *Multilateral Commercial Diplomacy: The General Agreement on Tariffs and Trade and its Impact on National and Commercial Policies and Techniques*, New York: Praeger, 1966.

Dahrendorf, Ralf, *Society and Democracy in Germany*, London: Hamish Hamilton, 1967.

Davenport-Hines, Richard, *The Macmillans*, London: Mandarin, 1992.

Davidson, Basil, *Who Wants Peace?* London: Union of Democratic Control, 1960.

Davies, Harold, *The Meaning of Berlin: A Reply to Lord Home's Yellow Book*, London: Gladiator Book Company, 1963.

Dean, Robert W., *West German Trade with the East: The Political Dimension*, New York: Praeger, 1974.

Deighton, Anne, *The Impossible Peace: Britain, the Division of Germany and the Origins of the Cold War*, Oxford: Oxford University Press, 1990.

Deighton, Anne (ed.), *Britain and the First Cold War*, London: Macmillan, 1990.

Denman, Roy, *Missed Chances: Britain & Europe in the Twentieth Century*, London: Indigo, 1997.

Dennis, Mike, *German Democratic Republic: Politics, Economics and Society*, London: Pinter, 1988.

DePorte, A.W., *Europe between the Superpowers: The Enduring Balance*, New Haven, CT: Yale University Press, 1986.

Deutschen Institut für Zeitgeschichte (ed.), *Jahrbuch der Deutschen Demokratischen Republik 1961*, East Berlin: Verlag die Wirtschaft, 1961.

Dilks, David (ed.), *Retreat From Power: Studies in Britain's Foreign Policy of the Twentieth Century* (2 volumes), London: Macmillan, 1981.

Dobrynin, Anatoly, *In Confidence: Moscow's Ambassador to America's Six Cold War Presidents*, New York: Times, 1995.

Dockrill, Michael and McKercher, Brian (eds), *Diplomacy and World Power: Studies in British Foreign Policy, 1890–1950*, Cambridge: Cambridge University Press, 1996.

Dockrill, Saki, *Britain's Policy for West German Rearmament*, Cambridge: Cambridge University Press, 1991.

Douglas-Home, Alec, *The Way the Wind Blows*, New York: Quadrangle/NYT Book Co., 1976.

Drzewieniecki, W.M., *The German–Polish Frontier*, Chicago: Polish Western Association of America, 1959.

Dyson, Keith (ed.), *European Détente: Case Studies of the Politics of East–West Relations*, London: Frances Pinter, 1986.

Eden, Sir Anthony, *The Memoirs of Sir Anthony Eden: Full Circle*, London: Cassell, 1960.

Eibl, Franz, *Politik der Bewegung: Gerhard Schröder als Außenminister 1961–1966*, Munich: Oldenbourg, 2001.

Eisenberg, Carolyn, *Drawing the Line: The American Decision to Divide Germany, 1944–1949*, Cambridge: Cambridge University Press, 1996.

Eisenhower, Dwight D., *Mandate for Change: The White House Years 1953–1956*, London: Heinemann, 1963.

——, *Waging Peace: The White House Years 1956–61*, London: Heinemman, 1966.

Ellison, James, *Threatening Europe: Britain and the Creation of the European Community, 1955–58*, London: Palgrave Macmillan, 2000.

End, Heinrich, *Zweimal deutsche Aussenpolitik: Internationale Dimensionen des innerdeutschen Konflikts 1949–1972*, Cologne: Wissenschaft und Politik, 1973.

Erwig, Rainier, *Stereotypes in Contemporary Anglo-German Relations*, London: Macmillan, 2000.

Etzemüller, Thomas, *Sozialgeschichte als politische Geschichte: Werner Conze und die Neuorientierung der westdeutschen Geschichtwissenschaft nach 1945*, Munich: Oldenbourg, 2001.

Evans, H., *Downing Street Diary: The Macmillan Years 1957–63*, London: Hodder and Stoughton, 1981.

Feinstein, Margarete Myers, *State Symbols: The Quest for Legitimacy in the Federal Republic of Germany and the German Democratic Republic, 1949–1959*, Boston: Brill, 2001.

Foot, Michael, *Aneurin Bevan: 1897–1960*, Brian Brivati (ed.), London: Indigo, 1999.

Frei, Norbert, *Adenauer's Germany and the Politics of Amnesty and Integration*, New York: Columbia University Press, 2002.

Freund, Michael, *From Cold War to Ostpolitik*, London: Oswald Wolff, 1972.

Frey, Eric G., *Divisions and Detente: The Germanies and their Alliances*, New York: Simon & Schuster, 1987.

Fritsch-Bournatzel, Renata, *Confronting the German Question: Germans on the East–West Divide*, Oxford: Berg, 1988.

Gaddis, John L., *Strategies of Containment: A Critical Appraisal of Postwar American National Security Policy*, New York: Oxford University Press, 1982.

——, *We Now Know: Rethinking Cold War History*, Oxford: Oxford University Press, 1997.

Gaddis, John L., Gordon, Phillip H., May, Ernest R. and Rosenberg, Jonathon (eds), *Cold War Statesman Confront the Bomb: Nuclear Diplomacy Since 1945*, Oxford: Oxford University Press, 1999.

Gaitskell, Hugh, *The Challenge of Co-existence*, London: Methuen, 1957.

——, *The Diary of Hugh Gaitskell 1945–1956*, Philip M. Williams (ed.), London: Jonathan Cape, 1983.

Garton Ash, Timothy, *In Europe's Name: Germany and the Divided Continent*, London: Vintage, 1994.

Gaulle, Charles de, *Memoirs of Hope: Renewal and Endeavour*, trans. Terence Kilmartin, New York: Simon & Schuster, 1971.

GDR Academy of Sciences, *Information GDR*, Oxford: Pergamon Press, 1989.

GDR Information Office, *White Book on the Bonn War Treaty*, East Berlin: Nationales Druckhaus, 1952.

Gearson, John P.S., *Harold Macmillan and the Berlin Wall Crisis, 1958–1962: The Limits of Interest and Force*, London: Macmillan, 1998.

Gearson, John P.S. and Schake, Kori (eds), *The Berlin Wall Crisis: Perspectives on Cold War Alliances*, Basingstoke: Palgrave Macmillan, 2002.

Gesamtdeutsches Bewesstein (ed.), *Deutschland in Europäischen Spannungsfeld*, Leer: Gerhard Rautenberg, 1963.

Gilbert, Martin, *Never Despair: Winston S. Churchill 1945–1965*, London: Heinemann, 1988.

Giles, Frank (ed.), *Forty Years On: Four Decades of Koenigswinter Conferences*, Blackpool: BPCC, 1989.

Goguel, Rudi and Pohl, Heinz (eds), *Oder–Neisse: Eine Dokumentation*, East Berlin: Kongress, 1956.

Gordon, Lincoln, Brown, J.F., Hassner, Pierre, Joffe, Josef and Moreton, Edwina, *Eroding Empire: Western Relations with Eastern Europe*, Washington: The Brookings Institution, 1987.

Gordon Walker, Patrick, *Political Diaries 1932–71*, Robert Pearce (ed.), London: The Historians' Press, 1991.

Gorgey, Lazlo, *Bonn's Eastern Policy, 1964–1971*, Hamden, CT: Archon Books, 1972.

Gossel, Daniel, *Briten, Deutsche und Europa: die Deutsche Frage in der britischen Außenpolitik, 1945–1962*, Stuttgart: Steiner, 1999.

Gotto, Klaus (ed.), *Der Staatssekretär Adenauers: Persönlichkeit und politisches Wirken Hans Globkes*, Stuttgart: Klett-Cotta, 1980.

Granieri, Ronald J., *The Ambivalent Alliance: Konrad Adenauer, the CDU/CSU, and the West, 1949–1966*, Oxford: Berghahn, 2003.

Gransow, V. and Jarausch, K. (eds), *Die deutsche Vereinigung*, Cologne: Wissenschaft und Politik, 1991.

Gray, William Glenn, *Germany's Cold War: The Global Campaign to Isolate East Germany, 1949–1969*, Chapel Hill & London: University of North Carolina Press, 2003.

Greenwood, Sean, *Britain and European Integration Since the Second World War*, Manchester: Documents in Contemporary History, Manchester University Press, 1996.

——, *Britain and the Cold War, 1945–1991*, London: Macmillan, 2000.

Grewe, Wilhelm, *Rückblenden: 1951–1976*, Frankfurt aM: Propyläen, 1979.

Griffith, William E., *The Ostpolitik of the Federal Republic of Germany*, Colorado: Westview Press, 1978.

Gromyko, Andrei, *Memories*, trans. Harold Shukman, London: Hutchison, 1989.

Groom, A.J.R., *British Thinking about Nuclear Weapons*, London: Frances Pinter, 1974.

Grosser, Alfred, *Germany in Our Time: A Political History of the Postwar Years*, London: Pelican Books, 1974.

Gruner, Wolf D., *Die Deutsche Frage: ein Problem der europäischen Geschichte seit 1800*, Munich: Beck, 1985.

Haase, Christian and Gossel, Daniel (eds), *Debating Foreign Affairs: The Public Dimension of British Foreign Policy*, Berlin: Philo, 2003.

Habel, Peter and Kistler, Helmut, *Kontorvers: Die Grenze Zwischen Deutschland und Polen*, Bonn: Herausgegeben von der Bundeszentrale Politische Bildung, 1970.

Hahn, Walter F., *Between Westpolitik and Ostpolitik: Changing West German Security Views*, London: Sage, 1975.

Hailsham, Lord, *The Door Wherein I Went*, London: Collins, 1975.

Hanreider, Wolfram F. (ed.), *West German Foreign Policy: 1949–1979*, Colorado: Westview Press, 1980.

——, *Germany, America, Europe: Forty Years of West German Foreign Policy*, New Haven, CT: Yale University Press, 1989.

Hanson, Philip, *Western Economic Statecraft in East–West Relations: Embargoes, Sanctions, Linkage, Economic Warfare, and Détente*, Chatham House Papers 40, London/Routledge & Kegan Paul Ltd., 1988.

Harrison, M.M., *The Reluctant Ally: France and Atlantic Security*, Baltimore, MD: Johns Hopkins University, 1981.

Hayter, Sir William, *The Kremlin and the Embassy*, London: Hodder & Stoughton, 1966.

Healey, Denis, *The Time of My Life*, London: Michael Joseph, 1989.

Heath, Edward, *The Course of My Life: My Autobiography*, London: Hodder & Stoughton, 1998.

Heidelmeye, Wolfgang and Hindrichs, Guenter (eds), *Documents on Berlin 1943–1963*, Munich: R. Oldenberg Verlag, 1963.

Heidemeyer, Helge, *Flucht und Zuwanderung aus der SBZ/DDR 1945/1949–1961: die Fluechtlingspoitik der Bundesrepublik Deutschland bis zum Bau der Berliner Mauer*, Düsseldorf: Droste, 1994.

Herwarth, Hans von, *Von Adenauer zu Brandt*, Munich: Propyläen, 1990.

Heuser, Beatrice, *NATO, Britain, France and the FRG: Nuclear Strategies and Forces for Europe, 1949–2000*, London: Macmillan, 1997.

Hillgruber, Andreas, *Europa in der Weltpolitik der Nachkriegszeit (1945–1963)*, Munich: Oldenbourg, 1981.

Hopkins, Michael F., Kandiah, Michael D. and Staerck, Gillian (eds), *Cold War Britain, 1945–1964: New Perspectives*, Basingstoke: Palgrave, 2003.

Horne, Alastair, *Macmillan: 1894–1956*, Volume I, London: Macmillan, 1988.

——, *Macmillan 1957–1986*, Volume II, London: Macmillan, 1989.

Howard, Michael, *Disengagement in Europe*, Harmondsworth: Penguin, 1958.

Hubatsch, Walter (with Johanna Schomerus and Werner John), *Die Deutsche Frage*, Würzburg: A.G. Ploetz, 1961.

Hurd, Douglas, *The Search for Peace: A Century of Peace Diplomacy*, London: Warner Books, 1997.

Husemann, D., *As Others See Us: Anglo-German Perceptions*, Frankfurt aM: P. Lang, 1988.

Institut für Zeitgeschichte (ed.), *Materialien zur revanchistischen Politik des Bonner Staates und der Landsmannschaften*, East Berlin: Redaktion Informationsdienste, 1964.

Jain, Rajendra K., *Germany, the Soviet Union and Eastern Europe 1949–1991*, London: Sangam Books, 1993.

Jaksch, Wenzel (trans. and ed. Kurt Glaser), *Europe's Road to Potsdam*, New York: Praeger, 1963.

James, Robert Rhodes (ed.), *Winston Churchill: His Complete Speeches 1897–1963, Volume VIII, 1950–63*, London: Heinemann, 1974.

——, *Anthony Eden*, London: Papermac, 1987.

Jaspers, Karl, *The Future of Germany*, University of Chicago Press, 1967.

Jebb, Gladwyn, *The Memoirs of Lord Gladwyn*, London: Weidenfeld & Nicolson, 1972.

Jenkins, Roy, *A Life at the Centre*, London: Macmillan, 1991.

Johnson, Lyndon, B., *The Vantage Point: Perspectives of the Presidency 1963–69*, London: Weidenfeld & Nicolson, 1972.

Kaiser, Karl, *German Foreign Policy in Transition: Bonn between East and West*, London: RIAA/Oxford University Press, 1968.

Kaiser, Karl and Morgan, R. (eds), *Britain and West Germany: Changing societies and the future of foreign policy*, London: RIAA/Oxford University Press, 1971.

Kaiser, Karl and Roper, John (eds), *British–German Defence Co-operation*, London: Jane's/RIIA, 1988.

Kaiser, Wolfram, *Using Europe, Abusing the Europeans: Britain and European Integration 1945–63*, London: Macmillan, 1996.

Kappelt, Olaf, *Braunbuch DDR. Nazis in der DDR*, West Berlin: Reichmann Verlag, 1981.

Keeble, Curtis, *Britain, the Soviet Union and Russia*, London: Palgrave Macmillan, 2001.

Keesing's Research Report (Number 8), *Germany and Eastern Europe Since 1945: From the Potsdam Agreement to Chancellor Brandt's 'Ostpolitik'*, New York: Scribner's, 1973.

Kennan, George F., *The Nuclear Delusion*, New York: Pantheon, 1982.

Kennedy, Paul, *The Realities Behind Diplomacy: Background Influences on British External Policy 1865–1980*, London: Fontana, 1981.

Kennedy-Pipe, Caroline, *Stalin's Cold War: Soviet Strategies in Europe, 1943–56*, Manchester: Manchester University Press, 1995.

Kettenacker, Lothar, *Germany Since 1945*, Oxford: Oxford University Press, 1997.

Khrushchev, Nikita, *Khrushchev Remembers*, introduction, commentary and notes by Edward Crankshaw; trans. and ed. Strobe Talbott, London: Andre Deutsch, 1971.

Kielinger, Thomas, *Crossroads and Roundabouts: Junctions in German-British Relations*, London: FCO & Bonn: Press and Information Office of the Federal Government, 1997.

Kilian, Werner, *Die Hallstein Doktrin: der diplomatische Krieg zwischen der BRD und der DDR 1955–1973*, Berlin: Duncker und Humblot, 2001.

Kipp, Yvonne, *Eden, Adenauer und die deutsche Frage: Britische Deutschlandpolitik im internationalen Spannungsfeld 1951–1957*, Paderborn: Ferdinand Schöningh, 2002.

Kirkpatrick, Ivone, *The Inner Circle*, London: Macmillan, 1959.

Kissinger, Henry A., *The Troubled Partnership: A Reappraisal of the Atlantic Alliance*, Council on Foreign Relations, 1965.

——, *The White House Years*, London: Weidenfeld & Nicolson and Michael Joseph, 1979.

Koerfer, Daniel, *Kampf und Kanzleramt*, Stuttgart: Deutsche Verlagsanstalt, 1987.

Köhler, Henning, *Adenauer: Eine Politische Biographie*, Frankfurt aM: Propyläen, 1994.

Kulturstiftung der deutschen Vertreibenen, *Materialien zu Oder–Neisse-Fragen: Eine Dokumentation*, Bonn: 1979.

Labour Party, *Talking Points: German Rearmament*, Labour Party Pamphlet, 1954.

——, *Economy for Rearmament: Who Controls West German Industry?* LRD publications, March 1954.

Lacoutre, Jean, *De Gaulle: The Ruler 1945–1970*, trans. Alan Sheridan, London: Harvill, 1993.

Lansing Dulles, Eleanor, *One Germany or Two? The Struggle at the Heart of Europe*, Stanford: Hoover Institute Press, 1970.

Laqueur, Walter, *Europe Since Hitler*, London: Pelican Books, 1972.

Large, David Clay, *Germans to the Front: West German Rearmament in the Adenauer Era*, University of North Carolina Press, 1996.

Larres, Klaus, *Politik der Illusionen: Churchill, Eisenhower und die deutsche Frage, 1945–1955*, Göttingen: Vandenhoeck und Ruprecht, 1995.

——, *Churchill's Cold War: The Politics of Personal Diplomacy*, London: Yale University Press, 2002.

Larres, Klaus and Meehan, Elizabeth (eds), *Uneasy Allies: British–German Relations and European Integration since 1945*, Oxford: Oxford University Press, 2000.

Larres, Klaus and Panayi, Panikos (eds), *The Federal Republic of Germany Since 1949: Politics, Society and Economy Before and Since Reunification*, London: Longman, 1996.

Lee, Sabine, *An Uneasy Relationship: British–German Relations between 1955 and 1961*, Brockmeyer: Bochum, 1996.

——, *Victory in Europe: Britain and Germany since 1945*, London: Longman, 2001.

Leffler, Melvyn P., *A Preponderance of Power: National Security, the Truman Administration, and the Cold War*, Stanford: Stanford University Press, 1992.

Leonhardt, Rudolf W., *This Germany: The Story since the Third Reich*, trans. Catherine Hutter, London: Penguin, 1966.

Louis, William Roger and Bull, Hedley (eds), *The Special Relationship: Anglo American Relations Since 1945*, London: Clarendon Press, 1986.

Loth, Wilfried, *Overcoming the Cold War: A History of Détente, 1950–1991*, Basingstoke: Palgrave, 2002.

——, (ed.) Europe, *Cold War and Coexistence, 1953–1965*, London: Frank Cass, 2004.

Luxmoore, Jonathan and Babiuch, Jolante, *The Vatican and the Red Flag: The Struggle for the Soul of Eastern Europe*, London: Chapman, 2000.

Macmillan, Harold, *Tides of Fortune 1945–55*, London: Macmillan, 1969.

——, *Riding the Storm 1956–1959*, London: Macmillan, 1971.

——, *Pointing the Way 1959–1961*, London: Macmillan, 1972.

——, *At the End of the Day 1961–1963*, London: Macmillan, 1973.

Marshall, Barbara, *The New Germany and Migration in Europe*, Manchester: Manchester University Press, 2000.

Mawby, Spencer, *Containing Germany: Britain and the Arming of the Federal Republic*, London: Macmillan, 1999.

Mayer, Frank A., *Adenauer and Kennedy: A Study in German–American Relations, 1961–1963*, London: Macmillan: 1996.

McDermott, Geoffrey, *Berlin: Success of a Mission?* London: Andre Deutsch, 1963.

McGhee, George C., *At the Creation of a New Germany: An Ambassador's Account from Adenauer to Brandt*, New Haven, CT: Yale University Press, 1989.

Mee, Charles L, *Meeting at Potsdam*, New York: Franklin, 1975.

Meissner, Boris (ed.), *Die Deutsche Ostpolitik 1961–1970: Kontinuität und Wandel: Dokumentation*, Cologne: Wissenschaft und Politik, 1970.

Merkl, Peter H., *German Foreign Policies, West and East: On the Threshold of a New European Era*, Santa Barbara: Clio Press, 1978.

Meyer, Enno, *Deutschland und Polen: 1914–1970*, Stuttgart: Ernst Klett, 1971.

Montagu, Ivor, *Germany's New Nazis*, London: Panther, 1967.

Moreton, Edwina (ed.), *Germany Between East and West*, Cambridge: Cambridge University Press/RIIA, 1987.

Morgan, Kenneth O., *Callaghan: A Life*, Oxford: Oxford University Press, 1997.

Morgan, Roger, *Britain and Germany since 1945: Two Societies and Two Foreign Policies*, The 1988 Annual Lecture, German Historical Institute London.

Morgan, Roger and Bray, Colin (eds), *Partners and Rivals in Western Europe: Britain, France and Germany*, London: Gower, 1986.

Morsey, Rudolf and Repgen, Konrad (eds), *Untersunungen und Dokumente zur Ostpolitik und Biographie*, Adenauer-Studien III, Mainz: Mattias Grünewald, 1974.

Münch, Ingo von (ed.), *Dokumente des geteilen Deutschland*, Stuttgart: Brentano, 1968.

Münger, Christof, *Die Berliner Mauer, Kennedy und die Kubakrise: Die westliche Allianz in der Zerreißprobe 1961–1963*, Paderborn: Schöningh, 2003.

Murray, Donette, *Kennedy, Macmillan and Nuclear Weapons*, London: Macmillan, 2000.

Naimark, Norman M., *The Russians in Germany: A History of the Soviet Zone of Occupation, 1945–1949*, Cambridge, MA: Harvard University Press, 1995.

Nationalrat der Nationalen Front des Demokratischen Deutschland, *Braunbuch: Kriegs- und Nazi Verbrecher in der Bundesrepublik*, East Berlin: Dokumentationszentrum der Staatlichen Archivverwaltung der DDR, 1965.

New York Times (ed.), *Portraits of Power*, London: Octopus, 1979.

Nicolson, Harold, *Diplomacy*, London: Thornton Butterworth, 1939.

Noakes, Jeremy, Wende, Peter and Wright, Jonathan (eds), *Britain and Germany in Europe*, Oxford: Oxford University Press, 2002.

Northedge, F.S., *Descent from Power: British Foreign Policy 1945–1973*, London: Allen & Unwin, 1974.

Northedge, F.S. and Wells, A., *Britain and Soviet Communism*, London: Macmillan, 1982.

Oppelland, Torsten, *Gerhard Schröder 1910–1989: Politik Zwischen Staat, Partei und Konfession*, Düsseldorf: Droste, 2002.

Osterheld, Horst, *Aussenpolitik unter Bundeskanzler Ludwig Erhard, 1963–1966: Ein dokumentarischer Bericht aus dem Kanzleramt*, Düsseldorf: Droste, 1992.

Osterheld, Horst, Prittie, Terence and Seydoux, François, *Konrad Adenauer*, Bonn: Aktuell, 1983.

Ovendale, R. (ed.), *The Foreign Policy of the British Labour Governments 1945–51*, Leicester: Leicester University Press, 1984.

Pabst, Wilfred, *Das Jahrhundert der deutsch–französischen Konfrontation*, Hannover: Niedersächsische Landeszentrale für Politische Bildung, 1983.

Peden, George C., *The Treasury and British Public Policy 1906–1959*, Oxford: Oxford University Press, 2000.

Persson, Hans-Åke, *Rhetorik und Realpolitik: Grossbritannien, die Oder–Neisse-Grenze und die Vertreibung der Deutschen nach dem Zweiten Weltkrieg*, Berlin: Berliner Wissenschafts-Verlag, 2001.

Perzi, Niklas, *Die Beneš-Dekrete: Eine Europäische Tragödie*, Vienna/Linz: Niederosterreichisches Pressehaus, St Pölten, 2003.

Pimlott, Ben, *Harold Wilson*, London: HarperCollins, 1993.

Planck, Charles R., *The Changing Status of German Reunification in Western Diplomacy, 1955–1966*, Studies in International Affairs Number 4, The Washington Center of Foreign Policy Research of the Johns Hopkins University School of Advanced International Studies, 1967.

Pollitt, Harry, *In Defence of Peace: The Case Against Rearming the Nazis*, London: Communist Party, 1954.

Prittie, Terence *Adenauer: A Study in Fortitude*, London: Tom Stacey, 1972.

Rees, G. Wyn, *Anglo-American Approaches to Security, 1955–60*, London: Macmillan, 1996.

Reichel, Peter *Vergangenheitsbewaeltigung in Deutschland: Die Auseinandersetzung mit der NS-Diktatur von 1945 bis heute*, Munich: Beck, 2001.

Rey, Marie-Pierre, *La tentation du rapprochement: France et URSS à l'heure de la détente, 1964–1974*, Paris: Sorbonne, 1991.

Rhode, Gotthold and Wagner, Wolfgang, *The Genesis of the Oder–Neisse Line: A Study in Diplomatic Negotiations During World War II: Sources and Documents*, Stuttgart: Brentano, 1959.

Richardson, J.L., *Germany and the Atlantic Alliance*, Cambridge, MA: Harvard University Press, 1966.

Robbins, Keith, *Present and Past: British Images of Germany in the First Half of the Twentieth Century and their Historical Legacy*, Göttingen: Wallstein, Verlag, 1999.

Roberts, Frank, *Dealing with Dictators: The Destruction and Revival of Europe 1930–70*, London: Weidenfeld & Nicolson, 1991.

Rogers, Daniel E., *Politics After Hitler: The Western Allies and the German Party System*, London: Macmillan, 1995.

Rostow, Walt, *The Diffusion of Power: An Essay in Recent History*, New York: IISS, 1992.

Rothwell, V.H., *Britain's War Aims and Peace Diplomacy 1914–1958*, London: Clarendon Press, 1971.

Rozek, Edward J., *Allied War Diplomacy: A Pattern in Poland*, New York: John Wiley, 1958.

Ruane, Kevin, *The Rise and Fall of the European Defence Community: Anglo-American Relations and the Crisis of European Defence, 1950–55*, London: Macmillan, 2000.

Rusk, Dean, *As I Saw It*, London: I.B. Tauris, 1991.

Salisbury, Keith, *Churchill and Roosevelt at War:The War they Fought and the Peace they Hoped to Make*, London: Macmillan, 1994.

Salzmann, Stephanie C., *Great Britain, Germany and the Soviet Union: Rapallo and After, 1922–1934*, London: Boydell, 2003.

Sanders, David, *Losing an Empire, Finding a Role: British Foreign Policy Since 1945*, London: Macmillan, 1990.

Sarotte, Mary, *Dealing with the Devil: East Germany, Détente and Ostpolitik, 1969–1973*, Durham, NC: University of North Carolina Press, 2001.

Schaad, Martin P.C., *Bullying Bonn: Anglo-German Diplomacy on European Integration*, London: Macmillan, 2000.

Schaffer, Gordon, *Do You Want War over Berlin?* London: Gladiator, 1961.

Schieder, Theodor (ed.), *Dokumentation der Vertreibung der Deutschen aus Ost-Mitteleuropa*, Volumes I–V, Bonn: Bundesministerium für Vertriebene, Flüchtlinge und Kriegsgeschädigte, 1953–1960.

Schlesinger, Arthur M., *A Thousand Days: John F. Kennedy in the White House*, London: Andre Deutsch, 1965.

Schmidt, F.J. (ed.), *Im deutschen Bundestag: Deutschland und Ostpolitik*, Volume II, Bonn: Bertlesmann, 1973.

Schmidt, Wolfgang, *Kalter Krieg, Koexistenz und kleine Schritte: Willy Brandt und die Deutschlandpolitik 1948–1963*, Wiesbaden: Westdeutscher, 2001.

Schroëder, Gerhard, *Decision for Europe*, London: Thames & Hudson, 1964.

Schütt, Siegfried, *Theodor Oberländer: Eine dokumentarische Untersuchung*, Munich: Langen Müller, 1995.

Schwartz, Thomas Alan, *Lyndon Johnson and Europe: In the Shadow of Vietnam*, London: Harvard University Press, 2003.

Schwarz, Hans-Peter (ed.), *Konrad Adenauer: Reden 1917–1967: Eine Auswahl*, Stuttgart: DVA, 1975.

Scott, L.V., *Macmillan, Kennedy and the Cuban Missile Crisis: Political, Military and Intelligence Aspects*, London: Palgrave Macmillan, 1999.

SED Abteilung Massenorganisation, *Warum ist die Oder–Neiße-Linie eine Friedensgrenze?* East Berlin, 1950.

Segal, Gerald, *The Great Power Triangle*, London: St Martin's Press, 1982.

Seppain, Hélène, *Contrasting US and German Attitudes to Soviet Trade, 1917–91: Politics by Economic Means*, London: St Martin's Press, 1992.

Shapley, Deborah, *Promise and Power: The Life and Times of Robert McNamara*, Boston: Little, Brown & Company, 1993.

Shuckburgh, Evelyn, *Descent to Suez: Diaries, 1951–56*, London: Weidenfeld & Nicolson, 1986.

Siegler, Heinrich von, *The Reunification and Security of Germany: A Documentary Basis for Discussion*, Munich: Siegler & Co. K.G. Verlag für Zeitarchive, 1957.

——, *Wiedervereinigung und Sicherheit Deutschland: zweite erweiterte Auflage*, Bonn: Verlag für Zeitarchive, 1957.

Smith, M., Smith, S. and White, B. (eds), *British Foreign Policy: Tradition, Change and Transformation*, London: Unwin Hyman, 1988.

Smyser, W.R., *From Yalta to Berlin: the Cold War Struggle Over Germany*, London: Macmillan, 1999.

——, *The German Economy*, London: St Martin's Press, 1993.

Sorenson, Theodore C., *Kennedy*, London: Pan Books, 1966.

Sowden, J.K., *The German Question 1945–1973: Continuity in Change*, Bradford: Bradford University Press, 1975.

Spaulding, Robert Mark, *Osthandel and Ostpolitik: German Foreign Trade Policies in Eastern Europe from Bismarck to Adenauer*, Oxford: Berghahn Books, 1997.

Steele, Jonathan (compiler and ed.), *Eastern Europe Since Stalin*, New York: Crane Russak, 1974.

Steininger, Rolf (ed.), *Die Ruhrfrage 1945–6 und die Entstehung des Landes Nordrhein Westfalen: Britische, französische und Amerikanische Akten*, Düsseldorf: Droste, 1988.

——, *Der Mauerbau: Die Westmächte und Adenauer in der Berlinkrise 1958–1963*, Munich: Olzog, 2001.

Stent, Angela, *From Embargo to Ostpolitik: The Political Economy of West German–Soviet Relations 1955–1980*, Cambridge: Cambridge University Press, 1980.

Stewart, Michael, *Life and Labour: An Autobiography*, London: Sedgwick & Jackson, 1980.

Stirk, Peter M.R. and Willis, David (eds), *Shaping Postwar Europe: European Unity and Disunity 1945–1957*, London: Pinter Publishers, 1991.

Strang, Lord, *Britain in World Affairs*, Westport, CT: Geenword Press, 1961.

Stromseth, Jane, *The Origins of Flexible Response*, London: Macmillan, 1988.

Swingler, Stephen, *Warning to the West! or The Consequences of German Re-armament*, London: Gladiator, 1961.

Szar, Zolton Michael, *Germany's Easterm Frontiers: The Problems of the Oder–Niesse Line*, Chicago: Polish Western Association of America, 1960.

Szkopiak, Zygmunt C. (ed.), *The Yalta Agreements: The White Book: Documents Prior to, During and After the Crimea Conference 1945*, London: Polish Government in Exile, 1986.

Tauber, Kurt P., *Beyond Eagle and Swastika: German Nationalism Since 1945*, 2 Volumes, Middletown, CO: Wesleyan, 1967.

Taubman, William, *Khrushchev: The Man and his Era*, New York: W.W. Norton, 2003.

Tetens, T.H., *The New Germany and the Old Nazis*, London: Secker & Warburg, 1961.

Thomas, George, *George Thomas, Mr Speaker: The Memoirs of Viscount Tonypandy*, London: Castle Books, 1985.

Thomas, H., *Armed Truce: The Beginnings of the Cold War, 1945–6*, London: Heinemann, 1987.

Thomas, Neil, *A Compromised Policy: Britain, Germany and the Soviet Threat 1945–6*, London: Minerva Press, 1994.

Thorpe, D.R., *Selwyn Lloyd*, London: Jonathan Cape, 1989.

——, *Alec Douglas-Home*, London: Sinclair-Stevenson, 1996.

Trachtenberg, Marc, *A Constructed Peace: The Making of the European Settlement 1945–1963*, Princeton, NJ: Princeton University Press, 1999.

Tratt, Jacqueline, *The Macmillan Government and Europe: A Study in the Process of Policy Development*, London: Macmillan, 1996.

Truman, Harry S., *Year of Decisions*, Memoirs, Volume One, New York: Doubleday, 1955.

——, *Years of Trial and Hope*, Memoirs, Volume Two, New York: Doubleday, 1956.

Tusa, Ann, *The Last Division: Berlin and the Wall*, London: Hodder & Stoughton, 1996.

Ulam, Adam, *Expansion and Coexistence*, New York: Praeger, 1968.

van Ham, Peter, *The EC, Eastern Europe and European Unity: Discord, Collaboration and Integration Since 1947*, London: Pinter Publishers, 1993.

van Oudenaren, John, Détente in Europe: the Soviet Union and the West since 1953, London: Duke University Press, 1991.

Vogt, Timothy R., *Denazification in Soviet-Occupied Germany: Brandenburg, 1945–1948*, Cambridge, MA: Harvard University Press, 2000.

Wagner, Wolfgang, *The Genesis of the Oder–Neisse Line: A Study in Diplomatic Negotiations During World War II*, Stuttgart: Brentano Verlag, 1957.

Watson, Alan, *The Germans: Who are they now?* London: Thames Methuen, 1992.

Watt, Donald Cameron, *Britain Looks to Germany*, London: Oswald Wolff, 1965.

——, *Succeeding John Bull: America in Britain's Place 1900–1975*, Cambridge: Cambridge University Press, 1984.

Wedermeyer, Paul, *Konrad Adenauer: The Authorised Autobiography*, London: Heinemann, 1957.

Westad, Odd Arne (ed.), *Reviewing the Cold War: Approaches, Interpretations, Theory*, London: Frank Cass, 2000.

Weymar, Paul, *Konrad Adenauer: The Authorised Biography* (trans. Peter de Mendelssohn), London: Andre Deutsch, 1957.

Whetten, Lawrence, *Germany's Ostpolitik: Relations between the Federal Republic and the Warsaw Pact Countries*, Oxford: Oxford University Press, 1971

White, Brian, *Britain, Détente, and Changing East–West Relations*, London: Routledge, 1992.

Wilkes, George (ed.), *Britain's Failure to Enter the European Community 1961–63: The Enlargement Negotiations and Crises in European, Atlantic and Commonwealth Relations*, London: Frank Cass, 1997.

Williams, Philip, *Hugh Gaitskell: A Political Biography*, London: Jonathan Cape, 1979.

Wilson, Harold, *Purpose in Politics*, London: Weidenfeld & Nicolson, 1964.

——, *The Labour Government 1964–70: A Personal Record*, London: Weidenfeld & Nicolson and Michael Joseph, 1971.

Windsor, Philip, *Germany and the Management of Détente*, London: Chatto & Windus, 1971.

Wiskemann, Elizabeth, *Germany's Eastern Neighbours: Problems Relating to the Oder–Neisse Line and the Czech Frontier Regions*, Oxford: Oxford University Press, 1956.

Wolfers, Arnold (ed.), *Alliance Theory in the Cold War*, London: The Johns Hopkins Press, 1959.

Wolfers, Arnold, *Discord and Collaboration: Essays on International Politics*, Baltimore and London: The Johns Hopkins University Press, 1962.

Wolff, Stefan, *The German Question since 1919: An Analysis with Key Documents*, London: Praeger, 2003.

Young, Hugo, *This Blessed Plot: Britain and Europe from Churchill to Blair*, London: Papermac, 1999.

Young, John W. (ed.), *The Foreign Policy of Churchill's Peacetime Administration 1951–55*, Leicester: Leicester University Press, 1988.

Young, John W., *Britain and European Unity 1945–1992*, London: Macmillan, 1993.

Zayas, Alfred M. de, *Nemesis at Potsdam: The Anglo-Americans and the Expulsion of the Germans*, London: Victor Gollancz, 1977.

Ziegler, Philip, *Wilson: The Authorised Life*, London: Weidenfeld & Nicolson, 1993.

Zubok, Vladislav and Pleshakov, Constantine, *Inside the Kremlin's Cold War: From Stalin to Khrushchev*, Cambridge, MA: Harvard University Press, 1996.

Journal articles and chapters from books

Acheson, Dean, 'The Practice of Partnership', *Foreign Affairs*, 41/2 (1963), 247–60.

Adamthwaite, Anthony, 'Introduction: The Foreign Office and Policy-Making', in

John W. Young (ed.), *The Foreign Policy of Churchill's Peacetime Administration 1951–55*, Leicester University Press, 1988.

Adenauer, Konrad, 'Germany and the Problems of Our Time', *International Affairs*, 28/1 (1952), 156–61.

——, 'Germany and Europe', *Foreign Affairs*, 31/2 (1953), 361–6.

——, 'Germany, The New Partner', *Foreign Affairs*, 33/1 (1955), 171–83.

——, 'The German problem, a world problem', *Foreign Affairs*, 41/1 (1962), 59–65.

Ahonen, Pertti, 'Domestic Constraints on West German Ostpolitik: The Role of the Expellee Organizations in the Adenauer Era', *Central European History*, 98/1 (1998), 31–63.

Albert, E.H., 'The Brandt Doctrine of Two States in Germany', *International Affairs*, 46/2 (1970), 293–303.

Aldous, Richard, ' "A Family Affair": Macmillan and the Art of Personal Diplomacy', in Richard Aldous and Sabine Lee (eds), *Harold Macmillan and Britain's World Role*, London: Macmillan, 1996.

Alexander, Philip, ' "We too mean business": Germany and the second British application to the EEC in 1966–67', in Oliver Daddow (ed.), *Harold Wilson and European Integration: Britain's Second Application to Join the EEC*, London: Frank Cass, 2003.

Andrew, Christopher, 'Anglo-American–Soviet Intelligence Relations', in A. Lane and H. Temperley (eds), *The Rise and Fall of the Grand Alliance 1941–45*, London: Macmillan, 1995.

Anthon, Carl G., 'Adenauer's Ostpolitik 1955–1963', *World Affairs* (Washington), 139/2 (1976), 112–24.

Arndt, Claus, 'Legal Problems of the German Eastern Territories', *American Journal of International Law*, 74/1 (1980), 126–8.

Aron, Raymond, 'French Public Opinion and the Atlantic Treaty', *International Affairs*, 27/1 (1952), 8–15.

Ausland, John C. and Richardson, Hugh F., 'Crisis Management: Berlin, Cyprus, Laos', *Foreign Affairs*, 44/2 (1966), 291–303.

Bader, W.B., 'Nuclear Weapons Sharing and "The German Problem" ', *Foreign Affairs*, 44/4 (1966), 693–700.

Baring, Arnulf, 'The Institutions of German Foreign Policy', in Karl Kaiser and Roger Morgan (eds), *Britain and West Germany: Changing Societies and the Future of Foreign Policy*, London, 1971.

Barker, Elisabeth, 'The Berlin Crisis 1958–62', *International Affairs*, 39/1 (1963), 59–73.

Barman, Thomas, 'Britain, France and West Germany: The Changing Patterns of their Relationship in Europe', *International Affairs*, 46/2 (1970), 269–79.

Baylis, John, 'Britain, the Brussels Pact and the Continental Committment', *International Affairs*, 60/4 (1984), 615–30.

Berger, Stefan and LaPorte, Norman, 'John Peet (1915–1988): An Englishman in the GDR', *History*, 89/1 (2004), 49–69.

Berger, Stefan and Lilleker, Darren, 'The British Labour Party and the German Democratic Republic during the era of non-recognition, 1949–1973', *Historical Journal*, 45/2 (2002), 433–58.

Bertram, Cristoph, 'West German Perspectives on European Security: Continuity and Change', *The World Today*, March 1971, 115–24.

Birrenbach, Kurt, 'The West German and German Ostpolitik – The German Opposition View', *The Atlantic Community Quarterly*, 9/2 (1971), 196–204.

Black, Jeremy, '"The Bitterest Enemies of Communism": Labour Revisionists, Atlanticism and the Cold War', *Contemporary British History*, 15/3 (2001), 26–62.

Blanke, Richard, 'The German Minority in Inter-war Poland and German Foreign Policy: Some Reconsiderations', *Journal of Contemporary History*, 25/1 (1990), 87–102.

Bluth, Christoph, 'British–German Defence Relations, 1950–80: A Survey', Karl Kaiser and John Roper (eds), *British–German Defence Co-operation*, London: Jane's/RIIA, 1988.

Bowie, Robert R., 'Tensions Within the Alliance', *Foreign Affairs*, 42/1 (1963), 49–69.

Brandt, Willy, 'The East–West Problem as Seen From Berlin', *International Affairs*, 34/3 (1958), 297–304.

——, 'German Policy Towards the East,' *Foreign Affairs*, 46/3 (1968), 476–86.

Brechtken, Magnus, 'Personality, Image and Perception: Patterns and Problems of Anglo-German Relations in the 19th and 20th Centuries', in Adolf M. Birke, Magnus Brechtken and Alaric Searle (eds), *An Anglo-German Dialogue: The Munich Lectures on the History of International Relations*, Prince Albert Studies vol. 17, Munich: K.G. Saur, 2000.

Brentano, Heinrich von, 'Goals and Means of the Western Alliance', *Foreign Affairs*, 39/3 (1961), 416–29.

Brzezinski, Zbigniew, 'The Challenge of Change in the Soviet Bloc', *Foreign Affairs*, 39/3 (1961), 430–43.

Brzezinski, Zbigniew and Griffith, William E., 'Peaceful Engagement in Eastern Europe', *Foreign Affairs*, 39/4 (1961), 642–54.

——, 'Moscow and the M.L.F.: Hostility and Ambivalence', *Foreign Affairs*, 43/1 (1964), 126–34.

Buffet, Cyril, 'De Gaulle, the Bomb and Berlin: How to Use a Political Weapon', in J. Gearson and K. Schake (eds), *Harold Macmillan and the Berlin Crisis: Perspectives on Cold War Alliances*, Basingstoke: Palgrave Macmillan, 2002.

Bullock, Alan, 'The German Communists and the Rise of Hitler', in *The Third Reich*, London: Weidenfeld & Nicolson for UNESCO, 1955.

Burr, William, 'Avoiding the Slippery Slope: the Eisenhower Administration and the Berlin Crisis: November 1958–January 1959', *Diplomatic History*, 18/2 (1994), 177–205.

Camps, Miriam, 'Britain, the Six and American Policy', *Foreign Affairs*, 39/1 (1960), 112–22.

Carr, G.A., 'The Involvement of Politics in the Sporting Relationships of East and West Germany 1945–1972', *Journal of Sport History*, 7/1 (1980), 40–50.

Clay, Lucius D., 'Berlin', *Foreign Affairs*, 41/1 (1962), 47–58.

Coker, Christopher, 'The New Barbarians', *Parliamentary Brief*, July 1993.

Cold War International History Project, Woodrow Wilson International Center for Scholars. Rough notes from a conversation (Gromyko, Khrushchev and Gomulka) on the international situation, n.d. (October 1961), online, available at: www.wilsoncenter.org.

Connor, Ian, 'The Integration of Refugees and Foreign Workers in the Federal Republic of Germany Since the Second World War', *German Historical Institute London, Bulletin*, 22/1 (2000), 18–31.

Conze, Eckart, 'Staatsräson und nationale Interessen: Die "Atlantiker-Gaullisten"-

Debatte in der westdeutschen Politik- und Gesellschaftsgeschichte der 1960er Jahre', in Ursula Lehmkuhl, Clemens A. Wurm and Hubert Zimmermann (eds), *Deutschland, Großbritannien, Amerika: Politik, Gesellschaft und Internationale Geschichte im 20. Jahrhundert*, Stuttgart: Steiner, 2003.

Croft, Stuart, 'British Policy Towards Western Europe: 1945–1951', in Peter M.R. Stirk and David Willis (eds), *Shaping Postwar Europe: European Unity and Disunity 1945–1957*, London: Pinter Publishers, 1991.

Crossman, R.H.S., 'British Labour looks at Europe', *Foreign Affairs*, 41/3 (1963), 732–43.

Dean, Robert W., 'Bonn–Prague Relations: The Politics of Reconciliation', *The World Today*, April 1973, 149–59.

Deighton, Anne, 'British West German Relations, 1945–1972', in Klaus Larres and Elizabeth Meehan (eds), *Uneasy Allies: British–German Relations and European Integration since 1945*, Oxford: Oxford University Press, 2000.

Diebold Jr, William, 'Britain, the Six and the World Economy', *Foreign Affairs*, 40/3 (1962), 407–18.

Dockrill, Saki, 'Retreat from the Continent? Britain's Motives for Troop Reductions in West Germany 1955–1958', *The Journal of Strategic Studies*, 20/3 (1997).

Dyson, Keith, 'European détente in historical perspective: ambiguities and paradoxes', in Keith Dyson (ed.), *European Détente; Case Studies of the Politics of East–West Relations*, London: Frances Pinter, 1986.

Erler, Fritz, 'The Basis of Partnership', *Foreign Affairs*, 42/1 (1963), 84–95.

——, 'The Alliance and the Future of Germany', *Foreign Affairs*, 43/3 (1965), 436–46.

Foerster, Roland G., 'Innenpolitik Aspekte der Sicherheit Wesedeutschlands (1947–1950)', in MGFA (ed.), *Anfänge Westdeutscher Sicherheitspolitik, 1945–1946: Band I: Von der Kapitulation bis zum Pleven-Plan*, Munich: Oldenbourg, 1982, 510–11.

Fulcher, Kara Stibora, 'A Sustainable Position? The United States, the Federal Republic, and the Ossification of Allied Policy on Germany, 1958–1962', *Diplomatic History*, 26/2 (2002), 283–307.

Garnett, John, 'BAOR and NATO', *International Affairs*, 46/4 (1970), 670–7.

Gearson, John P.S., Witness Seminar, 'British Policy and the Berlin Wall Crisis 1958–61', *Contemporary Record*, 6/1 (1992), 107–77.

Gelberg, Ludwik, 'The Warsaw Treaty of 1970 and the Western Boundary of Poland', *The American Journal of International Law*, 76/1 (1982), 119–53.

Geyer, Martin H., 'Der Kampf um nationale Repräsentation: Deutsche–deutsche Sportsbeziehungen und die "Hallstein-Doktrin"', *Vierteljahrshefte für Zeitgeschichte*, 44/1 (1996), 55–86.

Gillessen, Günther, 'Germany's Position in the Centre of Europe: The Significance of Germany's Position and Misunderstandings about German Interests', in Arnulf Baring (ed.), *Germany's New Position in Europe: Problems and Perspectives*, Providence, RI: Berg, 1994.

Gladwyn, Lord, 'The Necessity for European Political Integration', *International Affairs*, 45/4 (1969), 631–42.

Goebbels, Josef, 'Das Jahr 2000', *Das Reich*, 25 February 1945, 1–2.

Goldstein, Erik, 'Britain and the Origins of the Cold War 1917–1925', in Michael F. Hopkins, Michael D. Kandiah and Gillian Staerck (eds), *Cold War Britain, 1945–1964: New Perspectives*, Basingstoke: Palgrave, 2003.

Gordon Walker, Patrick,'The Labor Party's Defense and Foreign Policy', *Foreign Affairs*, 42/3 (1964), 392–402.

Grabbe, Hans-Jürgen, 'Konrad Adenauer, John Foster Dulles, and West German–American Relations', in Richard H. Immerman (ed.), *John Foster Dulles and the Diplomacy of the Cold War*, Princeton, NJ: Princeton University Press, 1992.

Griffiths, Richard, 'A Slow One Hundred and Eighty Degree Turn: British Policy Towards the Common Market. 1955–60', in George Wilkes (ed.), *Britain's Failure to Enter the European Community 1961–63: The Enlargement Negotiations and Crises in European, Atlantic and Commonwealth Relations*, London: Frank Cass, 1997.

Grosser, Alfred, 'France and Germany: Divergent Outlooks', *Foreign Affairs*, 44/1 (1965), 26–36.

Hallstein, Walter, 'Germany's Dual Aim: Unity and Integration', *Foreign Affairs*, 31/1 (1952), 58–66.

Harries, O., 'Faith in the Summit', *Foreign Affairs*, 40/1 (1961), 58–70.

Harrison, Hope, 'The Berlin Wall, Ostpolitik and Détente', in David C. Geyer and Bernd Schaefer (eds), *American Détente and German Ostpolitik 1969–1972*, Washington, DC: German Historical Institute, 2004.

Hassel, Kai-Uwe von, 'Détente Through Firmness', *Foreign Affairs*, 42/2 (1964), 184–94.

——, 'Organising Western Defense', *Foreign Affairs*, 43/2 (1965), 209–16.

Healey, Denis, 'When Shrimps Learn to Whistle Thoughts after Geneva', *International Affairs*, 33/2 (April 1957), 1–10.

Herter, Christian A., 'Atlantica', *Foreign Affairs*, 41/1 (1962), 299–309.

Herwarth, Hans von, 'Anglo-German Relations: I. A German View', *International Affairs*, 39/4 (1963), 513–22.

Hillgruber, Andreas, 'Adenauer und die Stalin-Note', in Dieter Blumenwitz (ed.), *Konrad Adenauer und seine Zeit*, vol. 2, Stuttgart: Deutsche Verlag Anstalt, 1976, 113–15.

Hogg, Quintin, 'Britain Looks Forward', *Foreign Affairs*, 43/3 (1965), 409–25.

Holdich, P.G.H., 'A Policy of Percentages? British Policy in the Balkans After the Moscow Conference of October 1944', *International History Review*, 9/1 (1987), 32–46.

Home, Earl of, 'Interdependence: the British Role', *International Affairs*, 37/2 (1961), 154–60.

Howard, Michael, 'Disengagement and Western Security', *International Affairs*, 34/4 (1958), 469–76.

Hughes, R. Gerald, '"We are not seeking strength for its own sake": the Labour Party and West Germany, 1951–64', *Cold War History*, 3/1 (2002), 78–84.

——, 'Unfinished Business from Potsdam: Britain, West Germany, and the Oder–Neiße line, 1945–1962', *International History Review*, 27/2 (2005), 259–94.

——, '"Possession is nine tenths of the law": Britain and the boundaries of Eastern Europe since 1945', *Diplomacy and Statecraft*, 16/4 (2005), 723–47.

——, '"Don't Let's be Beastly to the Germans": Britain and the German Affair in History', *Twentieth Century British History*, 17/2 (2006), 257–83.

Ihme-Tuchel, Beate, 'Das Bemühen der SED um die diplomatische Anerkennung durch Jugoslawien 1956/57', *Zeitschrift für Geschichtswissenschaft*, 42/8 (1994), 695–702.

Ingimundarson, Valur, 'The Eisenhower, the Adenauer Government, and the Political Uses of the East German Uprising in 1953', *Diplomatic History*, 20/3 (1996), 378–90.

Jenkins, Roy, 'British Labour Divided', *Foreign Affairs*, 38/3 (1960), 487–96.

Joffe, Josef, 'The View from Bonn', in Lincoln Gordon with J.F. Brown, Pierre Hassner, Josef Joffe and Edwina Moreton, *Eroding Empire: Western Relations with Eastern Europe*, Washington, DC: The Brookings Institution, 1987.

Kaiser, Karl, 'Germany's Unification', *Foreign Affairs*, 79/1 (1990–91), 179–205.

Kaiser, Wolfram, 'Money, Money, Money: The Economics and Politics of the Stationing Costs 1955–1965', in Gustav Schmidt (ed.), *Zwischen Bündnissicherung und privilegierter Partnerschaft: Die deutsch–britischen Beziehungen und die Vereinigten Staaten von Amerika, 1955–1963*, Bochum: Brockmeyer, 1995.

——, 'Against Napoleon and Hitler: Background Influences on British Diplomacy', in Kaiser Wolfram and Gillian Staerck (eds), *British Foreign Policy 1955–64: Contracting Options*, Basingstoke: Macmillan, 2000.

——, 'Trigger-happy Protestant Materialists? The European Christian Democrats and the United States', in Marc Trachtenberg (ed.), *Between Empire and Alliance: America and Europe during the Cold War*, Lanham: Rowman & Littlefield, 2003.

Karsten, Bernd, 'Pensionen für NS-Verbrecher in der Bundesrepublik 1949–1963', *Historische Mitteilungen*, 7/2 (1994), 262–82.

Kellen, Konrad, 'Adenauer at 90', *Foreign Affairs*, 44/2 (1966), 275–90.

Kennan, George F., 'Disengagement Revisited', *Foreign Affairs*, 37/2 (1959), 187–210.

——, 'On Peaceful Coexistence: A Western View', *Foreign Affairs*, 38/2 (1960), 171–90.

——, 'Polycentrism and Western Policy', *Foreign Affairs*, 42/2 (1964), 171–83.

Kennedy, John F., 'A Democrat looks at Foreign Policy', *Foreign Affairs*, 36/1 (1957), 46–54.

Khrushchev, Nikita S., 'On Peaceful Coexistence', *Foreign Affairs*, 38/1 (1959), 1–18.

——, 'A Call for a Treaty . . . renouncing the use of Force in the Settlement of Territorial and Frontier Disputes', London: Soviet Booklet, 2/2, 1964.

Kissinger, Henry A., 'The Search for Stability', *Foreign Affairs*, 37/4 (1959), 537–60.

——, 'Strains on the Alliance', *Foreign Affairs*, 41/2 (1963), 261–85.

——, 'Coalition Diplomacy in a Nuclear Age', *Foreign Affairs*, 42/4 (1964), 525–45.

Korbel, Josef, 'German–Soviet Relations: The Past and the Prospects', *Orbis*, 11/4 (1967), 1046–60.

Krebs, Ronald R., 'Liberation à la Finland: Reexamining Eisenhower Administration Objectives in Eastern Europe', *Journal of Strategic Studies*, 20/3 (1997), 1–26.

Kronsten, Joseph A., 'East–West Trade: Myth and Matter', *International Affairs*, 45/2 (1969), 265–81.

Kubricht, A. Paul, 'Politics and Foreign Policy: A Brief Look at the Kennedy Administration's Eastern European Diplomacy', *Diplomatic History*, 11/1 (1987), 55–66.

Larres, Klaus, 'Reunification or Integration with the West? Britain and the Federal Republic of Germany in the Early 1950s', in Richard J. Aldrich and Michael F. Hopkins, *Intelligence, Defence and Diplomacy*, Ilford: Frank Cass, 1994.

——, 'Preserving Law and Order; Britain, the United States and the East German Uprising of 1953', *Twentieth Century British History*, 5/3 (1994), 320–50.

——, 'Germany and the West: the "Rapallo factor" in German Foreign Policy from the 1950s to the 1990s', in Klaus Larres and Panikos Panayi (eds), *The Federal Republic of Germany Since 1949: Politics, Society and Economy Before and Since Reunification*, London: Longman, 1996.

——, 'Britain and the GDR: Political and Economic Relations, 1949–1989', in Klaus Larres and Elizabeth Meehan (eds), *Uneasy Allies: British–German Relations and European Integration since 1945*, Oxford: Oxford University Press, 2000.

——, 'Britain and the GDR in the 1960s: The Politics of Trade and Recognition by Stealth', in Jeremy Noakes, Peter Wende and Jonathan Wright (eds), *Britain and Germany in Europe*, Oxford: Oxford University Press, 2000.

Lee, Sabine, 'Anglo-German Relations 1958–59: The Postwar Turning Point?', *Diplomacy and Statecraft*, 6/3, (1995), 787–808.

——, 'Perception and Reality: Anglo-German Relations during the Berlin Crisis, 1958–1959', *German History*, 13/1 (1995), 45–69.

——, 'America and the Shaping of Post-War Germany', *German Politics*, 5/1 (1996), 145–50.

——, 'Pragmatism Versus Principle? Macmillan and Germany', in Richard Aldous and Sabine Lee (eds), *Harold Macmillan: Aspects of a Political Life*, London: Macmillan, 1999.

——, 'CDU Refugee Policies and the Landesverband Oder/Neiße: Electoral Tool or Instrument of Integration?', *German Politics*, 8/1 (1999), 131–49.

Leffler, Melvyn P., Review Essay, 'The Cold War: What Do "We Now Know"?', *The American Historical Review*, 104/2 (1999), 501–24.

Lemke, Michael, 'Kampagnen gegen Bonn: Die Systemkrise der DDR und die West-Propaganda der SED 1960–1963', *Vierteljahrshefte für Zeitgeschichte*, 41/1 (1993), 153–74.

Lewis, Flora, 'The Unstable States of Germany', *Foreign Affairs*, 38/4 (1960), 558–97.

Longden, Martin A.L., 'From "Hot War" to "Cold War": Western Europe in British Grand Strategy, 1945–1948', in Michael F. Hopkins, Michael D. Kandiah and Gillian Staerck (eds), *Cold War Britain, 1945–1964: New Perspectives*, Basingstoke: Palgrave, 2003.

Loth, Wilfried, 'Das Ende der Legende: Hermann Graml und die Stalin-Note: Eine Entgegnung', *Vierteljahrshefte für Zeitgeschichte*, 50/4 (2002), 653–64.

Ludlow, N. Piers, 'Germany, Britain, and the EEC, 1956–1972', in Jeremy Noakes, Peter Wende and Jonathan Wright (eds), *Britain and Germany in Europe*, Oxford: Oxford University Press, 2002.

Marchio, Jim, 'Resistance Potential and Rollback: US Intelligence and the Eisenhower Administration's Policies Towards Eastern Europe, 1953–56', *Intelligence and National Security*, 10/2 (1995), 219–41.

Mauer, Victor, 'Harold Macmillan and the Deadline Crisis Over Berlin 1958–9', *Twentieth Century British History*, 9/1 (1998), 54–85.

Mawby, Spencer, 'Revisiting Rapallo: Britain, Germany and the Cold War, 1945–1955' in Michael F. Hopkins, Michael D. Kandiah and Gillian Staerck (eds), *Cold War Britain, 1945–1964: New Perspectives*, Basingstoke: Palgrave, 2003.

May, Ernest R., 'The American Commitment to Germany 1949–55', *Diplomatic History*, 13/4, (1989), 431–60.

Middleton, Drew, 'Adenauer: Germany Reborn', in *New York Times* (ed.), *Portraits of Power*, London: Octopus, 1979.

Montias, John Michael, 'Communist Rule in Eastern Europe', *Foreign Affairs*, 43/2 (1965), 331–48.

Moreton, Edwina, 'The View From London', in Lincoln Gordon with J.F. Brown, Pierre Hassner, Josef Joffe and Edwina Moreton, *Eroding Empire: Western Relations with Eastern Europe*, Washington: The Brookings Institution, 1987.

Morgan, Roger, 'The British View', in Edwina Moreton (ed.), *Germany Between East and West*, Cambridge University Press/RIIA, 1987.

Morgenthau, Hans J., 'Alliances in Theory and Practice', in Arnold Wolfers (ed.), *Alliance Theory in the Cold War*, London: The Johns Hopkins Press, 1959.

Mühlen, Norbert, 'The Survivors', *Commentary*, 36/5 (1963), 23.

Nicolson, Harold, 'Diplomacy Then and Now', *Foreign Affairs*, 40/1 (1961), 39–49.

Niedhart, Gottfried, 'The British Reaction towards Ostpolitik: Anglo-West German Relations in the Era of Détente, 1967–1971', in Christian Haase and Daniel Gossel (eds), *Debating Foreign Affairs: the Public Dimension of British Foreign Policy*, Berlin: Philo, 2003.

——, 'The East–West Problem as Seen from Berlin: Willy Brandt's Early *Ostpolitik*', in Wilfried Loth (ed.), *Europe, Cold War and Coexistence, 1953–1965*, London: Frank Cass, 2004.

Northedge, F.S., 'Britain as a Second-rank Power', *International Affairs*, 46/1 (1970), 37–47.

Oppelland, Torsten, 'Domestic Political Developments I: 1949–69', in Klaus Larres and Panikos Panayi (eds), *The Federal Republic of Germany Since 1949: Politics, Society and Economy Before and Since Reunification*, London: Longman, 1996.

——, 'Gerhard Schröder and the First "*Ostpolitik*"', in Wilfried Loth (ed.), *Europe, Cold War and Coexistence, 1953–1965*, London: Frank Cass, 2004.

Owen, Henry, 'NATO Strategy: What Is Past Is Prologue', *Foreign Affairs*, 43/4 (1965), 682–90.

Pagedas, Constantine A., 'Harold Macmillan and the 1962 Champs Meeting', *Diplomacy and Statecraft*, 9/1 (1998), 224–42.

Paterson, William E., 'The German Social Democratic Party', in William E. Paterson and Alastair H. Thomas (eds), *Social Democratic Parties in Western Europe*, London: Groom Helm, 1977.

Petchatov, Vladimir O., '"The Allies are Pressing on you to Break your Will …": Foreign Policy Correspondence between Stalin and Molotov and other Politburo Members, September 1945–December 1946', Washington, DC: Cold War International History Project, 1999.

Piotrowicz, R.W., 'The Polish–German Frontier in International Law: the Final Solution', *British Year Book of International Law 1992*, Oxford: Oxford University Press, 1992.

Prittie, Terence, 'The Statesman: Historical Perspective', in Horst Osterheld, Terence Prittie and François Seydoux, *Konrad Adenauer*, Bonn: Verlag Bonn Aktuell GmbH, 1983.

Raack, R.C., 'Stalin Fixes the Oder–Neisse Line', *Journal of Contemporary History*, 25/4 (1990), 467–88.

Rapacki, Adam, 'The Polish Plan for a Nuclear-Free Zone Today', *International Affairs*, 39/1 (1963), 1–12.

Roberts, Frank, 'Is Germany's *Ostpolitik* Dangerous? A Diplomatic Balance Sheet', *Encounter*, May 1971, 62–8.

——, 'The German–Soviet Treaty and its Effect on European and Atlantic Policies: A British View', *The Atlantic Community Quarterly*, 9/2 (1971), 184–95.

Rogers, Daniel E., 'The Chancellors of the Federal Republic and the Political Legacy of the Holocaust', in Alan E. Steinweis and Daniel E. Rogers (eds), *The Impact of Nazism: New Perspectives on the Third Reich and Its Legacy*, London: University of Nebraska Press, 2003.

Schaad, Martin C., 'Bonn between London and Paris?', in Jeremy Noakes, Peter Wende and Jonathan Wright (eds), *Britain and Germany in Europe*, 2002.

Schake, Kori, 'US Policy in the 1958 and 1961 Berlin Crises', in John Gearson and Kori Schake (eds), *The Berlin Wall Crisis: Perspectives on Cold War Alliances*, Basingstoke: Palgrave Macmillan, 2002.

Schmidt, Gustav, '"Master-minding" a New Western Europe: the Key Actors at Brussels in the Superpower Conflict', in George Wilkes (ed.), *Britain's Failure to Enter the European Community 1961–63: The Enlargement Negotiations and Crises in European, Atlantic and Commonwealth Relations*, London: Frank Cass, 1997.

——, 'European Security: Anglo-German Relationships 1949–1956', in Jeremy Noakes, Peter Wende and Jonathan Wright (eds), *Britain and Germany in Europe*, Oxford: Oxford University Press, 2002.

Schroeder, Gerhard, 'Germany Looks at Eastern Europe', *Foreign Affairs*, 44/1 (1965), 15–25.

Schulz, Eberhard, 'Unfinished Business: the German National Question and the Future of Europe', *International Affairs*, 60/2 (1984), 391–402.

——, 'Berlin, the German Question and the Future of Europe: Long-Term Perspectives', in Keith Dyson (ed.), *European Détente: Case Studies of the Politics of East–West Relations*, London: Frances Pinter, 1986.

Schwartz, Thomas, 'The Berlin Crisis and the Cold War', *Diplomatic History*, 21/1 (1997), 140–8.

Shlaim, A., 'Britain, the Berlin Blockade and the Cold War', *International Affairs*, 60/1 (1984), 1–14.

Skubiszewski, Krzysztof, 'Poland's Western Frontiers and the 1970 Treaties', *The American Journal of International Law*, 67/1 (1973) 23–43.

——, 'Legal Problems of the German Eastern Territories', *The American Journal of International Law*, 74/1 (1980), 122–33.

Sommer, Theo, 'For An Atlantic Future', *Foreign Affairs*, 43/1 (1964), 112–25.

——, 'Bonn Changes Course', *Foreign Affairs*, 45/4 (1967), 477–91.

Steel, Sir Christopher, 'Anglo-German Relations: II. A British View', *International Affairs*, 39/4 (1963), 522–31.

Steininger, Rolf, 'Great Britain's first EEC failure in January 1963', *Diplomacy and Statecraft*, 7/2 (1996), 400–14.

Strauss, Franz-Josef, 'Soviet Aims and German Unity', *Foreign Affairs*, 37/3 (1959), 366–77.

——, 'An Alliance of Continents', *International Affairs*, 41/2 (1965), 191–203.

Stürmer, Michael, '*Ostpolitik, Deutschlandpolitik* and the Western Alliance: German Perspectives on Détente', in Keith Dyson (ed.), *European Détente: Case Studies of the Politics of East–West Relations*, London: Frances Pinter, 1986.

Tebinka, Jacek, 'British Memoranda on Changing the Curzon Line in 1944', *Acta Poloniae Historica*, 80 (1999), 167–94.

Thomson, David, 'General De Gaulle and the Anglo-Saxons', *International Affairs*, 41/1 (1965), 11–21.

Urban, G.R., 'Co-existence without sanctimony', in G.R. Urban (ed.), *Détente*, London: Temple Smith, 1976.

van Dojk, Ruud, *The 1952 Stalin Note Debate: Myth or Missed Opportunity?* Cold War International History Project Working Paper 14, May 1996.

Varsori, Antonio, 'British Policy Aims at Geneva', in Gunther Bischof and Saki Dockrill (eds), *Cold War Respite: The Geneva Summit of 1955*, Louisiana: Louisiana University Press, 2000.

——, 'Britain as a Bridge Between East and West', in Wilfried Loth (ed.), *Europe, Cold War and Coexistence, 1953–1965*, London: Frank Cass, 2004.

Wagner, R. Harrison, 'The Decision to Divide Germany and the Origins of the Cold War'. *International Studies Quarterly*, 49/4 (1978), 446–56.

Warner, Geoffrey, 'From Ally to Enemy: Britain's Relations with the Soviet Union, 1941–1948', in Michael Dockrill and Brian McKercher (eds), *Diplomacy and World Power: Studies in British Foreign Policy, 1890–1950*, Cambridge: Cambridge University Press, 1996.

Weigall, David, 'British Perceptions of the European Defence Community', in Peter M.R. Stirk and David Willis (eds), *Shaping Postwar Europe: European Unity and Disunity 1945–1957*, London: Pinter Publishers, 1991.

Whyte, Anne, 'Quadripartite Rule in Berlin', *International Affairs*, 23/1 (1947), 30–41.

Williams, Philip, 'Britain, Détente and the Conference on Security and Cooperation in Europe', in Keith Dyson (ed.), *European Détente: Case Studies of the Politics of East–West Relations*, London: Frances Pinter, 1986.

Wilmot, Chester, 'Britain's Strategic Relationship to Europe', *International Affairs*, 29/4 (1953), 409–17.

Wilson, D., 'Anglo-Soviet Relations: the Effect on Ideas and Reality', *International Affairs*, 50/3 (1974), 380–91.

Wolfe, James H., 'West Germany and Czechoslovakia: The Struggle for Reconciliation', *Orbis*, 14/1 (1970), 154–79.

World Survey, *The West German Federal Republic and the Ostpolitik in Election Year*, 50 (1973), London: The Atlantic Education Trust.

Wright, Jonathan, 'The Role of Britain in West German Foreign Policy since 1949', *German Politics*, 5/1 (1996), 22–34.

Wrigley, Chris, 'Now You See It, Now You Don't: Harold Wilson and Labour's Foreign Policy 1964–70', in R. Coopey, S. Fielding and N. Tiratsoo (eds), *The Wilson Governments 1964–1970*, London: Pinter, 1995.

Wurm, Clemens A., 'Britain and West European Integration, 1948–9 to 1955, Politics and Economics', in Jeremy Noakes, Peter Wende and Jonathan Wright (eds), *Britain and Germany in Europe*, Oxford: Oxford University Press, 2002.

"X", 'The Conduct of Soviet Policy', in *A Foreign Affairs Reader*, Washington, DC: Council for Foreign Relations, 1948.

Young, John W., 'Churchill's "No" to Europe: the "Rejection" of European Union by Churchill's Post-War Government, 1951–1952', *The Historical Journal*, 28/4 (1985), 923–37.

——, 'The Foreign Office, the French and the Post-war Division of Germany 1945–46', *Review of International Studies*, 12/3 (1986), 223–34.

——, 'Cold War and Détente with Moscow', in John W. Young (ed.), *The Foreign Policy of Churchill's Peacetime Administration 1951–55*, Leicester: Leicester University Press, 1988.

Index